"SHOW US LIFE"

Toward a History and Aesthetics of the Committed Documentary

Edited by
Thomas Waugh

The Scarecrow Press, Inc.
Metuchen, N.J., and London
1984

Acknowledgments begin on page vii.

Library of Congress Cataloging in Publication Data
Main entry under title:

"Show us life".

Includes bibliographical references and index.
1. Moving-pictures, Documentary--History and criticism--Addresses, essays, lectures. 2. Moving-pictures--Political aspects--Addresses, essays, lectures. I. Waugh, Thomas, 1948- .
PN1995.9.D6S5 1984 791.43'53'09 84-5603
ISBN 0-8108-1706-3

Manufactured in the United States of America

CONTENTS

ACKNOWLEDGMENTS

Seth Feldman: portions of "Cinema Weekly and Cinema Truth: Dziga Vertov and the Leninist Proportion" appeared in earlier forms in an article of the same title in Sight and Sound, XLIII, 1 (Winter 1973-74), pp. 34-37, and in Feldman, Evolution of Style in the Early Work of Dziga Vertov (Ph. D. dissertation, NYU, 1975; rpt. New York: Arno Press, 1977), used with permission of Sight and Sound and the author.

Vlada Petric: an earlier version of "Esther Shub: Film as a Historical Discourse" appeared as "Esther Shub: Cinema Is My Life," Quarterly Review of Film Studies (Fall 1978), pp. 429-448, used with permission of the author and Redgrave Publishing Company.

Bert Hogenkamp: "Workers' Newsreels in Germany, the Netherlands, and Japan During the Twenties and Thirties" is an abridged portion of the author's Workers' Newsreels in the 1920's and 1930's (London: "Our History" Pamphlet 68, History Group, CPGB, no date, no copyright [1977]), used with permission of the author.

Russell Campbell: "Radical Documentary in the United States, 1930-1942" is a revision of portions of the author's Ph. D. dissertation (Northwestern, 1978), reprinted as Cinema Strikes Back: Radical Filmmaking in the United States, 1930-1942 (Ann Arbor: UMI Research Press, Studies in Cinema, Series No. 20, 1982), used with permission of the author and of UMI Research Press.

Daniel Serceau: "The Communist Party and La Vie est à nous: Document and Fiction, Poetics and Politics," used with permission of the author.

Thomas Waugh: "Joris Ivens' The Spanish Earth: Committed Documentary and the Popular Front," a revision of parts of the author's Ph. D. dissertation, Joris Ivens and the Evolution of the Radical Documentary (Columbia, 1981), originally published as "'Men Cannot Act in Front of the Camera in the Presence of Death': Joris Ivens' The Spanish Earth," Parts I and II, Cineaste, XII, 2 (1982), pp. 30-33, and XII, 3 (1983), pp. 21-29, used with permission of the author and of Cineaste.

Bill Nichols: an earlier version of "Newsreel, 1967-1972: Film and Revolution" appeared as "Newsreel: Film and Revolution," Cineaste, V, 4 (1973), pp. 7-13, and is used with permission of Cineaste and of the author.

Dan Georgakas: "Finally Got the News: the Making of a Radical Documentary" is a slightly revised version of "Finally Got the News: the Making of a Radical Film," Cineaste, V, 4 (1973), pp. 2-6, and is used with permission of Cineaste and of the author.

Guy Hennebelle: "French Radical Documentary After May 1968" is a slightly edited translation of "Bilan et perspectives: un cinéma pour transformer le monde," and "Iskra: Le cinéma militant est une étincelle," originally published in Cinéma d'aujourd'hui, "Cinéma militant," (Dossier établi sous la direction de Guy Hennebelle, No. double 5-6, Mars-avril 1976), pp. 35-42, 189-198, and is used with permission of the author.

Claire Johnston and Paul Willemen: "Brecht in Britain: The Nightcleaners and the Independent Political Film," originally published as "Brecht in Britain: The Independent Political Film (on The Nightcleaners)", Screen, XVI, 4 (Winter 1975/76), pp. 101-118, is reprinted, slightly abridged, with permission of the Society for Education in Film and Television Limited and of the authors.

E. Ann Kaplan: "Theory and Practice of the Realist Documentary Form in Harlan County USA" appeared in an earlier form as "Harlan County USA: The Documentary Form," Jump Cut, #15 (1977), pp. 11-12, and is used with permission of Jump Cut and of the author.

Julia Lesage: parts of "Feminist Documentary: Aesthetics and Politics" appeared in earlier form as "Rape: Disarming Film Rape," Jump Cut, #19 (1978), pp. 14-16, and as "The Political Aesthetics of Feminist Documentary Film," Quarterly Review of Film Studies (Fall 1978), pp. 507-523; used with permission of Jump Cut and of Redgrave Publishing Company respectively, and of the author.

Barbara Halpern Martineau: "Talking About Our Lives and Experiences: Some Thoughts About Feminism, Documentary and 'Talking Heads'" is used with permission of the author.

Joan Braderman: "Shinsuke Ogawa's Peasants of the Second Fortress: Guerrilla Documentary in Japan," originally published as "Japan: Peasants of the Second Fortress" in Revolutionary Films/Chicago '76, sponsored by Chicago Tribune and the Film Center of the School of the Art Institute, Chicago, is used by permission of the Film Center and of the author.

Réal La Rochelle: "Committed Documentary in Quebec: A Still-Birth?" is used with permission of the author.

Margaret Cooper: "The Challenge of Radical Film Distribution: Conversations with Toronto's DEC Films Collective," originally published as "'We Don't Have Films You Can Eat': Talking to the DEC Films Collective," Jump Cut, #28 (1983), pp. 37-40, is reprinted, abridged by the author, with permission of Jump Cut and of the author.

Chuck Kleinhans: "Forms, Politics, Makers, and Contexts: Basic Issues for a Theory of Radical Political Documentary" is used with permission of the author.

Julianne Burton: "Democratizing Documentary: Modes of Address in the Latin American Cinema, 1958-1972" is used with permission of the author.

John Hess: "Santiago Alvarez: Cine-Agitator for the Cuban Revolution and the Third World" is used with permission of the author.

Victor Wallis and John D. Barlow: "Democracy as Participation: The Battle of Chile" is a much revised extension of Wallis's "Battle of Chile: Struggle of a People Without Arms," Jump Cut, #21 (1979), pp. 8-9, and is published here with permission of Jump Cut and of the authors.

Pierre Véronneau: "Children of Vertov in the Land of Brecht," originally published in Heynowski & Scheumann: Documentaire politique (Montreal: La Cinémathèque québécoise, 1979) and is reprinted here in translation with permission of the Cinémathèque québécoise and of the author. Excerpts from the working notebooks of Walter Heynowski and Gerhard Scheumann are reprinted in translation with the permission of the authors.

Steve Neale: "Notes and Questions on Political Cinema: from Hour of the Furnaces to Ici et ailleurs" is used with permission of the author.

Anand Patwardhan: "The Guerrilla Film, Underground and in Exile: A Critique and a Case Study of Waves of Revolution," excerpted from the author's Master's Thesis of the same title (McGill University, 1981), is reprinted with permission of the author.

John Ramirez: "The Sandinista Documentary: A Historical Contextualization" is used with permission of the author.

INTRODUCTION

WHY DOCUMENTARY FILMMAKERS KEEP TRYING TO CHANGE THE WORLD, OR WHY PEOPLE CHANGING THE WORLD KEEP MAKING DOCUMENTARIES.

Thomas Waugh

... we realized that the important thing was not the film itself but that which the film provoked. --Fernando Solanas, 1969[1]

Afraid that the discussion was getting too political, another of the censors said, "... We cannot show this film, c'est trop de réalité." --Joris Ivens, c. 1942[2]

... These people are seeing the cinema screen for the first or second time, they still don't understand the taste of "cine-spirits," and when real peasants appear on the screen after the "sugary actors" of the drama, they all liven up and try to look behind the screen. A real tractor about which they know only by hearsay crosses the field and ploughs it in a few seconds before the audience's eyes. Chatters, shouts, questions. "The actors" are forgotten. Now there are real things and people on the screen. There is not a single false theatrical movement to unmask the screen, to remove the peasant's trust. This sharp boundary between the reception of drama and documentary was noticeable whenever a first, second, or third film was being shown--everywhere where the poison had not yet penetrated deeply, where a demand for the venomous sweetness of fictional drama made up of kisses, sighs and killing had not yet been created.
This was at the time when only the outlines of the movement of Kino-Eye were drawn, when we had to decide whether we should keep up with fea-

> ture cinema ... or whether we should declare war on feature films and begin to construct cinematography anew. "Petrushka" or life? we asked the audiences. "Petrushka," the hopelessly infected answered. "We know about life already--we don't need life. Hide life, boring life from us." "Life," those who were not hopelessly infected and those who were not at all infected answered. "We don't know life. We haven't seen life, we've seen our village and ten verst around. Show us life."
> --Dziga Vertov, 1920[3]

Sixty-three years of film history have passed since Vertov's polemic in the third year of the Soviet Revolution, yet his distinction between "Petrushka" and "life" still rings true. Kisses, sighs and killings still lure us into movie palaces, but in order to be shown "life" we go elsewhere, to the austere environments of classrooms, libraries, and union halls--and occasionally to art cinemas or to a public television network--to watch 16mm documentaries drearily unwind. Vertov would find today's mass audiences incurably contaminated (though one thinks he would recognize the very contemporary but equally ingenuous French or Japanese peasants referred to in this collection) and would not be surprised that documentary has acquired this aura of dreariness, that the battle against "Petrushka" has long since been lost.

Yet, documentary can still set off a Vertovian sense of urgency and fervor in certain quarters; namely, wherever people are struggling against oppression.

Ever since Vertov first entered the Soviet newsreel initiative, activists on the left have continued to use the documentary medium to intervene wherever they have been challenging the inherited structures of social domination. This continuous tradition of radical documentary flourishes more than ever today as the front of radical change broadens and retrenches at the same time, and as technology becomes increasingly accessible. At a gathering of more than 500 radical media activists from the U.S. and Canada in 1979 (U.S. Conference for an Alternative Cinema, Bard College, New York), over eighty-five films were screened. Of these, fully seventy were documentaries. This book is about the rich and complex tradition whose contemporary manifestation was so evident at Bard. It is about both its founders and its divergent branches in the last generation, and about the practical and theoretical questions posed by these hundreds of films.

All of the films discussed by authors gathered here set about the job implied by the word documentary, but they also attempt to do much more. They attempt to act, to intervene--whether as gut-level calls to immediate, localized action, or as more cerebral essays in long-term, global analysis. They are all works of art, but they are not merely works of art (although some have been reduced to this role); they must be seen also as films made by activists speaking to specific publics to bring about specific political goals. Furthermore, a good many of the films treated in this book were made under an important additional assumption; if films are to be instrumental in the process of change, they must be made not only _about_ people directly implicated in change, but _with_ and _for_ those people as well.

This latter assumption is true of committed books as well, and, I hope, of this book in particular. This book was made principally for students and teachers of film and media studies, and of the social sciences--there is a serious gap in the college market which _Show Us Life_ can fill. But this book appears in the hope also that activists outside of the educational milieu--both those who make or use film and those engaged in other kinds of political work--will find it useful. Filmmakers are among the contributors to _Show Us Life_, I am glad to say, as are film programmers and distributors, and a vital part of the book's audience must be found among people using film in political struggles.

As targeted readers I am thinking particularly of "poor" and marginal film-makers/users, both those working within the framework of the traditional left and workers' movements, and those within the progressive mass movements of the seventies and eighties: the women's movement; minority, anti-racist and national movements; the environmental/anti-nuke/peace movement; lesbian and gay liberation groups; and other resistance movements enlisting prisoners, consumers, welfare recipients, immigrants, the handicapped, the elderly, the unemployed, and others on down the endless list of those disenfranchised under patriarchal capitalism. Filmmakers are working on fronts situated everywhere along this list, expanding the tradition of committed documentary around each one of these causes (though for reasons of space and effectiveness, and to avoid the shotgun scatter-effect of some anthologies, I have chosen to represent some but not all of these fronts in the book). In addition to oppositional filmmakers, I would like to reach also those filmmakers working within dominant media, for their role is a crucial one too.

All of these filmworkers and their fellow activists in non-cultural fields, then, are part of the target audience of this book. Committed film historians, critics, and theorists must address not only other scholars, but must also speak clearly and directly to non-specialists and activists in all spheres of our struggle.

Commitment

Before going further, I must narrow down to some degree what I mean by "committed documentary." I will try to elaborate both components of this double-pronged concept, "commitment" and "documentary," with some degree of concreteness, though my sense of them will be made clear enough in the following pages.

By "commitment" I mean, firstly, a specific ideological undertaking, a declaration of solidarity with the goal of radical socio-political transformation. Secondly, I mean a specific political positioning: activism, or intervention in the process of change itself. To paraphrase Marx, a committed filmmaker is not content only to interpret the world but is also engaged in changing it. But Marx's utopian ideal is expressed through very pragmatic applications by the filmmakers discussed here. Few would disagree with Iskra's reminder that filmmakers themselves cannot make revolutions but can only provide "working tools" for those who can.

Filmmakers on the left have always realized that film, like all cultural forms, is a bearer of ideology, and that even films which aspire to change are produced through and within the dominant structures of belief. How then can committed filmmakers escape the entrapment of traditional ideological forms and work within a truly revolutionary ideology? Not by finding and repeating a "correct" line, obviously, but by rooting them, work within actively ongoing political struggles; by making films, I repeat, not only about people engaged in these struggles, but also with and by them as well, and through this process, and with full awareness of the contradictions in play, hammering out the shapes of an evolving new revolutionary ideology around those struggles. This third and final criterion for commitment, this "subject-centered" or "contextual" ideal expressed in my string of emphasized prepositions, is as essential an element of my notion of commitment as the first two: ideological principle, and activist stance.

I like the way the complexity of this notion has been visualized and summarized by Miguel Littin, the Chilean filmmaker whose own commitment has been expressed on the boundaries of fiction and documentary:

> We have used a line from the poet Antonio Machado a lot in our political development: "Walker, there is no road/Roads are made by walking." But, concretely, in our country, cinema has to be the avant-garde of events, opening the way to the great revolutionary perspectives, clarifying what revolution is and at the same time being a witness to reality, but projecting it to future transformations ... and without demagogy.... There is a distinct difference in attitude between one who speaks to the public from a balcony and those who work with and among the people, with all the richness and dynamics that this implies; we ourselves are being transformed....[4]

A glance at the table of contents, however, is a reminder that this notion of commitment, so poetically expressed in the abstract, must be given concreteness within specific historical conjunctures. Throughout the sixty or so years of the historical scope of this anthology, commitment, with its revolutionary principle, activist stance and subject-centered base, has taken innumerable different concrete expressions. Typing up these manuscripts, I have been moved by the concrete poetry of place names that have come to symbolize for me this diversity: Fuenteduena, Sanrizuka, Santiago, Detroit.... The contexts in which the films spotlighted in this volume intervene vary as widely as these place names, and as the styles of the films themselves; they range from the euphoric dynamism of the first decade of the Soviet revolution to the desperate tension within the crumbling fortress of post-industrial capitalism, to fierce defiance on the Central American battleground. It goes without saying that the range of ideological coloring represented by the films (and not incidentally by the contributors to this anthology) is just as broad. The films--and the contributors--occupy virtually all of the gradations possible on the left side of the political spectrum, from the social democratic through the Marxist-Leninist to the left-libertarian. Some readers will undoubtedly find my non-sectarian criteria too broad, others will see them as too narrow, or skewed in other ways. I hope that the majority will agree that the spectrum I have chosen is a provocative demonstration of the range of history's opportunities and a confirmation that there is no simple rigid formula of committed film-making which can be applied to every historical problem. Let a hundred flowers bloom.

Obviously, not all of the films in this book fulfill the complex goal that I have set forward. History has seldom permitted the committed filmmaker the clarity of perception which we in retrospect invariably enjoy, and thus the committed filmmakers discussed in this volume have the retrospective privilege of error. Criticisms by Daniel Serceau, Russell Campbell and myself of filmmakers of the Popular Front on both sides of the Atlantic, for example, are to be read in the spirit of respect for their achievements and for the complex contradictions of the historical situation in which they found themselves. At the same time, some of the present authors stop short of direct criticism out of courtesy or solidarity, motivations that are perhaps misguided.

Even where clarity of perception existed, without error, history has not always permitted the committed filmmaker the full and unproblematical chance to live up to each facet of his or her own vision. To realize a vision of commitment at every stage of a film's trajectory has usually required a miracle of personal tenacity and historical fortuity, at the stage of a film's production, at the stage of its photography, editing and post-production, and at the final stage of its exhibition and consumption. The reader will have no trouble finding examples of films discussed in this volume which were unsuccessful in expressing the filmmaker's vision at any one of these three stages. In fact, it would be very surprising indeed if most of the films in this anthology did not express in some way various limitations and contradictions at some stage in their trajectory. Most of the articles included here are preoccupied in important ways with these gaps between political intention and achievement. It is only by exploring how committed artists of the past have come to grips with--or failed to come to grips with--their historical contexts that we can learn how to act within our own. In discussing the contradictions posed by the filmmakers included in this book--one artist speaking from a balcony (to use Littin's image), another failing to break out of the ahistoric avant-garde aloofness by which bourgeois culture sidetracks the political artist, another relying on authoritarian, individualist, or sexist modes of film production, another deploying mystificatory or illusionist filmic discourse, or still another working within the "System" without a precise strategic justification--the point is to perfect our own practice as filmmakers/users and activists by learning from their efforts and experience.

A further qualification of the notion of commitment is necessary. It is possible that the reader may have already inferred a further criterion from my emphasis on distribution, or from the fact that a significant proportion of the films in this book are aimed at popular audiences. A large number of films in fact attempt--and often succeed--to break out of the frequent bind of left cultural work, the restriction of appealing to a small, already politicized audience. However, this criterion of popular appeal is not absolute: given the complex dynamics of political media activism within the repressively tolerant, image-overloaded, post-industrial cultural environment, there is no necessary correlation between the size of a film's public (nor for that matter the size of its grain, its gauge, or its budget) and its political effectiveness. This selection includes both an Oscar-winner, Harlan County U.S.A., and The Nightcleaners (not even nominated!), a film whose defenders readily admit--upon questioning--that it was "badly received," all the while dismissing many of the activist premises of the last few pages as "conventional notions of agit-prop" and "a very functional, instrumental notion of cinema." The debate over this issue of audience, scarcely changed since similar debates in the twenties and thirties, continues to be a very lively one, as the reader will discover in Steve Neale's article and elsewhere in Show Us Life.

Documentary

The second component of this book's organizing concept, "documentary," is less elusive than "commitment," though equally problematical. For more than fifty years, "documentary" has been a mode of film discourse that is popularly understood, historically defined, and as readily assumed by filmmakers, film audiences and film critics as it was unwittingly by Vertov's "uncontaminated" peasants years before the term was even coined. The commonsense understanding of the label "documentary" combines ideas of nonfiction and education with social seriousness, noncommercial or alternative or television distribution, and of course Grierson's "creative treatment of actuality," the elements of creative shaping and actuality both being always understood (though in varying proportions for different audiences and different periods).

This taxonomical consensus is more or less universal, and, in my opinion, not especially problematical in itself: such a consensus of audience with practitioners (or as Bazin put it, a "common fund") must always be the departure point and basic object of genre studies.[5] However, this consensus has been attacked in the last decade by theorists who, like Steve Neale, Paul Willemen, and Claire Johnston, anthologized here, quite convincingly demonstrate that documentary must forfeit its claim to a privileged access to truth (including "pravda" and "vérité"), reality, and objectivity (though the last of these aspirations has never been claimed by most of the practitioners discussed here in the first place). Documentary, such theorists have shown, relies no less than any other filmic genre on its own systems of codes, conventions, and cultural assumptions and mediations. An obvious corollary of this insight, for some, is that a documentary that does not challenge the terms of its own conventions of belief, that does not subscribe to the aesthetic prescriptions of what has come to be known as "political modernism,"[6] is guilty not only of a fallacious realism but also of a political complicity. Thus, it is now a commonplace to read in undergraduate term-papers that documentary is no different from fiction (an assertion somewhat less subversive now than when Godard first called Lumière a storyteller and Méliès a documentarist some seventeen years ago) or that Harlan County is guilty of the most heinous illusionism.

What are the ramifications for this book of our new sophistication in looking at documentary, of its teetering on its ideological pedestal? Many, and at the same time, very few. The emergence of the view of documentary as an art form without any special transparency (it is uncertain whether the commonsense understanding of documentary will ever change that much) necessitates the alteration and enrichment of critical terms of reference, to be sure; they have been long in need of a tune-up in any case. Also on the agenda is a toughening of the standards of documentary historiography, long in need of antidotes to the "venomous sweetnesses" of the Riefenstahl/Flaherty/Grierson cultists (Bert Hogenkamp and Russell Campbell are only two historians who have made important advances in this direction). Perhaps more important, it is already apparent that the new theoretical awareness has enormously expanded the vocabulary of documentary filmmakers themselves. This expansion of documentary vocabulary has come, in fact, just in time to offset its impoverishment following, on the one hand, the enshrinement and then decline of the vérité movement, and on the other hand, the mass-immunization against that same vérité spread by television newscasting. Filmmakers as different as John Berger (Ways of Seeing), Joanne Elam (Rape), and Emile de Antonio (In the King of Prussia) have recently testified in their experiments with self-reflexivity or mixed modes to the most impressive addition to the documentary repertory since the advent of vérité. Their success has also hinted encouragingly about an availability and accessibility of the new image theory for the documentary public, just about the time that progressive/popular fictional filmmakers seem to have given up.[7] The sixty-year legacy of documentary activism that is the subject of this book is enriched rather than dissipated by our better understanding of the workings and the risks of documentary discourse. I hope that this anthology reflects this enrichment.

On a broader scale, the new documentary theory has never even threatened to dislodge documentary as an important and discrete arena of committed film practice. The new skepticism has not led radical film activists to abandon documentary in favor of Godardian introspection; far from it. As evidenced by the interview with the Iskra Collective and other entries in this volume, it has instead led them towards a greater precision about, and willingness to experiment with, political goals, target audiences, textual practices, and contextual relationships with subjects--in short, toward a fuller artistic maturity. In any case, documentary continues to be a privileged medium--indeed, the privileged medium--for committed artists and their publics, and a resource of first priority for the political activist. John Ramirez's intriguing piece on Nicaraguan cinema indicates that revolutionary societies today turn to documentary as an instrument of social construction no less enthusiastically than did the Soviets sixty-five, the Chinese thirty-five, and the Cubans twenty-five years ago. Lenin's dictum about the cinema being of first priority for the young revolutionary society, repeated at least twice in this volume (by no coincidence), seems to be taken up just as eagerly by the new societies of the Third World as it was by Vertov. This is equally true for Lenin's more detailed prescription for state film policy, the Leninist Film Proportion, a recommended ratio of fiction to nonfiction films for the early Soviet film industry. Thus, it is fitting that the Soviet experimentation with the new art form begins this volume, just as it is that our accounts of new documentary activity in the Third World end it.

The cycle begun in those mobile agit-train editing rooms along the Volga, and renewed in makeshift outdoor screening areas in the liberated zones of El Salvador, demands the comprehensive historical and theoretical study that this book inaugurates. This long-standing demand is heightened rather than undermined by the recent theoretical refinements in film studies: it would be foolhardy to deny that the films that constitute the subject of this anthology remain a coherent, authentic and largely untouched corpus for scholarly, ideological and political examination.

A few other remarks about documentary are also in order. Firstly, my focus on documentary does not mean that I deny the political potential of all other cinemas, notably of fiction. On the contrary, I certainly vouch for the potential of committed fiction. Indeed, Littin is only one among many filmmakers who have ultimately opted for committed fiction. (Is it incidental, however, that most of the healthy traditions of committed fiction display strong documentary influences--the Cubans, the early Soviets, the Italians from Zavattini to Rosi, filmmakers here in Quebec?) I accept without reservation such filmmakers' probable interest in fiction's ability to reach and move large numbers of people, to introduce political concepts into mainstream culture. All the same, committed fiction raises entirely different historical, theoretical and tactical questions from those raised by documentary. It is thus quite outside the scope of a volume that has already been forced for reasons of space to leave large geographical, historical and political domains of committed documentary unrepresented. Some readers may even wonder whether Jean Renoir's La vie est à nous should not also have been excluded on these grounds, with its didactic hybridization of agitprop fiction, newsreel documents and Party oratory, the ensemble undeniably weighted toward the first of these.

One further precision. By emphasizing analytic and activist documentary by my editorial selection, I do not mean to belittle the special power of those documentaries which reflect or observe the world without either the desire or the capability to engage in a direct strategy of changing it. Scientific study is, after all, a key precept of Marxist thought: many observational documentarists in the traditions of cinéma-vérité and direct cinema will continue to make important contributions by providing raw material for such study, as well as by gaining entry to media channels where radicals have no access. I am thinking, for example, of filmmakers like Frederick Wiseman, whom early Marxist theorists might have called "critical realists," and who deserve our careful consideration. Though I do not dismiss Wiseman, none of the filmmakers offered by this volume as models for political practice is content to remain at the observational level of Wiseman's work. Each one, in his or her way, endeavors to move beyond observation, and all of its inherent liabilities: humanist ambiguity, false objectivity, liberal empiricism, and the complicity of spectacle. They undertake rather to accede to the level of intervention, using Wiseman's language (if at all) only as an ingredient which other cinematic strategies must expand, transform, or deconstruct.

On the other hand, finally, compilation documentary, a prolific and creative radical tradition, represented here by its founder, Esther Shub, and some of its most interesting practitioners of the last twenty years, primarily from Latin America, belongs at the center of this book, indeed deserves a book all its own. Admittedly, my "subject-centered" ideal, expounded at the outset, has no obvious direct application to the admirable work these artists accomplish on their own terrain, the stock-shot library and the editing-room. Yet their project of radical historiography is second in importance to none, and, led by the work of Emile de Antonio, has been a major influence on radical documentarists of the seventies and eighties.

Toward an Aesthetics of Committed Documentary

This book appears at a time when documentary studies is finally entering its own within the discipline of film studies. It is no longer possible to complain, as Bill Nichols did in his seminal 1976 essay, "Documentary Theory and Practice," that the theoretical examination of the formal structures of documentary, its codes and units, is "scarcely begun."[8] Since then, there has been a small flood of new entries in the field, inaugurated in many ways by Nichols' work. The best of the new entries confront documentary in terms of the new methodologies developed in the seventies: semiotic/structuralist analysis; psychoanalytic approaches; formal(ist) analysis; ideological analysis; oral history; specialized technological, industrial, exhibition, and audience history. The once bleak picture now looks very lively, building expansively on the work of the pioneers of documentary studies, Erik Barnouw, Jay Leyda, and Lewis Jacobs.

As for political film itself, both fiction and nonfiction, its study is just as healthy, thanks largely to the exciting if unpaid periodical work of the last few years (rather than to the grace of the publishing industry). Too often, however, criticism of political film is still dominated by ad hoc critical principles, outdated conceptual models, and the all-too-frequent substitution of ideological fervor or indignation for solid analysis. The notable achievement in this area has been in the feminist camp, whose intellectual acuity and diversity, as well as enviable political strength, the reader will find well represented in this volume.

As for the hybrid field of political documentary proper, outside the feminist area, there has been a tremendous gap which I hope this anthology will help fill. We have still to muster a set of critical and theoretical principles for dealing with the aesthetics of a genre, political documentary, which refuses to meet any of the expectations of bourgeois aesthetics, modernist or otherwise. Instead of meeting the criteria of durability, abstraction, ambiguity, individualism, uniqueness, formal complexity, deconstructed or redistributed signifiers, novelty and so on, all in a packageable format, political documentaries provide us with disposability, ephemerality, topicality, directness, immediacy, instrumentality, didacticism, collective or anonymous authorship, unconventional formats, non-availability, and ultimately non-evaluability. No wonder we keep running into baffled dismissals such as that of Andrew Sarris in the face of the French collective work, Far from Vietnam: "Zero as art."[9] How then do we talk about films whose aesthetics consist in political use-value? What does the concept of an aesthetics of political use-value mean, beyond the fact, say, that The Spanish Earth raised enough funds to send eighteen ambulances to the Spanish front? The articles in this book, I hope, will advance us considerably in our search for an alternative, political aesthetics. They will also, I hope (and this may mean the same thing), occasion a certain re-cycling of many of the films covered, films whose original political context and thus "use-value" have lapsed, but which may find new uses and engage new aesthetics in new contexts.

Patterns of Change and Continuity

Show Us Life is organized into two historical blocks. This roughly chronological, historical arrangement seemed natural for a film genre whose roots in specific historical conjunctures are more evident (though perhaps not more determining) than for any other genre. The first and shorter block deals with the achievements of the pioneers of the committed documentary of the period between the Wars, in the Soviet Union, in Western Europe, and in North America. The second consists of a survey of contemporary work from the West and from the Third World (except for one entry, the "Second World" is conspicuous by its absence), from the last twenty-five years or so. This has been a period when the simultaneous resurgence of three only partly connected phenomena set off a renewal of the committed documentary whose abundance, diversity and fervor would surpass the legacy of the first period: 1) the entry of the Third World as a fully enfranchised player on the geo-political scene; 2) the emergence of the New Left in the "First World," and 3) the explosion of cinéma-vérité/direct cinema in the domain of documentary technology.

Two questions. First, why the gap between the two chronological blocks? It is not that committed documentarists disappeared for a decade or two during the War and the Truman-Eisenhower era. Far from it; their participation (some would say submersion) in the Allied wartime propaganda effort was a distinguished one, as was their intermittent but by no means inconsequential achievement in the Dark Ages that followed in both East and West. These subjects have been neglected and merit careful study (two of the most celebrated figures of this period, Leo Hurwitz and Joris Ivens, are discussed in this volume in terms of earlier work, and others, Andrew and Annelie Thorndike, the East German compilationists, as well as the Americans Sidney Meyers and Herbert Biberman, are invoked in passing); my leap over this fascinating period, however, results only from the cruel exigencies of space and the relative shortage of film historians working in the area. The task of defining the unbroken continuity between the thirties and the sixties is high on the agenda for the future.

A second question is about what tentative conclusions may be reached from such a juxtapostion of two distinct historical bodies of similarly motivated film activism. Though it is ultimately up to the reader to determine the fundamental continuities and ruptures between the two periods, and to draw the appropriate lessons from them, it is perhaps useful for the editor to sketch some of the more obvious contours in this introduction. The most basic pattern is that the three-part typology that I establish at the beginning of my essay on The Spanish Earth is quite constant throughout the entire scope of the book. I am referring to three distinct categories of interaction of historical context, political goal, and audience dynamic: 1) films of information, agitation and resistance whose primary audience is situated within the same pre-revolutionary political context as that depicted

(Native Land and Hour of the Furnaces may be considered prototypes here); 2) films of information and international solidarity depicting pre- or post-revolutionary situations for audiences outside of the context depicted (of which The Spanish Earth and The Battle of Chile may be considered prototypes, and of which Godard's contribution to Far from Vietnam and his Ici et ailleurs may be considered self-reflexive interrogations); 3) films of information and exhortation for audiences within the same post-revolutionary situation as that depicted (Vertov's Kinopravda series and the contemporary Cuban and Nicaraguan films entering this category). Of course, hybrids appear as often as the pure examples, and films shift from one audience/category to another in the course of their careers, as is vividly documented by Anand Patwardhan in his discussion of his own work.

Yet for all the apparent continuity in these three basic types of contextual political dynamics in the work of our two generations of committed documentarists, their films, obviously, do not look at all alike. Here is where the three determining factors I have mentioned come in: the enfranchisement of the Third World, the emergence of the New Left, and the explosion of cinéma-vérité. All have become interconnected to change the face of the contemporary committed documentary, with the technical transformations of the third factor often mirroring the significant ideological and thematic shifts occasioned by the first two. For example, the new lightweight cameras encouraged filmmakers to go beyond their traditional observational modes toward modes of participation and even of collaboration, intervention, and social catalysis. New stocks permitted new environments to be added to the documentary arsenal, for example leading feminists to add the iconography of kitchen-table rap groups to that of classical street-corner demonstrations, enabling them to translate into filmic practice the political practice of intervening in the personal sphere. On another level, new accessibility of film and video hardware dramatically multiplied forms of collective and grass-roots authorship to match the democratic aspirations of the new political movements. At the same time, increased access to the mainstream media added to the resources of compilationists; this enabled, on the one hand, filmic applications of new modes of social historiography (for example the forthcoming Before Stonewall), and on the other, new possibilities for montage subverters of the mainstream media, matching our increasing sensitivity to cultural aspects of domination (from Millhouse to The Atomic Café).

Perhaps most striking among the technical transformations was the new sound. The first generation of sound documentarists had neither the capacity for on-location recording and subject interviews, nor the ideological aspirations that have come to be connected with these tactics. Working within or alongside a centralist party formation, they were also constrained for the most part to make do with silent films or with voice-over narrators that seemed to mimic the hierarchical political organization. The era of the Nagra allowed filmmakers, virtually for the first time, to listen to and record their subjects in their everyday situations, an enormous potential leap toward the subject-centered ideals and rank-and-file agendas of contemporary liberation movements in both the First and the Third Worlds. The potential for "letting the people speak" has led to excesses, correctly criticized by Guy Hennebelle and admirably defended by Barbara Halpern Martineau. All the same, a general tendency of contemporaries has been, despite the "workerist"/ populist trap, toward anti-dogmatic, discursive, more open-ended, more flexible, and more democratic forms in a very literal sense, bringing political ideals of contemporary radicals much closer to the reality of filmic practice (Julianne Burton provides a thorough and provocative chronicle of this tendency in Latin America). The authorial voice has not disappeared, but it is now most often more collaborative, more sensitive, more intermittent, less prescriptive, less self-righteous.

Thematically, our two blocks of films in Show Us Life reflect, as might be expected, a certain evolution in the concerns and struggles of the Left through the last sixty years. The early films express the preoccupations of classical Marxism: exploitation and oppression under capitalism, the crises of capitalism, and the production, organization, struggles and victories of workers. Strikes and demonstrations are at the dramatic and visual center of these works, as Campbell and Hogenkamp both emphasize. During the Popular Front of the late thirties, the same themes are still central but have become modulated towards more conciliatory imagery, the utopia of world revolution having being postponed by the more immediate job of forming alliances in the struggle against fascism. The theme of the People's War enters the documentary repertory at this time, re-surfacing in our own era, with fascists now replaced by neo-imperialists, whether in Latin America (as amply demonstrated in this anthology) or in Indochina, Africa and the Middle East. All of the classical themes continue to preoccupy our contemporaries, of course, as a number of recurring titles in this volume testify, most notably Harlan County, USA. At the same time, however, the taking up of the camera by Third World filmmakers and by non-traditional radicals in the First World, from feminists to anti-nuclear activists and gay liberationists, has resulted in a staggering proliferation of new thematic interests in the contemporary committed documentary. From neo-imperialism to health care, from sexual violence to popular culture, each new theme is linked to a more general global analysis and comes out of the political practice that is the focus of this book. Interestingly, one theme omnipresent in the films of the pioneers (either explicitly or by conspicuous omission, as in the case of many Popular Front artists), the presence of the Party, has all but disappeared in contemporary work, with the only exceptions appearing in those situations where electoral politics is still on the agenda of the Left, as in France, or in a certain subgenre of compilation work, not without traces of nostalgia, pioneered chiefly by the New Day Films (Union Maids, Seeing Red: Portraits of American Communists).

One final note. As already hinted, I have had to be far more selective in my editorial choices than I would have liked; my original proposal was for an anthology double this length. I hope that it is immediately understood, then, that a focus on a particular film or filmmakers is usually based more on availability and representativeness than on an evaluative judgment. My decision to include Julia Lesage's remarkable piece on Rape, for example, instead of a treatment of This Film Is About Rape, is not meant to privilege Joanne Elam and her Chicago collaborators over Bonnie Kreps and the National Film Board of Canada's Women's Studio; the same for my focus on DEC Films rather than New Day Films, Quebec rather than Ireland, American blacks rather than the gay movement, Latin America rather than Africa, and so on. Fortunately, there is plenty of scope for sequels.

I am grateful to Barbara Halpern Martineau for the original idea for Show Us Life, which neither of us realized would take five years to realize, and for her input into its early stages; to Mark Leslie for help with translations; and of course to twenty-six patient and unpaid contributors whose interventions will, I modestly hope, inspire new energy and new recruits among committed documentarists. Show Us Life is dedicated to Julia, Chuck and John, who have demonstrated that political film criticism is an integral part of political film practice.

Notes

1 Fernando Solanas, "Cinema as a Gun," Cineaste, Vol. III, No. 2 (Fall 1969), p. 20.

2 Joris Ivens, The Camera and I (New York and Berlin, 1969), p. 99.

3 Dziga Vertov, "A Film-Show in a Village (1920)," Masha Enzensberger, trans., cited in Enzensberger's "Dziga Vertov," Screen, Vol. 13, No. 4.

4 "Film in Allende's Chile," interview with Miguel Littin by Gary Crowdus and Irwin Silber, Cineaste, Vol. IV, No. 4 (Spring 1971), p. 7.

5 Genre studies is a useful theoretical framework for the study of documentary, though, more properly speaking, documentary is not so much a genre as a genre-family that coincides with a distinct mode of filmic--and non-filmic--discourse and practice.

6 The concept of "political modernism" originates with Fredric Jameson, Aesthetics and Politics (London, 1978), and is developed by Sylvia Harvey, May '68 and Film Culture (London, 1978).

7 I am thinking for example of the Cubans' shift away from self-reflexive works like The Adventures of Juan Quin Quin (1967) toward conventional political melodramas like El Brigadista of a decade later.

8 Bill Nichols, "Documentary Theory and Practice," Screen, Vol. 17, No. 4, pp. 34-48.

9 Andrew Sarris, "The New York Film Festival," repr. in. Confessions of a Cultist: On the Cinema, 1955/1969 (New York, 1971), p. 317.

PART I

PIONEERS

Chapter 1

"CINEMA WEEKLY" AND "CINEMA TRUTH": DZIGA VERTOV AND THE LENINIST PROPORTION

Seth Feldman

More than is the case with any figure of film history, Dziga Vertov's standing has been the victim of rival contemporary claimants to his legacy. On the one side are adherents of the modernist avant-garde who appropriate Vertov as some kind of ancestor of Peter Kubelka. On the other side are those with special interest in documentary who argue for Jean Rouch, Frederick Wiseman or even the Maysles brothers as the rightful heirs. By willfully sidestepping Vertov's fervent political claims for his art, both positions seriously trivialize and distort Vertov's immense legacy. It is only through the solidly materialist historical scholarship on Vertov's actual texts and their contexts, scholarship that happily has not been too far behind the false prophets, that we are coming closer to an understanding of the real dimensions of his work. Stephen Crofts' and Olivia Rose's "An Essay Towards Man with a Movie Camera" is one example of such scholarship, and Seth Feldman's study of Vertov's early newsreel series, presented below, is another. This rare analysis of the formative stages of Vertov's artistic and political practice serves, among other things, to lay to rest some of the myths that inevitably accumulate around any artist whose actual work is seen so rarely, among them the myth that Vertov never worked with staging or mise-en-scène. It also reminds us of how urgent it is for all of Vertov's films to become available in the English-speaking world, not to mention full English translations of his many writings (which to date have been provided only very selectively by the various claimants). Only then will we be able to profit from the full legacy of this towering figure, the founding parent of radical documentary.

The name Dziga Vertov has come to be associated with the question of the role of the artist/intellectual in revolutionary activity. During his own lifetime, Vertov's definition of this role was a matter of contention in both the Soviet Union and the Western Left. Identified with the Russian/Soviet avant garde, Vertov could be seen either as a case study of the adaptation of avant-garde sensibilities to Marxist necessity or as the embodiment of reactionary formalist concerns. It was this latter interpretation that would destroy Vertov's career in the years after Stalin's proclamation of Socialist Realism as the only correct Soviet aesthetic. It would also serve to separate Vertov from the Russophile Western filmmakers who would serve as the core of the American and British documentary film of the 1930s.

Vertov's standing as a revolutionary filmmaker was rehabilitated only after his death in 1954. The first, though generally unrecognized, step in this process is the association made by Georges Sadoul between Vertov's work and the documentary movement emerging in France in the late 1950s. Sadoul's translation of Vertov's term, Kinopravda, as "cinéma vérité" was, at first, accidental. But upon reflection, Sadoul recognized that the immediacy and freedom of movement inherent in Vertov's newsreels and silent features were, in fact, prerequisites for the direct cinema movement.[1] A few years later, Jean-Luc Godard asserted the failure of cinéma vérité to achieve the standard of materialist analysis set by Vertov's work. In naming his political filmmaking collective the Dziga Vertov Group, Godard established Vertov as more than a prophet of direct cinema and video style. Rather, to Godard and to subsequent materialist analysts of Vertov's work[2] the ostensibly Formalist concerns of the Soviet documentarist were no more nor less than a Marxist rethinking of cinema's functions.

As a result of this recent rethinking of Vertov's role, films such as The Man with the Movie Camera, Enthusiasm and Three Songs About Lenin may be viewed outside of their previous associations with the purely modernist avant-garde. By the same token, the "death sentence" passed by Vertov and his colleagues on the narrative feature film was more than a call for a return to a primitivist sensibility.[3] Rather, it is the first declaration that the progressive cinema cannot coexist with an intrinsically bourgeois narrative code. The lesson taught by Vertov's films and writing is that film form is not an arbitrary experimental pursuit. Rather, it is the repository of film's potential as a tool for understanding and influencing social change.

But how did Vertov learn that lesson? It is our contention here that Vertov's style and formal concerns were a direct product of the needs of the post-Revolutionary situation in the Soviet Union. Vertov recognized historical necessity in the same way that Lenin recognized it in his dictum that cinema would be the Revolution's most important art form. And much to the annoyance of other Soviet filmmakers who, from the first, wished to re-establish the pre-Revolutionary feature industry, Vertov insisted on Lenin's proviso to that much quoted assertion: that some 75 per cent of cinema resources would be earmarked for the production of informational films.

In adopting and advocating this "Leninist Proportion," Vertov was also reflecting the initial response of the Russian avant-garde to the Revolution. That movement rejected fictionalization and abstraction in favor of direct engagement in the construction of the Communist State. Mayakovsky, sitting on the State Museums Committee, passed a death sentence of his own on all the materials captured from the old regime. The poet dedicated his efforts toward the writing and illustration of informational wall posters. Other artists turned their talents toward the design of more efficient clothing, structures and implements. On their part, the original impetus of the Formalist critics was to reduce artistic and social manifestations to universal scientific principles. The ultimate goal was to make universally accessible what had previously been obscure elitist pursuits.

Beyond all these considerations was the very survival of the Revolution. Nowhere is this seen more clearly than in the first two newsreel series produced by Vertov. Kinonedelia (Cinema Weekly) consisted of 43 weekly issues released during 1918 and 1919, the height of the Civil War. In form, they appear to differ little from other newsreels of the period. Yet, as seen below, in the selection of items and their juxtaposition lay the basis for an analytic use of reality.

Vertov's second newsreel series, Kinopravda, consists of 23 issues released between 1922 and 1925. Their construction reflects the movement in revolutionary struggle away from physical combat to the struggle for ideas. It was during the production of Kinopravda that Vertov made his most fervent demands for the new understanding of cinematic form. And it is within those Kinopravda issues that Vertov most clearly questions the uses of reality in a Socialist State and the role of those assigned to perceive it.

Dziga Vertov's introduction to cinema, according to Alexander Lemberg's account,[4] took place sometime during the Kerensky period. Vertov had been experimenting with the recording of sound. Using a Pathéphone he had attempted to record and edit street and factory noises. Meeting Lemberg at a "poet's café" Vertov discovered that his ambition of capturing and editing reality could be better achieved through cinema. Lemberg, a newsreel cameraman, agreed to teach Vertov the basics of the medium. By the time of the October Revolution Vertov was ready to take his place as a Soviet cinéaste.

The immediate results of the Revolution were not encouraging to any would-be filmmaker. As neither film stock nor film equipment had ever been produced in Russia, the Bolsheviks, in the face of a trade embargo, could make no promises of supplies. What little stock and equipment remained in the country was largely in the hands of those hostile to the new regime. But on March 4, 1918, some five months after the Revolution, the first step was taken to provide the Government with an agency for cinema production. On that date, the Praesidium of the Soviet of Workers', Soldiers' and Peasants' Deputies of the City of Moscow decreed that an inventory be made of all cinema equipment in the city and forbade further hoarding of equipment and stock. Two weeks later NARKOMPROS, the People's Commissariat of Education, took control of the resources of the Skobelev Committee, the state film production unit under Kerensky. But it would not be for another two months that the equipment so taken would be allocated to the only group within NARKOMPROS with any idea for its use, the self-proclaimed Moscow Kino Committee.

Handed their equipment on May 26, the Committee, under the direction of Mikhail Koltsov, was able to release Kinonedelia No. I one week later. Whatever part Vertov, as the Committee's secretary, played in this first production was probably eclipsed by the skills of the cameramen Lemberg, A. A. Levitskii, P. K. Novitskii, G. B. Giber, Eduard Tisse, P. V. Ermlov and others. While these men went out in search of news, Vertov watched how the fragments of what they shot were pieced together by his future wife and editing assistant, Yelizaveta Svilova. By the time Koltsov was called to the front in the summer of 1918, Vertov had gained the acumen to take over the entire operation.

The primary task he inherited from Koltsov was to emphasize the establishment of Bolshevik authority throughout the expanses of what was to become the USSR. Amid interventionist invasions and the emerging forces of the Civil War, the most important message *Kinonedelia* had to deliver was that the new government was continuing to function and was establishing roots deeper than those of the ephemeral regime that had so recently fallen. To achieve this end, *Kinonedelia* relied on conventional newsreel images whose power can only be appreciated if they are seen in the context of their times. Item one in *Kinonedelia No. I* consists of nothing more than the dedication of a monument to Marx in Moscow. We see speakers standing at the base of a large bust of Marx, and later a parade. But what we are also seeing is the opening of a new set of eyes, the first images that Soviet film was able to produce of the achievement of Communism in Russia. The simple item is a dedication to the future of *Kinonedelia*, its purpose and its audience. It is also a self-congratulatory proclamation by those who, only fifteen months before, had been ruled by a medieval monarchy.

Approximately one third of the items in *Kinonedelia* deal with this theme of the establishment of the Soviet State. They range from shots of children on a peasant commune to the meeting of the VI Extraordinary All-Russian Congress of Soviets. In some cases, it can be assumed, the presentation of these items was primarily informative, telling people about new and unfamiliar institutions. In other cases, depending on how well informed a particular audience was, such items could have the equally useful function of reinforcing previously publicized information by the addition of photographic "proof."

Complementing the items on new institutions are film portraits which served to introduce the new leaders of the Soviet Government and armed forces, lending an air of reality to figures who had been publicized by other media. In two instances, however, the images of leaders take on a more important function. In Kinonedelia No. 22, shots of Lenin recovering from wounds are inserted as a reassurance to those concerned about him after Dora Kaplan's assassination attempt. A similar item, contradicting rumors of the death of E. K. Breshko-Breshovskaya, also recognizes and reacts to a specific question in the mind of a potential audience.

Soviet leaders were not the only political figures presented to the public by Kinonedelia. Film portraits of enemies appeared with some frequency; and the device of portraying the enemy among items concerning the new regime was consistent with the theme of conflict that runs through the newsreel series. As the Civil War intensified, the juxtaposition of images of pro- and anti-Soviet leaders was complemented by a growing number of items concerning battles and trials of anti-government figures.

As the number of items concerning conflict increased, so did the sophistication and intensity of montage with which these conflicts were presented. Early news stories about the Civil War are placed almost haphazardly. An item entitled "Workers Appeal for the Defence of the Socialist Nation" (in No. 4) can almost be mistaken for another "human interest" story, sandwiched as it is between an item on the Kazan Station in Moscow and a part of the regular "Petrograd in These Days" series. But a vastly improved presentation of war news can be seen in Kinonedelia No. 19. In item four, we are shown a sequence which begins with shots of a dead sailor, continues with shots of the interventionist arms used to kill him and ends with a pan around newly captured territory. The sailor, the mute evidence of the invaders and the long shot of the captured land together achieve a montage effect, creating a motif present in no single image. It is only because the three images are put together the way they are that we know a battle has taken place.

The montage structure of Kinonedelia No. 19 does not end with item four. Item five is a series of shots of the Ukrainian Nationalist leader Skoropadskii leading public prayers against the Soviets. Item six, announcing the execution of an enemy, follows as if to predict the fate of anti-Soviet figures such as Skoropadskii. Item seven is then presented with a dual effect. While it too announces the death of an enemy leader (Bochkareva, the commander of the reactionary Women's Fighting Battalion), it leaves as the final image of the entire newsreel shots of Bochkareva at a moment of power. By using these old shots of Bochkareva, Vertov achieves a montage collision between images of the counter-revolutionary in action and the news transmitted by the title. The net effect is to reiterate the overriding theme of these last four items: the Revolution's inevitable triumph over its enemies.

A third kind of montage that Vertov began to develop in *Kinonedelia* was the more formal cutting between images which was later to become his trademark. In *Kinonedelia No. 30*, one can all but feel Vertov's exhilaration when, for the first time, he cuts purely on motion. The shots are taken from the front of a train as it goes around bends in a snow-covered mountainous area. As the cars begin to swing to screen right, there is a sudden cut and they are seen going off to screen left. The sequence is continued in this manner for a total of five edits in the space of a little less than a minute of screen time. The pace, of course, is ridiculously slow. Nevertheless, it creates within the viewer the sense of cinematically augmented motion, the production of movement that could not exist without cinema. In later manifestoes, Vertov was to refer to this aspect of his work as the Cinema Eye: "I am eye. I am a mechanical eye. I, a machine, am showing you a world the likes of which only I can see."

While what was to become the Cinema Eye is just barely apparent in *Kinonedelia*, the second of Vertov's major principles, Life Caught Unawares, played a prominent part in the newsreels. As it came to be defined in later writings and films, Life Caught Unawares meant the creation of a sense in the viewer that the activities of the subject on the screen had not been affected by the presence of the camera. The hidden camera, a favorite device of Vertov's cameraman brother Mikhail Kaufman (who did not join Vertov until 1922), played a small role in creating these images. More often, and more significantly, Vertov would depend on his subject being too busy to call attention to the camera's presence. In later films, particularly *Man with the Movie Camera* (1929), this technique was developed into a kind of barometer of social involvement. In *Man with the Movie Camera*, only the social outcast and the NEP-man call attention to the camera, true participants in Socialist activities having no time to "mug."

In *Kinonedelia*, Life Caught Unawares is used as both

an organization and an ideological tool. What now look like rather anodyne shots of people strolling through parks, listening to concerts and standing in queues in front of city shops, in 1918 and 1919 took on altogether different meanings. The shots of queues, for instance, worked to counteract a traditional town/country animosity that had intensified in Russia during the period of War Communism. They were evidence to country people that those in the cities were suffering privations similar to their own. Conversely, simple shots of farm activities were aimed at city people alarmed by rumors of rural food hoarding. Taken together, items of this sort were meant to produce the impression of a growing bond between rural and urban areas engaged in a shared struggle against equal hardships. The official admission that these hardships existed undoubtedly helped the credibility of Kinonedelia (and of the government that sponsored it). Furthermore, the images of citizens from all over Russia working to achieve Communism created, over the weeks, a continuing travelogue of social progress, a theme more explicitly developed in later Vertov films like A Sixth of the World (1926).

Ideologically, this emphasis on the common man as news had ramifications for both Socialist art and cinema history. While cinema itself was nothing new to the Russian people, the idea of a cinema which placed them on a screen so recently reserved for actors and dignitaries was not only a novelty (boosting distribution) but a celebration of their victory in the class struggle. And, just as it was appropriate for the first Socialist cameras to be turned upon the common man, it was equally fitting that Vertov, a neophyte filmmaker, should all but quote the earliest works of his medium, the studies of home life and street scenes with which Lumière began world cinema. The images produced by Life Caught Unawares represented the first cinema products since Lumière in which the camera had not been a self-conscious factor in the arrangement of the images it produced. To Vertov, this meant that the filmmaker could be accepted into the new society as a fellow-worker rather than as a boss (as he was in fiction film) or a dispassionate observer (as he was supposed to be in contemporary newsreels).

This conception of the filmmaker as a fellow-worker may be traced back to the attitude expressed by the Moscow Kino Committee toward their predecessors in Kinonedelia No. I. In the last item of that issue, a shot of the moribund Skobelev Committee was placed after the title: "The Skobelev Committee at the End of the Holiday." Nor did this proclamation of new vigor prove to be an idle boast. By the time the Soviet Government had nationalized cinema production in August 1919, Vertov had not only produced all of Kinonedelia[5] but had also edited three short compilation films: Battle at Tsaritsyn, The Trial of Miranov and The Unearthing of the Remains of Sergei Radonezhskogo (all 1919). At the time of nationalization, he was working on Anniversary of the Revolution (1919), a twelve-reel compilation film chosen by Lenin as one of the first Soviet works of art to be sent abroad. By the time he began work on Kinopravda in June 1922, Vertov had, besides supervising film work at the front, edited the thirteen-reel compilation film History of the Civil War (1922) as well as the shorter films All-Russian Elder Kalinin and The Agit Train of the Central Party (both 1921).

These last two films are indicative of Vertov's interest in new methods of distribution. Both grew out of his travels with Soviet President Kalinin on the agit-train Lenin in 1920. Using a specially designed film car aboard the agit-train (in much the same manner as Medvedkin some dozen years later), Vertov composed a continually changing travelogue, showing audiences newly edited films while shooting their reactions and their surroundings for insertion into the films they were watching. Vertov repeated this technique during his travel on the agit-steamer Red Star, the result being the film Instructional Steamer "Red Star" (1924). The technique of including audience response as part of a film's content would be repeated in A Sixth of the World and would be a central motif in Man with the Movie Camera.

When Vertov returned to Moscow to make Kinopravda, he brought with him the ability to liberate film from the conventions of the film theatre and make it part of the architecture of the Soviet City. The Kinoks (practitioners of the Cinema Eye), as Vertov's production group began to call themselves, were as serious about distributing films as they were about making them. Kinopravda No. 9 shows the Kinoks setting up a mobile projector and having an image on a portable screen in what they claim to be 90 seconds from their time of arrival at any location. Vertov also hoped that accessibility to cinema would not be limited to a passive audience. In 1923, an effort was undertaken to organize clubs of cinema correspondents along the lines followed by the American Newsreel organization of the 1960s. Unfortunately, the scarcity of materials in the USSR limited this proposed cinema network to films such as Kinopravda

No. 19, made during the travels of the Moscow-based film-workers.

Exercising his role as a fellow-worker, Vertov's main concern in the first Kinopravdas was to help organize public assistance for victims of the 1922 famine. In items concerning the famine, he tempers the shock of images taken in the devastated areas with other images of a Soviet government taking steps to alleviate the situation. As in the Kinonedelia item concerning Bochkareva, he experiments with collisions between the message on the title card and the shots that follow. In one instance, we are told that sightseeing flights over Moscow have been organized as a fund-raising device to help the famine areas. But what we actually see on the screen are images of a modern airplane and a vast Soviet city. The sense of urgency produced by the title card collides with the sense of reassurance provided by the images, to leave the viewer with the net impression that the problem will eventually be solved.

Kinopravda's evolution from a conventional news-oriented newsreel to a project encompassing these many experiments in the format of the short documentary began with Kinopravda No. 13. To better understand the change in the newsreel, it is valuable to compare Kinopravda No. 13 with the issue that preceded it. Both Kinopravdas deal with the celebration of the fifth anniversary of the October Revolution. Kinopravda No. 12 treats the celebration as a set of news items, presenting them in a fundamentally journalistic manner. All of the items are presented as having taken place the week of the celebration (three of them are, in fact, dated) and each item is kept isolated from the others by explanatory title cards.

The most important editing in Kinopravda No. 12 exists between items rather than within them. The largest, most "newsworthy" item, the anniversary celebration in Red Square, is covered in item one. The second item, showing a meeting of workers and peasants in a village outside Moscow follows as if to continue the spirit of the larger demonstrations but in the microcosm of a village setting. Items three and four repeat this macrocosm/microcosm pattern by covering a large workers' demonstration, followed by a smaller meeting to celebrate the opening of workers' houses. The fifth item also continues the microcosm motif by covering a "Party for Three Generations." The "party" is actually a ceremony in which Pioneers are sworn into the Komsomol; Komsomol members are sworn into the Party and all gather around an "October child" who represents the generations yet to come. The ceremony is thus a microcosm of the various generations passing the torch of Party loyalty, a situation which, we are led to believe, is true throughout the nation. This theme of unity through a meeting of representatives is furthered in the sixth and last item of the issue in which workers from the Far East meet Moscow workers and Soviet leaders.

Kinopravda No. 13, like Kinopravda No. 12, begins with the coverage of the demonstrations marking the fifth anniversary of the Revolution. As previously noted, however, these images have been set off by the title: "FIRST." The non-specificity of the title and the title that immediately follows it ("FIVE YEARS OF OCTOBER") serves to free the images of this first part of the issue from any necessary connection with the actual demonstrations. The first images of these demonstrations are followed by a sequence of airborne shots of cities, villages and factories from all around the Soviet Union. Just as spontaneously as it left the Red Square demonstrations, the newsreel returns to them through shots of various Russian leaders, a portrait of Lenin and the slogan from Lenin's speech of the day.

Having declared its geographical freedom, Kinopravda No. 13 displays a similar temporal freedom in the section following the titles "SECOND" and "FIVE YEARS OF STRUGGLE." This section is entirely composed of shots from the Civil War, the famines and the first years of the NEP. This recounting of the past serves to set up the third and longest of the sections, which roams not only through time and space but also through levels of humor and seriousness (by following a parade of sculptured caricatures of political enemies with a show of military strength), and even delves into self-reflection by using sequences from previous issues of Kinopravda. Kinopravda No. 13 is, in short, fulfilling the principle of the "Cinema Eye" by extending the perception of a given event to include phenomena existing beyond the time and space open to human perception. It is the first time in any of his surviving work that Vertov pulls an event apart and shapes it in this manner.

The strategies of Kinonedelia No. 13 would be repeated in later issues. Kinopravda No. 17, for instance, uses these same techniques in its coverage of the Agricultural and Home Industries Exhibition held in Moscow. The issue begins not with shots of the Exhibition but rather with shots depicting an unspecified area during a famine. Shots then follow of a harvest and of Soviet President Kalinin among peasant children. This sequence might have stood as a simple introduction to the Exhibition--once again, as in Kinopravda No. 1, showing a food crisis and its solution via Government intervention. Vertov was not, however, content to let this stand as the introductory sequence. In the following shots children are seen writing and sending a telegram. From the text of the telegram, we learn that the children are writing to Lenin to wish him a speedy recovery. There is, however, no mention of the Exhibition. This is left up to Lenin who, in a telegram having nothing to do with the first one, writes: "All Union Exhibition, from my soul I wish you progress." In this way, by taking completely disparate items as the material for his introduction to the Exhibition, Vertov not only provides a reason for the Exhibition's existence but also manages to link its opening to Lenin's recovery which, in turn, is linked to the well-being of the nation as a whole.

The coverage of the Exhibition itself is structured with a complexity matching its introduction. Vertov chose to compose Kinopravda No. 17 before the opening of the Exhibition. Thus, the shots of the Exhibition are entirely made up of construction workers building it. Nor are all these workers seen at the Exhibition site. Shots take us to factories, railway terminals and out into fields where workers and peasants are--or so the editing implies--working on projects for the Exhibition. It is only toward the end of the issue that the camera returns to the Exhibition site, where it follows Lunacharsky, the minister in charge, on a tour of inspection and observes the raising of the flag. As a final gesture, Kinopravda No. 17, having expanded the exhibition both temporally and geographically, portrays it with an animated map.

To appreciate the uniqueness of the kind of treatment given to an event by Vertov in the later Kinopravdas, one need only compare them to the other newsreels of the day. The American newsreel industry which, according to Fielding, "established its leadership in the international newsreel business"[6] in the early 1920s, increasingly modeled itself on what Vertov regarded as the "newspaper newsreel":

> The preponderance of journalistically trained and print-oriented personnel ... contributed in larger measure to the newspaper like structure and style

> of the American newsreel, with the fragmented succession of unrelated "stories," the titles composed in the manner of front page headlines, and the practice of beginning each issue with the major news event of the day, followed by successively less important subject matter.[7]

This situation would not change until the 1930s, when the possibility of spoken commentary encouraged analysis of events and eventually the introduction of The March of Time and its imitators.

Of course, seeing Kinopravda merely as a precursor of The March of Time not only does the series an injustice but, more importantly, represents a misreading of the historical context within which the Soviet newsreel series was developed. Kinopravda, no less than any other work produced during the 1920s in the USSR, was part of the discovery and exploration of montage as a formal means of materialist deconstruction. This is seen quite clearly in Kinopravda No. 18. The largest item in that issue is the coverage of a Communist "Christening," a ceremony similar to that seen in Kinopravda No. 12. Here, though, the cutting is far more sophisticated, working its way toward a crescendo in which the participants in the ceremony and the factory machinery around them join in the singing of the "Internationale." Very few words from the anthem are seen in titles. But, in the rhythmic cutting of some 60 four- to eight-frame shots, Vertov works toward a synesthetic re-creation of the musical accompaniment.

This particular item also illustrates a difference in emphasis between Kinonedelia and Kinopravda. Within the item, we are shown workers shutting down their machines to attend a ceremony honoring the newly born "October baby." The baby is passed among a small group of Party members, Komsomols and Pioneers, gifts are presented to the parents, and the singing of the "Internationale" begins. It is at this point that the machinery seems to set itself in motion and join in the singing, for the montage finale described above.

From the stiff, nervous performances of the participants in the ceremony, it is apparent that Vertov in this sequence has little use for Life Caught Unawares. Nor is this the only Kinopravda item which looks posed. In a sequence in No. 8, showing eager citizens snapping up news of the trial of the Social Revolutionaries, we see Vertov and his brother in the back seat of a speeding car taking a newspaper from a boy running alongside. Other shots within Kinopravda are as, if not more, evidently contrived.

But if Vertov seems in Kinopravda at times to abandon Life Caught Unawares, he does so in the fervor of creative freedom which characterizes this new stage of his work. The success of Kinonedelia and of the compilation films guaranteed him government support (one instance in which the availability rather than the scarcity of stock and equipment encouraged montage experimentation). During the production of Kinopravda, Vertov had a large stock of archive material on which to draw. He had a large and competent staff. Producing another newsreel series (Goskinokalendar) concurrently with Kinopravda gave him a second large stock of facilities, as well as an overview of Soviet current events. At the same time, Goskinokalendar, a more conventional newsreel, relieved him of the necessity of presenting "straight" news in Kinopravda.

Consequently, Kinopravda existed as a purely experimental venture in the cinematic interpretation of current events. The Cinema Eye was given a free hand in constructing and reconstructing those images which the news produced. Cameras were cranked at a multitude of speeds and mounted on every conceivable vehicle. Animation became a regular feature, Vertov remembered having invented entire new genres: "Review films, sketch films, verse films, film poems and preview films made their appearance.... Considerable work was done in the utilization of new methods for subtitling, transforming titles into pictorial units equal to the images."

Trying to do everything cinema could do, Vertov inevitably transgressed the boundaries of Life Caught Unawares. He found that one of the most useful capabilities of cinema was that of reproducing a posed or acted event. In Kinopravda No. 18, the nature of the story to be covered dictated the filming of people who were all too obviously altering their actions to suit the requirements of the camera.

However much the coverage of ceremonies may have presented a problem in this early work, the idea of the ceremony served in Vertov's later films as an effective compromise between the demands of Life Caught Unawares and the need to present images that furthered the theme of a given film. While, strictly speaking, the orchestra conductor in Enthusiasm (1930) is not changing his actions for the benefit of the camera, he is still providing Vertov with the performance called for at that point in the film. This is not to say that the staged scene did not remain a part of Vertov's repertoire of cinematic devices for the rest of his career. It is merely to point out that the staged event, taken in conjunction with the demands of Life Caught Unawares, produced, as a hybrid, an interest in ceremony that provided one of Vertov's most frequently recurring themes.

Another motif running through all Vertov's films is his fascination with machinery, as demonstrated by the use of the machine in Kinopravda No. 18. Machines are employed metaphorically in sequences like that in Kinopravda No. 8, in which army tanks are almost literally converted into ploughshares as they are used to pull earth-moving devices leveling the Moscow airport. Machines may also be used for humor, as in a sequence in Shagai Soviet (1926) in which buses and trucks decide to hold a political rally without their drivers. But as Vertov himself stressed in the manifesto We, machines are used most significantly when they are being integrated (via the Cinema Eye) into the life of man:

> We discover the soul of the machine, we are in love with the worker at his bench, we are in love with the farmer on his tractor, the engineer on his locomotive.
>
> We bring creative joy into every mechanical activity.
>
> We make peace between man and machine.
>
> We educate the new man. [8]

Man and his machinery are thus montage elements in the creation of a cinematic integration which, the Kinoks hoped, would reflect a similarly successful integration in the society of "the new man." In much the same way as man and his machines, man and his history are integrated in what is the longest and perhaps the most powerful of the Kinopravda issues. Kinopravda No. 21 is a 795-meter essay on the effect of Lenin's life and death upon the Russian people. Using the interpretative option of the series, Vertov chose not to treat Lenin's death as a news story but rather to collect all possible relevant images, produce his own animations, and carefully compose a montage around a set of subtitles which read like lines from a Mayakovskian poem.

The length and complexity of Kinopravda No. 21 are indicative of Vertov's growing impatience with the newsreel genre. In 1924, he had been given his own unit--Kultkino--within the Moscow Film Studio. But even then his plans went beyond Kultkino and toward the production of factual films that would involve ordinary citizens in a nationwide exchange of revolutionary images. The first manifestation of this effort was the feature-length film Kinoglaz (Cinema Eye, 1924). That work, expanding the montage lessons of Kinopravda, was to have been the first of six explorations by the extended Kinok group.

Little came of Vertov's ambitious plans for mass film production. In 1925, after the release of Kinopravda No. 21, he constructed an issue around the peasants' response to Lenin's teachings. The last Kinopravda, No. 23, celebrated the coming of radio. Characteristically the film used stop-action techniques to demonstrate the construction of a crystal set and antenna. More importantly, it defined Soviet radio as a medium that would be acquired and listened to on a collective basis.

The following year, 1926, was decisive for Vertov, for the Kinoks and for the form of revolutionary cinema. Vertov released Shagai, Soviet (Stride, Soviet!) and his most ambitious work, Shestaya chast mira (A Sixth of the World). This latter film, commissioned by Gostorg, the State Export Agency, took the Kinoks around the entire nation to shoot a panorama of Socialist production. The footage was then edited so as to de-emphasize the ethnic and geographical distances covered. Instead, the nation's workers are brought together in a careful, extended montage rhythm. What could have been a travelogue or an exploitative peek at exotic peoples became an ode to the unifying force of socialist production.

A Sixth of the World cost Vertov his job at the Moscow Film Studio and, in retrospect, could be seen as the beginning of the end of his career. The film's contrasting of Soviet production with Western decadence made it unusable as a sales tool for Gostorg. Its message--that foreign exports were part of the struggle for socialism--ran counter to the conciliatory tone of the NEP.

There was a more important reason for Vertov's banishment from Moscow. By 1926, the Leninist Proportion had become an embarrassment for Soviet cinema. The feature film industry had re-established itself. Moreover, the films that had begun to win international recognition were the feature works that responded to but, essentially, recognized the predominant narrative code. Eisenstein, Kuleshov and Pudovkin were the codifiers, interpreters and apostles of Griffith's aesthetic. Despite their revolutionary plots, these Soviet features offered, through their very accessibility, the conciliatory message that Vertov had refused. Compared to films like Battleship Potemkin, By the Law and Mother, Vertov's work was overly parochial and a bit anachronistic.

Perhaps what Vertov leaves us in these two newsreel series is the true news, a kind of reality that can be read only by those in sympathy with the moment. Kinonedelia and Kinopravda tell us that every period is to be interpreted through its own form. As Godard realized in *his* Dziga Vertov films, these works were not the prophecy of some future technology or style. Nor were they models to be slavishly followed in the correct interpretation of contemporary politics. They are, finally, the assertion of that need for interpretation and the embodiment of a still ongoing search for radical documentary form.

Notes

1 Georges Sadoul, "Actualité de Dziga Vertov," Cahiers du Cinéma, 24, No. 144 (June, 1963), pp. 22-23.

2 A particularly important work in this regard is Stephen Crofts and Olivia Rose's "An Essay Toward Man with a Movie Camera," Screen, 18, No. 1 (Spring, 1977), pp. 9-58.

3 Vertov's contempt for narrative cinema is most clearly seen in his manifesto, "Kinoki. Perevorot" ("Kinoks. Revolution") which originally appeared in Lef, No. 3 (June-July, 1923), pp. 135-43. It appears in English in Film Culture, No. 25 (Summer, 1962), pp. 50-54 (and reprinted in Film Culture Reader) in Cinema, No. 9 (1971), pp. 25-28, and in Screen, 12, No. 4 (Winter, 1971), pp. 52-58.

4 Alexander G. Lemberg, "Dziga Vertov prikhodit v kino" ("Dziga Vertov Comes to Cinema") in Iz istorii kino; materialy i dokumenty. Edited by S. Ginzburg et al. Vol. 13. Moscow: Akademiia Nauk SSSR, pp. 39-49.

5 Sadoul questions Vertov's editorship of Kinonedelias Nos. 38, 39, 41 and 42. See Sadoul's "Bio-Filmographie de Dziga Vertov," Cahiers du Cinéma, 24, No. 146 (August, 1963), pp. 21-22.

6 Raymond Fielding, The American Newsreel, 1911-1967 (Norman, Oklahoma, 1972), p. 128.

7 Ibid. p. 135

8 Dziga Vertov, "My. Variant manifesta" ("We: a Variant of a Manifesto"), Kinofot, No. 1 (August 25-31, 1922), p. 12. The manifesto is translated in Lutz Becker's "Film in October" in Art in Revolution edited by Brian Dunce (London, 1971), pp. 83-87, 95-97.

Chapter 2

ESTHER SHUB: FILM AS A HISTORICAL DISCOURSE

Vlada Petric

Like Vertov, Esther Shub is another pioneering figure in the tradition of the committed documentary whose stature is unjustly obscured by the lack of availability of her work. In fact, the situation is even more critical than with Vertov: no film undergraduate from the hinterlands has not seen Man with the Movie Camera, but how many have seen The Fall of the Romanov Dynasty, the only one of Shub's works to be generally accessible? Vlada Petric and Jay Leyda have been virtually the only popularizers and interpreters of Shub's work in the English-speaking world. Petric's essay here goes a long way toward remedying our neglect of Shub's thought, with its abundance of excerpts from her untranslated writings, and fills in much detail about her relationships with Vertov and Eisenstein. The next step on the agenda, beyond the indispensable job of bringing her films back into circulation, will be a detailed textual and contextual analysis of the individual films themselves.

> It is amazing how many unexpected solutions come up when you hold film stock in your hands. Just like letters--they are born from the tip of the pen. --Shub

Esther Shub, along with Dziga Vertov, must be considered the most avant-garde Soviet filmmaker in silent documentary cinema. Admitting that she got her "schooling" from Vertov's films, Shub saw cinema as a constructivist enterprise, i. e., a montage structure composed of archival footage. Hence she would select only existent film shots to construct new cinematic structures as an engineer would construct a building or machine. Vertov also considered himself an "engineer," but he and his kinoks[1] photographed "Life-As-It-Is" without a preplanned script. In contrast to Vertov, Shub used prewritten scripts for her films, but both fought uncompromisingly against "staged" cinema with actors and sets.

When Shub started her career as a filmmaker, there was another prominent woman filmmaker in the Soviet Union--Olga Preobrazhenskaya, who directed several feature films, including both Women of Ryazan (1927) and The Quiet Don (1930). However, Shub's interest lay not in the feature film, but in the documentary. She belonged to the revolutionary filmmakers who wanted to change the very ideas about cinema and at least diminish the influence of the traditional (bourgeois) cinema in the new society. Shub's most important contribution was the establishment of a specific cinematic genre, the so-called compilation film, movies made exclusively from existing documents, mainly stock footage taken by many, often unknown, cameramen. Working with newsreel material (kinokhronika), Shub discovered some crucial principles of editing and intertitling, which were further developed by Eisenstein, Vertov, Pudovkin, and Kuleshov.

Shub was born to a family of landowners in a remote Russian village in the Chernigov district in the Ukraine on March 3, 1894. She attended elementary school in a nearby provincial town and studied literature in Moscow a few years before the October Revolution. Most of her time in Moscow was spent with the family of Alexander Ertel, a writer famous at the time, whose home was regularly visited by important literary and theater people, including the great poets Mayakovsky and Khlebnikov, the writer and poet Bely, and the painter Burlyuk. They all belonged to the avant-garde movement which fought against traditional art as well as the official cultural policy imposed by the Tsarist government. After the revolution Shub dropped her study of comparative literature so that she could attend the seminar of The Institute for Women's Higher Education given by progressive scholars and social activists of Moscow. While studying at the Institute, she applied for a job in the government, feeling that she could contribute something to the culture of the new regime; thus she became one of the officers in the Theater Department of Narkompros.[2]

In the beginning she was involved in theater and collaborated with Meyerhold and Mayakovsky, but later, in 1922, she joined the staff film company, Goskino, and began to learn about cinema. She soon became an expert in re-editing films imported for Soviet distribution, while producing herself both compilation and documentary films. Shub remained in Goskino until 1942 when she was nominated chief editor of Novosti Dnya (The News of the Day) in the Central Studio for Documentary Film in Moscow. In 1933-35 Shub supervised the montage workshop in Eisenstein's class in VGIK.[3] During the war she edited newsreels and continued to teach montage in VGIK when the school moved to Alma Ata in Kazakhstan. Her closest friends in the film world were Sergei Eisenstein, Vsevolod Pudovkin, Dziga Vertov, and Viktor Shklovsky. She wrote two books, In Close Up, 1959, and My Life--Cinema, 1972.[4] Shub died in Moscow, September 21, 1959, leaving to the history of cinema the following films:

Padenie dinastii Romanovykh (The Fall of the Romanov Dynasty), 1927
Velikiy put' (The Great Road), 1927
Rossiya Nikolaya II i Lev Tolstoi (The Russia of Nicholas II and Lev Tolstoi), 1928
Segodnya (Today), 1930
K-SH-E (Komsomol--Leader of Electrification), 1932
Moskva stroit metro (Moscow Builds the Subway), 1934
Strana Sovietov (The Country of the Soviets), 1937
Ispaniya (Spain), 1939
20 let sovetskogo kino (Twenty Years of Soviet Cinema), 1940
Fashizm budet razbit (Fascism Will Be Destroyed), 1941
Strana rodnaya (The Native Country), 1942
Sud v Smolenske (The Trial in Smolensk), 1946
Po tu storonu Araksa (On the Other Side of the Aras River), 1946

In addition to these films, Shub edited many documentaries for the younger filmmakers and conceived scores of newsreels dedicated to various political, public, and cultural events of the country. One of the most successful was her two-hour newsreel about the International Congress of the Democratic Federation of Women, held in Moscow in 1946.

Undoubtedly, Shub's most significant works are her three compilation films that cover Russian history spanning three decades: Russia: 1897-1912; The Fall: 1912-1917;

and The Road: 1917-1927. Prior to producing these films, she viewed close to one million meters of newsreel footage, from which she selected shots to be included in the final versions of her three films, making altogether 6,000 meters. These three films are, in fact, the visual history of Russia from the end of the last century through the October days, and closing with the Tenth Anniversary of the October Revolution.

The greatest problem Shub faced was digging up all the existing film material, which, after the Revolution, had been largely taken out of the country and sold to foreign producers (mostly American) or destroyed by the bad conditions in the film archives and production companies in Russia. She began at the last moment to search for all the footage related to Russian history, visiting many archives and storage places of the pre-revolutionary newsreel companies, "Kino-Moskva," "Pathé," and "Gaumont" in Moscow, Leningrad, and Kiev as well as in The Moscow Museum of the Revolution. She persuaded the government to buy the important 2,000 feet of negative about the February Revolution of 1917, including rare shots of the Tsarist period, sold in the United States immediately after the Revolution. She then began extensive research into the historical background and the selection of relevant material that could support her historical point of view.

The crucial issue in this type of filmmaking is to present the visual data in such a manner that the author's ideological attitude comes through without distorting the documents themselves. Shub emphasized this issue by saying: "The intention was not so much to provide the facts, but to evaluate them from the vantage point of the revolutionary class. This is what made my films revolutionary and agitational--although they were composed of counter-revolutionary material" (251). She had in mind footage taken from films made by anti-Marxist filmmakers which supported the Tsarist policy.

When she began editing her first film, its working title was February because Shub wanted to concentrate on the February Revolution of 1917. But as her concept developed in the course of editing, she expanded the film into a three-hour movie, with the new title, The Fall of the Romanov Dynasty. Although she was working simultaneously on a second film, The Great Road (also called Ten Years), she completed The Fall earlier in the same year (1927). Paradoxically, she found greater difficulty in collecting material for the second film, although it covered the first decade following the October Revolution, while the first film was composed of footage shot at the turn of the century. Not only was she compelled to find some of the crucial material for this film in the United States (including the famous shots of Lenin in his private home with his wife Krupskaya), but she also found the Soviet newsreel produced after the Revolution less interesting than the footage depicting life in the period before the Tsar's fall. In a 1927 interview, she stated frankly: "After the Civil War, Soviet newsreel concentrated on parades, meetings, arrivals, departures, delegates and the like, while there was almost no record of how we transformed the country to a new political economy and carried out the consequent construction."[5] Therefore she had to shoot the old documents, letters, photographs, objects and newspapers herself to compensate for the lack of film material. Inevitably, additional shooting was necessary for The Fall: Shub filmed 1,000 of the total 6,000 feet. The completed film, The Fall of the Romanov Dynasty, was conceived as a visual chronicle with three themes: a) Tsarist Russia in the years of the "black reaction" and the situation in Europe during the same period; b) World War I; and c) The February Revolution and the period 1912-1917.

As mentioned above, Shub was an expert in editing and subtitling foreign films prepared for Soviet movie theaters. Importation of foreign films increased during the period of the economic crisis, that is, in the years of NEP[6] when thousands of light entertainment films were widely shown in the Soviet Union. Shub reedited more than 200 foreign films and ten domestic feature films, thus acquiring great skill in montage. Most of these films were serials, with continuous action divided into episodes and designed for those European countries where films were still shown in two or three evenings. In order to keep the audience informed about the plot, each episode had a short "montage summary" of the preceding episode. Shub's job was to make one full feature film out of several episodes. To achieve this, she had to cut the introduction, then shorten and rearrange the sequences according to new titles that were not required to repeat already known facts as they often did in a three-part movie. In the course of time, Shub collected many shots from various films. She played with them, creating new montage units on the editing table, thus experimenting with the method known as the "Kuleshov Effect,"[7] which marks the starting point of the Soviet montage school.

Eisenstein used to watch Shub while she was doing these exercises. He even participated in one of them, reediting Fritz Lang's Dr. Mabuse (1922). Shub recalls this in her memoirs:

> Eisenstein reedited with me the adventure-detective film which dealt with speculators on the stock exchange, swindlers, mistresses and aristocracy. The title of the film was Dr. Mabuse. We reedited it many times, so that instead of several series, it became a feature with normal duration. We changed the narrative structure of the film as well as the intertitles. Even the film's title was changed: it became Gilded Mould (Pozolochennaya gnil'). As the introduction to the film we included a long title which read: The international war brought imperialist Germany to division and the capitalist crash. At the same time, when the working class makes incredible efforts to maintain its existence and fight against foreign and domestic bastards, the men who did not participate in the war avoided experiencing its horrors, and during the war led empty lives, full of speculation and adventures. They still continue this type of life after the war, a life of debauchery and manipulation" (75).

The above quotation is interesting as a document of the NEP period in Russia, and the way intellectuals tried to justify the sudden shift of concept in Soviet culture after the first revolutionary radicalism. The economy was at the edge of total collapse, so that Lenin was forced to permit, to a certain degree, the revitalization of private enterprise both in villages and cities, which consequently brought some loosening of ideological restraints in art. Overnight profit became the most important goal for all public activities, and the old type of show business began to flourish again, especially in Moscow and Leningrad. All the true revolutionaries and artists who dreamt of the new society, including Mayakovsky, Vertov, Brik,[8] as well as Shub, faced this new trend toward cheap entertainment with great pain, yet tried to adjust to the new policy as an "inevitable step" in the evolution of Socialism.

This is how Shub described those odd days of NEP in the Soviet Union:

> In the beginning I did not understand the meaning of the New Economic Policy, but when I realized what it really was, I lost my inner peace. Moscow suddenly became strange to me. Shadows of the past unexpectedly spread over my dear city. Again, marquees, advertising signs, trivial magazines, fancy restaurants, cabarets, casinos, night-clubs, "Nep-projects," and "Nep-men." It was the resurrection of the old days which we thought had gone forever.

Then Shub quotes the names of night-clubs, restaurants, luxury stores and popular magazines--even elegant apartments where one could entertain young ladies. No wonder that a woman like Shub, a true artist and an honest revolutionary, was disappointed with the new situation. Mayakovsky, Vertov, and many other revolutionaries had the same reaction. After all, they were giving their energy and talent to the creation of a new art, and contributing to workers' emancipation, when suddenly the ghost of the old bourgeois "mesmerizing art" spread over the Soviet Union like the plague.

Shub remembers how once, as she was working intensively on editing newsreels as well as studying at the Institute for Women's Higher Education, her friends invited her to dinner in one of the secluded Moscow apartments where they met an elegant lady covered with diamonds and gold, who acted as the hostess at a party where meals were served on china dishes and in crystal glasses (68). This happened at the same time as Vertov and his group known as "kinoks" were cruising along the Volga region filming thousands of children literally dying of hunger. But, concludes Shub in her memoirs, "that was only one aspect of life, an inevitable stage resulting from the NEP" (68). There were only two choices: either to accept the fact, or to withdraw into herself and her work. She never revisited that fancy Moscow apartment to spend, as she put it, her entire month's salary on a single dinner. She returned to her editing room and stayed there until the end of her life. The result of her work and her devotion to cinema testifies to her uniqueness both as an artist and a human being.

Before going into a closer analysis of Shub's major films, let me mention her relationship to other Soviet revolutionary filmmakers of the twenties. Most of all she was influenced by Eisenstein and Vertov, each in a different way.

From Eisenstein she learned about complex montage structures and a method of shooting staged events so as to mimic life's authenticity; this she believed was more important than anything else in cinema. In late 1927, Shub visited Leningrad and lived in the same hotel ("Europe") where Eisenstein's crew stayed while working on October. She spent most of her time with Eisenstein in the Winter Palace, observing the shooting and later discussing the montage structure of specific sequences with Eisenstein and his assistant, Alexandrov. "For me that was the best school for mastering the art of filmmaking" (114), she wrote later. In addition, Shub maintained a lengthy correspondence with Eisenstein, (mostly while he was working in Mexico, during 1931), discussing various problems of montage and the necessity "of developing one's concept of reality in the process of shooting, and only then subordinating the material to the director's vision" (116).

In spite of all her admiration for Eisenstein's intellect and genius, Shub never rejected her own concept of cinema; that is, her great concern for ontological authenticity,[9] which was to her the most important feature of the film shot. This is where she was closest to Vertov's method of "Cinema-Eye" (Kino-Glaz) and his strategy of shooting life "unawares" (varsplokh). Shub admitted that frankly:

> My study of cinema was not in a school. My university was the editing table, my friends, cameramen, several directors of feature films, and Dziga Vertov. Although we often argued with him--I could not accept his total disavowal of films based on scripts--I admired his great talent.... Vertov was an innovator, a creator, a seeker of new paths in documentary film.... Nobody understood the way he did that the right material does not come to the filmmaker out of the clear blue sky, but that it is always the result of the filmmaker's and cameramen's mutual action on the spot.... In 1925, Vertov made Lenin's Film-Truth, discovering a new type of film journalism (newsreel) as a substitute for the so-called cultural film propagated and encouraged by RAPP[10] (85, 206, 305).

Shub was one of the most objective (and constructive) critics of both Vertov's and Eisenstein's work, never going to extremes, while pointing to their faults and/or valuable qualities. She remained outside the existing antagonistic groups which--for strategic reasons--often undermined the significance of one artist over another. In contrast, Shub judged films according to their own values, regardless of to which group the filmmaker belonged. Even as the wife of A. Gan (the editor of the Constructivist journal Kino-fot), who attacked Eisenstein's theory of "Typage" (nonprofessional actors) and his concept of the staged mise-en-scène, Shub never changed her admiration for Eisenstein; on the other hand, this did not diminish her respect for Vertov.

In return, Shub had an equivalent influence on both Eisenstein and Vertov, which they acknowledged. Her recollection of the period when Eisenstein attended and participated in Shub's reediting of imported commercial movies has already been quoted above. But her greatest influence on Eisenstein was during her viewing and selecting of the newsreel footage for The Fall of the Romanov Dynasty. She wrote:

> He used to come to my editing room, not once, but many times, particularly when I was looking over the old footage about the February events in Leningrad and Moscow, and I think that he reconstructed the July revolt in Leningrad (October) directly under the impression of what he saw while viewing the old footage with me (74).

Obviously it was not merely the experience of viewing old footage that Eisenstein received from Shub; they discussed the material endlessly and experimented with montage by putting together different shots. Her memoirs are full of interesting conversations with Eisenstein, for whom she had great admiration. Shub's relationship to Vertov, however, was less intimate, but more dynamic and controversial. Although she admitted that "in the final account, through all our discussions, I was his pupil," she did not accept Vertov's method, and never stopped criticizing his irreconcilable antagonism to any kind of staged cinema. As one may assume, the influence was mutual, and Vertov himself admitted this by describing their discussions in his own way in his diary and by considering Shub one of the most significant figures in Soviet documentary film of the silent era.[11] Mayakovsky also praised Shub as "the most artistic (khudozhestvennaya) of all Soviet filmmakers, because in her films montage involves real facts, without the slightest rearrangement of reality or subsequent shooting."[12]

Above all, Shub and Vertov were ardent advocates of factualism (i.e., using the camera for recording authentic facts) in cinema and emphasized the paramount significance of ontological authenticity for the film image. They felt that ontological authenticity was the most proper way to separate cinema from literature and theater as well as from traditional aesthetics. They rejected the claim that an image was bad if it candidly depicted the outside world. On the other hand, they found that pictorial stylization of the photographed event, and especially its theatrical arrangement, was an attitude inherited from the fine arts and imposed on cinema. In painting this concept has its own justification for reasons thoroughly explained by art historians. In cinema, however, this principle has no validity because the representational aspect of motion pictures goes beyond mere truthfulness of the image to its prototype. Yet, ontological authenticity is not the ultimate goal of the film image, as it is in naturalistic painting or naturalistic literature. Rather, the strong representational nature of the motion-picture image is only a means by which this medium is capable of revealing some of the intrinsic features of reality, those features that cannot be perceived by the naked eye or brought out in a dynamic way by any other medium.

With such a radical concept of the relationship between film and reality, Shub and Vertov had to negate all basic aesthetic laws established by traditional documentary cinema. It is no surprise that Vertov went to extremes in denying actors, decor, and script in cinema. However, while Vertov was absolutely unyielding and aggressive due to his explosive temperament, Shub always found the necessary balance between documentary and narrative film. Therefore, she was accepted by the theorists of both unstaged and staged cinema. _Lef_ and its Futurist editors continuously took her work as the example of the "cinema of fact" because her concept of the newsreel as "visual documentation of history" was in harmony with the Futurist and Constructivist idea of "factual art" in general. Mayakovsky, Brik, Tretyakov and Chuzhak, as the editors of _Lef_, often quoted Shub's films in their attacks on "imaginative art," such as novels and plays based on invented stories and dramatized events. Most of the discussions of film in _Lef_ dealt with Shub's, Vertov's, and Eisenstein's works. Later, when Eisenstein fully opted for staged cinema, and after he decided to cast a worker (Nikandrov) to play Lenin in _October_, Mayakovsky, Brik and Tretyakov attacked him and praised only Shub and Vertov.[13] Mayakovsky was especially fond of Shub's film The Fall of the Romanov Dynasty. In his speech delivered at the meeting in honor of the Tenth Anniversary of the Soviet Cinema (in 1927), Mayakovsky raved about the "extraordinary films created by Esther Shub," while at the same time he ridiculed Eisenstein's decision to "stage [instsenirovka] Lenin in October."[14]

Viktor Shklovsky wrote extensively about Shub in his book For Forty Years, emphasizing her great sensitivity in selecting the right image out of thousands and giving it proper meaning through its relation to other images.[15] In his memoirs, Shklovsky also recalls how Shub was effective in reediting foreign films. The modern film theorists in the Soviet Union increasingly refer to Shub's writings on documentary film. Two of the most sophisticated among them, Tatyana Selezneva[16] and Sergei Drobashenko,[17] in their books on the evolution of the theory and practice of the Soviet documentary tradition, often quote Shub and compare her concepts with Vertov's. Selezneva and Drobashenko particularly emphasize the problem of ontological authenticity in the works and writings of Shub and Vertov. There were occasions when Shub was as militant as Vertov, which was justified by the tough conditions surrounding documentary filmmaking in the Soviet Union. In her 1929 article, "The Unstaged Cinema," Shub discussed the traditional division between artistic film and documentary film. She found that such a division was useless because "the idea of 'artistic movies' also includes such 'examples' of the past as The Crippled Master" (262). She intentionally chose the title of a trivial melodrama to characterize the style of conventional entertainment movies. What bothered her most was the fact that the official Soviet production film companies of the 1920s continued to make films of that kind. She wrote:

> This is the type of film encouraged by our film companies, and made by directors, the best cameramen, an entire army of actors, script-writers, artists, architects, propmen and other professionals. An enormous amount of money is spent on films like these. To imitate life, to enact and show arranged (staged) events on the screen is the method we call "staged cinema." Then there are "cultural films" which, in fact, do not exist. The term has been invented by people who do not know or do not want to recognize that a new trend in documentary cinema exists. As a result, the reality of today's

> Soviet cinema means staged films, in addition to the fact that most of them are artistically insignificant.... We, filmmakers of unstaged films, have a different notion of what cinema should be like. We do not need studios or actors, we do not need designers, painters, and scripts. There is nothing we can learn from fictional literature or from beautifully composed images. The real world of this planet, the real environment and technological ambience in which we live, the real things around us, ordinary people in actions, events of the day occurring by chance or by necessity, men equipped with scientific knowledge, men capable of pushing science forward, men fighting heroically to gain control over the natural elements--all this is the material of our films. We want to collect these facts and organize them into film-things related to science, technology, pedagogy and the vital tasks of today's life. We want to make films which will propagate the war against our class enemy, films which will courageously disclose both the failures and successes of a unique endeavor in the world, the endeavor to build socialism, which is our ultimate objective (263-264).

This quotation is obviously reminiscent of Vertov's early proclamations, both in its emphasis on factualism as the main feature of the documentary film, and in the style of writing, a vocabulary full of revolutionary zeal. It is the same language which characterized Vertov's "We" manifesto of 1922 or the proclamation "Kinoks Revolution" of 1923, in which staged cinema was denounced as the "opiate of the masses," and films with actors and based on scripts, the "poisonous bourgeois psychodramas."[18]

Shub's concept of documentary film was similar to Vertov's on both the theoretical and ideological levels. Ontological authenticity was the center of their theorizing about unstaged cinema. Vertov called it "Film-Truth" (*Kinopravda*), while Shub referred to it as "authentic material" (*podlinnii material*). According to her: "Authentic material is something that gives life to a documentary film, regardless of the fact that it might be composed of archival footage or shot by the filmmaker" (263). But unlike Vertov, Shub considered it possible to apply the idea of ontological authenticity to staged films, believing that a documentary can be authentic even if the filmmaker shoots the material following a preconceived script. She even invented a term for this hybrid genre, calling it an "artistic documentary film" [khudozhestvennyi dokumental'nyi fil'm], which "insists on showing on the screen all the dramatic events of everyday life, real people in action and conflict, without staging the events, but by recording segments of real life" (296).

Shub's concept of montage was not schematic, but rather intuitive and associative. She had a marvelous feeling for rhythm and movement, a true sense for selecting and putting the right shots together. Her ultimate goal was to comment upon events by the very juxtaposition of shots which, as such, preserve their own authenticity. Sergei Yutkevich recalls how he tried to obtain theoretical advice about editing from Shub. He asked her: "Please, Edi [that is how close friends used to call her], tell me why I have to place this shot here and not there? How much must I cut off from this long shot? One meter or two? And why just that much? Tell me the secret of how you decide about all this?" The answer was straightforward: "There is no secret. There are no rules whatsoever. One only needs to master the sense of the part within the whole."[19]

Like Vertov, Shub developed a "montage way of thinking," and she considered that "the true filmmaker possesses the capacity to find the most vivid and most emotional way of revealing all that is hidden in the filmed material." As for the final order of the shots, she could not give any rule as to how to achieve the correct montage tempo and how to bring forth the meaning of the juxtaposed shots. Hence, she repeatedly stated that one can learn only through practice:

> I began by simply watching films in the auditorium, then analyzing them on the editing table, which is essential for every director. This helped me understand how to judge correctly the technical execution and composition of the shot. Slowly I developed the capacity of memorizing each shot, particularly its inner content, rhythm, movement, and tempo in general. Then a moment always arrived when I began to feel sure at what point it was necessary and imperative to cut from a long to a medium shot, or from a medium shot to close-up, and vice versa. Finally, I became fully aware of the magic power of the scissors in the hands of some-

> one who uses montage to express himself visually as he uses the alphabet to express himself verbally (76).

Shub's concern for ontological authenticity was reconfirmed in her attitude toward sound films. In her 1929 article, "The Arrival of Sound in Cinema," she wrote:

> For us documentarists it is crucial to learn how to record authentic sound: noise, voices, etc., with the same degree of expressiveness as we learned how to photograph authentic, non-staged reality. Therefore, we have little interest in what presently goes on in the film studios, in those hermetically insulated theatrical chambers dotted with microphones, sound intensifiers, and other technological props. We are interested in the experimental laboratories of the scientists and true creators who can function as our sound operators (270).

She strongly opposed the postsynchronization and dubbing of feature films in the studio, and discarded any imitation of real sound. After her visit to the German sound film studios in Berlin, she concluded that the post-synchronization of films after they have been completed as silent movies kills their ontological authenticity because they have "no connection with the film's essence in general: the sound becomes dead, metallic, unnatural, and stifled" (271). Among the examples she gave was von Stroheim's silent film, The Wedding March (1928), "which was synchronized in German post factum, and thus entirely killed by the sound. The exaggerated, rough, and inadequate sound destroyed the subtle irony of this film" (271). Evidently, at that time the technical facilities of sound recording were not sophisticated enough to permit a truthful auditory recording of reality, as it was indeed possible to capture the visual aspect of life by the camera. Yet it is important to note that Shub, along with Vertov,[20] immediately sensed the necessity for direct sound recording and thus anticipated modern sync-sound cinema. With a continuous concern for authentic facts in documentary film, particularly in the sound era, both Shub and Vertov urged technicians to construct microphones and portable sound recording systems capable of capturing all sorts of authentic sounds simultaneously with shooting the image on actual locations.

Shub's compiled film trilogy is, in essence, a long newsreel put together on the basis of an ideological concept which chronologically follows a historical course of events. Her greatest talent was in conveying her viewpoint without distorting the authentic impact of the selected footage. It was a difficult task because there was not enough footage to begin with. For example, she found only eight meters of the footage shot about Tolstoi, his wife Sophia Andreevna, and their daughter Sukhotina, about 100 meters of Yasnaya Polyana, 100 meters of Astapov and over 200 meters of Tolstoi's funeral. Yet Shub decided to make a film about Tolstoi as "the center of historical change" by focusing on his religious and philosophical theories as well as the social circumstances in which he lived and worked. In order to document the social background of the period, Shub turned to newsreels photographed by various foreign cameramen visiting Russia at the turn of the century and, especially, the footage which belonged to the Tsarist photo archive. In addition, she photographed many historical objects related to Tolstoi and the landscape of Yasnaya Polyana. After seeing the material many times, she did not begin immediately selecting the shots. Prior to that she undertook considerable research about the period, interviewed many personalities involved in the events, and discussed the subject with her friends and collaborators. Then she wrote an impressionistic but extremely visual script in the style Eisenstein used to notate the order of images to be shot the next day in Odessa for his Battleship Potemkin. Here is the synopsis of the film's beginning as found in her notebook written in 1928:

> Russia at the dawn of the decline of a feudal-
> landowner society, and the rise of capitalism.
> Enormous space--without roads.
> Manors of the noblemen and landlords.
> Endless fields, forests and rivers.
> Millions of peasants, mostly illiterate,
> and "liberated."
> Living in ruins...
> In the cold...
> In hunger...
> Death.
> Homeless life...
> Full of squabbles,
> Of superstition,
> Of a desperate appeal to God...
> Of seeking oblivion in vodka.

The railways, factories, and warehouses under construction.
The big commercial establishment developed by the exploitation of the cheap labor of the peasants escaping the rural areas.
Cities controlled by the merchants and industrialists.
Poverty and suffering of the working class.
The coronation of Nicholas II.
The family estate of the Counts Volkonsky--Yasnaya Polyana.
Tolstoi's ancestors--tsar's servants--serfs.
Count Lev Nikolaevich Tolstoi--the repentant nobleman...
Outward humbleness...
Rejection of luxury...
Working by himself (without making use of someone else's work).
The continuation of the typical life led at the court and enjoyed by the landlords.
Yasnaya Polyana--like any other village.
Documents of the actions S.A. Tolstoi performed as a landlord.
In these conditions appears the protest of Lev Tolstoi against the autocracy, the violence of the government, exploitation (documents).
The protest against social hypocrisy, lies, misery and oppression of the working mass (documents).
Tearing off the mask from the Orthodox church and priests (documents).[21]

As one can see, this is a typical shooting script (découpage) composed of the specific shots which Shub already had in mind, followed by her laconic comments on the events, i.e., the ideological statements which she planned subsequently to develop and visualize. The structure of the script is chronological, with strong emphasis on the ideological aspect of the historical process. Obviously, after viewing the archival footage, Shub was inspired by specific visual facts; but in the course of structuring the material in written form, she developed her own vision of the historical events and included in it her personal ideological view of history. Her goal was to restore for the contemporary viewer the time when the Revolution of 1905 was defeated, those days when in the first few months of 1906 about a thousand men were executed without trial, when the wildest oppression struck peasants and workers, the dramatic period when Tolstoi preached that "Evil must be opposed by non-resistance, instead of violence," so that his death became a symbol of the beginning of the decay of the monarchy.

The result of this project turned out to be one of the most authentic cinematic documents of the silent era, containing many genuine data about the historical events and, at the same time, revealing a personal attitude toward the objective facts. As Shub put it, "each of my compilation films was also a form of agitation for the new concept of documentary cinema, a statement about unstaged film as the most important cinematic form of the present day" (262).

In many of her articles, Shub gives detailed instructions of how the compilation film as well as the true documentary newsreel have to be conceived and realized on the basis of absolutely different principles from those used in narrative and staged films. "The failure of most films made without a literary script, actors, decor, and other features of the staged cinema results from the fact that they are, in essence, conceived as fictional, dramatic and entertainment films" (246). This means that Shub structured her compilation films as "cinematic essays," and in this way her work differs radically from other documentary films of the period; the film chronicles before the 1920s were composed of unstructured newsreel footage merely illustrating various historical events without any conscious ideological attitude.

The Fall of the Romanov Dynasty (covering the footage before 1912 and including all the available material) is less dynamic than The Russia of Nicholas II and Lev Tolstoi (which goes up to 1917). But the authenticity of the rare old shots in The Fall (many of which were photographed by Alexander Drankov, one of the first Russian cameramen) gives them invaluable significance as documents. Shub elaborates extensively on the problem of structuring the newsreel material. The inclusion of all the unique footage arranged in a relationship that would allow her message to come through clearly and expressively was one of her major difficulties. In her article, "Yasnaya Polyana," Shub discusses the structure of the sequence involving Tolstoi. She quotes the list of sixty-four shots (including those showing objects she photographed subsequently) which present Tolstoi in his *milieu*, from the earliest footage showing Tolstoi and his wife Sophia Andreevna sitting on the bench in their garden, to the end, when masses of people on their knees pay their last tribute to the genius while his coffin is laid in the grave. The real cinematic impact of this sequence comes from the intricate relationship between the original newsreel footage on the one side, and objects, documents, or places subsequently photographed by Shub on the other side and related to the intertitles. Thus she created a cinematic collage of the past events seen from the contemporary standpoint, and proved that this medium offers an ideal possibility for historical discourse.

The problem of intertitles was one of the most discussed aspects in Lef's article dealing with cinema, often illustrated by examples from Shub's films. While Shklovsky, Tretyakov, and Brik criticized Vertov's intertitles, particularly in his films A Sixth of the World (1926) and The Eleventh Year (1928), as being redundant and too grandiloquent, they found Shub's intertitles functional and complementary to the image. This does not mean that Shub avoided the use of political slogans as intertitles; but she used them with greater economy and with the right sense of where to include them. For example, in The Fall, the idea of the decline of the monarchy is conveyed by the montage of various details of Tsarist symbols--golden armor, court paraphernalia, and the monument to Alexander II--with the intertitle "Down With the Tsar, the Bourgeoisie, the Capitalists, and the Provisional Government." In fact, the intertitle is a document in itself since it represents the slogan commonly used by the Bolsheviks.

Shub used other montage devices with the obvious intention of expressing her own comment upon the documentary facts. For example, in The Fall, she cuts directly from the shot of the landlord walking idly over the field to the shot of the ragged peasant exhausted from work. She uses even more blatant ideological parallel editing in The Great Road, based on the alternation of the Rockefeller close-up with the long shot of the crowded stock market, implying that Rockefeller is the king of the financial world.

This type of montage was criticized by some Soviet theorists of the period as a method alien to the very nature of documentary film because it mutilated the authenticity of the documentary fact. It was considered a forceful link between facts which were not actually connected in reality. However, the critics of Lef magazine defended Shub by claiming that she established an ideological reality through her method of montage. Among them was V. Pertsov, who in his famous article, "The 'Play' and Demonstration," stated:

> What Shub and Vertov did is pure oratorical journalism expressed by cinematic language. Montage is an active method of analysis and synthesis. If material is correctly analyzed regarding the place, time and content of the shots, if the hidden meaning of the footage is revealed not merely by the geography of its actual occurrence, but also by the possibility of juxtaposing the shots within a given theme, then the editor can add his personal voice to the chosen facts. Then, although the objective meaning of the specific shot may be in discord with the real life situation in which the shot was photographed, the ideological link between them creates another, ideological level of authenticity. For to edit facts means to analyze and synthesize, not to catalogue them.[22]

Since Shub had more material for The Fall than for The Russia, she could select the shots with dynamic composition executed by an often hand-held camera, as well as shots which were sometimes photographed from a plane. As a result, the editing pace in The Fall changes demonstrably throughout the film. In the beginning, shots are rather chronologically organized and intercut by informative titles conveying just facts. Later, when the mobilization begins (in World War I), the editing becomes more dynamic, with many details included; the intertitles are more emphatic and emotional. As Shub explains in her 1928 article, "My First Work," the basic problem of The Fall was structural. Her main concern was to achieve a balance between the material showing the Tsar, his family, and Russian politicians of the period, on the one hand, and the people, peasants, workers, and ordinary citizens on the other. With this in mind, she had to sacrifice many fascinating shots in order to provide the audience with the right historical perspective. She emphasized mass movement as the symbolic forecast of the events to come. She used many long shots of demonstrations in Petrograd and Moscow during 1917 to give a feeling of atmosphere and environment. Some of these shots have been used many times in various compilation films made later by other directors. Eisenstein and Pudovkin, as has already been mentioned, reconstructed some of these events in October (the street demonstrations), Battleship Potemkin (long views of the Russian fleet), and The End of St. Petersburg (the famous high-angle shot of the citizens in top hats standing in front of the stock exchange, and the wounded soldiers dying in water-filled trenches).

Like other Soviet revolutionary filmmakers, Shub wanted to make films for ordinary people, mainly workers and peasants, but never by compromising or by lowering her artistic standards. She invested all her creative energy into educating common citizens and helping them understand real art and complex cinematic structures. Eisenstein, Vertov and Dovzhenko had similar attitudes toward so-called "difficult" films. Unfortunately, some of their most avant-garde films such as October, The Man with the Movie Camera, and Zvenigora were severely criticized for being "inaccessible" and difficult to understand. They contradicted this criticism by using Mayakovsky's strategy in handling such attacks launched against his poetic style when he read his poems to a large audience. He told them: "If you do not understand a poem, you cannot immediately claim that it is the writer who is the fool."[23] Shub was particularly resolute in defending serious and complex films. When Shklovsky wrote that Dovzhenko's Ivan (1932) was a failure because it was not accessible to the mass audience, Shub responded in the most emancipated manner:

> Not long ago Mayakovsky was also criticized for not being comprehensible to the large audience. Therefore today's critics have no right to say: "This is an important work of art, but it is a failure." This is incomprehensible. The task of a true critic is to create the climate for such "difficult" works. When an important achievement in the arts takes place, the critic's duty is to help it with his pen so that a temporarily incomprehensible work soon becomes comprehensible to everybody (280-281).

Shub's book of memoirs is loaded with similar statements which prove that she was a woman of great personal integrity, considerable courage, and innate cinematic consciousness. Her intellectual predilection did not prevent her decision to make films for the common people. But instead of entertaining them, she insisted on educating them. Her recollection of the past events and personalities who created the Soviet cinema of the 1920s is emotional and nostalgic, never sentimental or conceited.

Shub dedicated separate chapters of My Life--Cinema to Mayakovsky, Gorky, Vishnevsky, Tynyanov, Eisenstein, Vertov, Pudovkin and Joris Ivens. In a unique way, she succeeded in conveying her great emotional involvement, her critical attitude, and her personal impressions and opinions about these people as human beings and creators. Her book also includes some of her unrealized projects: a documentary about Mayakovsky; a travelogue of Turkey; and two scripts for compilation movies, "The Great Fatherland's War, 1941-45" and "Moscow in 800 Years." All these projects were conceived with the ideological-theoretical concept Shub formed in the silent era: no staged events, no actors, no decor. But the prewritten script--yes! She worked intensively on many scripts and wrote them in such a manner that the visual structure of the proposed film would be apparent. Her scripts are composed in an emotional essayist style which could serve as a guideline in selecting specific facts from reality by finding actual events that would fit the filmmaker's vision of the overall film's structure.

One of her most fascinating scripts is "Women" (in seven parts), written during 1933-34 and designed to show Soviet women in historical context and through their socio-psychological evolution from 1914 to the early 1930s. The poetic, visual, and analytic style of Shub's writing is best illustrated by this script. It can be read as a poem in prose which stimulates a series of images with a distinct meaning. The reader will be able to judge for her or himself from the translated segment of "Women" I have published elsewhere.[24] Hopefully, everybody will agree that Shub was indeed a filmmaker with an extraordinary visual imagination, infallible sense of structure, sharp intellect, and great love of poetry. She knew how to build a vision of the past by unifying scattered film footage which would have been lost forever if she had not collected it and organized shots into a coherent as well as meaningful whole. She succeeded in achieving this by developing her own method and mastering her technique of "the sense of the part within the whole."

In her 1927 article, "We Do Not Reject the Element of Mastery," she insisted that only "with great skill is it possible to create a documentary film out of newsreel material and make it better than a fictional film ... everything depends on method" (249). Obviously the "method" was the key point of Shub's cinematic structuring and means of conveying her view of history. One could say that Esther Shub was the first Cinematic Historian, in the sense of "writing history with lighting,"[25] as President Woodrow Wilson said of Griffith's The Birth of a Nation. But while Griffith in his film "reconstructed" a moment in American history, Shub subsequently "wrote" the history of the Soviet revolution using authentic images as "letters" for composing words and sentences while "typing" them on her editing table. For Esther Shub, Moviola was "le stylo," her sharp "writing pen." She used this medium as a "language," not in a strict linguistic sense, but as a system of communication; hence, her films illustrate and explain history through motion pictures more clearly than any written document.

In conclusion I would like to quote the last paragraph of an excellent essay on Shub written by Sergei Drobashenko, the most authoritative theorist of Soviet documentary film (and the author of a book on Vertov). Considering Shub and Vertov the greatest documentarists of Soviet cinema, Drobashenko states:

> Like Vertov, Shub developed many modes of film journalism and documentary filmmaking that are now widely used. The political method of compiling archival footage found in the recent works of filmmakers, like A. and A. Thorndike,[26] the Soviet director A. Medvedkin[27] and many others, has its roots in the historical documentaries made by Shub at the end of the 1920s. Her films The Great Road, Country of the Soviets, On the Other Side of the Aras River, and The Native Land[28] anticipated a number of important Soviet documentaries such as Unforgettable Years by I. Kopalin[29] and other films which document the historical evolution of the Soviet Union. Shub's remarkable work, Spain, resolved the problem of the documentary approach to war for the first time in Soviet cinema. Her film On the Other Side of the Aras River initiated a whole series of documentaries concerning the liberation of foreign people struggling against national oppression and world colonialism. All of Shub's work demonstrates originality, inventiveness and a great artistic sense. Therefore her practical and theoretical legacy merits rigorous scholarly research.[30]

Notes

1 Kinok(s) is the name which Vertov invented for his collaborators, a group of directors, cameramen, editors, and technicians who fought for "unstaged,"

"non-acted" cinema such as in the Kinopravda (Film-Truth) newsreel series produced in the early 1920s. Among the kinoks were Vertov's wife, Yelizaveta Svilova, the editor, and his brother, Mikhail Kaufman, the cameraman in The Man with the Movie Camera.

2 Narkompros stands for People's Commissariat of Education in the Soviet Government, founded in 1917 and headed by Anatoly Lunacharsky from 1917 to 1929. Lunacharsky was a former Social-Democrat who joined the Bolsheviks in 1904 and actively participated in the October Revolution.

3 VGIK stands for the All-Union State Institute of Cinema, the highest film school in the Soviet Union (Moscow). Eisenstein and Kuleshov were among the first teachers of VGIK.

4 Esther (Esfir) Shub, Zhizn moya--kinematogra [My Life--Cinema] (Moscow: Iskusstvo, 1972). All the quotations in this article are taken from this book, which also includes Shub's first book, Krupnyn planom [In the Close-Up]. The number of the page is indicated in the parentheses following each quotation.

5 Jay Leyda, Kino (New York: Collier Books, 1973), pp. 224-225.

6 NEP stands for the "New Economic Policy", a hybrid economic plan initiated by Lenin's famous speech to the Tenth Convention of the Communist Party in March 1921, when he declared: "We are in a condition of such poverty, ruin and exhaustion of the productive powers of the workers and peasants that everything must be set aside to increase national production." Often referred to as "Capitalism in the Soviet Union," the NEP period lasted from 1922 through 1927, with considerable impact on Soviet art throughout that time.

7 "Kuleshov Effect" is the name of the experiment Lev Kuleshov made with his students in his Film Workshop in 1920. Juxtaposing different shots (the face of the actor Ivan Mozhukin, a bowl of soup, a woman in a coffin, and a girl playing with a toy bear), Kuleshov demonstrated that for the viewer the expression on the actor's face radically "changes" depending on the image that follows or precedes the close-up.

8 As one of the editors of Lef magazine (chief editors were Mayakovsky and then Tretyakov), Osip Brik was one of the most severe critics of the narrative, fictional cinema. He wrote that it is necessary to "expel romanticism and sentimentalism from the Soviet cinema, declaring once and for all that we do not make films to excite ourselves or experience happiness and grief, but to show real facts and objectively depict real events on the screen." Novy Lef, no. 2 (1927), p. 28.

9 Ontological authenticity, or onto-authenticity, is a term which defines the illusionistic and factual denotation of motion picture photography, implying that the objects and events actually existed in front of the camera at the time when the image was exposed. By its very nature (i.e., ontology), the motion pictures projected on the screen make the viewers believe that the events occur "for real." This impression is particularly relevant for documentary film as well as those fictional genres which emphasize the realism of the film image, like Italian neorealism or French cinéma-vérité. André Bazin talks about this phenomenon in his essay, "The Ontology of the Photographic Image," in What Is Cinema? Vol. 1 (Berkeley: University of California Press, 1967), pp. 9-16.

10 RAPP stands for the Russian Association of Proletarian Writers, a professional organization which through the 1920s gathered predominantly traditional writers together who followed the trend and concept later defined as Socialist Realism. They strongly believed in literary tradition and insisted upon the centrality of Party ideology in literature and art in general. Thus, they essentially differ from the avant-garde movements such as Futurism, Constructivism and Formalism, which flourished in the early days of the Soviet Republic.

11 Dziga Vertov, Stat'i, denvniki, zamysly [Articles, Journals, Projects], ed. Sergei Drobashenko (Moscow: Iskusstvo, 1966), p. 153.

12 Vladimir Mayakovsky, "Puti i politika Sovkino" [The Road and Politics of Sovkino], Polnoe sobranie sochinenii (Moscow: GIKL, 1959), Vol. 12, p. 356.

13 Novy Lef, No. 4, 1928, p. 30.

14 Vladimir Mayakovsky, Polnoe sobranie sochinenii, Vol. 12, p. 359.

15 Victor Shklovsky, Za sorok let [For Forty Years] (Moscow: Iskusstvo, 1965), p. 208.

16 Tatyana Selezneva, Kinomysl' 1920'kh godov [Film Thought of the 1920s] (Moscow: Iskusstvo, 1972, p. 43.

17 Sergei Drobashenko, Fenomen dostovernosti [Phenomenon of Authenticity] (Moscow: Nauka, 1972), p. 45.

18 Vertov's two most important articles explaining his revolutionary concepts of documentary cinema are: "My. Variant manifesta" [We. A Version of the Manifesto], Kino-fot, Nos. 1 and 2, Moscow 1922, and "Kinoki, Perevorot" [Kinoks. Revolution], Lef, No. 3, Moscow, 1923.

19 Sergei Yutkevich, "Volshenitsa montazhnogo stola" [The Sorceress of the Editing Table], a preface to Shub's book, My Life--Cinema, p. 6.

20 Vertov demonstrated his concept of sound cinema in his (and the Soviet Union's) first sound film, Enthusiasm (1931), and in many of his articles, some written long before the advent of sound. In his 1925 article, "Film-Truth and Radio-Truth," he discussed the possibility of applying the principle of "Life Caught Unawares" to the registration of sound. The most important of Vertov's articles on sound film is "The First Steps" (1931), in which he anticipates the sync-sound technique, i.e., the direct sound recording of reality with portable equipment.

21 Shub, Zhizn' moya - kinematograf, pp. 153-154.

22 Vladimir Pertsov, " 'Igra' i demonstratsiya" [Play and Demonstration], Novy Lef, No. 11-12, Moscow, 1929 p. 35.

23 Herbert Marshall, Mayakovsky (London: Dennis Dobson, 1965), p. 66.

24 "Esther Shub's Unrealized Project: Women," Vlada Petric, trans., Quarterly Review of Film Studies, Fall 1978, pp. 449-456.

25 Thomas Dixon, Southern Horizons: An Autobiography, ms. in the possession of Mrs. Dixon, Raleigh, North Carolina, cited in Eric Goldman, Rendezvous with Destiny (New York: Knopf, 1966), pp. 176-77.

26 Andrew and Annelie Thorndike are East German film-makers who made the four-hour compilation movie, The Russian Wonder [Das Russische Wünder], 1958-63.

27 Alexander Medvedkin is the author of the famous early Soviet sound (i.e., musically accompanied) comedy, Happiness [Shchaste'e] (1933-34), who, after the war, made several documentaries about countries of Africa and the Far East.

28 The Native Land [Rodnaya strana] (1943-45) is a long documentary made by a group of Armenian directors under the supervision of Alexander Dovzhenko and Esther Shub.

29 Ilya Kopalin was one of the most prominent members of Vertov's group of Kinoks.

30 Sergei Drobashenko, "Esther Shub--Segment of a Monograph," Voprosy kino iskusstva, No. 8, Moscow 1964, p. 266.

Chapter 3

WORKERS' NEWSREELS IN GERMANY, THE NETHERLANDS AND JAPAN DURING THE TWENTIES AND THIRTIES

Bert Hogenkamp

Recent excavations of radical cultural movements in the Europe of the decades between the wars, of which Bert Hogenkamp's ongoing work is the most notable in the area of cinema, reveal that Vertov's dream of a vast network of kinoks' circles, democratizing artistic production in the service of the Revolution, was often as close to realization in the capitalist West as it ever was in the Soviet Union. Hogenkamp's glimpse of the political and artistic practice of the network of progressive non-professional film groups in Germany, the Netherlands, and Japan (space does not permit a survey of related activity in France, the U.K., and Belgium) lays the groundwork for continued research and archival restoration in this area, and, as he mentions, uncovers uncanny anticipations of similar work undertaken in the early years of the contemporary New Left.

In the course of the last decade, at the same time as the commercial cinema newsreel went into decline and lost any major impact on public opinion, young, radical film collectives in Western Europe and the USA began to adopt the newsreel as a vehicle for counter-information. Thus came into existence the Newsreel Collectives in the USA and Great Britain, the Cinetracts of May 1968 in Paris, the Cinegiornali in Italy, the newsreels of the Amsterdams Stadsjournaal (Amsterdam City Newsreel). In Japan the

the Communist Party had already been producing its own "Akahata News" (Red Flag News) since February 1961. These counter newsreels, putting into practice possibilities neglected by their commerical counterparts, transformed both the form and content of the medium.

Yet it is often forgotten that once before, and this time when the commercial newsreel was at the height of its influence, the working-class movement made sustained attempts to turn this format to its own use. The American film pioneer Tom Brandon speaks of a "missing chapter in film history" in referring to the history of the workers' film movements of the 1920s and '30s. The very existence of these movements has been ignored by the standard works of bourgeois film historians. It is not surprising therefore that the later generation of newsreel collectives knew hardly anything about the efforts made in the '20s and '30s to produce newsreels for the labor movement.

While a great deal has been written about the working-class press, much less is known about attempts to use more modern means of communication like the cinema, radio and, recently, television. Of all film formats the newsreel probably shows more affinity to the daily and weekly newspaper. This article will discuss the newsreels produced by workers' film movements in Germany and the Netherlands during the 1920s and '30s. In particular it will examine the objectives which those producing the newsreels set themselves, the forms of organization adopted for distribution and showing and the success of these newsreels in counteracting the influence of the bourgeois newsreel.

1. The Working-Class Movement and Film

The organized working-class movement was comparatively late to realize the value of the film as a medium of propaganda and education. For a long time the working-class movement stuck to its traditional means of propaganda, the written and spoken word. In the first years of the cinema the trade unions and the socialist parties rejected films even though the workers were the most frequent visitors of the cinema. The thought that the cheap entertainment provided by the cinemas would keep the workers away from the class-struggle was predominant. This negative attitude went even so far that a plan was developed in German social-democrat circles to boycott the film and to prevent working-class families from visiting the cinema.[1] While the Catholic Church had discovered very early the educational and propaganda value of the new medium, the working-class movement was hard to convince. During the First World War the belligerent powers used to the full the possibilities that the medium offered. The Russian October Revolution was an important event for the film as well: in the first workers' and peasants' State the new medium was to be developed to an unrivalled height.

In his Conquer the Film (1925) Willi Muenzenberg tells how shortly after the First World War some Leipzig workers, after seeing an anti-Soviet film, stormed the projection room, destroyed the projection equipment and burned the film.[2] Muenzenberg compares this incident with the destruction of mechanized looms by the British weavers during the Industrial Revolution. He concludes that the revolutionary working-class movement has to use the film to its own end, instead of trying in vain to destroy it. Workers' International Relief (WIR), the relief organization headed by Muenzenberg, frequently used propaganda films for its campaigns. The WIR even established its own production company, Mezhrabpom, with offices in Berlin and Moscow.

The big wave of classic Soviet films during the second half of the '20s put an end to all doubts about the value of the film medium. Most social-democrat and communist parties started using the film for educational and propaganda purposes. Cautious attempts were made to start the production of workers' feature films. The high expenses involved in making feature films turned out to be a great hindrance and limited their production. Documentaries--cheaper to produce--therefore got more attention.

2. Working-Class Movement and Newsreel

After "discovering" the film medium of the '20s, two courses were open to the working-class movement regarding the newsreel. It could try to get itself presented in the commercial newsreel as advantageously as possible (or the least disadvantageously according to its strength). What the results of such a policy can be is shown by the following event. The Dutch Social-Democratische Arbeiders Partij (SDAP, Social-Democrat Workers' Party) used to put its films out to contract to the commercial newsreel firm Polygoon, which in turn imposed the following conditions:

Polygoon would put an item about an important SDAP event in its weekly newsreel if the film service of the SDAP bought a film about this same event from Polygoon. This kind of barter was very profitable for Polygoon. By using the same material twice the expenses were brought down, while Polygoon kept complete control of its own newsreel and obtained a degree of control of the form and content of the SDAP films. As a gesture of courtesy Polygoon used to send socialist-minded cameramen to the events. The SDAP had to pay a very high price for its attempts to obtain a spot in Holland's foremost newsreel. Not only did it not obtain control of the way it was going to be presented in the newsreel, but also it lost any control of the production of its own films.

The situation in the Netherlands was an exception that confirmed the rule that it was virtually impossible to exercise influence on the bourgeois newsreel, and then only at a very high price. The "whistle-concert" in the cinema was frequently used by the workers as a method of criticism of the newsreel, but proved not to be very effective. Usually the cinema manager changed the "controversial" newsreel, but the newsreel was to be changed anyway within three days (with twice-weekly newsreels). There was only one conclusion: the working-class movement had to take the production of newsreels in its own hands. Only workers' newsreels could overcome the quantitative (too little attention paid to the working-class movement) and qualitative (this attention expressed itself in a negative way) shortcomings of the commercial newsreels. In 1929 the film critic of The New Leader, writing under the penname of "Benn," put it this way:

> We could have a newsreel showing the industrial and political demonstrations; the social causes leading up to strikes; co-operative activities; the effects of the miners' eight-hour day on the miners and their families; the contrast of nine-in-a-room in workers' homes with one-in-nine-rooms in homes of the upper-class, etc. instead of the newsreel I saw last week. It consisted of the following items: First, two schoolboy football teams playing for some trophy or other; second, Princess Mary opening a building; third, the erection of a stand on a racing track, and racing ponies engaged in trial runs on the track; fourth, the Prince of Wales opening the Newcastle Exhibition; fifth, Captain Campbell failing

in his attempt to beat Major Segrave's motor-racing speed-record; sixth, the King being removed from Bognor to Windsor on his recovery from illness.[3]

From 1928 to 1939 efforts were made in numerous countries to produce workers' newsreels that showed not "simply sport and royalty, royalty and sport" but "matters of vital importance to the workers."[4] I will describe some of these workers' newsreels and in doing this I hope not only to tell how and by whom they were produced, but also the efforts that were made to show them to a wide working-class audience.

3. Germany: Zeitbericht-Zeitgesicht (1928)

Before Hitler's seizure of power, but when the Weimar Republic was already on its last legs, a workers' film society was formed in Berlin. It arranged film shows and would have shown newsreels of its own, but the censorship banned them. So they bought old UFA newsreels, which had long finished their run and had been approved by the censorship in their time. From these we cut newsreels. For instance, in the "Dogs' beauty contest" overwhelmingly glamorous ladies held expensive lapdogs in their arms. Next to this was "One who did not take part in the contest": a blind beggar and his "seeing eye" watchdog, watching over his miserable master in the cold of the winter. Then "St. Moritz": skating rinks and the guests on the terrace of a luxury hotel. "This, too, is St. Moritz": a melancholy procession of ragged, hungry snow-shovellers and rink-sweepers. "Brilliant military parade" followed by "Disabled ex-servicemen begging in the streets." There were no other captions. The police were itching to ban these newsreels but could not do so, as they were all respectable UFA newsreels, every one of them approved by the censorship. Only the order of showing had been altered a little.[5]

Thus Béla Balázs years later recalled the newsreel of the Volksfilmverband (Popular Assocation for Film Art). Thanks to the attention paid to this newsreel by Balázs and Kracauer in their theoretical works on the film,[6] it has become quite famous.

In January 1928 an appeal for the foundation of a Volksfilmverband, signed by a large group of progressive artists and intellectuals, was launched. Follwing the example of the Volksbuehne, the German social-democrat theater movement, this assocation tried to "rescue" the film for large working-class audiences: "... film has to become what it can and must be: A means to spread knowledge, illumination and education, notions, thoughts and ideas--a means to approach and reconcile the nations--a living, active factor in daily life as well as the spiritual and artistic life." In February 1928 the Volksfilmverband started its work. Chairman of the board became the writer Heinrich Mann. Kaethe Kollwitz, Erwin Piscator and Rudolf Schwarzkopf among others were members of the board: a kind of cultural united-front therefore, an idea that found its expression too in the list of honorary members.[7] A magazine appeared, Film und Volk (Film and People), edited by Franz Hoellering, former editor of Willi Muenzenberg's Arbeiter-Illustrierte-Zeitung (Workers' Illustrated News).

On February 29, 1928, the first filmshow of the Association took place. Scheduled were the newsreel of the Volksfilmverband, Zeitbericht-Zeitgesicht (News of the Times--Face of the Times), and Pudovkin's The End of St. Petersburg. But, as chairman Heinrich Mann remarked in his opening speech: "You are going to see--or rather you would have seen now--a newsreel such as you probably have not seen very often."[8] Zeitbericht-Zeitgesicht was in fact forbidden by the censorship. The newsreel was composed by Ernst Angel and Viktor Blum from old, already censored newsreel footage; yet the censorship refused to give permission for its showing at the opening performance of the Volksfilmverband. Only when a good many cuts had been made in the newsreel was the association permitted to show it publicly, even to juvenile viewers. By then the Volksfilmverband had decided not to show it, since it then retained almost nothing of its original character, and instead Film und Volk announced that the association intended to produce its own weekly newsreel within the near future.[9] It all went a bit differently from the way Béla Balázs wants us to believe.

In the course of the year the Volksfilmverband developed into a powerful film society organization with sections in most of the big cities in Germany. At that time there was no bourgeois film society movement in Germany such as existed for example in France, the Netherlands and Great Britain. This did not make the work of the association easier, as the support of progressive bourgeois film societies in the struggle against censorship was missing. On the other hand the Volksfilmverband could take an example from the Volksbuehne-movement, in which the German working-class had struggled since 1890 for a politically and artistically exemplary theatre.[10] The plan to produce a newsreel of its own was never realized, but the Volksfilmverband became involved in 1929 in the production of the documentary film Hunger in Waldenberg (Shadow of the Mine). Not until the Volksfilmverband joined the Interessegemeinschaft fuer Arbeiterkultur (Interest-community for Workers' Culture), the cultural organization of the KPD, in the summer of 1929, did the association lose its character as a politically neutral film society organization. Only then were the exact aims of the association clearly formulated: "the struggle against film censorship and reactionary cultural tendencies."[11] The Volksfilmverband soon became, however, a victim of the economic crisis, although the Hamburg and Stuttgart sections carried on until 1933.

The conception devised by the makers of Zeitbericht-Zeitgesicht--to give a new meaning to existing film material by reediting the sequence--became well known thanks to Balázs and Kracauer. In Germany Werner Hochbaum made the film Zwei Welten (Two Worlds), in which he opposed the world of the rich to the world of the poor by using existing film material (for example from his own fiction film, Brueder [Brothers]).[12] The Dutchman Joris Ivens used this method too, as did the Belgian Henri Storck in his film Histoire d'un Soldat Inconnu (History of an Unknown Soldier).

4. Netherlands: VVVC-Journaal (1930-31)

> Up to this time my experience in idea editing had been rather sparse. My earliest experience was some time in 1929 when I was given charge of the film programs for a series of workers' cultural and educational Sunday mornings. On Friday nights we would borrow a number of commercial newsreels. On Saturday we would study the material in the newsreels in relation to the international and national situation of the week, re-edit them with any other footage we happened to have available to us giving them a clear political significance, print new subtitles (the films were still silent) showing relationships between events which newsreel companies

> never thought of, and which would certainly have shocked them if they had ever seen our uses of their "innocent" material. For example, we could relate the injustice of an American lynching with the injustice of the Japanese aggression in Manchuria, making a general statement about injustice which we would then localize with a current event in our own country. Previously miscellaneous material was knit together into a new unity, sometimes with the addition of a spoken word on the public address system or some cartoons, photographs or photostats of an editorial from the Dutch conservative press. After our Sunday morning show was finished we would take the film apart again, restore its original form and return it to the newsreel companies who were none the wiser![13]

> For the Party we used to show newsreels on Sunday mornings to the workers. That was on the Haarlemmerdijk in Amsterdam. We hired cinema-newsreels and cut them into pieces. We put in between shots from the Russian Revolution and from the construction of socialism there. After the performances the newsreels were hurriedly restored to their old state.[14]

From these two quotations--the one completing the other--it appears that Joris Ivens took the trouble to edit a series of newsreels, to be shown in performances for workers, from 1929 onwards (whether this date is correct remains to be seen). Especially thanks to the second quotation, it is not very difficult to identify these newsreels: it concerns the newsreels of the Vereeniging voor VolksCultuur (Association for Popular Culture).

The Vereeniging Voor VolksCultuur

In January 1928 the Vereeniging voor VolksCultuur (VVVC) was founded with the aim "to facilitate the organization of film, cabaret and other performances, and in such a way that undesirable interference from authorities who are not kindly disposed toward us can be limited to a minimum."[15] The foundation of the VVVC has to be seen as an attempt by the Communist Party of Holland to increase the effectiveness of its filmshows (because that's what it was all about in the beginning). The Dutch sections of the Workers' International Relief (WIR) and the International Labour Defence (ILD), both closely connected with the CPH, had gained experience in the exhibition of films in the preceding years. Films like His Call, War to the War and In the Clutches of the White Terror were shown. The CPH itself had organized performances of Potemkin and Mother for its members, especially in Amsterdam. Performances of the latter film, forbidden by the censorship, provoked fierce reactions from local authorities, including police interference. Undoubtedly the increasing censorship was one of the reasons for the foundation of the VVVC. Another reason might have been the success enjoyed by the film service of the social-democrat Instituut voor Arbeiders Ontwikkeling (Institute for Workers' Education).

An organization like the VVVC had a double function. First of all it fought against the censorship that victimized especially Soviet films, and secondly it made a point of producing its own films. Besides the exhibition of Soviet films like Bed and Sofa, Potemkin, The Forty-First and others, the VVVC started the production of its own films. Arm Drenthe (Poor Drenthe), a film about Holland's poorest province, made by Communist MP Louis de Visser and Leo van Lakerveld, secretary of the ILD, was the first VVVC film.[16] Next the VVVC imported two German films, Red Front and Bloody May Day,[17] which were promptly forbidden by the censorship committee under the leadership of the social-democrat Van Staveren.

Early in 1930 the work of the VVVC rather stagnated. Evidently FIM-film, the main distributor of Soviet films, took a position against CPH organizations, which made it much more difficult to hire Soviet films.[18] Leo van Lakerveld, the then-secretary of the VVVC, wrote an angry letter in January 1930, in which he condemned the acts of the Party-secretariat and argued that it "undermined the carefully built up VVVC-work."[19] One has reason to suppose that his warning was heeded, for the VVVC's activities expanded considerably during the rest of 1930.

The Newsreels

The first VVVC-newsreel was shown September 28, 1930 in the Cinema Royal, Amsterdam. De Tribune wrote:

"The VVVC-newsreel--which turned out to be nothing else than a common bourgeois newsreel, but for this occasion a bit re-edited and provided with new titles--really hit the nail on the head. It made it clear to those present how such topical news on the screen, shown every week in all theaters, has been viewed. It was wittily accompanied by Bern. Drukker with improvised organ-playing."[20] In contrast to subsequent numbered newsreels nothing further is to be found on this newsreel. One can assume that it had been edited the way Ivens has described above then restored to its original form, and returned to the distributor the next day.

The next VVVC-morning--this time in the biggest cinema of the city, Tuschinsky--saw the premiere of the so-called Tribune-film, Breken en Bouwen (To Break and to Build). The title of this film refers to alterations being made at the premises of De Tribune, alterations which were carried out by Party members in their spare time. During the various actions to save this daily newspaper (in that period De Tribune was attacked from many sides) in December 1930 and January 1931, the film was intensively used.

The "first" VVVC-newsreel (the unnumbered one from September not counted) was premiered on November 16 in Amsterdam. De Tribune called the newsreel "a fine choice of images from the Southern part of the Soviet Union, from Baku, Kharkov, Kiev, elucidated by some spoken texts and parts of an older film in which we see Lenin and Stalin 'in action,' and later a beautiful series of images showing how the Russian comrades celebrate their October."[22] The newsreel was, according to De Tribune, "shot personally by one of the friends of the VVVC in the Soviet Union!'" The identity of this friend of the VVVC is not disclosed (the names of the members of the VVVC film collective were as a matter of course never mentioned). A cautious supposition points, however, at least in the direction of Joris Ivens, for Ivens had just made his trip through the Soviet Union and moreover he had visited some of the cities that were shown in the newsreel.[23]

About the second VVVC-newsreel (première on December 26, 1930 in the Tuschinsky and Corso cinemas, Amsterdam) De Tribune wrote: "The VVVC-newsreel, now a regularly returning attraction of the Sunday-mornings of the big cultural organization, was devoted this time to the work of the ILD. In the limelight was a series of images shot by the VVVC-film collective of a canvassing and collection-tour in the Amsterdam Jordaan (a workers' district; BH) and worked up and edited into an older series of images. In this way the VVVC is gradually building up an archive of newsreels of its own, that will render an excellent service in extending this mass-organization over the whole country."[24] The newsreels were also scheduled on the programs of other VVVC-sections.

In 1931 three more newsreels were brought out. On newsreel No. 3 De Tribune wrote: "This newsreel has been composed by a master hand, it is more eloquent than the best of our writers or speakers, it is an uncommon force in recruiting for the Party of Lenin, Liebknecht, Rosa Luxemburg!"[25] In the monthly bulletin of the VVVC, De Sovjet-Vriend (The Soviet Friend), the contents of this newsreel has been summed up: "The Terror in Europe and America; Life, work and death of Lenin; the Construction in the Soviet Union."[26] Newsreel No. 4 got the title "The face of two worlds: The Russian and German revolution." Newsreel No. 5 was titled "The Intervention is near." The content of this newsreel, a two-reeler: "The powers that drive to the war; the terror throughout the whole world; the demonstration of the ILD on March 8 and the behavior of the police on the Ledscheplein; Fascism (Mussolini, Hitler, the Pope); the counter-revolution a gas attack (sic); the construction in the Soviet Union; the Red Army is on guard."[27] This newsreel was the last and undoubtedly the most ambitious of the series.

Why the VVVC-film collective did not continue the series is hard to discern. Perhaps the departure abroad of Joris Ivens was a reason. One important change cannot be left unmentioned: in March 1931 the VVVC changed its name into Vereeniging van Vrienden der Sovjet-Unie (VVSU; Association of Friends of the Soviet Union). On the first Sunday morning performance in Amsterdam, organized by the VVSU under its new name, a newsreel was shown.... It was a newsreel made in the Soviet Union![28]

The film collective is mentioned once more in the summer of 1931, when it filmed a national meeting of the VVSU and the ILD on August 30 in Amersfoort. This newsreel, showing among other agit-prop theater-groups from Amsterdam and Arnhem, was shown on Sunday, September 27, in Cinema Royal, Amsterdam. It was the last film of the collective.

How Did the VVVC-Newsreels Function?

Having described the contents of the VVVC-newsreels, I want to try and establish how the newsreels functioned by posing some questions.

Where were the newsreels shown? Apart from the Tribune film, Breken en Bouwen, that was used in special campaigns to support the paper, all the newsreels were shown in the popular VVVC performances. In view of the frequency of the performances it seems hard to believe the story that each of the newsreels was especially edited before each performance and afterwards sent back to the distributor. Referring to the premiere of newsreel No. 2., De Tribune remarks that the newsreels could "render an excellent service in extending this mass-organization." The VVVC was very busy in establishing sections all over the Netherlands; in Apeldoorn, Arnhem, Groningen, Haarlem, Leeuwarden, Leiden, Lemmer and Utrecht, In January 1931 it claimed 6,000 members.[29] The newsreels were shown frequently in programs organized by the local sections.

What did a VVVC-program look like? The most important part of the VVVC mornings or evenings was the (Russian) feature-film. Sometimes an artist performed, a small orchestra (that very often had to accompany the silent feature-film as well) played, and an edition of the VVVC-newsreel was shown. Before the performance and during the interval De Tribune, the VVVC-organ De Sovjet-Vriend and other publications were canvassed. Sometimes a speech was made, introducing the program or referring to some current event. The Amsterdam section undoubtedly had the most comprehensive program, with singing, dancing and recitation.[30]

How many people visited these performances? In other words: how many people saw the VVVC-newsreels? This question cannot be answered with accuracy. In the report that appeared regularly in De Tribune sometimes the number of spectators is mentioned. In view of the membership of the VVVC, amounting to some 7,000 to 8,000 in the spring of 1931, one can suppose that each issue of the VVVC-newsreel was seen by 4,000 to 5,000 people on average. Amsterdam and Haarlem (with respectively 2,000 and 1,300 members) were the largest sections. The absence of Rotterdam, the big port, is conspicuous.

How did the people react? In the reports in De

Tribune reactions to the newsreels were very enthusiastic. Therefore they were assigned a special role in extending the VVVC. Occasionally something of the audience reactions during the exhibition of the newsreels filtered through. The arcors (worker-correspondents) who wrote a small report on the performances outside of Amsterdam, mentioned among others: "The appearance on the screen of Stalin was greeted with thunderous applause, and the Red Army was received with the Internationale and shouts of Red-Front,"[31] "Stalin was greeted with applause"[32] and "elicited from those present spontaneous cheers."[33] From Apeldoorn comes the only negative reaction: "Three young men tried to create confusion with anarchistic methods during the exhibition of this newsreel (No. 4; BH) by whistling, shouting, singing, etc. In no uncertain way it was made clear that the great majority of those present did not like this kind of behavior."[34]

As a conclusion it can be noted that the VVVC-newsreels were part of a program that consisted further of a feature-film and one or more other forms of entertainment, and that was seen with a good deal of enthusiasm by 4,000 to 5,000 members of the VVVC, spread over a dozen cities.

The VVVC-Newsreels and the CPH

Following the example of Germany, where, under the umbrella of the Interessegemeinschaft fuer Arbeiterkultur (Interest-community for Workers' Culture), the KPD organizations were active in almost all cultural areas, the CPH worked hard from 1931 onwards in developing its own proletarian cultural expressions in all their forms. Thus the Vereeniging van Arbeiders-Fotografen (Workers' Camera Assocation) and various agit-prop theater-groups were founded early in 1931. In view of the past of the VVVC it is not surprising that the VVVC-film collective was the first to come into the open. The VVVC was undoubtedly trying to make its programs as attractive as those of the commercial cinemas, and the (relatively cheap) production of its own newsreels offered an excellent opportunity to do this.[35] The production of fiction films of its own, however, is never even mentioned, as contrasted with Great Britain for example.[36] The presence of Joris Ivens as an experienced filmmaker was, of course, an important factor, but the VVVC had proved already with Arm Drenthe that it was able to produce its own films.[37] The idea of editing various kinds of film material (existing and newly shot) can be attributed to Ivens, who might have read about the way the German newsreel Zeitbericht-Zeitgesicht was made.

The VVVC-newsreels were made with the purpose of making clear the political line of the CPH--a political line that was suppressed in or distorted by the Dutch bourgeois newsreels. Therefore it is no wonder that four of the five editions were devoted largely to the Soviet Union.

The newsreels fulfilled an important function regarding Soviet feature-films. For these films were made in the first place for exhibition in the Soviet Union and tried accordingly to show the reality in the Soviet Union. This reality did not have much relation to the experience of the Dutch workers. Only the newsreels could relate the situation in the Netherlands and the situation in the Soviet Union to each other, and in this way provide audiences with a better insight into the political situation (and at the same time improve the reception of the Soviet films). In the quotation at the beginnig of this chapter Ivens mentions the example of "injustice" and how this theme was linked with events in different countries. In view of the way the newsreels were shown, one can on the other hand assume with some caution that they were probably more suited for "recognition" than for "consciousness-raising." The audiences to which they were shown must have been, generally speaking, Party-members and sympathizers. Only in Amsterdam and Haarlem, where really large sections existed, can the presence of members who were not strictly familiar with the Party line be supposed.

The VVVC-newsreel could have been an important start for the development of a workers' film movement in the Netherlands. Yet it was not until 1934 that a workers' film collective appeared as a successor of the VVVC-film collective. Why this long interruption? Why was the work of the VVVC-film collective not carried out? To answer these questions further research is needed, in which the recollections of former participants will be decisive, because no more details can be gathered from the reports in De Tribune.

As far as is known none of the VVVC-newsreels has survived. A unique occasion to get further acquainted with the start of a Dutch workers' film movement--that is the qualification one can give to the work of the VVVC-film collective--has therefore been lost.

5. Japan: Prokino-News (1930)

In 1928 the NAPP (All-Japanese Congress of the Association for Proletarian Art) was founded. The CPJ concentrated all its cultural work in the NAPP. One of the NAPP organizations was the League for the Proletarian Cinema (Prokino): this started its work in 1929. The exceptional side of Prokino was that it used practically only small film. Some members had already gained experience in filming strikes and demonstrations in 1927 and 1928 with 9.5mm cameras (the usual format for amateur filmmakers in the pre-war period). The first 16mm film that Prokino made was The Funeral of Yamamoto. Yamamoto was a Communist MP who had been murdered by a right-wing terrorist. This film--one of the few Prokino films that have survived--shows workers' delegations on their way to pay Yamamoto their last respects. It must have been made in difficult circumstances. In 1930 the first newsreel of Prokino, Prokino-News No. 1, was brought out. This newsreel has unfortunately not survived and nothing is known about its content. Prokino had active groups in Tokyo and Kyoto. A cautious supposition regarding the content of Prokino-News No. 1 would point towards a choice from the material shot by, for example, these Tokyo and Kyoto groups. It is also unknown whether more editions of Prokino-News appeared.

Choosing to work with small film, Prokino placed itself automatically outside the commercial cinema system that only used the inflammable 35mm film stock. "Exhibition is possible in all small halls and even in peasants' huts. Because the white terror in Japan forces the comrades there to do their filmwork (shooting and exhibition) almost always illegally, this small film method is of great importance."[38] Prokino tried to do filmwork at the grassroots, because the cinemas were closed to the movement. Notwithstanding the severe repression, Prokino succeeded in doing a lot of important work until its dissolution in 1934. Two of the few films that have survived make this clear. Earth (1930) is a film about the struggle of peasants and workers against the expropriation of a plot of arable land by a big factory. 12th May Day in Tokyo (1931) shows impressive images of May Day in Tokyo: workers are searched by policemen, some speakers are prevented from giving a speech by the police, the WIR distributes food, masses of workers are assembling wearing headbands with slogans and carrying their banners.

It is not possible to treat the influence of the Prokino movement extensively within the framework of this article. The exemplary role of Prokino must be stressed, however. In an interview Tom Brandon mentions that the Japanese movement was an example for the Workers' Film and Photo League in the USA when it started.[39] In Germany and Great Britain, too, the activities of Prokino were discussed and imitated. The use of 16mm film offered Prokino the advantage of being less exposed to the interference of the police, but also it made it possible to work at a grassroots level. Prokino no longer directed itself to the places of exhibition that were created and controlled by capitalism--the cinemas--but to forms of organization created by the workers and peasants themselves, like trade unions, peasant-leagues, cooperatives, etc.[40]

6. Conclusions

> When we speak of the content of a newspaper we mean the principle of organization and cultivation of the newspaper's capacities--aimed at the class-cultivation of the reader.
> (...)
> Though proletarian newspapers and bourgeois newspapers may have equal factual capacities, this is what sets them poles apart in content.[41]

Following the reasoning of the great Soviet film director and theoretician Sergei Eisenstein, one can wonder what the principles of organization of the workers' newsreels have been. In other words, how far did the workers' newsreels answer to the need of proletarian news coverage? Were they really "the eye (and ear) of their class," to quote this well-known remark on the German worker-photographer?

In Misère au Borinage (Misery in Borinage)--a film on the aftermath of the big miners' strike in Belgium, made in 1933 by Joris Ivens and Henri Storck--one sees a worker having to borrow a bicycle in order to go and get a loaf of bread from his parents-in-law who live more than a mile away. On his way he cycles past bakeries, of which the shop windows are full of bread. Simply because he does not have the money to buy a loaf of bread at the nearest shop, he has to cycle more than a mile in order to obtain this basic necessity of life. In Workers' Topical News No. 1 one sees the food kitchen of the WIR. Workers are handing over a voucher and get a cup of tea and a slice of bread. A group of men and women pose giggling in front of the camera, their mouths stuffed with bread. In Workers' Newsreel Number 12 workers demonstrate for higher unemployment benefits and winter relief. In Workers' Topical News No. 2 one sees shots of contingents of Hunger Marchers on their way to London. On their banners slogans like "We are marching against starvation" and "We demand full maintenance" can be read. These four examples show events that were caused by the same phenomenon: the economic crisis. But one sees a totally different approach in the re-enacted documentary of Ivens and Storck, on the one hand, and in the workers' newsreels on the other.

On the basis of a content-analysis it is not very difficult to ascertain that all the workers' newsreels were devoted to social and economic issues that concerned the working-class in general. This is what set them apart from the bourgeois newsreels. Another question is whether the workers' newsreels found a way to treat the individual experiences of the workers (as Ivens and Storck did in their Misère au Borinage not only in the sequence described above, but in other sequences of this film as well). The workers' newsreels showed, however, only the organized working-class actions like protest-demonstrations, Hunger Marches, workers' sport contests, congresses, May Day celebrations, etc.[42] These were collective experiences. The individual experiences of the workers were not treated in the workers' newsreels. This is what made them less suited for exhibition to unorganized workers who could not immediately recognize their own experiences in the films. The case of the German Arbeiter-Illustrierte-Zeitung shows clearly the possibilities of such an approach. The fact that the individual experiences of the German workers got so much attention in this photo-magazine (many of the photo-stories were made by worker-photographers themselves), made it widely read among non-organized working-class families.[43]

One can, of course, wonder whether the newsreel is the right film format for such an approach. Regarding this one can pose the question whether the workers' newsreels did not let their principle of organization be dictated too much by the bourgeois newsreels. It is conspicuous that the experimental Soviet newsreel Kinopravda (Film Truth), directed by Dziga Vertov from 1922 to 1924, was not imitated by the West European and American workers' film organizations. Two reasons can be given. Vertov's work (his films as well as his writings) was not very well-known outside the Soviet Union. Further it is striking that, if workers' newsreels were mentioned in the workers' press (the possibility to produce them, their merits, etc.), they were considered as a counterpart to the bourgeois newsreels and not as an extension of the Soviet newsreels.

Most of the workers' newsreels were simple newsfilms, covering certain working-class activities. Only a few tried to go further. In the VVVC-newsreels an effort was made to show more of the causes of phenomena like fascism, the intervention-war against the Soviet Union, etc. The American Film and Photo League tried to show more of the background of events in its news-reviews like America Today. The French Film Service of the Federation of the Seine always placed its newsreels of Popular Front demonstrations in a wider historical context: the Popular Assembly on July 14, 1935 was linked with the capture of the Bastille on July 14, 1789; Léon Blum, the hero who has survived an attempt at murder, was compared with Jean Jaurès, the murdered socialist martyr; a demonstration at the Mur des Fédérés was the occasion for a lesson on the Paris Commune in 1871. If one would apply the characterization of the newsreel of Baechlin and Muller-Strauss, quoted at the beginning of this article, consistently, these newsreels were not newsreels. Their makers obviously knew better, because they did call them newsreels.

A normal distribution of the workers' newsreels in the cinemas was out of the question. How, then, was it possible to reach the largest possible working-class audience? Principally existing organizations were used. Through these organizations a public of mainly organized workers was reached, while the organization in question could use the film show as an extra attraction to convince non-members to join. Especially for this kind of film show the coming of the small film played an important part. A second method of reaching a wide working-class audience was to organize film shows in normal cinemas for workers (and with an entrance fee that they could afford). The film program could act as the attraction that would bring in the unorganized workers as well. In practice the possibilities to do this were limited. For example, no big advertising campaigns could be set up in order to reach workers who did not read newspapers like L'Humanité, De Tribune or the Daily Worker. Most of these workers' film societies disappeared after a short period of prosperity.

The commercial newsreel firms had an enormous apparatus at their disposal for the exchange of film material. The international firms had contracts with the much smaller national firms that would guarantee a mutual exchange of news-items. This method was very profitable for the international firms: it lowered their costs (they did not have to send newsreel-teams on expensive trips all over the world) and it made the national firms completely dependent on them. In the article of Tischler a proposal is made for the establishment of an exchange of newsreel-footage on a national scale. In Great Britain the Film and Photo League tried to work in a similar way, for example, by requesting its members to film the passing of Hunger Marchers through their village or town and send in the materials to the League's headquarters in London, where it could be edited.

Whatever the criticisms on these workers' newsreels may be, the most important fact should not be forgotten: they have left a filmed record of many working-class activities that would otherwise not have survived.

Notes

1 Willi Muenzenberg, "Erobert den Film 1", in: Willi Luedecke, Der Film in Agitation und Propaganda der revolutionaren Arbeiterbewegung 1919-1932, Berlin 1973 (Oberbaumverlag) p. 78.

2 Willi Muenzenberg, op. cit., p. 80.

3 Benn, "Why Not A Socialist News Reel?" in: The New Leader, 31 May 1929, p. 2.

4 Arthur West (Ralph Bond), "News-Film Dope. Sport, Royalty and Militarism," in: Daily Worker, 18 August 1930, p. 5.

5 Bêla Balâzs, Theory of Film (Character and growth of a new art), London n.d. (Dennis Dobson), pp. 165-166.

6 See: Siegfried Kracauer, "Die Filmwochenschau" in: Die Neue Rundschau 1931 (Vol. 42, no. 2), pp. 573-575; Siegfried Kracauer, From Caligari to Hitler, A Psychological History of German Film, Princeton (University Press), pp. 192-193; Béla Balázs, Der Geist des Film, Halle 1930 (Verlag Wilhelm Knapp) p. 212.

7 Gertraude Kuehn, Karl Tuemmler, Walter Wimmer (eds.), Film und revolutionaere Arbeiterbewegung in Deutschland 1918-1932. Dokumente und Materialien zur

Entwicklung der Filmpolitik der revolutionaeren Arbeiterbewegung und zu den Anfaengen einer sozialistischen Filmkunst in Deutschland. Berlin/GDR 1975 (Henschelverlag), Vol. II, p. 237.

8 Film und Volk, Vol. I, no. 2, p. 4.

9 Ibid., p. 22.

10 See: Heinrich Braulich, Die Volksbuehne, Theater und Politik in der deutschen Volksbuehnenbewegung. Berlin/GDR 1976 (Henschelverlag).

11 Film und Volk, Vol. III, no. 1, p. 38.

12 Film im Klassenkampf, Retrospektive zur XVI. Internationalen Leipziger Dokumentar- und Kurzfilmwoche 1973, Berlin/GDR 1973 (Staatliches Filmarchiv der DDR), p. 18.

13 Joris Ivens, The Camera and I, Berlin/GDR 1969 (Seven Seas), pp. 96-97.

14 Joris Ivens, Een revolutionair met een kamera, no place, no date, p. 14.

15 De Tribune, 28 January 1928, p. 5.

16 De Tribune, 16 May 1929, p. 2 and Roode Hulp, 1929; no. 3, p. 4.

17 De Tribune, 28 November 1929, p. 1. Blutmai 1929: a documentary made by Piel Jutzi about the shooting of Berlin workers on May Day 1929 by order of the social-democrat police-commissioner Zoergiebel. Roter Frontkaempferbund: a documentary made by Carl Junghans about a meeting of Red Front-fighters in 1928 in Berlin.

18 De Tribune, 28 January 1930, p. 6.

19 De Tribune, 29 January 1930, p. 3.

20 De Tribune, 29 September 1930, p. 4.

21 De Tribune, 27 October 1930, p. 1.

22 De Tribune, 17 November 1930, p. 4.

23 Joris Ivens, op. cit., pp. 51 ff.

24 De Tribune, 27 December 1930, p. 4.

25 De Tribune, 28 January 1931, p. 4.

26 De Sovjet-Vriend, no. 2-3, March 1931, p. 5.

27 De Tribune, 20 March 1931, p. 6.

28 In 1931 the Dutch newsreels went over to sound (Ch. Boost, op. cit, p. 63). How far was this a reason for not continuing with the VVVC-newsreel? To answer this question one has to know at least if the Sowkino-newsreel, shown on April 19, 1931, was a sound newsreel (which is not mentioned in De Tribune).

29 De Tribune, 21 January 1931, p. 6.

30 The agit-prop theatre that would become a regular part of the VVSU-performances was not introduced in the Netherlands until the spring of 1931. See: Projektgroep "literatuur-sociologie" I, Links Richten tussen partij en arbeidersstrijd, Nijmegen 1975, Vol. II, pp. 440 ff.

31 De Tribune, 22 December 1930, p. 4. on the exhibition of newsreel no. 1 in Utrecht.

32 De Tribune, 2 January 1931, p. 4 on the exhibition of newsreel no. 1 in Groningen.

33 De Tribune, 27 January 1932, p. 4 on the exhibition of newsreel no. 1 in Haarlem.

34 De Tribune, 22 May 1931, p. 3.

35 Ralph Bond, at that time leader of the British Federation of Workers' Film Societies--the British equivalent of the VVVC--stresses the need to imitate the program of the commercial cinema in the best way possible. See: Ralph Bond, "Workers' Film: Past and Future," in: Labour Monthly, Vol. 58, no 1 (January 1976), p. 28.

36 See: Bert Hogenkamp, "Film and the Workers' Movement in Britain, 1929-1939," in: Sight and Sound, Vol. 45 no. 2 (Spring 1976), pp. 69-71.

37 It has been recently established that Ivens was in fact camera operator for the 15-minute Arm Drenthe--Hogenkamp's original supposition was perhaps truer than he realized (T. W.).

38 Korea Senda, "Proletarische Film-Bewegung in Japan," in: Arbeiterbuehne und Film, Vol. XVIII no. 2 (February 1931), pp. 26-27.

39 "Pioneers: An Interview with Tom Brandon," in: Film Quarterly, Vol. XXVI no. 5 (Fall 1973), pp. 12-24.

40 The information for this chapter was found in: Kazuo Yamada, "Das soziale Erwachen des japanischen Films," in: Eckhart Jahnke, Manfed Lichtenstein, Kazuo Yamada, Dokumentarfilm in Japan, Seine demokratische und kaempferische Traditionen, Berlin/GDR 1976 (Staatliches Filmarchiv der DDR), pp. 29-40.

41 Sergei Eisenstein, "Perspectives" (1929), in: Jay Leyda (Ed.), Film Essays and a Lecture by Sergei Eisenstein, New York, Washington, 1970 (Praeger), p. 40.

42 With the exception of Zeitbericht-Zeitgesicht, which is by any standards an exceptional workers' newsreel.

43 For the Arbeiter-Illustrierte-Zeitung see: Aesthetik und Kummunikation no. 10, January 1973); Gabriele Ricke, Die Arbeiter-Illustrierte-Zeitung, Hannover, 1974) Internationalismus Verlag); Heinz Willmann, Geschichte der Arbeiter-Illustrierten-Zeitung 1921-1938, Berlin, 1975 (Das europaeische Buch). An attempt in Great Britain to set up a similar photo-magazine failed after one issue of this Workers' Illustrated News had been brought out.

Chapter 4

RADICAL DOCUMENTARY IN THE UNITED STATES: 1930-1942

Russell Campbell[1]

The rediscovery of the work of the Film and Photo League and of Frontier Films was the most exciting revelation of the seventies for the cultural activists of the American New Left. It meant that there was a dynamic radical cultural tradition in the United States after all, many of whose central figures were still alive. Though elements of the rediscovery were controversial (a few outraged denials that the "Comintern connection" established by Russell Campbell below had ever existed), for the most part the effect was an enormous shot-in-the-arm for committed film production, as well as the occasion for the restoration of a long-suppressed cultural and political heritage. Once again an immediate priority is the restoration of the actual films and their re-entry into circulation; in the meantime, Campbell's excellent textual analysis of representative works, carefully situated historically, must serve in their stead.

Part One: The Film and Photo League

The Workers' Film and Photo League in the United States (known as the Film and Photo League after 1933) was part of an extensive cultural movement sponsored by the Communist International and its affiliated national parties in the inter-war period. Specifically, it was a section of the

Workers' International Relief (WIR), American chapter of the Comintern-linked Internationale Arbeiterhilfe (IAH), founded at Lenin's instigation in Berlin in 1921.

The IAH's chief function was providing food, clothing and shelter for strikers and their families. But its activities extended also into the mass media and many cultural fields. Thus in the United States the WIR organized, during the early thirties, revolutionary drama groups (the Workers' Laboratory Theatre), dance troupes (the Red Dancers), symphony and mandolin orchestras, bands, choirs, art workshops, etc.

The head of the IAH, the remarkable Communist entrepreneur and propagandist Willi Münzenberg, was particularly interested in film because of its potential for reaching a mass audience. Münzenberg's commitment to an alternative, working-class cinema was expressed in his 1925 pamphlet, Erobert den Film! (Capture the Film!), and in practice in the considerable activity in film production, distribution and exhibition undertaken in Germany and the Soviet Union by IAH organizations such as Prometheus, Weltfilm and Mezhrabpomfilm.

In the US the IAH affiliate, at first known as the Friends of Soviet Russia, had been involved with film distribution since its founding in 1921. Throughout the twenties it arranged nationwide release of documentaries about the Soviet Union designed to counteract the hostile propaganda emanating from Hollywood, and beginning in 1926 it also handled non-theatrical distribution (and, effectively, exhibition) of Soviet features. This distribution arm of the WIR was to become closely allied with the Workers' Film and Photo League.

The WIR had also been responsible for the production of at least two documentary films, about the Communist-led textile strikes in Passaic, New Jersey in 1926 and Gastonia, North Carolina in 1929. But as the nation entered the Great Depression there was no permanent production crew available to undertake ongoing filmic coverage of working-class events. The necessity for such a group soon became apparent. On March 6, 1930, a Communist-sponsored demonstration of the unemployed resulted in probably the largest such crowds in US history jamming into New York's Union Square, but the capitalist press minimized the event and commercial newsreels of the demonstration were suppressed at the behest of

New York police chief Grover Whalen--no doubt partly because they exposed the brutality of his officers in action. As the economic situation worsened, protest marches, rallies, and manifestations of all kinds became more frequent, and the bourgeois media continued to ignore or distort them. It was clear that there was an urgent need, at the very least, for workers' newsreels.

In May, Daily Worker film critic Samuel Brody wrote:

> I want once more to emphasize the news-film is the important thing; that the capitalist class knows that there are certain things that it cannot afford to have shown. It is afraid of some pictures....
>
> Films are being used against the workers like police clubs, only more subtly--like the reactionary press. If the capitalist class fears pictures and prevents us from seeing records of events like the March 6 unemployment demonstration and the Sacco-Vanzetti trial we will equip our own cameramen and make our own films.[2]

Less than two weeks later, again in the Daily Worker, the call for workers' movie production was reiterated. Radical poet and film critic Harry Alan Potamkin argued:

> The German workers have started well. There is no need to begin big. Documentaries of workers' life. Breadlines are picket lines, demonstrations and police attacks. Outdoor films first. Then interiors. And eventually dramatic films of revolutionary content. Workers' organizations should support a group to be pioneers on this important front.[3]

Even as the call was being made, cinematic forces on the Left were being quietly mobilized. In New York a photography group with ties to the WIR had been in existence for several years. This was the (Japanese) Workers' Camera League (also known as the Workers' Camera Club and the Nippon Camera Club), which concentrated on photographs of proletarian life and the class struggle. In the spring of 1930 the Workers' Camera League combined forces with the International Labor Defense (ILD)--the Communist legal-aid organization parallel to the WIR--to form the Labor Defender Photo Group, whose purpose was "to get pictures of the class struggle for use in working-class papers and magazines," particularly the ILD's Labor Defender. The Defender group possessed two motion-picture cameras and shot a newsreel of the May Day parade.[4]

More workers' newsreels followed, but production seems to have been too haphazard to satisfy the partisans of radical cinema. In December 1930 the Workers' Camera League was reorganized under the auspices of the WIR into a body which could sustain political filmmaking and photography on a systematic, ongoing basis. The new organization evidently absorbed the Labor Defender Photo Group and was named the Workers' Film and Photo League.[5]

The key New York WFPL participants at the beginning were Samuel Brody, Lester Balog, Robert Del Duca and, a little later, Leo Seltzer. Of the group members Del Duca had the most practical experience, having worked as a newsreel cameraman and laboratory technician; Brody was clearly the theoretician and political overseer. Balog was "mainly an inside man--he worked on art work and editing."[6] Seltzer, with an interest in engineering and background as an art student, became in time probably the League's single most active filmmaker. Dissemination of the group's program was enthusiastically undertaken by its unofficial spokesman, Harry Alan Potamkin. Handling the WIR's Film Department, and thus intimately involved with arranging distribution and exhibition of--and often finance for--the League's productions, was Tom Brandon, a former student who had worked as a truck driver before becoming an organizer for the WIR.

Total membership in the League, including the photo section, fluctuated (according to Brody) between 75 and 100, and was "mainly working-class with a sprinkling of middle-class intellectuals sympathetic to our progressive goals."[7] The core group of 1931 was augmented notably by a handful of enthusiasts excited by the artistic possibilities of the film medium, including Lewis Jacobs, Leo T. Hurwitz, David Platt, Jay Leyda (for a short period prior to his departure for the Soviet Union), Irving Lerner, and Ralph Steiner. For the most part these men were less involved with the League's production work than with its other activities: publications (program notes, Filmfront, contributions to the Daily Worker and New Theatre); lectures and discussions; film series screenings; photographic exhibitions; anti-censorship agitation; boycott campaigns; film school and photo courses. By 1934 Balog was in California (where, as a member of the San Francisco FPL, he was jailed for showing Road to Life and Cottonpickers' Strike to agricultural workers); and in the fall of that year Hurwitz, Lerner and Steiner broke away to form Nykino. Soon after, Seltzer secured work as a filmmaker with the WPA, and most of the League's production in the last year or two of its existence seems to have been handled by Del Duca, Julian Roffman, and Vic Kandel. Nancy Naumburg and James Guy did pioneering work, with the League's assistance, on the dramatized political documentary in 16mm.

The kernel of the League's work was the production of newsreels. Leo Seltzer insists that the group was not challenging Hollywood on its own terms, by manufacturing motion pictures as merchandise. Hence it is probably more correct to speak, for the bulk of (W)FPL output, not of individual films, but of "footage"--news film which was processed and printed rapidly and then roughly edited for the quickest possible screening and maximum impact. Once the topical moment had passed, of course, the footage became available for recutting into later compilation documentaries, and it is to this class that most of the League's major productions--National Hunger March, Bonus March, Hunger 1932--belong.

Though the newsreels did sometimes receive theatrical screenings (particularly during 1932-33, at New York's Acme Theatre), they were more often shown by League members themselves in a more political context, at Communist functions, in union halls, or at meetings of fraternal societies, nationality groups, or workers' clubs. Most importantly, Seltzer recalls, they were shown during strikes:

> Whenever there was a picket line we covered it and came back and showed the pickets themselves on the picket line. It was a tremendous morale booster. Plus maybe a Russian film, or maybe the Taxi film [a 1935 FPL production], or the waterfront film [Marine, 1934, also FPL], to give them an idea other people were also struggling for better conditions. We had some footage of the Kentucky strike, and the Pittsburgh strike. I don't know who shot the Pittsburgh film, but I went back with a projector to show it to the miners who were

> still blacklisted. They were still living in tents for the second winter. And I remember I went into the town and we stretched this sheet between two houses--the sheriff's and the deputy's house on either side--and we expected to be shot at any minute while projecting the film.[8]

Taking films to the workers became a potent organizing device.

As might be expected, the content of (W)FPL newsreels and longer films was conditioned by the particular campaigns being undertaken by the CP. Here it is essential to recall that the period 1929-34 was one of militant class struggle for the world Communist movement. Party strategy in the US (as elsewhere) was to build the strength of the movement by stimulating recruitment into: a) the "revolutionary" unions--those affiliated to the Trade Union Unity League (TUUL); b) the Party's "mass organizations"--of which the WIR was one; and c) the Party itself.

Thus the footage devoted to the miners' strikes of 1931 and 1932 played its part in assisting the drive to organize the coalminers of western Pennsylvania, eastern Ohio, Kentucky and Tennessee--then destitute and disillusioned with John L. Lewis's leadership of the United Mine Workers--into the TUUL-affiliated National Miners Union (NMU). On the West Coast there was an energetic campaign to build the Cannery and Agricultural Workers Industrial Union, reflected in several of the Los Angeles WFPL productions.

Organization of the unemployed was undertaken via the Unemployed Councils around the demands for immediate relief and a comprehensive program of social insurance. These demands were dramatized by numerous local and two national hunger marches. The national marches, held in December 1931 and December 1932, became occasions for coordinated newsreel coverage by WFPL camera crews around the country--the WIR arranging the filmed record along with food, shelter and medical care for the marchers. A hunger march in Detroit on March 7, 1932, filmed by members of the local League, became a massacre when police opened fire and killed four demonstrators; the film survives.

The Bonus March of 1932 was not Communist-led, but the Party did try to extend its influence among the out-of-work veterans through the participation of its "mass organization," the Workers Ex-Servicemen's League (WESL), whose banners are prominent in the powerful League film devoted to the march, camp, and eviction.

The Scottsboro Case was used by the Party to focus attention on lynch law in the South and the oppression of blacks generally; it conducted a militant defense through the International Labor Defense and held many rallies demanding the release of the accused youths. This activity was reinforced by several newsreels and a short film made for the ILD, with assistance from the League, by Leo T. Hurwitz, entitled The Scottsboro Boys.

Other films focused on further pressure points in the class struggle and helped fulfill the League's reported purpose of "the taking of newsreels of demonstrations, meetings, Party activities and other affairs of immediate, daily concern to the American working class."[9]

Cinéma-vérité has dulled our appreciation of participant camerawork, but in the thirties the hand-held, close-range cinematography of street actions which the League footage offered must have struck spectators with great novelty and force. Leo Seltzer has stressed the importance of his physical involvement in the events he was shooting in conveying excitement, and writing of his participation in the filming of Hunger 1932, Brody makes a similar point. Brody, however, lays emphasis--as Seltzer does not--on the political commitment of the filmmakers:

> I was a member of a group of four cameramen sent by the New York section of the Workers Film and Foto League to cover the activities of Column 8 of the National Hunger March on its way to Washington from New York City.
>
> Soon there will be shown to the workers of New York the evidence gathered by the keen eyes of our cameras. This evidence is totally unlike anything shown in newsreels taken by capitalist concerns. Our cameramen were class-conscious workers who understood the historical significance of this epic march for bread and the right to live. As a matter of fact, we "shot" the march not as "disinterested" news-gatherers but as actual participants in the march itself. Therein lies the

> importance of our finished film. It is the viewpoint of the marchers themselves. Whereas the capitalist cameramen who followed the marchers all the way down to Washington were constantly on the lookout for sensational material which would distort the character of the march in the eyes of the masses, our worker cameramen, working with small hand-cameras that permit unrestricted mobility, succeeded in recording incidents that show the fiendish brutality of the police towards the marchers.... [10]

It was in camerawork, and not in editing, that the newsreels were distinguished, but in the longer compilation films there are some striking sequences of montage in the Soviet manner. Bonus March, for example, edited by Seltzer and Balog, opens with a prologue which sketches the background to the contemporary situation. A model of savage political comment in film, this sequence achieves, through skillful intercutting of documentary footage with strong iconic significations, a biting attack on imperialist war and its patriotic trimmings, on the capitalist economy, and on the pretensions of religion. The sequence is constructed as follows:

> TITLE: "1917 ... " / swinging sign: "Go Places with the US Army"--travel photographs, picture of ship, etc. / sign: "Adventure Over the World," and doughboy picture / mass parade of troops / battlefield: tanks and troops advance / swinging sign: "Travel--US Army" / cannon fires / another cannon fires / "Travel--US Army" sign / shells explode, blowing up building / battlefield: shells explode / "Travel--US Army" sign / tank flattens tree / soldiers leap into trench / ship on sign "Go Places with the US Army," swinging / battleship / ship on sign / battleship / ship on sign (FLASH) / ship's cannon is raised / interior of gun barrel, ZOOM IN / ship's cannons fire / another battleship / battleship / (DIFFERENT ANGLE) battleship smoking / German warplane / explosion in the trenches / dead on battlefield / garden party, for injured and maimed servicemen / servicemen line up to be greeted / servicemen shake hands with VIPs /

man on crutches, legless man / shaking hands / nurses attend to servicemen / shaking hands / stretcher patient wheeled up / US flag / cathedral / another cathedral, TILT DOWN / down-and-out unemployed man on bench, head in hands / cathedral, TILT DOWN / priest in street / heroic statuary / sign: "Catholic Charities, St. Francis Xavier's Parish" / US Eagle sign on Bank of United States building / same man on bench / sign: "The Salvation Army--Jesus for the Bowery" / CLOSE-UP, man on bench / older unemployed man / bindlestiffs in street / sign: "The Salvation Army--The Bowery for Jesus"; people walk past / sign in stones: " ... body a seat and we have been setting down ever since"; Hooverville, water in background; TILT UP / same sign, on riverbank, cabin in the water behind; PAN to reveal waterside Hooverville shacks / shacks, and inhabitant / HIGH ANGLE, bread line: "Emergency Food Station, The Salvation Army" / (DIFFERENT ANGLE) bread line / STRAIGHT OVERHEAD, bread line; TILT UP revealing its length / OVERHEAD (CLOSER SHOT), men in bread line / (STREET LEVEL; MEDIUM SHOT) men in bread line, reading newspapers; PAN as they inch forward.

Following documentation of agitation by the Workers Ex-Servicemen's League, the march to Washington, the encampment, and demonstrations, the film begins its sequence of the eviction with a quick reprise of the opening statement--a title "1917 ... " and shots of marching troops, tanks on the battlefield, an explosion, the wounded given a garden-party reception--then "1932 ... " and the US infantry attacks down Pennsylvania Avenue, backed up by the cavalry, and the armored division.

The surviving issue of the League news magazine, America Today, offers another example of creative montage used to make a political point forcefully and economically. As part of a sequence on Fascism, Seltzer intercut some footage of Franklin D. Roosevelt (which actually depicted him signing legislation repealing Prohibition) with shots of warships at maneuvers. The CP line at the time was that Roosevelt was preparing for aggressive war, and that the New Deal represented incipient Fascism. The sequence is cut as follows:

> troops parade through streets / Mussolini salutes / troops march, give Fascist salutes / Fascist salute, PAN to reveal arm is Hitler's / US battleship, TILT UP to following ship / FDR signs document, reaches for blotter, lays it down, makes a fist to blot / navy cruiser, cannons fire / (FRONT VIEW) guns are raised / interior of gun barrel / cannons fire / FDR looks up and smiles / dark cloud, DISSOLVE to NRA Eagle sign and inscription: "We Do Our Part."

Seltzer was quite content working strictly within a newsreel/documentary mode. By 1934, however, some dissatisfaction was being felt among other League members with this approach. It was in recognition of this and anticipation of arguments to come that Brody wrote an article, "The Revolutionary Film: Problem of Form," defending the FPL's traditional aesthetic commitment. The riposte came in New Theatre three months later, when Hurwitz described the work being done by an experimental group at the League's Harry Alan Potamkin Film School, and stated:

> ... the plan is to develop this experimental group into a production group within the Film and Photo League for the purpose of making documentary-dramatic revolutionary films--short propaganda films that will serve as flaming film-slogans, satiric films and films exposing the brutalities of capitalist society.[11]

The plan encountered rough going, and the issue remains a controversial one among former FPL members. There is not space here to develop the ramifications of the dispute, which centered on financial priorities rather than either/or aesthetic choice, but the upshot was that the FPL did not approve Hurwitz's proposal for a "shock-troupe of full-time film workers," and in the fall of 1934 he, Steiner and Lerner broke away to form the nucleus of a radical filmmaking collective known as "Nykino."

Meanwhile, in September, the FPL rededicated itself to the business of unvarnished newsreel production at a National Conference held in Chicago. Reference has so far been made primarily to the New York section of the League, but in fact branches existed in many cities of the country.

Detroit, Chicago, and Los Angeles were the most active in terms of production, but there were strong groups also in Boston, Philadelphia, Washington, D. C. and San Francisco, and local FPL organizations were reported at one time or another in Pittsburgh; Hollywood; New Haven, Connecticut; Cleveland; Laredo, Texas; Madison, Wisconsin; and Perth Amboy, Newark, and Paterson, New Jersey.

The Conference resolved that, "The tremendous growth of the working-class movement coupled with the increase of strikes and class warfare makes it imperative for the Film and Photo League to concentrate its best film and photo forces on the field of battle, adequately to record the vital events of our time." 16mm was adopted as the basic stock for local use, 35mm being retained for original photography at the national level. A National Film Exchange was set up, and a National Executive Committee elected, with David Platt as National Secretary and Tom Brandon a member.

Work continued. In 1934-35 Leo Seltzer produced, with Ed Kern, his much-praised Marine, and Nancy Naumburg, with James Guy, directed two longish political films (with acted sequences), Sheriffed and Taxi, the latter of which became an official FPL production. All these films are lost, and reviews provide only frustrating hints as to their content and technique.

After a spate of productivity in the first half of 1935, the League began to lose ground. The WIR was weakened by the annihilation of the IAH in Germany under the Nazis, and seems to have ceased activity by mid-decade. The New York FPL continued as an independent entity, but without the organizational backing, financial support, and political direction its parent body had been able to provide, it experienced an uphill struggle. In September 1935, League members collaborated in the creation of the New Film Alliance in an effort to divest themselves of many of the FPL's non-production commitments (their hopes for it were not to be fulfilled). A few films continued to be produced, but by June 1936, when the League's film section announced a move to new headquarters, activity was very sporadic. The last film to be released under the Film and Photo League's name, Getting Your Money's Worth (1937), was, according to its director Julian Roffman, not in fact a League project, and a press report claiming the FPL was "still kicking around in this vale of tears" was Roffman says, "a whistling-in-the-dark effort and a thumbing of noses at the forces that had gutted the organization by their forming of other groups and cliques."[12] Meanwhile, though, the stills section had re-emerged as the Photo League and was to become a significant force in documentary photography for many years to come; another offshoot, Associated Film Audiences, was monitoring Hollywood productions for reactionary content; and the group of filmmakers who had split to form Nykino were consolidating their position as the newly formed non-profit production company, Frontier Films.

Part Two: Frontier Films

Frontier Films was incorporated in March 1937. The members of its production collective had all participated in the experimentation of the Nykino years; they included Paul Strand (president), Leo Hurwitz and Ralph Steiner (vice-presidents), Lionel Berman (executive director), Willard Van Dyke, Ben Maddow (known as "David Wolff"), Sidney Meyers ("Robert Stebbins"), Irving Lerner ("Peter Ellis") and Jay Leyda ("Eugene Hill"). Their intention was to make high-quality social documentaries with a progressive viewpoint.

The problem of financing was the initial hurdle to be overcome, and it was to continue to dog the collective for the five years of its existence. The group was committed to produce sound films of a professional standard on 35 mm with a crew which received at least a minimal salary, all of which pushed costs up compared with those of the Film and Photo League. Frontier hoped to make inroads into the commercial theatres and to reach an expanding non-theatrical market, but though it achieved some success in these areas, financial returns remained low. As a result the company was forced to rely on donations for survival, and fundraising became a perennial and time-consuming task. Some money was contributed in small amounts by supporters in the unions and elsewhere, but the major income came in the form of substantial gifts or soft loans from a handful of wealthy sympathizers.

During 1937-38, Frontier Films produced four short documentaries on political themes. Heart of Spain and Return to Life dealt with medical services in Republican Spain and the war against fascism. China Strikes Back celebrated the recent unification of forces in China (led by Mao Zedong and Chiang Kai-shek) to combat Japanese invasion. The only domestic production, People of the Cumberland, was a study of the work of the Highlander Folk School in Tennessee: its role in stimulating the revival of folk arts and in attacking poverty in the depressed Cumberland Plateau region by assisting in union organization.

Most of Frontier's energies in the next few years were absorbed by the group's major production, and the culminating achievement of the radical film movement of the decade, the feature-length Native Land. Co-directed by Hurwitz and Strand, photographed by Strand, and edited by Hurwitz, Native Land drew on the talents of many others, including Maddow, who hammered out the script in collaboration with the directors: Marc Blitzstein, who composed the score; Paul Robeson, who sang and spoke the narration; and, in miniature roles, a clutch of New York actors, many of whom had been associated with left-wing theatre.

The subject of Native Land is the American working people of the Depression years and their efforts to organize despite brutal opposition. The conflict is seen in terms of the violation of civil liberties by fascist-minded corporations and thugs working in their interests; by means of frequent references to the Bill of Rights, the film's rhetoric seeks to legitimize the workers' cause, stigmatize the violent and underhand tactics of the employers, and promote an alliance in defense of democracy.

The immediate inspiration for the film was a series of hearings conducted in 1936-37 in Washington by the La Follette Civil Liberties Committee (a subcommittee of the Senate Committee on Education and Labor). In support of the National Labor Relations Board, which was being frustrated by right-wing industrialists in its efforts to enforce the 1935 Wagner Act and thus guarantee the right of collective bargaining, the La Follette Committee exposed corporation techniques of union-smashing by the employment of labor spies, and of strike-breaking by means of munitions stockpiling and vigilante force. Its indictment of labor espionage was given popular treatment in Leo Huberman's The Labor Spy Racket, published in September 1937 and an acknowledged stimulus for Native Land.

Native Land's screenplay is built around factual incidents. They include the murder of a union farmer in Michigan in 1934, and of a labor organizer in Cleveland in 1936; the shooting down of two Arkansas sharecroppers (one black, one white) by deputies, again in 1936; the infamous Shoemaker killing of November 30, 1935, in which the Ku

Klux Klan tarred and feathered progressive candidates in a local Florida election; and the Republic Steel Massacre of Memorial Day, 1937. A lengthy central sequence exposing the modus operandi of spies in a labor union is a dramatized version of facts revealed in the Senate Committee hearings, and a briefer section is devoted to the Committee's investigatory procedures. Bracketing the portrayal of these selected events are documentary montages illustrating the themes of the historical legacy of the Bill of Rights and the modern transformation of American life through industrialization. Other threads inserted into the pattern involve the everyday work and recreation of Americans, militant unionists parading in the streets, the intimidation of a pro-union shopkeeper, police attacks on demonstrators, and an angry clergyman speaking out against repression.

In structure Native Land is deliberately "dialectical," alternating sequences of light and dark, advance and setback; and of documentary (the general) and drama (the specific). This bold experiment, prefigured only in earlier productions of the Frontier group, was unprecedented on this scale in the American cinema. It was the outcome of years of theoretical discussion, and represented a striving for a Marxist aesthetic bridging Stanislavsky and Brecht, which would be both emotionally involving and intellectually informative (a useful comparison is Steinbeck's contemporaneous The Grapes of Wrath, which counterpoints the Joads' story with chapters of generalized narrative and commentary).

Central to the dialectical concept was that the situation dealt with in the film was not fixed but fluid; history was in the process of being shaped, and there were no crippling defeats to mourn nor final victories to celebrate. In Hurwitz's view, such a conception ruled out the possibility of a conventional dramatic climax and resolution. Moreover, concern with an abstract notion--liberty--as the driving force of the film required that the individual dramas, though factual, be subordinated to an overall pattern in which discursive documentary segments would also have a place.

From this structure Native Land derives much aesthetic power. For being anchored in a documentary base, the miniature dramas stand out the more vividly in their separate qualities: the lyricism of the Michigan sequence, with its billowy clouds, sturdy white draft horses, the rude plow turning the soil; the desolate pain of the Arkansas sequence, the hunted sharecroppers fleeing through the swamps; the garish horror of KKK torture by night in Florida.

Strand's photography helps: it is in a sharp, documentary style that occasionally achieves great beauty. The acting performances, modeled on the practice of the Group Theatre--to which several of the actors including Howard Da Silva and Art Smith were attached--are marked by a low-key psychological realism that is both unobtrusive and compelling. And there are moments when Blitzstein's score keys the action to a sharp emotional pitch, as when, in the Arkansas sequence, Robeson's voice breaks into the mournful spiritual, Dusty Sun.

Likewise, through being counterposed with the individual incidents, the generalized documentary segments covering developments on a national scale are charged with a greater tension. Among the best of these is the latter section of the opening montage, which depicts post-Civil War America in imagery of molten iron, locomotive wheels, steam engines, trains, girders, bridges, factories, pylons, high-tension wires, smokestacks, oil tanks, cranes, pipelines, sky-scrappes--all cut to a fast, nervous rhythm. Interposed within this sequence are shots of the Statue of Liberty and the Stars and Stripes--and at this point the question of ideology is ineluctably posed.

Although not released until 1942, Native Land was conceived and largely filmed in the years 1937-39, and it is quintessentially a product of the People's Front era. CPUSA secretary Earl Browder had declared, in conformity with decisions promulgated by the Communist International at its Seventh World Congress in 1935, that the crucial political struggle of the day was not socialism vs. capitalism, but democracy vs. fascism. And democracy in the United States was to be preserved, the argument ran, by a vigorous defense of those civil liberties which were the heritage of the revolutionary history of the American people, and which were now menaced by powerful reactionary forces with fascist tendencies.

The impact of this political line is to be observed in the battle lines drawn up in the film. In the aggressive class-struggle period of the early thirties, for example, churchmen and small business operators were consigned wholesale by the Communist Left to the enemy camp; in Native Land a conspicuous attempt is made to win their support and recognize their potential contribution to the anti-fascist cause. Significantly, the state is now also viewed as a potential ally: the traditional democratic process (demonstrations and writing to Congress) by which pressure is put on government is endorsed, the La Follette Committee is extolled, and the film is awash with patriotic imagery: statues of Washington, Jefferson, and Lincoln, the Flag, the Statue of Liberty, the dome of the Capitol Building.

The symbols of national tradition could in this way, it was thought, be reclaimed for the working class and its new allies and turned against those class descendants of the bourgeois pioneers (termed "the fascist-minded on our own soil" in an opening title) whose practice mocked their ancestors' pretensions. But thus recasting the class struggle into terms of democracy vs. fascism meant, for the filmmakers, that the people be confronted by a single, monolithic menace.

"Conspiracy" screams a title superimposed over an animated sequence of the film, and the narration explains that the Senate Committee has uncovered "a plan with a single aim, backed by millions of dollars, by the resources of the biggest corporations." The conspiracy, whose "secret connections" and "interlocking parts" have been exposed--a spider's web is drawn over a map of the US to make the point--is under the direction of "a handful of fascist-minded corporations"--which remain unspecified.

But it is extremely unlikely that the sporadic outbursts of anti-union violence in the thirties--such as those depicted in the film--were all directed from a single source, and in applying a grid which fit for Italy, Germany or Spain to the quite different situation in the United States the filmmakers restricted their ability to clearly identify the enemy--and consequently, it may be argued, they obscured the nature of the various struggles to be waged. Among those responsible for the anti-labor outrages it portrays, Native Land of course names the Ku Klux Klan along with its brother organizations, the Black Legion, Associated Farmers, Silver Shirts, and Christian Front. The police departments of Chicago, New York, San Francisco, and other cities are by implication held liable for their violent attacks on demonstrators, and the sheriff and his deputies of Fort Smith, Arkansas, are flagrantly guilty of murder. But on the crucial questions of who is behind the smooth hit-men who leave Fred Hill dead on his Michigan farm, who hired the unseen killer of the organizer in Cleveland, who employed the treacherous labor spies or the pockmarked thug of Memphis who runs the grocer out of town, the film is evasive.

Despite its tributes to the triumphant struggles waged by "the plain people" of America, Native Land--and this is one of its most striking characteristics--is a film which dramatizes defeats. We learn that Fred Hill spoke up at a farmers' meeting, but we are not shown the meeting (nor do we discover what he spoke about); we see him hoisting his son on to a horse, washing up, chatting with his wife--and then his murdered body. The Cleveland labor organizer is merely a corpse: the film's focus is on the maid who finds him. The important movement to organize share-croppers during the mid-thirties is represented by the shooting down of two activists. Likewise, the labor espionage section concentrates on the destructive maneuvers of the spies; the Memphis grocer is shown, not helping unionists, but being driven out of town for doing so; the socialist leaders of the Modern Democrats in Florida, active opponents of the Ku Klux Klan, are depicted only in their role as recipients of torture; the Republic Steel strikers and their supporters are simply massacre victims.

Except for the angry unionists who are restrained by their president from assaulting the exposed labor spy (for fear of adverse publicity), the protagonists of Native Land are not fighters: they are, as the narrator remarks over shots of workers heading off to their jobs, "little people," the "innocent ones" who "never hurt anyone, never could." These working people are shown mostly at play: ping pong and checkers at the union hall, a steamboat excursion, visiting the parks and the zoo. The film fails to trace the source of working-class strength: the power to strike. Strikes, in fact, are not even mentioned on the soundtrack--an extraordinary omission in a film celebrating the victories of the union movement in the thirties.

In general, Native Land takes a working-class conservative-defensive line. The Democratic system (the Bill of Rights, the Senate Committee, the administration of Roosevelt--whose portrait appears almost as an icon on the walls at union headquarters) is pictured as responsive to labor's needs. Soviet ideology was associated with the collectivization and mechanization of agriculture: as if to remove any hint of contamination by it, Native Land's first hero/martyr is a family farmer who works his own land with a horse plow--and is manifestly content. Work is seen as fulfilling. The mass unemployment of the Depression years (in 1939, there were still nine and a half million jobless) is scarcely alluded to. No change in life style is proposed: the film celebrates in happy imagery and upbeat song the working family's morning routine, the pastimes of a summer holiday. People, we are told, don't want very much out of life.

It is overstating the case to claim, as Ernest Callenbach does, that the film "assumes a prior Golden Age--apparently the heroic pioneer period--when men were men, invented liberty and equality, and lived happily without oppression."[13] On the contrary, Native Land insists that Americans have had to fight for their freedom in every generation. Yet the myth of a pre-existent harmony lingers in several sequences: an early morning montage in which America wakes up to the cheerful strains of a Blitzstein song, a Memorial Day holiday with people on swings and skates and slides and watching the seals at the zoo. Central to both is the iconography of children at play, that stereotypical imagery of an untroubled age. These sequences, like those (in Heart of Spain and Return To Life) of Madrid before the shells and bombs explode, represent the calm before the storm: they propose that American working people are basically and normally happy and satisfied with their lives, that they have moderate desires, and that they have done nothing to deserve the murderous repression exercised upon them. If their demands (like those of the Arkansas sharecroppers, who asked only ten cents more for their cotton) are modest, it is all the more outrageous that they should be shot down for making them.

Such a rhetorical structure has the effect of making Native Land appear, in some respects, backward-looking beside, say Van Dyke and Steiner's The City (1939), which is saturated with naive American optimism. The City also turns to the past--in fact recreates a supposed prior harmonious age in some detail--but its major emphasis is on the transformation of living conditions prevalent in contemporary industrial society in the utopian community to come. Its solution is, however, politically fanciful, as the Frontier filmmakers were quick to point out. Native Land, being more "realistic," is concerned with protecting the gains of the past rather than projecting a future of radical social change.

At a time when the Nazis were on their way to subjugating Europe, it was an understandable preoccupation. The question which Native Land provokes--and it is relevant to the People's Front strategy as a whole--is whether

America's "native fascists" were seriously comparable to Hitler; whether, in fact, the situation justified the sacrifice of radical working-class initiatives in the interests of a broad-based defensive coalition whose political goals were vague and whose unity would be welded by fervent invocation of the patriotic ideals of a bygone age.

Notes

1 This article is based on my Northwestern University Ph.D. dissertation, Radical Cinema in the United States, 1930-1942: The Work of the Film and Photo League, Nykino, and Frontier Films, now published as Cinema Strikes Back: Radical Filmmaking in the United States, 1930-1942 (Ann Arbor: UMI Research Press, 1982). Part One was published in slightly different form in Jump Cut, No. 14 (1977) and is reproduced with permission. Portions of Part Two were included in my article on Native Land in Revolutionary Films/Chicago '76 (1976) and are reprinted with the permission of the Film Center, School of the Art Institute of Chicago. I do not mean the title to be exclusive: there were, of course, other radical filmmakers working independently of (though in touch with) the Film and Photo League or Frontier Films, such as Herbert Kline (in the later thirties) and Joris Ivens.

2 S[amuel] B[rody], "The Movies as a Weapon Against the Working Class," Daily Worker, May 20, 1930, p. 4.

3 Harry A. Potamkin, "Workers' Films," Daily Worker, May 31, 1930, p. 3.

4 New Masses, VI, No. 2 (July 1930), p. 22; Labor Defender, April 1930, p. 76.

5 See Daily Worker, December 4, 1930, p. 2, and December 11, 1930, p. 2.

6 Leo Seltzer, in Russell Campbell, "'A Total and Realistic Experience': Interview with Leo Seltzer," Jump Cut, No. 14 (1977), p. 25.

7 Brody, in Tony Safford, "The Camera as a Weapon in the Class Struggle: Interview with Samuel Brody," Jump Cut, No. 14 (1977), p. 28.

8 Seltzer, loc. cit., p. 27.

9 S[eymour] S[tern], "A Working-Class Cinema for America?" The Left, I, No. 1 (Spring 1931), p. 71.

10 Brody, "The Hunger March Film," Daily Worker, December 29, 1932, p. 4.

11 Leo T. Hurwitz, "The Revolutionary Film--Next Step," New Theatre, May 1934, p. 15.

12 "Film and Photo Demise Greatly Exaggerated," Daily Worker, April 30, 1937, p. 9; Julian Roffman, letter to author, October 26, 1977.

13 Ernest Callenbach, "Native Land," Film Quarterly, XXVII, No. 1 (Fall 1973), p. 61.

I would like to thank the many former participants who helped me with my research into the radical film movement of the thirties, and in particular, Leo Hurwitz, David Platt, Julian Roffman, Leo Seltzer, and the late Tom Brandon. --R. C.

Chapter 5

THE COMMUNIST PARTY AND LA VIE EST A NOUS: DOCUMENT AND FICTION, POETICS AND POLITICS

Daniel Serceau*

La Vie est à nous would never, of course, have received the attention it has were it not for the identity of its chief collaborator, Jean Renoir. Daniel Serceau's goal here is not to debate the authorship of the film, however. Auteur or no auteur, La Vie would merit careful analysis as one of the first big-budget features in the West to aim explicitly at a non-politicized mass audience with the purpose of communist (electoral) mobilization. Despite its aborted career, and even if the Popular Front had not won the 1936 French elections, La Vie remains a key cultural document of that momentous experiment in leftist strategy, of an era that retains much exemplary value as well as much glamour for contemporary radicals. Serceau's scrutiny may dissipate some of the glamour but it has the salutory effect of restoring the film to its historical context, an effect not always sought by auteurists. Though Serceau does not over-emphasize the theoretical implications of the interplay of actuality, didactic sketches, and direct-address appeal that constitutes the principal textual strategy of the film, his minute criticism of its ideological implications adds greatly to our understanding of a basic model in the history of left film activism:

*Translated from the French by Mark Leslie and Thomas Waugh.

what might be called the "sketch-film", a didactic hybrid of fiction, semi-documentary, actuality and essayistic material, anticipated by Brecht and Dudow's Kuhle Wampe (1932), and refined by many later examples, from Native Land (1942) to Salt of the Earth (1954), from Two or Three Things I Know About Her (1966) to Coup pour coup (1971), from The Seventeenth Parallel (1967) to Hombres de Mal Tiempo (1968), from Far from Vietnam (1967) to Germany in Autumn (1978).

La Vie est à nous (Life Belongs to Us), although overt propaganda for the French Communist Party (PCF), functions primarily in the manner of the classical fiction film. It makes use not only of documentary techniques but also of mise-en-scène, used effectively to create the desired meanings....

The film opens with the illusion of an "objective" documentary, elaborating France's riches, which is soon revealed by the narrative to be the depiction of a schoolteacher's geography lesson. The documentary images thus yield to the spectacle of a classroom, probably in a Paris suburb, where working-class children are sitting, shabbily dressed. The lesson ends. As the children leave the room one by one, the teacher (Jean Dasté), stroking a pupil's head, murmurs to himself, "poor children," questioning in a sense the function of his own teaching. In this way, he verbalizes--outside the class, since he respects the neutrality required by his position--the contradiction of his own work, which exposes these children to images of a kind of wealth they will never know.

In the street, where the obvious state of poverty accurately reflects the average living conditions in the working-class neighborhoods of the thirties, the children remark upon the flagrant contradiction between their daily lives and what they're being forced to learn in school, the contradiction between the enormous accumulated wealth of "France" and the destitution in which they and their families live.

This is the most immediate level of discourse in the film, that is, its linear sequence of events. But the real discourse operates on another level through the constant dynamic of an essential element of the mise-en-scène which nevertheless is external to it: the audience, at each moment of the screening, perceives the film not as a film which they believe as it unfolds before their eyes, but as their own representation which they identify nonetheless as a reality. Thus the "documentary" is simply the depiction of a lesson, both the documentary and the lesson appearing separately as an image of France (the expression of her Truth), though both of them are actually only discourses. Here the principle of the mise-en-scène consists of playing on the representations formed each moment by the audience, and, through the dialectical system of their constant interplay, elaborating a discourse which is no longer only the sum of all the successive representations but the product of their synthesis.

In following what it believes to be a documentary, the audience tends to identify the run-down of the wealth of "France" as being that of the "entire country." The documentary's ideological purpose becomes clear: by using the French audience's spontaneous identification with the "national community" (hence their nationalism), the film gives a sense of pleasure, even of pride, the spectacle of riches functioning as the internalization of their own belongings. The division of society into classes, which can be here very accurately specified as the private appropriation of the national product, is covered by the audience's identification with the "nation."[1]

This effect on the audience is then expressed within the film itself in the form of the pupils' questioning of each other. They internalize this identification, but incompletely, because the contradiction with their own experience is too flagrant. In this sense, within the film, the pupils, or at least an aware few of them, represent (or come close to representing) spectators of their own class.

Our discovery of the classroom within the frame transforms the cinematic nature of the images (they change from documentary to fiction), but not their ideological value. The filmic depiction of the lesson still retains the illusion of truth. The teacher's exclamation occasions our first doubt, but it's only the presence of the children in the street, the visible display of contradiction and, above all, its verbalization by the children that gives the lesson and the images their full ideological value. At the same time, two ideas concerning bourgeois education are advanced. The teacher, despite his knowledge (of social reality) and his own class position, plays by the rules, conveying "bourgeois" knowledge to the children as universal knowledge. Thus, the criticism of bourgeois education does not take place inside the educational institution, but outside.

The schoolteacher's "playing by the rules" is not the only issue here. Also at stake is the actual method of acquisition of knowledge and of access to truth in the dialectical relationship uniting experience and theory. Without Theory, the children confronted with the spectacle of the street cannot understand anything, or rather, cannot understand that they don't understand. (With a very Renoiresque attitude, one of them uses his imagination. Retelling some maternal wisdom, but misunderstanding it, he claims to be wealthy.) But the children's awareness of street life, without completely invalidating the theoretical knowledge acquired in the geography lesson, is enough to contradict it and to make it strange (since it is not obviously a lie).

Is this criticism of the French school system intentional? Probably not. The metaphor of the school is used primarily as a didactic tool. La Vie est à nous not only depicts what is, while criticizing it (critical realism), but also provides an explanation of the perceived contradiction (the role of the Chorus), and a political strategy for resolving it. By substituting one kind of knowledge for another, the film takes on, acting for and in the name of the PCF, the theoretical function which every Marxist party must (or should) practice: to be, regardless of any electoralist goal, the agent of consciousness and scientific knowledge among the masses.

In this sense, in a Marxist tradition I would risk calling academic, does this PCF-sponsored film go beyond the mode of representation to which Renoir had until then restricted himself--critical realism? No, and for two reasons. Renoir, from at least La Chienne on, always situated the behavior of his characters within their social and class determinations. As for La Vie est à nous, it in no way aims at the effective transformation of society. A propaganda film, it serves first the campaign interests of the PCF. Consequently, as we shall see, it caters to the different strata of French society much more than it demands the transformation of their ideological and class positions.

The evocation of Soviet Russia and of the fathers of International Socialism (obviously purged of any allusion to its "renegades") does not fail to appear in the film. This is somewhat surprising in the electoral context of 1936 when the PCF is attempting to prove its patriotism. But it is a reference that signifies its will to carry high, all alone, the banner of the Revolution. Symptomatically, the allusion to the events of February 1934 is missing two compromising historical facts: the participation of PCF militants in the February 6 riots (L'Humanité had, moreover, called them to demonstrate that very morning); and the February 12 strike organized by the CGT[2] and which the Humanité of the 11th supported, on Moscow's orders, it appears. Only the demonstration of the 9th, to which L'Humanité had given the call on the 8th (that is, two days after the strike order of the CGT) is referred to in the film. The sectarianism of the beginning of the thirties and the falsification of history for propaganda purposes are, in fact, still on the agenda, despite the new strategic directions of the Party, or at least its official ones.

The PCF Political Line as the Basis for "La Vie est à nous"

This line, as we know, is linked to the evolution of PCF strategy after 1934, and is explained in part by the rise of fascism all over Europe, and, in part, by the stabilization and strengthening of "Stalinist counter-revolution" in the USSR.

The year 1931 marks the definitive conclusion to the sectarian period of the PCF where the "class against class" tactic prevailed, making Social Democracy the principal enemy. A new policy is developed: On the international front, the principal task becomes the "defense of the homeland of socialism." This results in the subordination of the proletariat's struggles to the defense of the USSR's interests, world revolution no longer appearing to be the best weapon against capitalist encirclement. Two methods are proposed to achieve this. The first is to make use of inter-imperialist contradictions to prevent the formation of a front of bourgeois states against the USSR. The second is to transform the working classes of different capitalist countries into pressure groups intended to break the anti-Sovietism of their respective bourgeoisies. In fact, the Popular Front aims at creating a "vast popular coalition" against fascism.

On the domestic front, from 1934 on, the PCF transforms both its analysis of political and economic responsibilities and the system of class alliances that it wants to set up. The enemy is no longer capitalism as such, but it is the so-called "200 families," in other words, the monopolist upper bourgeoisie.[3] The PCF clearly states that it will not take France out of the capitalist camp.

> France does not belong to the French;
> She belongs to the 200 families,

says the Chorus in the film. This is also a source of the virulent nationalism and patriotism of the Party, presented from that time on as the party of the "great reconciliation of the French nation."

As a result, the PCF attempts to create a union of all the anti-monopolist social classes. From 1934 on, "the platforms of the Party endeavor to create the basis of a program founded on the aspirations of all social strata affected by the policies of the upper bourgeoisie."[4] Politically, the alliances are made with the Socialist Party and the Radicals, the PCF proving itself to be in practice more flexible with the Radicals than with the Socialists. And, in terms of class, in addition to the industrial working class and the semi-proletariat, the Party must win over large sectors of working-class peasants and the middle classes.

La Vie est à nous, then, acts as a strict cinematic application of this new strategy.

Cahiers du cinéma[5] notes that: 1) the schoolteacher's lesson is largely borrowed from the report of Thorez (the PCF secretary whose oratory appears in the film) to the 8th Congress; and 2) this report provides the film with its organizing principle except for one important variation--"whereas Thorez goes from the exposé of the situation of the working classes ... to the international situation and to the rise of fascism in France, the film reverses this order and leads the three fictional episodes into the speeches of the political leaders."[6]

In effect, the denunciation in the film of the 200 families begins a series of sequences showing French, Italian, and German fascists. As for the 200 families, we follow them whether it be in their High Society activities or in their economic practices (e.g., the character played by Brunius lamenting that he has to bring about a new reduction in his staff). The goal is obvious: to crystallize the audience's class hatred against a bourgeoisie depicted in its most insolent luxury and, the condition that makes this possible: daily exploitation and oppression of workers today, and fascist violence tomorrow.

It is not a coincidence that the sequence concludes with a parade of French fascists watched by a petty bourgeois, standing on the sidewalk, who exclaims "Nothing can stop those people!" But a worker getting down from a lamp-post replies, "The Communist Party can!"[7] Propaganda for the Party is essentially linked to the anti-fascist struggle, as well as to the rallying-cry to overturn the 200 families. The PCF puts on a democratic face and presents itself as the instrument for achieving a unified movement in spite of all class contradictions, from the proletariat up to and including certain segments of the bourgeoisie. This unitary perspective, as we know, is "the union of the People of France."

But, simultaneously, the fascist specter (for indeed it is one, the film dwelling at length on the terror and violence that fascism sows in its path--murders of Party members, the Ethiopian war, riots, the skull-and-crossbones insignia, etc...) reminds all the different social strata aimed at by this alliance of the seriousness of the international situation. This leads to the audience's desire for an effective response to the fascist peril, a response which the PCF (through the episode of the petty bourgeois, already mentioned) claims alone to be able to provide, precisely through its ability to attract the middle classes. The equation "fascism equals the upper-class monopolies" is now fully operational. Against fascism, the union of the People of France now appears urgent and indispensable. It represents a proper working alliance as it isolates the fascists, while uniting all those who suffer from Big Capital, whose political expression is fascism.

The Three Sketches of "La Vie est à nous"

We must not, however, deceive ourselves as to the actual political purpose of La Vie est à nous. It is less a blueprint for an alliance of different social groups (based on a community of certain interests, certainly, but in which class differences and class interests remain present and perceived as such), than it is of winning their adherence to the Communist Party.[8] This is perfectly transparent in the film:

1) The sequence on fascism opens with nothing other than, on the one hand, the presentation of the PCF (the PCF and not the Popular Front, don't forget) as the only protection against fascism, and, on the other hand, with a sequence promoting the PCF newspaper, L'Humanité (ending with the slogan "Vive l'Humanité").

2) The sequence with the young unemployed man does not propose anything other than joining the C. P.

To show, no doubt, how much L'Humanité is the paper of all the different social groups affected by the crisis, the film opens up--by means of the metaphor of the Humanité editor Cachin opening three letters from his enormous pile of mail--three fictions. These three letters--"autonomous" fictions inside La Vie est à nous--recount three individual cases, signifying the capitalist oppression experienced by each of the social classes that must make up the Union of the People of France: the industrial working class, the landless peasantry, and the wage-earning petty bourgeoisie.

1. A Worker Gets Fired

In a workshop a time-keeper watches the pace on the line. An old worker, employed by the company for many years, nears retirement. He doesn't work fast enough. He is fired. Immediately the Party cell gets organized. A tract is written at night, a plan of action drawn up. One Communist, wanting to resort to force, is shouted down by his comrades. They decide on a strike. The boss attempts to get them back to work with empty promises. One older worker, afraid and respectful, is ready to give in, but the Communist leader intervenes. The fired worker will be rehired. This is, in essence, the first sketch. Three elements stand out:

1) The condemnation of violent action.

2) The avant-garde role of the Communist leader. Conscious of the paternalism of the management, he intervenes in time to "rectify" the behavior of his comrades, victims of their class alienation.

3) Intense, but not over-jubilant feelings of victory and, above all, of power result from the strike. In an organized concerted effort, illuminated as we have seen by the C. P., the working class confronts management arbitrariness and omnipotence. The propaganda goal is fulfilled.

However, this sequence raises another issue. Straight off, the firing takes on a dramatic flavor, with talk of suicide. Regardless of its probability (indeed a man can think of suicide), this over-dramatization of the story makes perfect sense for the strategy of an opposition party which, to fight off its adversary, must paint society as black as possible. Once again the specter of death haunts the protagonists.

Moreover, the sequence describing the onslaught and "misdeeds" of fascism ends on a "special effect": the skull insignia caught in a whirlpool effect, finally stopping, held on the screen as the definitive sign of fascist politics, the final stage to which it will ultimately lead humanity. The PCF thus takes on an appropriately life-affirming meaning. The old worker not only gets his job back. His family is actually saved from a potentially ruinous disaster (his daughter, furthermore, brings her babe-in-arms to visit the Communists). Here is a reminder of the boss's role, whose self-interest causes misery and ultimately death. The bosses' power, fascism, the upper bourgeoisie, and the 200 families are all lined up symbolically together, under the same symbolic definition, as murderous forces of Darkness and Destruction. Opposed to the radiant, prosperous and dynamic France of the first images of the "documentary" is another France, the France of misery and suffering, caused by the 200 families (c.f., Brunius playing the Knight of Industry claiming the "necessity" of layoffs), whose specter the PCF will chase away, restoring the joy of life: it brings back the possibility of life through the possibility of work. This romantic life-affirming day-dream thus replaces a more detailed political plan of action. It also prefigures the start of La Marseillaise, made by Renoir two years later (where a peasant kills the Seigneur's pigeon to satisfy his hunger), and is at work throughout La Vie est à nous. More about this later.

2. Some Peasants Get Repossessed

A family of tenant farmers cannot pay back its debt to the landowner. The landowner decides to seize their possessions. A bailiff prepares to auction them off. A Communist peasant brings his friends, however, and during the sale, they let the potential buyers know what they're getting in for. The peasants' goods are thus rebought for practically nothing by the farmer and his Communist friends.[9]

This sketch obviously fulfills the same propagandistic function as the preceding one. The C.P. is appealing to a new class, the landless peasants (they are farmers or sharecroppers). Each of the social categories targeted electorally by the C.P. (workers, peasants, at least landless ones, middle classes), sees itself in a specific sketch integrated into the PCF global strategy. The Communist leader (Gaston Modot) this time belongs to the family but is rejected by it for his political opinions. As with the parallel worker (in the previous story) he is therefore "persecuted for his convictions," activism thus appearing to be a test, or even a priestly vocation, devoid of any secondary benefits.

Somewhat surprisingly, the strategy used by the Communists resorts, if not to violence, at least to its threat. One of the buyers even has his foot trampled on by one of the communists before he stops bidding. Whether intentional or not, the sequence liberates and satisfies the class violence which so far had been channelled strictly through trade-union legality. In the unfolding of the story, the sequence becomes indisputably linked to all the usual populist imagery of a super-hero defeating a representative of the dominant classes who is particularly cruel towards his "subjects." The sequence actually works as revenge, operating in an almost magical manner in that victory appears certain and meets no opposition whatsoever. The sequence satisfies the audience, which triumphs vicariously over all the social forces oppressing them. The "peasant question" is therefore not dealt with analytically, but emotively. All the contradictions and economic problems are mystified in favor of a direct "class against class" confrontation in which one legal entity (the exploited) takes the place of another (the exploiters). In the style of certain TV series or comic strips, we put ourselves in the World of the Omnipotent, of a guardian force which magically resolves existential unhappiness.

3. The Unemployed Engineer

A young electrical engineer (René) can't find work. He can no longer accept living off his girlfriend, a worker. He leaves her place and gets a job as a car washer. One day, a client complains that his car isn't ready on time. René's boss fires him on the spot. In the street the same client offers him help ... on condition that he join a fascist league. Desperate and hungry, the young man is taken in by two C. P. militants. At their headquarters a celebration is being readied. The engineer quickly becomes part of this new community. He is given food to eat, fixes an electrical breakdown, and takes care of the lighting....

Cahiers du cinéma rightly emphasizes the special treatment of this third and last sketch. It is longer and more carefully produced than the preceding ones. Symptomatically(?), Jean Renoir is said himself to have directed it. One thing seems sure. The relationship between the young man and his working-class girlfriend, the directing of the actors, the use of depth of field, and the entire mise-en-scène of the beginning of the sketch "denote" Renoir. Situated at the end, it becomes all the more important. Would the "Party" have treated this sketch with any special attention? The explanation offered by Cahiers du cinéma is plausible:

> In 1936 ... what is at stake for the C. P. is gaining votes.... The C. P. speaks primarily, at this historical moment, to the middle classes, to that segment of the petty bourgeoisie susceptible of aligning itself with the positions of the proletariat.

Although the first of these quotations seems indisputable, the second poses problems. The engineer sketch clearly caters to the middle classes in terms of the qualitative value of their work. "All the same, a man like you," says Ninette, René's friend, "you're worth a thousand times more than they (the bosses). You are really someone, you come from a prestigious school, you have a degree. What's more, you even told me that some of them have no education."[10] Here Renoir introduces a class distinction between the engineer and his girlfriend, the worker. Is it indicative of the C. P.'s thinking that throughout the sketch it does not introduce a contradiction between René and the working class?[11] Ninette, all the same, spontaneously states her feeling that there is a hierarchical differentiation between her friend and herself (which, moreover, coincides with the male-female division). She admires her lover for his level of education, and his technical and scientific skills. Implicitly (and Nadia Sibirskaia's acting as Ninette forcefully emphasizes this), she makes René into a man superior to his bosses no doubt, but also superior to herself.

Such a couple, in the perfect unity of their amorous harmony, does not lack political significance. Only unemployment, caused by the 200 families, manages to separate them. This conjugal union achieves a class union, articulating the lack of contradiction and even any form of division between the working class and professionals. No longer is the "Union of the People of France" to be accomplished through a system of alliances and compromises. It will be accomplished through the symbiosis of a world without contradiction, where each class can unite with others without losing any of its own identity. La Vie est à nous, far from aligning the petty bourgeoisie with the position of the proletariat (as stated by Cahiers), fastens on to petty bourgeois ideology to elevate it to the ranks of the dominant class once the parasitic upper bourgeoisie has been eliminated. From this perspective, the film clearly defends the interests of the petty bourgeoisie, not only in the short term; it also presents it as a political force assuming and fulfilling its historical future. The power of Money and Birthright pales in comparison with that of Knowledge and Skills, here affirmed in its new and unique legitimacy.

Once again it is a question of snatching the petty bourgeoisie away from fascism. But that political force has no influence on René. His recruitment is made on the basis of a particularly disagreeable deal (a job in exchange for Party membership). René's attitude thus brings up the simple moral, necessarily shared by the majority or even all of the spectators. Strictly political interests or temptations don't exist. Fascism as a mass phenomenon, particularly within the petty bourgeoisie, is concealed if not denied. La Vie est à nous, a propaganda film, thus distinguishes itself from any pedagogical film. It does not explain the phenomena that it claims to combat, and substitutes a moral judgment for an analysis of their political content. René simply experiences fascist corruption. The encounter with the Communists thus works as the opposite of the preceding one. The corruption and the repugnant commerce of the fascists is contrasted with the generosity and altruism of the Communists.

Cahiers has commented at length, and correctly so, on the modalities of this encounter, which has three principal components:

1) René finds human warmth and moral support in the C.P., the opposite of what he has just known. Here he finds a totally altruistic solidarity and the feeling of a true fraternity.

2) By coming to the help of his "comrades," he makes use of his training again, and becomes part of the community on the basis of his acquired skills. In fact, his goal was not only to find work but to be employed at the level of his qualifications. His temporary function of electrical repairman is obviously the symbolic achievement

of this. The Party allows him (and above all, will allow him) to become again what he really is, an electrical engineer.

3) Finally, there is the encounter with the "Chorus," whose function it is to summarize and distill the lesson of the film. The agent of René's coming to consciousness, it also offers its representation. This coming to consciousness can be synthesized in this way: René finds the solution to his isolation and his despair through the prospect of the unification of the working masses under the leadership of the C. P. Thus, whereas the factory worker and the farmer found in the Party the instrument of a concrete, immediate solution to their oppression, and were invited to join it on this basis, the engineer enters the Party, or at least sympathizes with it, for essentially "lyrical" reasons. That is, it is enthusiasm for a radically new world in itself that causes René's transformation, from desperation and unemployment, into the germ of a new militant, joyful and alive again. This transformation is expressed and functions through the poetic element of the "Internationale." I say poetic because in the film the "Internationale," as a song, essentially draws on its emotional power to exercise its power of suggestion on the feelings and the desire for revolt of the proletariat and oppressed classes. The singing of the "Internationale" thus allows the C. P. to obtain an easy consensus and to avoid characterizing more precisely the new world it is advancing as its vision. Moreover, it appears from this sketch that there is no other solution to René's unemployment than the victory of the Left in the next elections. Unlike the cases of the peasant and the worker, no form of grass-roots organization is suggested to him as an instrument for struggle. His social and economic oppression appear to be directly linked to the domination of the 200 families and can only be abolished along with them.

Therefore, it is false to maintain, as _Cahiers_ does, that "for Bertheau,[12] the movement to communism is clearly a removal from his class." _La Vie est à nous_ requires nothing of the kind from him. To vote Popular Front is not to vote for the disappearance of his class privileges or status, but to abolish the type of oppression that capitalism (or rather the 200 families) exerts on them. Bertheau regains his identity as a professional within the Party. The Popular Front will not do more than this for him. Today, hope, confidence in the future, human fraternity in this association of good friends that is the Party; tomorrow, the elimination of unemployment, the use of his skills in a job that satisfies him. Bertheau does not have to renounce his situation for the simple reason that the union of "all the monopolist classes" is not based on the defense of the interests of the most exploited; it actually is made up of an association of all the interests affected by the domination of monopoly capitalism, but the presentation is empty of all contradictions between these groups. In this way, each class can support the union without having to change its own identity in any way. La Vie est à nous, an electoralist film, nowhere mentions any kind of proposal for transforming the relations of production, or social, political or ideological relations. It asserts itself basically as a propagandist and opportunist discourse of seduction, essentially aimed at the middle classes.

The entire sketch draws its unity from a life-affirming kind of metaphor, thus becoming part of the discourse of the rest of the film. René gets ready to leave his friend. To cheer him up, she prepares, with her back to him, a nice omelette, for which the eggs, she says, didn't cost her much. He leaves immediately. After being fired from his job, he joins a soup line, but is turned away because the soup has run out. Discouraged, he collapses in a doorway, the camera at his level. Two silhouettes frame him menacingly. The silhouettes, however, are two C. P. activists who take him to their headquarters. He repairs the electrical breakdown. He is given a sandwich, which he wolfs down while directing a spotlight towards the Chorus. In one of the very last sequences we find him beside Ninette, radiant, moving ahead arm in arm in the crowd, singing the "Internationale."

The strictly political opposition, Fascist/Popular Front (or "Dictatorship of the Proletariat"), does not appear at all in this part of the film. Just as fascism becomes represented by the image of the skull-and-crossbones, the Popular Front, or rather, a vote for the C. P., is associated with "life," whose signs are essentially those of light (the lanterns of the meeting-place as opposed to the shadow of the street), of song (the Chorus), of warmth (both biological and emotional), of the group (the loneliness of the sidewalk is contrasted with this community of work and song), and finally, in an absolutely basic way, of nourishment. Fascism and Communism thus appear as two radically different metaphors, two principles which are much more poetic than political.

Of course, the effects of each on the living conditions of the proletariat and agricultural workers have been demonstrated, but the final sequence, which absorbs and fulfills the Union of the People of France into the "Internationale" and the forward march of all the protagonists, speaks primarily to the audience's poetic imagination. It is this that carries off their adherence, that is substituted for any definition of a political program, and that informs the advent of Communism, identified from this point on as nothing but "life itself." This slippage from the Political to the Poetic, from analysis to dreams, from the world of compromises and negotiation to that of lyrical effusiveness is thus the essential characteristic of the film, its "symptom"--present, for that matter, in the title. "La Vie est à nous" ("Life Belongs to Us") summarizes the entire film in its desire to promise Everything and to say nothing but its actual function: to work as propaganda.

Notes

1 All this is interesting in comparison with Renoir's La Marseillaise, made two years later, also with PCF collaborators.

2 Georges Lefranc, Histoire du Front Populaire, Chapter 1; the Confédération generale du travail is the Communist-dominated trade-union umbrella organization; L'Humanité is the PCF newspaper.

3 cf. the 8th Congress of the PCF, Villeurbanne, January 22-25, 1936.

4 Histoire du Front Populaire, p. 282.

5 Cahiers du cinéma, #218 (March 1970), p. 17.

6 Ibid.

7 Then follows the sequence of propaganda for the paper L'Humanité, easily the rival of certain commercials for the big dailies.

8 Symptomatically, the two goals were somewhat confused, both electorally and organizationally.

9 This sketch is said to have been directed by J. Becker.

10 The script for the sketch is provided by Premier plan, #22/23/24.

11 On the same theme, see C. Goretta's The Lacemaker, and also La Chienne, Nana, and Mme. Bovary, in which Renoir recognizes how much class differences inevitably alter love relationships.

12 René is played by Julien Bertheau.

Chapter 6

JORIS IVENS' *THE SPANISH EARTH*: COMMITTED DOCUMENTARY AND THE POPULAR FRONT

Thomas Waugh

Joris Ivens was the progressive filmmaker of the late thirties whose international prestige extended furthest beyond the actual borders of the left. His reputation has waned very little to this day, except perhaps in the English-speaking world, where his stunning epic of the Chinese Cultural Revolution, *How Yukong Moved the Mountains*, was clumsily distributed in the late seventies, and where he continues to face grudges held over from the McCarthy era (the omission from Richard Roud's mammoth *Cinema: A Critical Dictionary* of the author of some fifty films and the subject of a dozen book-length studies and double that many major retrospectives over the years!) *The Spanish Earth* is the best known and perhaps the best of the films of this dean of the socialist documentary, but is also a document firmly rooted in the culture and politics of its era. I offer a detailed analysis of those roots below.

In July 1936 when General Franco launched his revolt against the Spanish Republic, Joris Ivens, the 38-year-old Dutch avant-gardist-turned-militant, was in Hollywood showing his films to film industry progressives. One year later, Ivens was in Hollywood again, this time officiating at the world première of *The Spanish Earth* before a glittering cross-section of the same community. A hasty, spontaneous response to the Spanish plight, directed by a Dutchman who spent only a few months in the U. S. , Spanish Earth was also the prototypical cultural product of the American left in the era of the Popular Front, a time when the left was closer to the American mainstream than at any time previously or since.

The Spanish Earth represents also the convergence of two basic traditions of radical filmmaking in the West, of which Ivens has been the chief pioneer and standard-bearer throughout his 55-year career. It is the definitive model for the "international solidarity" genre, in which militants from the First and Second Worlds have used film to champion each new front of revolutionary armed struggle, and of which the current El Salvador films are only the most recent chapter. It is also the model for the more utopian genre in which the revolutionary construction of each new emerging socialist society is celebrated and offered for inspiration for those still struggling under capitalism, a genre for which Nicaragua and Zimbabwe have offered the most recent stimuli.

And for filmmakers engaged in the less romantic dynamics of domestic struggles, with documentary continuing to be the first recourse of radical artists on every continent (despite recent theoretical challenges to its hegemony within political film), Spanish Earth remains a film of utmost pertinence. A special Ivens issue of Cinéma politique, a French review of militant cinema, listed in 1978 the major issues of contemporary radical cinema and declared Ivens' relevance to each one: "the relationship of form and content; collective work; the use of re-enactment in documentary reportage; the role of the party, political direction, and the commissioned film; the opposition between amateur and professional (here one might add the increasingly important intermediate category of 'artisanal'); the marginalization of militant cinema in relation to traditional film distribution; exoticism, the romanticism of the distant valiant struggle, opposed to everyday struggles, and traversed by the complex notions of cultural neo-colonialism." What is striking about this list is that, aside from a few overtones of seventies jargon, it could just as easily have been written during the period of Spanish Earth, so little have the "issues" preoccupying radical culture changed in the intervening years.

Spanish Earth, finally, has a central place within the evolution of the documentary form, aside from its strategic ideological position. It defines prototypically the formal and technical challenges of the thirty-year heyday of the classical sound documentary, 1930 to 1960, in particular its first decade. It confronts, with still exemplary resourcefulness, the problems of sound and narration; the temptation to imitate the model of Hollywood fiction with mise-en-scène, individual characterization, and narrative line; the catch-22's of distribution, accessibility, and ideology; the possibilities of compilation and historical reconstruction, and of improvisation and spontaneity.... Once again this list sounds surprisingly contemporary.

Joris Ivens disembarked in February 1936 in New York for what was to become a decade of work in the United States, the second decade of his career. He was entering a political context strikingly different from the familiar ones of Western Europe and the Soviet Union, where his output had included avant-garde film poems (such as Rain, 1929), epics of collective labor in both his native Holland (Zuiderzee, 1933) and the Soviet Union (Komsomol, 1932), industrial commissions (such as Philips-Radio, 1931), and militant denunciations of the capitalist system (Borinage, 1933, and The New Earth, 1934).

The left intellectual milieu to which Ivens and his co-worker/editor Helen Van Dongen attached themselves upon their arrival was deeply concerned by the buildup to war already evident in Ethiopia, China, Germany, and soon, Spain. Ivens had made his previous political films during a period when the international socialist movement had been oriented toward militant class struggle. Borinage and The New Earth had reflected this orientation with their uncompromising political postures and their confrontational rhetoric and form. In the U. S., the militant newsreel work of the Film and Photo League had matched this tendency in Ivens' work.

The militant era and the Film and Photo League, however, were both on their last legs at the time of Ivens' arrival. The Nazis had eradicated the Workers' International Relief, the Berlin-based, Comintern-sponsored parent body for radical cultural groups throughout the capitalist West. But the main reason for the about-face of mid-decade was an official change of policy promulgated by the Communist International at its 1935 World Congress and obediently followed by all the national parties including the CPUSA. The crucial political struggle of the day was to be not socialism vs. capitalism, but democracy vs. fascism. CPUSA chief Earl Browder declared that democracy in the United States was to be preserved by a vigorous defense of civil liberties, increasingly menaced by fascist reaction at home and abroad. The earlier view of Roosevelt as war-monger and of the New Deal as incipient fascism yielded to a new image of Roosevelt as champion of democratic rights and of the state as potential ally of progressive forces. Communists were to be ready to participate in joint action within popular fronts with the Socialist parties, civil libertarians, and liberal intellectuals. American Communists thus allied themselves enthusiastically with the social programs of the New Deal.[1]

Leftist cultural strategy inevitably followed suit. The militant vanguardism symbolized by the FPL and the John Reed Clubs of proletarian culture was replaced by efforts by left cultural workers to express themselves with the mainstream of American culture. They were largely successful: the last half of the decade saw the left achieve its point of maximum impact within American culture and a close interaction between the cultural and political spheres. The influx of leftist intellectuals and artists from Europe, most of whom were political refugees from fascism (unlike Ivens--yet), stimulated this interaction, and the active involvement of the state in the cultural domain sustained it. The Federal Arts project of the Works Progress Administration was launched in the fall of 1935 and the same year saw the Farm Security Administration of the Resettlement Administration move into the field of still photography. The New Deal would expand into motion pictures the following year and enlist the talents of hundreds of leftist artists, including Ivens himself, before the decade was out.

The documentary movement was another dominant influence on Ivens' American cultural context. This movement shaped not only all the arts during this period, even modern dance, but also the humanities and the social sciences, and the fields of journalism, education, and, yes, advertising. At the center of this current was the work of still photographers, such as Dorothea Lange, Walker Evans and Margaret Bourke-White, who began photographing the economic crisis in the first years of the decade. The infusion of state sponsorship into the documentary movement after 1935 ensured that the still photographs of the ravages of the Depression would become its most recognizable artistic legacy, but they do not represent its full scope. Photographers and filmmakers, especially those on the left, spread out from providing local evidence of hunger, unemployment, and police repression, as the first FPL images did, to shaping encyclopedic manifestos in which the entire politico-economic and cultural system would by analyzed, challenged, and sometimes celebrated, all of which Frontier Film's Native Land did when it was finally released in 1942 and Ivens set out to do in his never-completed New Frontiers (1940).

At first, the left documentary constituency thrived mostly on imports. Soviet documentaries, for example, were continuously on view in New York and other large centers throughout the thirties--Vertov's Three Songs of Lenin was a hit in 1934. British films were also prestigious and popular, beginning with Grierson's Drifters (1929), which appeared in New York in 1930.

The first documentaries by American directors to play theatrically in New York, outside of the FPL agitprop milieu, appeared in 1934: Louis de Rochemont's unsuccessful Cry of the World and Flaherty's Man of Aran, produced under Grierson's British wing. However, the appearance of Time-Life's March of Time the following February, injecting dramatic and interpretive elements into the traditional newsreel, precipitated a floodtide of new documentary work in the U. S. The non-theatrical showing of Ivens' films in the spring of 1936 added to the momentum. By this time, interest in documentary was so high that the work of the obscure Dutchman was praised rapturously, not only in leftist periodicals but in the liberal media as well. The National Board of Review Magazine's discovery of The New Earth led to the introduction of the nonfiction category to its influential annual ratings. Ivens' cross-country campus tour, organized by an FPL offshoot, the New Film Alliance, is a good index of the scale of the documentary movement in 1936. It extended, as I said at the outset, as far as Hollywood.

The Rockefeller Foundation and the Museum of Modern Art were important institutional props to the growing movement. The latter sponsored the official Washington premiere of Pare Lorentz's New Deal-funded Plow That Broke the Plains in May 1936, presenting a program that also included five European documentaries. White House staff, diplomats, and members of the Supreme Court all showed up. Buoyed by this sendoff, Plow went on to 16,000 first-run showings and raves in every newspaper. The World's Fair in 1939 became the showcase for this first phase of the documentary movement, with Ivens' work much in evidence.

The strong popular foundation of documentary culture was essential to Ivens and other leftist filmmakers. Unquestionably a mass phenomenon, its artifacts ranged from

Life magazine to I Am a Fugitive from a Chain Gang (1932). For socialists in the era of the Popular Front, mandated to enter the politico-cultural mainstream after years of marginality, to seek out allies among "unpoliticized" classes and groups, and to combat fascism on a mass footing, here was a vehicle for their aims. For socialist filmmakers still too distrustful of monopoly capitalism and the entertainment industry to attempt an infiltration of Hollywood, the independent documentary seemed to offer a cultural strategy that was as clear as black and white.

What was less clear at mid-decade was the direction that the socialist documentary of the future would take. Members of the Film and Photo League were sharply divided as to whether they should take advantage of the gathering stream of the documentary movement, as shown by the box-office success of The March of Time, or whether they should stick to their original "workers' newsreel" mission, with its marginal base and confrontational aesthetics.

Leo Hurwitz, a chief architect of the decade, as early as 1934 established three priorities for radical filmmakers, which ultimately became part of a new consensus during Ivens' first years in the U. S. :[2]

1. Mass access for radical film work through commercial or theatrical distribution. Leftists were greatly encouraged by the work of their colleagues in Hollywood who had contributed to such "progressive" films as Fritz Lang's Fury (1936) and the Warner Brothers' biographies such as The Story of Louis Pasteur (1935). The New Film Alliance, Ivens' hosts, sponsored symposia on The March of Time and on progressive commercial features from pre-Hitler Germany such as Mädchen in Uniform (1931) and Kameradschaft (1931). Ivens repeatedly praised such films on his tour and stressed the importance of "combining our work with the mass movement," and, as he would put it a few years later, of "break[ing] into commercial distribution [in order to] recover the social function of documentary." [3] Significantly Van Dongen stayed behind in Hollywood to study narrative editing. Where an earlier generation of documentarists, including both Ivens and the FPL, had assimilated the technical and aesthetic strategies of the European and Soviet avant-gardes, the generation of the Popular Front was looking west.

2. The development of new "synthetic" film forms. Hurwitz argued that the form of the earlier newsreels had

simply been an economic and technical necessity, not an ideological or aesthetic choice per se, and that these forms must now give way to sophisticated hybrid forms including "recreative analysis and reconstruction of an internally related visual event," or, in other words, mise-en-scène. He stressed the professionalism of the required new filmmakers who would replace the earlier amateur and artisanal cadres. This position was anathema to Hurwitz's opponents, who invoked Soviet authority and the name of Vertov, conveniently overlooking that reconstruction or mise-en-scène had long since taken a central place in the master's work. Ivens' films, screened repeatedly for the New York radicals upon his arrival, unambiguously bolstered the Hurwitz side with their rich mix of actuality, compilation, mise-en-scène, narrative, and even scripting (in his Soviet film Komsomol). "We must learn," he argued in a manifesto of the early forties, "to think of documentary as requiring a wide variety of styles--all for the purpose of maximum expressiveness and conviction."

3. More profound political analysis. For Hurwitz the early FPL newsreels of strikes and demonstrations had been too "fractional, atomic, and incomplete" for adequate political analysis. The new "synthetic" forms would facilitate more "inclusive and implicative comment," and could "reveal best the meaning of the event." This "meaning" was to be a deeper, materialist analysis of the class struggle within capitalist society, and the forward movement of the working class, in both world-historic and individual terms, not just in the local and collective terms that the workers' agitprop newsreels had seemed to emphasize. Once again, Ivens found himself on Hurwitz's side of the debate. Earlier films, he stated in a lecture on his tour, including his own, were "just seeing things, not understanding." Art must have a "definite point of view," and must express this without "aestheticism" or sentimentality. "The difference between newsreel and the documentary film" he later explained, is that "the newsreel tells us where-when-what; the documentary film tells us why, and the relationships between events ... and provides historic perspective." The new "deeper approach," in particular the tactic of introducing identifiable characters into nonfiction filmmaking (which Ivens began calling "personalization" soon after his immersion in the U.S. milieu), is capable of "penetrating the facts ... achieving a real interrelation between the particular and the general."

The debate among leftist filmmakers was accompanied

by organizational changes. Nykino, a new film production outfit, had been formed by Hurwitz and his allies as early as the fall of 1934, in order to put into practice the new priorities. The East Coast radicals were thus already set on a path closely parallel to that traced by the films Ivens showed in New York in 1936, that is, the evolution from agitational newsreel work to more systematic and ambitious explorations of new outlets, new forms, and deeper analysis. Ivens' effect, then, was one of reinforcement of direction already chosen and tentatively tested, or, as Hurwitz would put it, "a very important stimulus and source of encouragement." Another Nykino leader described it as "a turning point ... a shot in the arm ... assistance from a recognized filmmaker who confirmed the theories of Nykino." Ivens' Soviet credentials--he was fresh from almost two years within the Soviet film industry--added in no small way to the impact of this encouragement.

Ivens officially cemented his affiliation with the Nykino tendency in the spring of 1937 when that group inaugurated yet another production company, fully professional this time, to accomplish their goals: Frontier Films. Though in Spain at the time, Ivens joined the dazzling array of American artists and intellectuals who signed up as founding members of the Frontier production staff, board of directors, or advisory board. The Popular Front line was doing all right: both the West Coast and the East Coast were well represented, from Melvyn Douglas to Lillian Hellman, from liberals to fellow travelers to party members. Ivens had clearly aligned himself with the winning side. In fact, he had anticipated the Frontier Films approach the previous fall when he had enlisted many of the same luminaries to provide mainstream support--both moral and financial--for his first American film, Spanish Earth.

As soon as it first became apparent that the Franco rebellion posed a serious threat, Ivens had got together the group of leftist artists and intellectuals who were to become the producing body for a Spanish film. Their idea was to bolster American support for the Republican cause by means of a short, quickly made compilation of newsreel material. This would explain the issues to the American public and counter the already skillful Franquist propaganda. They called themselves Contemporary Historians, Inc., and had as their spokespeople the Pulitzer poet Archibald MacLeish and the novelist John Dos Passos, both well-known fellow-travelers. The functioning producer was to be Herman Shumlin,

Hellman's Broadway producer, with Hellman and Dorothy Parker rounding out this core group. Helen Van Dongen was to put together the film. It soon became clear, however, that not enough good footage was available and that even the shots at hand were of limited use since they were taken from the Franco side--burning churches and the like--and were expensive and difficult to pry out of the notoriously reactionary newsreel companies. The group then decided to finish the project as quickly and cheaply as possible, which Van Dongen did using a Dos Passos commentary and relying on Soviet footage of the front. This feature-length work, called Spain in Flames, was hurriedly released in February 1937. Meanwhile, the producers decided to put most of their hopes on a film of greater scope to be shot from scratch on Spanish soil, personally underwriting a budget of $18,000. Ivens would direct.

As the autumn progressed, the need for the film became more and more urgent: the left press began denouncing the German and Italian interventions and the Western democracies began nervously discussing neutrality. By the time Ivens arrived in Paris in the first bitter January of the war, a tentative scenario in his pocket, he had already been preceded by the first of the International Brigades, and by a growing stream of Western artists, intellectuals, and activists, including filmmakers from the Soviet Union and England.

In Valencia, suddenly the new Republican capital because of the presumed imminence of the fall of Madrid, Ivens and John Ferno, his old cinematographer from the Dutch days, joined up with Dos Passos and got right to work. They soon concluded, however, that their script was unworkable in the worsening situation. Drafted by Ivens together with Hellman and MacLeish, it emphasized the background to the war and a diachronic conception of the Spanish revolution, calling for considerable dramatization. The Republicans they consulted urged them instead to head straight for Madrid to find their subject in the action on the front line. As the film's commentary would later make clear, "Men cannot act in front of the camera in the presence of death."

The abandoned script merits a brief look, however, as an indicator of where American radical documentarists saw themselves heading in 1936. Based largely on dramatized narrative and semi-fictional characterization, its only American precursors would have been the films of Flaherty, some scattered FPL shorts, and Paul Strand's anomalous Mexican Redes, completed but not yet released at this point. The more likely model was the Soviet Socialist Realist semi-documentary epic, of which Ivens' own Komsomol (1932) was an important prototype.

The Spanish Earth script followed the chronology of a village's political growth over a period of six or seven years, from the fall of the monarchy until the fictional retaking of the village from Franquist forces during the present conflict. A single peasant family was to be featured, particularly their young son, whose evolution would be emblematic of the Spanish peasantry's maturation during those years. The village would be a diagrammatic cross-section of Spanish society as a whole, and various melodramatic or allegorical touches would highlight the various social forces in play: there were to be representative fascists, militarists, landowners, clergy, intelligentsia, even German interventionists and the ex-king! Ivens was clearly intending to expand his first experiments along these lines in Komsomol and Borinage (where striking miners had re-enacted their clashes with police and bailiffs, the latter impersonated by strikers in theatrical costumes). The script called for some elements of newsreel reportage to be worked in as well.

The final version of Spanish Earth turned out to be much more complex formally than the original outline called for, an improvised hybrid of many filmic modes, but certain elements of the outline remained. The most important of these was the notion of a village as a microcosm of the Spanish revolution. The chosen village, Fuenteduena, was ideal in this and every other respect. Its location on the Madrid-Valencia lifeline was symbolically apt, a link between village revolution and war effort. It was also visually stunning, set near the Tagus River amid a rolling landscape, and accessible to Madrid. Politically too, the village was ideal: the community had reclaimed a former hunting preserve of aristocrats, now fled, and had begun irrigating their new land. The filmmakers could thus keep their original theme of agrarian reform and hints of the original dramatic conflict between landowners and peasantry.

As for the original cloak-and-dagger plot about the young villager, Ivens and his collaborators attempted to telescope it into a simple narrative idea involving Julian, a peasant who has joined the Republican army. Even this scaled-down role was only partly realized since Julian disappeared in the frontline confusion after his village sequences had been filmed.

Julian, an undistinctive-looking young peasant, appeared in only four scenes of the final film, stretched out by the editor to a maximum: a brief moment on the Madrid front where he is seen writing a letter home, the text provided in an insert and read by the commentator; a scene where he is seen hitching a ride back home on leave to Fuenteduena, with a flashback reminder of the letter; next, his reunion first with his mother and then with his whole family; and finally, a sequence where he drills the village boys in an open space. The footage was insufficient even for these scenes, so that the commentator must ensure our recognition of Julian by repeating his name and fleshing out the details of the narrative. The reunion scene would be the biggest challenge to editor Van Dongen. She was to improvise with covering close-ups of villagers apparently shot for other uses, and ingeniously fabricate a fictional mini-scene from unrelated material, where Julian's small brother runs to fetch their father from the fields upon his arrival. The family thus shown in this sentimental but effective scene would be largely synthetic. After Julian's disappearance, a symbolic close-up of an anonymous soldier was taken for the defiant finale of the film.

But this forced postponement of Ivens' dream of "personalization" did not stand in the way of other efforts to heighten the personal quality of the film. At every point in Spanish Earth, the filmmakers would intervene in the post-production to make individual figures come alive dramatically: through the commentary, as when a briefly seen Republican officer is identified by name and then laconically eulogized when it is disclosed that he was killed after the filming; or through complex editing procedures, as when a miniature story of two boys killed in the bombing of Madrid is chillingly wrought out of non-continuous shots and a synthetic flash-frame detonation; or through lingering close-ups of anonymous bystanders and onlookers, some of whom are even dramatized through first-person commentary. Several years later, Ivens would conclude that such vignettes, "hasty and attempted identities now and then walking through a documentary," had fallen short of his goal of continuous "personalization," and that his next project on the Sino-Japanese front, The Four Hundred Million, had been no less frustrating. It would not be until Ivens' third American film,

The Power and the Land (1940), that the relative luxury of peacetime filmmaking would allow him to experiment with fixed characters developed consistently throughout an entire film--in this case, a wholesome American farm family.

"Personalization" was not the only aspect of the Fuenteduena shooting that imitated Hollywood narrative. Using their heavy tripod-based Debrie camera, Ivens and Ferno developed a kind of documentary "mise-en-scène," a collaborative shooting style "staging" "real" actors in "real" settings that eventually made up about two-fifths of the finished film. Ivens' mise-en-scène was an even more aggressive intervention in the events being filmed than Flaherty's collaboration with his subjects. Ivens matter-of-factly used the vocabulary of studio filmmaking such as "retake" and "covering shot"; on location, he set up shot-countershot constructions with his peasant subjects that aimed at the spatio-temporal continuity of studio fiction of the period, complete with complementary angles of a single action and insert close-ups of detail. This approach enabled not only a clear chronological summary of the Fuenteduena irrigation work as it progressed before the camera--Ivens' emblem of the Spanish revolution--but also the balanced and lyrical, even romantic, framings and movements that idealized the workers and their relationship to the Spanish earth. (See Photos, page 117.)

Ivens was of course not alone in "setting up" his subjects: the other major documentarists of the period, from Basil Wright to Pare Lorentz, all used variations of the same method. It is this element that looks most dated to our cinéma-vérité-trained eyes. For Richard Leacock, narrative mise-en-scène led to the "dark ages of the documentary," and for modernist critics like Vlada Petric, mise-en-scène meant the "[abandonment of] the concept of film as a genuine visual art which draws its content from those kinesthetic qualities only cinema can bring to life...."[4] Ivens, however, did not often have to answer to such ahistoric criticism at the time. The interventionist orthodoxy of the late thirties was no less universal than the "vérité" orthodoxy is today (or, rather, was until recently, now that films such as The Life and Times of Rosie the Riveter are challenging the voyeuristic "hands-off" mystique of filmmakers like Leacock and Wiseman). Filmmakers and critics of the late thirties agreed on the need for a dramatization of the factual, its "vivification," as some put it. This trend was

The mise-en-scène mode: the villagers of Fuenteduena seen examining the dry earth they will soon irrigate (above), and (below) buying "union-made" bread in the village bakery. Joris Ivens' mise-en-scène, undertaken in collaboration with the subjects, depicts the exemplary figures in typically low-angle "romantic" medium-close framings.

partly in reaction to the impersonality of the newsreels and the other journalistic media. "Was I making a film or just newsreel shots?" Ivens would ask of Spanish Earth. Truth was not a function of phenomenological scruple but of political principle. Truth was not to be found on the surface of reality, but in deeper social, economic and historical structures. The aesthetic of naturalist spontaneity in film was to be distrusted as much as "spontaneism" in the arena of political strategy. The generation of filmmakers who developed mise-en-scène as a documentary mode believed, like their cousins the Socialist Realists, that their work had the purpose not only to reflect the world but to act upon it, to change it. This was true even for liberals and social democrats like Lorentz and Grierson, who did not subscribe to Marxist ideals. Ivens' primary question was not whether he had shown the "truth" but whether "the truth has been made convincing enough to make people want to change or emulate the situation shown to them on the screen."

This is not to say that documentary mise-en-scène would have appeared to thirties spectators in the same way as fictional narrative cinema. An overwhelming network of "documentary" codes prevented it from doing so, from non-synchronous sound to non-made-up faces, to specific marketing approaches, to the replacement of "psychological" typing by "social" typing.

Mise-en-scène, however, a luxury affordable in the calm of Fuenteduena, was rarely possible on the front lines. In Madrid, the filmmakers attached themselves to the communist-affiliated Fifth Regiment in the Casa de Velasquez. Here they shot the siege of the city from the point of view both of its defenders in the frontline suburbs and of the air-raid shelters within the city itself. By the time of the key battle of Brihuega (Guadalajara) in March, Ernest Hemingway, a recent convert to the Republican cause, had replaced Dos Passos as the production's guide and literary mentor. At Brihuega, buoyed by an important contingent of the International Brigades, the Republicans won a major victory against a twelve-to-one firepower disadvantage and prevented the besieged capital from being cut off. The battle's additional political significance was the incontrovertible proof it offered that organized Italian units were taking part: Italian casualties and their letters home are shown in a particularly moving scene of Spanish Earth (a scene that would lead to a fruitless screening at the League of Nations). Brihuega features prominently in the last half of the final version of Ivens' film. The battle material, from both Madrid and Brihuega, as well as from one other village that the filmmakers shot under bombardment, has a style whose spontaneity is diametrically opposite to the orderly, lyrical mise-en-scène of Fuenteduena.

The "spontaneous" mode, relying primarily on the crew's two small hand-cameras, is notable for the unrehearsed flexibility and mobility required to cover the soldiers and civilian victims who could not "act before the camera." This mode, as Ivens had not foreseen while scriptwriting in New York, would make up more than half of the finished film. With this style, the camera operator, rather than rearranging an event in front of the lens, follows it spontaneously--the storming of a building, a run-for-cover during an air-raid, the evacuation of children, panic in the streets of the bombed-out village. The principles of spatio-temporal continuity were left for the editor to find in the cans: it was too dangerous for the operator to think about retakes and reverse shots. "Spontaneous" shooting provided spectators with its own distinctive documentary codes, distinct from those of mise-en-scène material which was often present, as in Spanish Earth, in the same film or even the same sequence: unmotivated and random detail of behavior or atmosphere, the flouting of taboos on out-of-focus material, looking at the camera, illegibility, etc., (see photo, page 120). The mystique of "life-caught-unawares" was still an essential element of the documentary sensibility despite the universal acceptance of mise-en-scène. Because of this mystique, "spontaneous" elements often had the greatest impact on spectators, or at least on reviewers: the reviews of the day never failed to mention a woman seen wiping her eye amid the rubble of her village. The great sensitivity of "spontaneous" material such as this in Spanish Earth has confirmed Ivens' reputation as a major inheritor of Vertov and a precursor of cinéma-vérité.

It was in Madrid also that Ivens shot some material in a third cinematographic mode that constitutes only a fraction of the finished film but deserves brief mention nonetheless. What I am referring to is static, controlled images of public events, taken with a heavy, stationary camera. I call this the "newsreel" mode because its repertory is identical to that of the newsreel companies of the period--ceremonious long shots of files of dignitaries, cheering crowds, military parades, or beauty contests. Though Ivens and other leftists and liberals usually avoided "newsreel" shooting,

The "spontaneous" mode: village women fleeing aerial bombardment, caught by a small portable camera in the heat of war. (Photo: Nederlands Filmmuseum)

as much out of distaste for clichés and superficiality as from any ideological scruple, the opportunity to use a borrowed newsreel sound truck to record a People's Army rally was one that Ivens could not refuse, (see photo, page 121). Newsreel-style cinematography was the only means by which thirties documentarists could attempt synchronous sound on location--twenty years would pass before technology would catch up, in the television age, with the aspiration to hear as well as to see "life-caught-unawares." In any case, the rally scene of Spanish Earth featured the stirring oratory of La Pasionaria and other Republican leaders (some redubbed in New York because of technical problems), and, for this reason, as well as for its skillful editorial compression, would avoid the pitfalls of the mode. It was up to Riefenstahl and the Nazis to elevate to a new artform the "newsreel" clichés of orators intercut with cheering crowds. The only phase of Ivens' career to depend on this mode was his Cold War exile in East Germany, where he presided over several official rally films of the fading Stalin era.

Spanish Earth, then, unexpectedly became a cinematic hybrid in the uncontrollable laboratory of war and revolution. In this, as a compendium of different filmic modes, it was typical of most documentaries of the late thirties. Other national traditions were varying the hybrid model according to local factors. Grierson's British directors tended to use mise-en-scène more than Ivens, even resorting to studio work on occasion; Cartier-Bresson's cinematography for Frontier

The "newsreel" mode: La Pasionaria, symbolic Communist spokesperson of the Republican cause, addresses a rally of the People's Army in one of the rare synch-sound recorded scenes of The Spanish Earth. (Photo: Nederlands Film-museum)

Films' second Spanish project, Fight for Life (1938), was more "spontaneous" than any other comparable film. However, the general trend was towards greater and greater use of mise-en-scène. In this respect, Ivens' evolution paralleled the work of almost every documentarist of the period. Whereever circumstances and resources permitted--which was not always the case as the buildup towards world war continued--documentarists almost unanimously built up the mise-en-scène components of their hybrid works, experimenting more and more with characterization, narrative vocabulary, and even scripting. Writers became standard crew members, not only for commentaries but to provide plots, continuity, and dialogue. During the forties, this mode became the basic component of most documentaries, rivaled only by the compilation mode for which the War had created a special market, and the dominance of mise-en-scène would continue right up until the explosion of cinéma-vérité in the late fifties.

Meanwhile Helen Van Dongen had begun assembling the consignments of rushes in New York as they arrived from Spain, wiring the filmmakers whenever she thought that a given topic was now well covered or that another was weak. When the shooting wound up in May, she began in earnest, shaping images shot according to each of the three modes outlined above according to the methods of narrative continuity that she had perfected in her recent Hollywood apprenticeship. Individual sequences began emerging--the Fuenteduena irrigation project, civilians under bombardment, the Madrid and Brihuega fronts--each built strictly with the sequential and temporal logic of short fictive units. Obviously, the "spontaneous" rushes presented the most challenge since they had not been shot "for the editor." But she responded with ingenuity, building up to each split-second bomb impact with systematic precision, and then having the clearing smoke reveal the rubble and the panic, or following each Republican artillery shot with an image denoting an on-target hit. Part of her skill was in picking out visual motifs to assure a narrative fluidity; images of children in a bombed-out street, or a repeated glimpse of an ambulance or an artillery shell, for example, would underline an implied continuity. Sometimes a minor but identifiable bystander would function as a hinge for a continuity: her choice to cut at the point when a background figure in the People's Army rally blows his nose has drawn the admiration of at least one critic. Seldom before had the principles of fictional narrative editing been so skillfully and unobtrusively adapted for the purposes of nonfiction. The abandonment of the modernist-derived editing strategies of the young Ivens in his avant-garde days--for example, unsettling contrasts in scale, angle, and movement direction, or ironic or dialectical idea-cutting, often Soviet-inspired--was a price that Ivens and Van Dongen were willing to pay to achieve the Popular Front goal of speaking the narrative film language of the people.

Within the emerging film as a whole, Van Dongen alternated short scenes of the military struggle and the social revolution, interweaving the themes of the combat in Madrid and Brihuega with the progress of the Fuenteduena irrigators. Two stunning scenes depicting the bombardment of civilians were placed at a climactic point about two-thirds of the way through the fifty-two-minute film, so that the concluding movement, the victorious battle interpolated with the completion of the irrigation system, seems like a defiant riposte of the people against their oppressors. A coda alternates single shots of water rushing through the new irrigation trough and images of a lone rifleman firing, so that the two themes, defense and revolution, are summarized and fused, two dimensions of a single struggle.

The alternating pattern of civilian and military struggles was therefore not just an effective editing device but a crucial ideological statement. In countering images of victimization with images of resistance and revolution, Spanish Earth articulates a world view that sees people as agents of history, not its casualties. The final word is given, not to the airborne mercenaries and their bombs, but to the people rooted in the central symbol of the film, the earth. And in alternating the military resistance with the civilian struggle, Spanish Earth equates them, merges them into the ideological concept of the people's war. Ivens would return again and again to this visual and ideological construct as he continued to chronicle the people's struggles of our era from China and the Soviet Union to Cuba and Vietnam, each time echoing the Spanish Earth equation of peasants in their fields and soldiers on the frontlines, of hoes and guns.

Ivens and Van Dongen brought to the soundtrack of Spanish Earth the same embrace of popular narrative film language as was evident in the shooting and editing, and the same creative resourcefulness in integrating it to their political task. The modernist virtuosity and clamorous experimentation of Ivens' early sound documentaries yielded to the subdued purposefulness of the Popular Front. The sound effects were innovative to the extent that Van Dongen experimented with more convincing laboratory synthesis (on-location sound effects were still primitive) and varied the newsreel cliché of wall-to-wall noise with moments of well-chosen silence and subtle transitions. However, the sound effects functioned essentially as support for the narrative thrust of the film, heightening the especially powerful scenes such as the bombardment episodes, injecting dramatic and informational energy into scenes that were less interesting visually, such as the long-shot Brihuega ones, and in general providing "realistic" background texture to each of the film's narrative lines.

Continuing the Popular Front practice of lining up prestigious contributors, Ivens recruited two of the best-known East Coast composers to handle the music: Marc Blitzstein, the in-house composer of the New York left, and Virgil Thomson, who had been widely acclaimed for his brilliant folk score for The Plow that Broke the Plains. Blitzstein and Thomson, pressed by the filmmakers' tight schedule, compiled Spanish folk music, both instrumental and choral, for the score. This choice reflected not only their haste but also the influence of the documentary movement on musical taste of the late thirties and the impact of Plow. The filmmakers fit the music to the images with discretion and sensitivity, with expressive pauses that contrast sharply with the "wall-to-wall" tendencies of the period, even of "prestige" films like Triumph of the Will and Man of Aran. The tedious over-synchronization that is also noticeable in these two films was likewise avoided, with general atmospheric matching being the guiding principle instead: sprightly dance rhythms accompany the villagers at work in the field and a soft dirge-like choral piece follows the village bombardment with just the right understated elegiac touch.

It was the commentary, however, that attracted more attention than any of the other soundtracks, and not only because of its star author. Hemingway's text is a high point in the benighted history of an artform of dubious legitimacy, the documentary commentary, and unusually prophetic in its anticipation of future developments in documentary sound. What was most striking to contemporary spectators was its personal quality. Ivens, Van Dongen and Hellman made a last-minute decision to replace Orson Welles' slick reading with a less professional recording by Hemingway himself. This voice, with its frank, low-key roughness, added to the text's aura of personal involvement. It was a striking contrast to the oily, authoritarian voice-of-God for which The March of Time was famous and which most documentaries imitated. Instead of an anonymous voice, the commentator became a vivid character on his own terms, a subjective witness of the events of the film, a participant. Though this function of the narrator was already common in Popular Front print journalism, Hemingway's contribution to Spanish Earth set off a trend in documentary film that would last throughout World War II, with filmmakers as different as Flaherty, John Huston and Humphrey Jennings benefiting from his example; it was an effective substitute for the still impossible ideal of using sound to make subjects come alive on location.

Hemingway's text had other innovative aspects too: its obliqueness, its variations in tone, its detail and immediacy, its multiplicity of postures towards the spectator, its ability to be at times dramatic and at times lyrical or reflective without being overbearing. Most remarkable, perhaps, was its restraint. Ivens and Hemingway concentrated on "let[ting] the film speak for itself," on avoiding words that would duplicate the image-continuity, on providing "sharp little guiding arrows" of text, "springboards," often at the beginning of a scene, to invite the audience's involvement. The commentary's role as information and exposition was secondary. Not surprisingly, it is in the strongly narrative mise-en-scène passages set in Fuenteduena that the commentary intervenes least, and in the extreme long-shot accounts of artillery and infantry combat where it is, of necessity, most present, and, arguably, most effective. Hemingway's text was ultimately laid over only one-fifth of the image-track. This was an all-time record for conciseness in the classical documentary (during the war, Frank Capra's Why We Fight films would sometimes approach four-fifths and the Canadian National Film Board films did so regularly), but Ivens' record was often rivaled by some of his more visually oriented contemporary documentarists.

A careful look at the commentary in Spanish Earth, as well as in most films by the "art" documentarists of the day, undermines a prevailing current myth of how sound operated in the classical documentary. This myth depicts the classical sound documentary as an "illustrated lecture," a film whose dominant diegesis was a direct-address commentary to which images played a mere supporting role.[5] Trained within the silent avant-garde cinema, Ivens and Van Dongen had nothing but contempt for this "illustration" approach, and usually succeeded in avoiding it, commissioning commentaries only after an autonomous image-continuity had been established and then reducing them ferociously. Most of the British directors in the Grierson stable did the same, as did Flaherty, Lorentz, and Vertov. Jennings and Riefenstahl did away with the commentary almost completely. Van Dongen had her own simple test of silencing the soundtrack to test the visual sufficiency of a given film. Spanish Earth must be seen as a highlight of a whole tradition of experiments in sound-image structures that fought against the voice-of-God tedium of the newsreels (and the later wartime compilation films) in search of creative alternatives for the still-new audio-visual artform. Our sense of documentary history must be revised to accommodate this tradition, just as the dream-factory/assembly-line model of Hollywood history has long since been shaped to account for the Capras and the Fords.

Hemingway's commentary was delivered live at a June preview of Spanish Earth, in silent rough-cut, at the Second National Congress of American Writers, a grouping of leftist and liberal writers. Hemingway declared to the assembly that "Spain is the first real battlefield in an evil and international conflict that is certain to recur elsewhere," something presumably most of those present already knew. In order to ensure that the film would reach those who did not already know this, a massive publicity campaign got underway. In July, a White House preview led to a plug in Eleanor Roosevelt's column, the impossible dream of all Popular Front filmmakers. Immediately thereafter, Ivens and Hemingway arrived in Los Angeles for huge sell-out premières and private fund-raising screenings within Hollywood's progressive circles, where $20,000 was collected for Republican medical relief.

The glitter and the publicity photos with Joan Crawford were not for the sake of vanity. The West Coast connections were deemed essential to the filmmakers' hopes for commercial distribution. Political documentaries had never received distribution by the "majors" up to this point, but the overwhelming feeling was that a breakthrough was imminent, thanks to Lorentz's obstinate and successful campaign the previous year to distribute Plow through independent exhibitors. But the fanfare was deceptive. Variety summed up Ivens' predicament on July 21:

> This can make money where any picture can make money but it won't make it there. It won't make it there because it won't get in there. It will have to depend as it did here in its world premiere, on lecture halls which are wired for sound and can gross enough in one performance to justify a week's buildup.

Nothing is new under the sun. The filmmakers resigned themselves to the traditional marginalized distribution that political, documentary, and Soviet films had always relied on. The film opened August 20th at the 55th Street Playhouse. While this art-house was one level above the usual Soviet purgatory downtown, Ivens' disappointment was profound, and record-breaking capacity crowds scarcely consoled him. However, the film's small leftist distributor, Garrison Films, still tried to repeat Plow's success. The ads played up the Hemingway name so much that Spanish Earth was often called a Hemingway film, a prestige-oriented tactic that was buoyed by the film's inclusion in the National Board of Review "ten best" list for 1937. Audiences more interested in entertainment were assured how undocumentary the film was: it was "The Picture with a Punch," and a "Dramatic Story of Life and People in a Wartorn Village in Spain." Further publicity resulted from short-lived censorship squabbles in Rhode Island and Pennsylvania. A review in The Nation, appearing during the film's third New York month, while acknowledging the bind of independent distribution, optimistically reported that Ivens was making progress and announced that more than 800 theaters across the U.S. had been signed up (Nov. 20). The real figure was closer to 300. In other words, the film made an enviable splash in the art-house/political circuit, but a mere ripple in the commercial sea. Ivens would not achieve his breakthrough until his own New Deal-sponsored film, Power and the Land, in 1940.

Looking back at his most famous film (for Cinéma politique) from the vantage point of the late seventies, Ivens felt that he could identify a certain impact that Spanish Earth had exerted on its own period:

> Of course you must not think that you are going to change the world with a film; all the same, there have been examples in history of films that have helped the revolution, like the Soviet films at the beginning of the October Revolution. In my own life, I saw the influence of Spanish Earth also: ... it really provided information about a problem that spectators were not very familiar with, and it helped the anti-fascist movement enormously ... directly even. People gave money for the International Brigades. There *are* militant films that have enormous power, and that is linked to the moment at which they are shown.

Ivens' estimation is not unreasonable. Although his film had no impact on the League of Nations or the Western governments, it was part of the expanding cultural and political movement of the Popular Front period, providing an impetus while it was still growing in influence and expanding its base.

As part of this movement, Spanish Earth reflected many of its cultural and ideological tactics that were not directly related to the Spanish subject. The agrarian theme, for example, with its basic icons of bread, earth and water, was central to the Depression imagination. Ivens' climactic image of water rushing through a new irrigation trough had already appeared in King Vidor's Our Daily Bread (1934) and Vertov's Three Songs of Lenin (1934), and impoverished migrant workers and sharecroppers had been the focus of countless photographic essays and books, as well as Lorentz's first two films. The Fuenteduena peasants were thus recognizable, universal, as were Hemingway's vague references to the "they" who "held us back." Yet Ivens' Socialist-Realist-tinted vision of the cheerful collective work of his villagers lacks the plaintive, almost defeatist feeling of most American or Western European agrarian imagery. The primitive irrigation project of Spanish Earth will seemingly feed an entire besieged capital. What is more, the collective, non-hierarchical initiative of the peasants is behind this success, not the expertise of the New Deal agronomists who dispense their advice on crop rotation upon the helpless denizens of Lorentz's films from on high.

All the same, Ivens' refusal of Socialist Realist dogmatism in his vision of collective work has a certain Popular Front ring to it. There is a clear division of responsibilities among the workers, and the Mayor displays a kind of leadership, even delivering a sub-titled speech announcing the project. Ivens carefully avoids all possible innuendos of collectivization, forced or otherwise; authority springs, spontaneously, out of an implied tradition of folk common sense. Though the Fuenteduena scenes establish a full catalogue of the material terms of the village collective, with impeccable Marxist attention to the forces of production, it does so in a way that lets the signals of tradition, exoticism and patience, conventionally attached to the peasant icon in Western culture, overshadow the signals of revolutionary change. Discretion is the distinguishing feature of this vision of the agrarian revolution taking place in the Spanish countryside during the Popular Front.

Another theme emerges in Spanish Earth for virtually the first time in Ivens' career: the family. This theme revolves primarily around Julian's homecoming sequence, but it is also notable elsewhere: in the images of two distraught mothers, one trying to load her children on an evacuation truck in besieged Madrid, the other in the bombed village inconsolably bewailing her slaughtered children, and in a young soldier's good-bye to his wife and child before the final battle, elevated by Hemingway into a symbol of the strength, courage and tragedy of the family unit at war:

> ... they say the old good-byes that sound the same in any language. She says she'll wait. He says that he'll come back. Take care of the kid, he says. I will, she says, but knows she can't. They both know that when they move you out in trucks, it's to a battle.

Compared to later populist-agrarian films like Flaherty's The Land (1940-42), Ford's The Grapes of Wrath (1940) or Renoir's The Southerner (1945), the family accent in Spanish Earth is decidedly minor. Nevertheless, it clearly points to Popular Front strategy of recuperating the values of mainstream culture: idealized families were highly visible in Frontier Films productions as well.

Spanish Earth, the first of the major anti-fascist films with wide distribution, initiated a preoccupation with military imagery that would dominate the screens of the next decade, and does so in a specifically Popular Front manner. Beyond Ivens' respectful treatment of soldiering as work, not surprising in the work of a filmmaker who had romanticized the construction of North Sea dikes and Soviet blast furnaces, his emphasis is on the humanity of the Republican troops. The soldiers are presented as little men, non-professionals. Shots showing "unsoldierly" signals--untidiness, awkward drilling, grins at the camera--are present throughout. In one sequence about life in camp, the emphasis is on everyday non-military activities such as getting haircuts, eating, reading newspapers; the implication is that the stake of the war is the quality of everyday life. In the parade scenes, there is more interest in the rawness of recruits eagerly joining up than in the precision of seasoned troops, more interest in small irregular groups than in the symmetrical formations of Riefenstahl's films.

The Nazi ballets of banners and boots have nothing in common with the "human" scale and detail of Ivens' People's Army.

At the same time, Ivens' attitude towards the Communist Party, its participation in the Republican government, and its leadership of the People's Army follows the usual Popular Front practice of "self-censorship." Specific political affiliations, whether of Ivens' subjects, his hosts, or of Ivens himself, were not a topic for discussion. A film courting mass distribution and Eleanor Roosevelt, as well as following the CPUSA line, declined of necessity to identify the line-up of Communist speakers during the People's Army rally scene: for example, La Pasionaria, José Diaz and the others appear as "the wife of a poor miner in Asturias," a "member of Parliament," etc. Explicit political labels complicated the broad-based popular coalitions that were the mainstay of the Popular Front, as well as the effectiveness of Republican propaganda within the Western democracies. The existence of the International Brigades, composed primarily of Western leftists, passes unmentioned. Other important gaps in Ivens' coverage of the war are conspicuous: Soviet aid to the Republicans; the question of the Church, a major focus of pro-Franquist propaganda; the identification of the enemy--the Italians and the Moroccan mercenaries are discussed in surprisingly respectful or pitying terms, but the Spanish classes who supported Franco's insurrection are omitted, as is the name of Franco, and even the word "fascist" (other than in one excerpted speech); and finally, acknowledgement of the political struggle going on within the Republican camp at the time, which would later come to a head in the Communist-Anarchist showdown in Barcelona near the end of the war. Although this latter decision to underline Loyalist unity is hardly surprising, there are works, André Malraux's L'Espoir (1937), for example, that reflect the diversity within the Republican ranks in a positive way.

Of course, all of these elisions can be justified in terms of dodging domestic red-baiters, religious groups, and censors (who had the habit of cutting hostile references to "friendly" powers such as Italy), but they are also part of a systematic effort to depict the war as a simple non-ideological struggle of "little people" against "rebels" and invaders. The stakes of the war came across as "democratic" in a very loose sense, rather than those of class struggle. Ivens was perfectly consistent with CPUSA policy, which preferred in the late thirties to call its ideology "Americanism," stressing "democracy" and "civil liberties" rather than class allegiance, and soliciting the support of non-left unions, the middle classes, elected officials, liberal intellectuals, and even the clergy.

Ivens' carefully constructed image of the Spanish war and civil revolution succeeded on that level without a doubt. The New York Times was persuaded after seeing the film that the "Spanish people are fighting, not for broad principles of Muscovite Marxism, but for the right to the productivity of a land denied them through years of absentee landlordship" (Aug. 21). Spanish Earth was the first film to formulate the concept of the people's war, a concept that would gain considerably in currency over the next generations of world history, and to insert this concept into mainstream public discourse. Of course, the price Ivens and his contemporaries paid for this achievement--the soft-pedalling of specific radical programs and identity, the adoption of popular filmic forms--is fiercely debated even to this day. But it was a price that the filmmakers of the Popular Front paid in full conscience....

What of Spain? How successful were the filmmakers in their short-term pragmatic objectives? The commercial success of their film in its art-house/political circuit quickly accumulated the funds to buy eighteen ambulances, which were sent to Madrid for assembly and deployment. Late in the war, when the situation was hopeless (for ambulances save lives, not wars), Hemingway gave a special presentation of Spanish Earth in Barcelona, where a real air-raid temporarily interrupted Van Dongen's synthetic ones. The film was revived in New York in February 1939, just in time for the final triumph of Franco. Its next revival came upon the death of Franco in 1975, throughout Europe and nowhere more eagerly than in Spain, a monument to the struggles two generations earlier of the Popular Fronts of both the Old World and the New, inspiration and instruction for the struggles that are still ahead.

Notes

1 The most detailed and reliable account of the ideological context of the films of the American Popular Front is Russell Campbell's 1978 dissertation for Northwestern, now published as Cinema Strikes Back: Radical Filmmaking in the United States, 1930-1942

(Ann Arbor: UMI Research Press, 1982), to which I must acknowledge my indebtedness. William Alexander's Film on the Left: American Documentary Film, 1931-1942 (Princeton, 1981) is a less comprehensive, more easily available treatment of the same subject.

2 A compact 1934 statement of Hurwitz's position, "The Revolutionary Film--Next Step," is anthologized in Lewis Jacobs' popular The Documentary Tradition, from which the quotes in this discussion are taken.

3 Quotations from Ivens' writings and speeches of the period are from his lecture notes for his American tour, preserved in the Nederlands Filmmuseum, Amsterdam, or from his well-known autobiography, The Camera and I (New York, 1968), in its final or early versions, for which some parts, also available in Amsterdam, began appearing as early as 1938.

4 Leacock, cited by Campbell, Radical Cinema, p. 413; Petric, Soviet Revolutionary Films in America (1926-35), dissertation, NYU, 1973, pp. 460-62.

5 This incomplete and misleading description of the classical sound documentary can be found even in such otherwise groundbreaking articles on documentary as Bill Nichols' "Documentary Theory and Practice," Screen, (v. 17, n. 4) and Annette Kuhn's "Desert Victory and the People's War," Screen, (v. 22, n. 2).

PART II

CONTEMPORARIES: THE WEST

Chapter 7

NEWSREEL, 1967-1972: FILM AND REVOLUTION

Bill Nichols

Newsreel, through all its various stages of political and chronological evolution as well as through its bi-coastal bifurcation, will always remain the exemplary political filmmaking enterprise for North American radicals, the group that first tested the water at the dawn of the New Left. It is thus fitting that Bill Nichols' study of the collective's first years should launch the section of Show Us Life devoted to our contemporaries. Steering resolutely clear of the mystification that pioneers usually command, Nichols' case study of certain representative films from both coasts is especially interesting for its insight into how organizational contexts intersected with aesthetic, ideological and political priorities.

Newsreel stepped into a vacuum. Left film culture in America withered away in the late thirties and early forties with the demise of the Film and Photo League and Frontier Films. The Hollywood left never sought to supplement or replace it. Television's entrenchment as a mass medium coincided with the onset of the Cold War. It had little, if any, room for radical viewpoints. During the fifties, individuals like Leo T. Hurwitz continued to make leftist films. Distributors like Tom Brandon managed to carry politically progressive films and to import eastern

European ones; and exhibitors like Amos Vogel, of Cinema 16 in New York, screened a wide-range of controversial or broadly "subversive" film. But, on the whole, the sense of a dynamic and wide-spread leftist film culture remained eclipsed by the combination of mass commodity culture and a political left, exemplified by (but not limited to) the CPUSA, which had great difficulty understanding or supporting the role of culture in political struggle. To this day the cultural activist runs the risk of criticism for opportunism--that is, for self-promotion or for "premature" expenditures of valuable resources on secondary concerns in the face of pressing social and economic struggle.

As much as any leftist filmmaking group, Newsreel exemplified the possibilities of a left cultural revival. It never spanned a very large swath of filmmaking possibilities, eschewing fiction for documentary and agit-prop, but it rekindled the possibilities of collective effort, alternative distribution, and organizational continuity that are essential prerequisites for a broader range of activity. Its own partial eclipse--by a host of other filmmaking groups (Kartemquin, New Day Films, Pacific Street Collective, Cine-Manifest); by individuals, newcomers who by the mid-seventies had access to institutional sources of funding that eluded Newsreel (Cinda Firestone, Connie Field, Lorraine Gray, Glen Silber, Alan Francovich); and by the continuing, innovative work of older independent filmmakers like Saul Landau or Emile de Antonio--attests to the vitality of a culture Newsreel helped to foster, certainly not single-handedly and sometimes by negative example. But when viewed in retrospect, the early years of Newsreel bear witness to many of the issues, debates, and strategies with which other groups and many individuals, then and since, have also had to contend. This account tries to lend some specificity to the events of those years, but leaves for another occasion the chronicling of the subsequent history of left film culture in America.

Newsreel was officially constituted in New York City in December, 1967. In contrast to the San Francisco center which was formed a few months later, New York Newsreel was composed of two similar but very distinct groups. At the core was a nucleus of some nine or ten white, middle-class males who had been involved in independent, Leftist film production.[1] The members of this nucleus were generally wealthy or had skills that kept them economically well-off; they had initiated the idea of a Newsreel group (after some of them had experimented with Alpha 60, a more conventional filmmaking collective/company that did not succeed) and they formed the initial leadership.

Surrounding the nucleus were less tightly-knit clusters of individuals from a similar white, middle-class, college-oriented background but who were generally lacking filmmaking skills and, often, experience and proficiency in political work. For many of them, Newsreel served as a rite de passage between the campus or personal indignation and collective action in the "real world." Most of them, however, found it difficult to break into the core of leadership elite, to gain a knowledge of filmmaking skills or even to make their voices heard effectively.

The earliest priorities were on productivity, confrontation and survival. The latter was accomplished by fund-raising and by acquiring the exclusive rights to a number of foreign-made, Leftist films (numerous films from or about Cuba and Vietnam, for example), a field in which Newsreel played an extremely valuable role. Other groups, like Tricontinental or its successor, Unifilm, later specialized in the distribution of Third World films across a broader artistic front than Newsreel's restricted emphasis on topical documentary, but in the late sixties and early seventies Newsreel was often the sole source of many Third World films. It helped demonstrate the importance of and need for such material and helped draw the American left into Third World struggle. New York Newsreel also helped establish links with, or partly inspire, European filmmaking groups that were part of the wide-spread sense of foment and possibility so noticeable in the late sixties.

Newsreel's stress on productivity meant that little long-range coordination or planning took place; members were free to propose and make films more or less on their own and then distribute them as Newsreels. Consequently, there was no particular "line" to the films, their quality was frequently quite low, and members of the nucleus tended to dominate the filmmaking process. Very rarely, for example, were women or Third World members behind a camera or in front of an editing table.

Where films had been hand grenades for Eisenstein and bullets for the Film and Photo League, they were seen as "can openers" by Robert Kramer, a leader in the early New York Newsreel group: "We want to make films that unnerve, that shake people's assumptions, that threaten, that do not soft-sell, but hopefully (an impossible ideal) explode like grenades in people's faces."[2] Kramer's views were indicative of prevailing New Left attitudes. The concepts of confrontation and polarization were in their ascendancy in 1968 and it is not surprising that Newsreel likened its grainy, jerky images to "battle footage" and its propaganda role to guerrilla warfare (carried to a frightening self-defeating conclusion in Kramer's feature film, Ice).

This essentially amorphous, ultrademocratic structure remained intact until 1969 when a period of intense deliberation brought several changes. Confrontation theory continued to play a major role and, in fact, Newsreel extended its field of attack. Previously, Newsreel had produced and distributed films on the premise that organizers "out there" (presumedly SDS members or community organizers of various sorts) would put the films to work. What they discovered was that there were precious few organizers with an ongoing constituency and that many of these belonged to the Old Left with whom Newsreel was not eager to cooperate. Consequently, Newsreel itself became more directly involved in distribution and began to send speakers from the group to screenings of their films. The process was never systematized, however. Each speaker worked largely on his own and no attempt was made to establish correlations between specific films and the reaction they got from various audiences.

The basic concept, however, was a vital one and clearly defined Newsreel's commitment to the political use of film. The screening-discussion format took them beyond the idea of providing alternative interpretations to events that could then be disseminated in the same fashion as the mass media's information. Newsreel began to argue that the film should never stand alone and that the structure of the screening had as much priority as the structure of the film. This principle, calling the viewing context an organizational responsibility, proved a distinctive feature of Newsreel's work. Independent filmmakers could not afford to make an extended commitment to leading or structuring discussion and tended to limit their involvement to the needs of promotion. The principle never became fully implemented (something like a party structure would probably be necessary for that); but it placed into sharper relief, for other activists to see, the question of audience and of the viewing event itself as a vital part of the politics of filmmaking. And while they developed the rationale for this approach largely by trial and error, it bears a close resemblance to the position adopted by Fernando Solanas and Octavio Getino, and shares the same underlying expectations:

> [This type of screening] provokes with each showing, as in a revolutionary military incursion, a liberated space, a decolonized territory. [The screening becomes a political event] which according to Fanon, could be a 'liturgical act, a privileged occasion for human beings to hear and be heard.'[3]

During this period, New York Newsreel continued to be dominated by the nucleus of activist/filmmakers and a point of view which Robert Kramer defined as a flexible position "between empiricism and dogmatism."[4] Essentially, this point of view (most obvious in films that Kramer or Fruchter had a large hand in, like Amerika, Summer '68, People's War or Ice) meant presenting actual material with a minimum of political analysis laid over it. Empiricism was defended as a method of choice because Marxism as they saw it (though they were speaking mainly of its vulgarized forms) had become narrow and rigid, dogmatically tied to a "correct line," and, therefore, idealist. Empiricism, on the other hand, acknowledged the uniqueness of the historical moment and allowed an unbiased look at "real needs" and "real conditions."

The concept bore more relation to cinéma-vérité than to empiricism as a scientific method. It called for a depiction of the face of social action and conflict independent of what was perceived as the overly conceptualized analysis of different political groups. When it came time to indicate how the real needs or conditions so depicted could be altered, Kramer and Fruchter were at more of a loss. Frequently they posed alternatives, but without an explicit understanding of how these alternatives might be achieved they often had a utopian aura.

Nonetheless, the group began to tend toward a less totally open-ended structure for itself. The sheer weight of numbers (New York Newsreel had between 50 and 70 members during this time) and the felt need for more democratic procedures contributed to a process of reevaluation and restructuring in which the group's nucleus still managed to hold a disproportionate degree of power.

A more radical restructuring of Newsreel took place in late 1969-early 1970 and revolved around the woman's question and the principles of Chairman Mao. Criticism/self-criticism became a way of formally incorporating more individuals into the democratic and bureaucratic process. When what had become the arteriosclerotic forms of democratic centralism were larded with this principle, they regained a flexibility and accountability--although never miraculously. The exact degree of success inevitably depended upon the people themselves.

For Newsreel this methodology coupled with the woman's question to bring much of the incipient chauvinism, elitism, individualism and subjectivism to the surface. The women organized discussion sessions and quickly discovered that "[the few women] who were active and spoke up, who worked and edited films, were not criticized at all. [The men] had never really thought about who the women were, what they did and what they thought." Men, however, received substantive criticism from other men; for the women, the only question was why they didn't act like men.

The criticism/self-criticism sessions were quite a revelation and precipitated a period of struggle and indeterminacy that persisted for the better part of a year. Gradually, the internal patterns of struggle began to form most clearly around three areas: the nature and role (within Newsreel) of women's liberation; the class composition of the group; and the acquisition of skills and control of the filmmaking process. A corollary argument that had begun some time before dealt with Newsreel's role in the Movement. Many argued that Newsreel should concentrate on filmmaking as a propaganda unit; others, including Fruchter and Kramer, urged a more active organizing role where members would work with a particular constituency, provide political leadership and also make films. For both groups the screening-discussion concept as it was practiced represented a hit-and-run operation of limited value: where they differed was on how to concentrate their efforts for maximum effect--on making the films or on mobilizing the people.

Gradually, the struggles began to resolve themselves and most, if not all, of the nucleus drifted away. Women and Third World members assumed a major share of the leadership roles; a priority on recruiting Third World members was established; skills were systematically taught to everyone in the group; filmmaking was given precedence over organizing, and the entire organization (after another period of hesitation lasting several additional months) chose to adopt the principles of democratic centralism. The control of filmmaking decisions thus moved out of the hands of the previously experienced and independently wealthy and into the hands of a collective structure. Some regretted the loss of autonomy and the sense of group spontaneity that had prevailed, and went elsewhere. Others felt a primary allegiance to the Movement and left to do organizing or other kinds of Movement work as Newsreel began to restrict its range of operation to film production. And by this point (in 1970), groups like the Black Panthers, Young Lords, La Raza, and Black Workers caucuses had developed a network of organizers capable of conducting screenings-discussions on a more ongoing basis than Newsreel itself could sustain. New York Newsreel chose to relate to its constituency primarily through film and video-tape skill-training programs which allowed for prolonged relationships and also furnished points of contact with needs and problems from which their own films could be formulated.

Confrontation was no longer the order of the day; the stress instead was on principled unity and cooperation. The membership had become much more decidedly working-class and had adopted a dynamic methodology that no longer contradicted but grew from Marxism.

The early New Left's aversion to Communism in particular and Marxist theory in general certainly influenced the thinking of Newsreel spokesmen like Robert Kramer. But within two years, the practical experience of Newsreel--like that of the Left as a whole, in confronting questions of class, race, and sex as well as the more topical issues of the war in Vietnam and the draft--compelled a search for a conceptual model, an explanatory theory. Although modifications were plentiful ("new working class" theory, elaborations of feminist theory, the theory and practice of Mao Zedong, Frankfurt School-based cultural theory), Marxism gained greater and greater acceptance as the frame within which debate could most profitably occur. (Other anti-imperialist, anti-war, anti-authoritarian elements of the New Left continued to balk at the acceptance of Marxism. Such elements tended to constitute the counter-culture as a more "life style"-oriented movement, a movement that only exercised marginal influence on Newsreel's organization or choice of film topics.)

Some of the films made during the latter half of

the period from 1968 to 1972 give a good indication of Newsreel's continuing search for forms and topics that would be compatible with the group's changing consciousness of its own nature and role. Make-Out, for example, from New York Newsreel, suggests a resourceful continuation of an anti-didactic spirit within a far less confrontational context--so much so that, at first, Newsreel hesitated to distribute it widely lest its open-ended structure be incorrectly interpreted.

Make-Out is Newsreel's only fiction film done on a collective basis. The others, Ice and In Passing, were primarily individual projects to which the group lent their aid but later chose not to distribute. Make-Out is not a personal vision but a collective one. Its structure is simple and its point unmistakable despite its lack of a political point of view transcending the situation portrayed: we see a boy and a girl in a parked car. The boy begins to neck with her while we hear her thoughts on the soundtrack. She wonders what he's heard about her. She wishes he would say something, say he likes her, for instance, but no. Instead he plods awkwardly along and her thoughts remain self-enclosed, impossible to communicate. The film (only 10 minutes long) ends with a disc jockey's voice announcing a commercial: "You're finding out what it's like to be feminine and it's a gas."

The conception and realization of Make-Out are economical and provocative. The voice-over commentary works in effective counterpoint to the visuals, and undermines the realistically portrayed encounter that we might otherwise think normal. The counterpoint also lends itself to the blossoming of another quality that is seldom found in Newsreels: a sense of humor.

By the same token, Make-Out reaches no conclusions, offers no models, gives no answers. The girl in the car is left to struggle with her budding consciousness essentially alone, much like the more politically advanced heroine (relatively) of Godard's Struggles in Italy. But instead of reacting to this less demonstrative, less analytical film by scuttling it, Newsreel recognized that it had an important role to play. Make-Out can be highly effective within a screening context where the girl's thoughts in the film can be completed and studied, where women in the audience do not leave with their thoughts about the film short-circuited inside them as the character's were, and where the audience gains a sharper understanding of the need for collective action by the very process of discussing the film. New York Newsreel, for example, screened the film for high school girls who identified with it immediately and where it opened up a wide range of questions that allow a perspective or line to build up around the film. Make-Out opened up many possibilities that New York Newsreel would explore further as its internal coherence, political theory and community orientation continued to develop.

New York Newsreel also gave considerable attention to the question of the prison system. In the early seventies, they made three films that explore the issues of what incarceration is like on a daily basis, of how events like the Attica Prison uprising (September 1971) could occur, of how prison labor is exploited, and of whether prisons may not be considered as a metaphor for the condition of all Third World minority groups within the United States. Of the three films (In the Event Anyone Disappears, Teach Our Children, and We Demand Freedom), In the Event demonstrates the greatest control in terms of subject-matter and gave a promising indication of the level of work Newsreel could produce.

In the Event Anyone Disappears makes fewer of the metaphorical allusions to society-as-prison that are perhaps too prevalent, and open-ended, in We Demand Freedom. Instead it concentrates on the experience of being in prison but still implicitly likens this experience to that of the Third World person struggling to survive in the everyday world.

In describing the film, a Newsreel person explained, "Mainly, what we tried to show was the exploitation of the work force inside the prison."[5] That may be too strict an interpretation of the film's emphasis, however, since the film also examines the oppressive conditions under which prisoners live whether working or simply surviving, and the nature of the prison/prisoner interface represented by guards, rehabilitation programs and medical services. Overall the film subsumes the discussion of exploitation in the prison work-place into a broader consideration of oppression in prison generally. It also likens the experience of Third World people, whether in prison or not, in terms of both exploitation and particular forms of oppression. Like the other two films, In the Event deemphasizes the distinctive function of prison, which is to segregate physically those who have been judged outside the legal bounds of our existing socio-economic system. Prisons give heightened institutional focus to the boundaries of the permissible in our society, and follow, quite dramatically, the fault lines of social contradiction, especially in terms of class and race. Newsreel's films, though, tended to regard prison as an extension of the oppression minority group members' experience outside prison. This appropriate, but more metaphorical, view is a recurrent motif in all three prison films, particularly We Demand Freedom, where it is, in fact, a central theme.

Interviews with prison inmates dominate In the Event with frequent cutaways to images of the prison system at large. Sound contributes in several ways to the overall development of the film, especially when it provides added specificity and credibility through sync interviews. Location sounds, or noise, also play a major part in the creation of mood, especially the sounds of the prison workshops and small factories. The noise is incessant and deafening. The ambient sound often engulfs voice-over commentary. The prisoners' voices appear to bob up during the sync interviews from beneath a sea of drowning sounds. The result effectively suggests the alienation of labor and the isolation of the prisoner within his environment.

Interviews elaborate the exploitative nature of prison work, Newsreel's intended theme. A black prisoner, for example, states in tight closeup to the camera, "I make 85¢ a day." The wage scale at his prison runs from 60¢ to $1.00 per day, which he explains pits the prisoners against one another. A little later in the film a prisoner speaks about prison workshops as "big business." These comments are tucked into the middle of the film without sufficient explanation of the distinctive functions of work and surplus-value inside the prison system. They are well-made points, tied to convincing shots of the prison workshops that evoke the iconography of nineteenth-century sweatshops, but the film clearly stresses economic exploitation as a common experience of Third World people wherever they might be, rather than further describing its more precise role within the prison system.

Other prisoner interviews relate additional tales of oppression. These include a description of prisoners left to die when medical aides refused to administer treatment outside normal clinic hours, of overcrowding in prison cells, of an education program taught in English to a prison population made up largely of Puerto Rican men who only spoke Spanish, and of guard brutality. A black prisoner gives an example of a guard who called a prisoner out of his cell to take a phone call and then beat him up. Toward the end of the film, this theme is taken up again by a prisoner who informs us, "In the event any of us disappear, just remember that we all got good hearts." In the Event's overall treatment of prison brutality graphically illustrates the kind of thinking that the prison system encourages among its functionaries:

> You have handed over to us robbers and murderers because you thought of them as wild beasts; you asked us to make domesticated sheep of them on the other side of the bars which protect you; but there is no reason why we the guards, the representatives of "law and order," we the instruments of your morality and your prejudices, would not think of them as wild animals, just the same as you.[6]

In general, Newsreel's prison films made the group one of the most important single sources of film material on this subject. These three films represent a large part of Third World Newsreel's filmmaking work in the early seventies and have been quite valuable in the hands of community and political groups. Although the exact nature of their political thrust can be debated, all three films work on a level to which their intended audiences can relate. The choice of emphasis on oppression and on the commonality of Third World people's experience of capitalist institutions may be a problematic choice in some respects, but this can be debated precisely among those people Newsreel wants to reach rather than among more marginal groups (such as film critics or cadre-type political organizations). These films, intended for situations where discussion accompanies the screening, encourage the audience itself to make many of the connections and ferret out many of the implications which more traditional (and less progressive) situations leave for critics to discover and communicate. Critics unfamiliar with this context often overemphasize faults apparent to audiences as well, and fail to see how a film like In the Event Anyone Disappears stimulates group discussion and heightens consciousness about a particular issue. Newsreel's films compare favorably with other, better-known prison documentaries like Cinda Firestone's Attica, but they have suffered from not being directed toward the kind of liberal, middle-class audience for which most critics write.

The other film-producing center, San Francisco Newsreel, was formed in the Spring of 1968. From the start there were significant differences from New York. Both shared an affinity with the then-flourishing counter-culture. Both were anti-capitalist, anti-imperialist, but also anti-Marxist. San Francisco Newsreel, however, did not have virtual class divisions within its membership. There was no filmmaking or activist elite and few, if any, individuals with personal resources sufficient to finance their own films. Hence filmmaking decisions from the start were shared by larger clusters of people and their consequences more generally diffused.

San Francisco began moving toward democratic centralism well ahead of New York, but like New York, they first passed through a bourgeois-democratic phase in which there were work-teams with relative autonomy and a central steering committee. Many members, in fact, were not involved in filmmaking or in distribution at all, but ran a communal garage, a movement center, a health clinic and other political projects. For a while it appeared that San Francisco Newsreel was a group of Leftist organizers who happened to have a few films. When this diffuseness of purpose became coupled to an absence of funds in late 1969, San Francisco Newsreel moved into a period of crisis that only slackened many months later.

The crisis led to a split among the members into two groups which developed position papers, argued their cases, but finally agreed they could not work toegther any longer. The smaller faction left and the remaining members instituted new procedures designed to see them through their financial crisis. One of the most revolutionary of these measures for the individual members was a work furlough program combined with a planned economy. Certain members would take working-class jobs for set periods of time while the others devoted themselves full-time to film production and distribution. The jobs filled a number of needs: they provided income of which all but a living stipend was administered by Newsreel collectively; they formally eliminated the discrepancy between members who had to work and those who did not; and they provided important exposure to the working-class milieu in which Newsreel sought to make most of its films.

San Francisco Newsreel also established a more disciplined form of democratic centralism (ahead of New York) and established a set of film priorities of which completion of The Woman's Film was foremost. There were three women in charge of the film, which meant that many of the men took jobs to see the project through. They also initiated a study program of film theory and history which was, remarkably, the first such program at any Newsreel center (collective study had previously been limited to political and historical topics). And they attempted to define more precisely "for whom" their propaganda was intended.

Newsreel had always been a predominantly white group. Their films, however, often focused on black and other minority groups, of which the series of four films on the Black Panthers are the most obvious example. San Francisco saw this as not altogether desirable and called for films "aimed at the white segment of the working-class because we are best equipped (being white) to serve them.... Our films will comment on the racism, male chauvinism and the petty-bourgeois ideology of the white working-class which we see as the three main obstacles that divide the working-class." This decision to acknowledge their own racial composition and work primarily with the white working-class was a major one and reflected an important step away from the romantic and voyeuristic tendency to glorify other races and other cultures from the outside. On the other hand, it was perhaps a very obvious decision that blacks had been urging white radicals to accept for years in order to form the basis for united action. Many activists now recognize a need for multi-national, radical groups, but it may be difficult for film propagandists to fill that need when there is still such a paucity of organizing material aimed directly at the white worker.

San Francisco Newsreel's attempt to resolve the question of "for whom" coincided with other debates about the composition of the group, particularly the number and effective voice of minority group members. The result was a continuing tension throughout this period, but when we look at their overall film production, certain patterns do begin to emerge. One of these was the tendency to document major political events or groups (like the Panthers, People's Park and San Francisco State Strike) rather than analyze more institutional sources of exploitation or oppression (as the New York Newsreel films on the Army, ROTC and New York Subway system). And compared to the short but diffuse anti-war movement films with which New York began, San Francisco started with the Black Panthers.

Black Panther was San Francisco's first film and was at the time Newsreel's most widely distributed film. Together with Columbia Revolt, it stabilized Newsreel as a financially solvent group. The film itself is simply conceived: interviews with Huey P. Newton (in Alameda County Jail), Eldridge Cleaver and Bobby Seale, intercut with one another and with shots of Black Panthers practicing close-order drill and also demonstrating outside the Alameda County Courthouse/Jail. The interviews are mixed with sufficient cutaways to keep them from creating a static impression: a particularly effective combination is a long tracking shot (from a car) of a black ghetto area coupled to Bobby Seale's description of the Party's 10-Point Program. The connection is oblique but not obscure. Instead of an obvious translation of Seale's description into shots of police brutality, avaricious businessmen, over-crowded jails and welfare lines, we see only the outer shell, the general milieu, within which the struggle for black liberation must take place. The image leaves the Party's program unfixed to a narrowly specific example, joins it with the entire black community and unifies it through a single take. It is, I believe, one of the rare examples of superior artistry in Newsreel films.

While the propaganda value of Black Panther has become somewhat eroded today, Newsreel's next major film, Oil Strike, retains a currency that transcends the immediate issues of striking workers. Shot in the oil refinery area of Richmond, California (just north of Berkeley but far removed from it in almost every way except geographically), the film describes the workers' demands, documents their disillusionment with democratic processes and concludes with a rally calling for student/worker unity--a fairly uncommon event at worker rather than student meetings. Oil Strike uses "enemy footage" to great advantage--the introduction consists of the concluding minute or so from a pro-company documentary describing the many advantages of working for Standard Oil. A voice-over commentary then describes the workers' demands (traditional trade union ones--a pay hike, medical insurance and a pension program) which the company refused to negotiate.

The most revealing part of the film for a Movement with many voices urging radicals to give up on the reactionary white worker lies in the interviews with white workers and their wives. One woman says, "I have no more respect for the law." A man explains, "I was a law-abiding citizen. I always figured the cops were there to protect me, but now I see that's only if I don't get out of line." Other workers say they've discovered that both the police and their own lives are controlled by corporate giants and invisible businessmen. Whereas the insights may be old hat to the New Left, they are searing indictments from the forgotten worker. His rhetoric may be less catchy, his analysis less penetrating, but for those who consider revolution impossible without working-class leadership, they are the most exciting words of the film.

The emotional climax of Oil Strike comes when we learn that a worker died after being run over by a scab-driven truck. The camera follows the funeral procession in tracking shots that parallel the company gates, draped with black ribbons. The sequence is reminiscent of the tracking shot that accompanies Bobby Seale's description of the 10-Point Program and effectively conveys the workers' solidarity against a backdrop of corporate domination (the refinery with its long, slender chimneys is plainly visible in the background). This emotional climax also corresponds to the strike effort that died without winning its objectives, and it has far broader impact than the more usual climactic montage of riot footage. Nonetheless, the climax turns from a study of process--the radicalization of white workers--to an emotional and moral appeal. We do not hear from workers how they responded to this unnecessary death. The event is related to the viewer by voice-over commentary as though this were our "real" point of contact (sympathy, outrage) rather than an understanding of our common cause with the workers' budding revolutionary consciousness. Failing to situate the death within the workers' context, it takes on a timeless quality (the Unknown Worker sort of idea) which can be moving, but only at the expense of its most integral rootedness in historical conflict.

The Oil Workers' union is predominantly white, a factor which the film does not stress and whose implications it does not explore. Nonetheless, Oil Strike remains one of the most explicitly working-class-oriented films that Newsreel has made and is consequently of great organizing value.

Another film of considerable importance is The Woman's Film. It has sparked considerable interest and gained a very diverse distribution--from women's discussion groups to the Museum of Modern Art.

Basically a series of interviews with black, Chicano and white working-class women, The Woman's Film comes closer than any other Newsreel to cinéma-vérité technique. Newsreel is not wholly comfortable with the technique, however, and the discomfort sometimes works to undermine its aesthetic premises. Cinéma-vérité, for example, seeks to detect rather than invent plot and to disclose that which is more than that which should, or might, be. For Newsreel, portraying what is cannot suffice when their intention is to reveal the inadequacy of that condition. In The Woman's Film, for example, the different interview sections imply the presence of a revolutionary process that can transcend the present-day reality of the women. But the links between these sections are not altogether evident. The sense of process itself becomes invented rather than detected. Why these women have rejected the myths that obscure their oppression by glorifying it and why these women foresee a class struggle and revolution rather than democratic reform is not at all apparent. Nor do we gain a broader view outside of their personal, but mainly politicla, commentary. The women remain subjects of the camera rather than autonomous individuals with distinctive lives. We see only a minimal fraction of their daily lives, and even then the women give most of their attention to the camera, speaking directly to it, rather than dealing with the rest of their surroundings.

As in Oil Strike, the intended audience can identify with the women as their sisters, but unlike the example of the strike, there is no galvanizing incident and no indication of which, if any, slower process of edification and redirection led them to their conclusions, thus biasing the film toward the predisposed, if not the already convinced.

Finally the film brushes against but never tackles what San Francisco Newsreel defined in its position paper as a priority: creating propaganda for the white working-class that would combat racism. Although one of the women, Florence, is active in "Why Not Whites?," a group trying to organize white mothers eligible for welfare that obviously must deal with racist arguments, the film never explores this issue nor Florence's impressions of it. None of the other women in the film discusses racism specifically or reflects any particular awareness of the importance of the question to their situation and objectives. The omission perhaps indicates the central dilemma that the filmmakers faced--to let the women speak for themselves, à la cinéma-vérité, and yet to present their own, Marxist perspective on the situation and its solution. Nonetheless, the omission is an egregious one that blunts the film's organizing importance and indicates that a white filmmaking group is not necessarily on safer ground when it turns its camera to whites instead of blacks.

The weight of these criticisms may seem to relegate the film to the second rank of Newsreels but, in fact, the intensity of critical engagement with the film is a measure of its strength. The Woman's Film represents a more serious attempt at a fusion of art and propaganda than the majority of Newsreels: it does not present charismatic leaders who have advanced beyond the average viewer's consciousness, nor events that are not analyzed--both situations that may leave many viewers feeling on the outside of a closed circle. The film does possess a coherence and a revelatory quality that, at moments, can be astounding, especially when the women relate some of their own, very personal experiences. Their stories, in fact, have a captivating quality similar to the anecdotes in Godard's films, and with far less oblique political implications. The protagonists are strong, perceptive women who bear witness to the strength and self-awareness of the working class. They conquer stereotypes and demolish myths. Despite its flaws, The Woman's Film is one of Newsreel's greatest accomplishments.

A final consideration of Newsreel's work involves a look at their treatment of what Marcuse called the "reality-transcending dimension." Newsreel films generally adhered very closely to the here and now and gave little consideration to the idea of revolution as a facet of consciousness as well as of immediate and specific political struggle. The films assume that the viewer has already evolved the faculty to conceive of an altered social fabric as something other than chaos or destruction. The films do not seem to acknowledge the fact that many people today have experienced an atrophying of this faculty. It is precisely this form of awareness, for example, that The Woman's Film abruptly unleashes when we hear the women conclude that there will have to be violent confrontations before their most basic needs are fulfilled. How they acquired a consciousness of this reality-transcending element within a milieu characterized by its absence is the least explored facet of their political nature. Their stories of oppression and struggle could be matched by even more compelling tales of hardship (such as the Queen for a Day show used to trade in, and where the connection was never made at all). Newsreel tended to accept the women's level of consciousness as normative (it is, after all, that of their own peer group), an exemplary form of awareness for others, but not a truly unusual one worthy of deep examination in its own right.

Dziga Vertov's conception of a "New Man" who would be born by the camera eye has scarcely been elaborated since, and Newsreel is no exception to this general neglect. Propaganda that is at odds with the prevailing situation and its patterns of acceptance and acquiescence is in special need of this supplementary dimension to both rational and emotional appeals. It faces the task of carving out still obscure categories of perception and setting them in sharp relief to those that dominate social, political and economic relationships.

Questions of subjectivity and consciousness have gained a place on the political agenda largely through the work of the women's movement. Concern with the politics of the everyday, the domestic, and the personal have contributed to an increased attentiveness to the problem of finding visual representations for a reality-transcending dimension within the terms of the typical and everyday itself, rather than in finely-worked rhetoric and slogans of leaders, parties or groups. The Newsreel films discussed here bear witness to the search for an emergent, representable dimension of what might be within what is. It is a search Newsreel and other Left filmmaking groups will be challenged to continue amid the changing, historical forms of contradiction and struggle.

Notes

1 Among these were Robert Kramer and Norman Fruchter, whose comments are featured in an article on Newsreel in Film Quarterly (Winter, 1968).

2 Ibid.

3 Fernando Solanas and Octavio Getino's "Towards a Third Cinema," first appeared in Tricontinental (Havana)

and has been reprinted in English in Cineaste, Vol. LV, No. 3, and in Bill Nichols, ed., Movies and Methods (Berkeley and Los Angeles, 1976), pp. 44-64.

4 New York Newsreel, "Towards a Redefinition of Propaganda," Leviathan, Vol. I, No. 6 (Oct.-Nov. 1969).

5 Interview by the author with Chris Choy, Third World Newsreel, New York, December 1974.

6 John K. Simon, "Michael Foucault in Attica," Telos, No. 19 (Spring, 1974), p. 157.

Chapter 8

FINALLY GOT THE NEWS: THE MAKING OF A RADICAL DOCUMENTARY

Dan Georgakas

Newsreel's foray into Detroit's union and racial politics in the late sixties was never judged by any of the participants to have been an unqualified success. Nevertheless, Dan Georgakas' analysis of the film that resulted, Finally Got the News, is a stirring case study of the practical and theoretical challenges of subject-centered political documentary filmmaking.

Finally Got the News was recognizable as a classic as soon as it was released in the winter of 1969/1970. [1] What made the film so distinctive was that it was made under the direct supervision of working-class blacks who advocated a Marxist approach to black liberation issues. The League of Revolutionary Black Workers, the organization the film was intended to publicize, no longer exists; but the film's political and class perspectives remain dynamic. Scenes of the city of Detroit--people pouring in and out of the automobile plants, the Diego Rivera murals in the Art Institute, the permanent smog overhanging Ford's River Rouge complex, the gigantic counter which minute by minute records car production by the edge of a major expressway like a capitalistic holy grail--all fuse to give a powerful impression of what the realities of living in Motor City are all about.

This was the site of the Insurrection of 1967, a

violent uprising which brought flames and rifle fire to the doorway of General Motors, an insurrection primarily carried out by workers, not youth or the permanently unemployed, an insurrection in which the majority of the snipers captured by police were Appalachian whites! Finally Got the News provides a view from the inside of the frustration that precipitated the revolt and the continuing alienation felt on automotive shop floors. More than a decade after its release, when the Public Broadcasting System, the educational television network, was selecting radical films of the 1960s and 1970s for a special series, Finally Got the News was rejected as too inflammatory.

The film originated as a project of Newsreel, a New York-based filmmaking collective that was then primarily composed of white males and was politically identified with the New Left. The objective was to make a film about Detroit blacks in much the way other films had been made of the Black Panther organization. The Newsreel filmmakers had read about DRUM (the Dodge Revolutionary Union Movement), a group of revolutionary black workers that operated at the main Dodge factory in Detroit. DRUM had carried out several successful strikes and had given birth to similar groups in other factories. Eventually the different factory units had merged with community, student, and support groups to form a League of Revolutionary Black Workers.[2]

Most of the individuals involved in Newsreel in the late 1960s supported the Black Panther/Weatherman thesis that the second American revolution would be led by a relatively small group of elite professional revolutionaries, with a following made up primarily of what traditional Marxists had called lumpen proletariat and the movement called "street people." The Newsreel group most interested in Detroit had a more working-class orientation than most of their compatriots and were anxious to document what black industrial workers were doing and thinking.

A small Newsreel contingent headed by Jim Morrison arrived in Detroit in June of 1969. They soon gathered League documents and recorded twenty-two hours of interviews with League spokespeople. This raw material was favorably received by New York Newsreel, but there was some hesitation about providing the funds needed for a film. An exasperated Morrison took fund-raising into his own hands in an ill-fated hash-smuggling scheme that netted him a ten-year sentence in a Canadian jail.[3] Shortly after Morrison's arrest, the main body of Newsreel came up with funds and a unit in Detroit could begin to work. From the onset, the group had two factions. Stewart Bird, Rene Lichtman, and Peter Gessner, the three Newsreel people who had the biggest role in making the eventual film, always saw their task as that of making a documentary that would accurately reflect the strategy of the League. The opposing faction felt that both the white and black radicals in Detroit needed an injection of Black Panther/Weatherman-style action. Rather than concentrating on filmmaking, this group proceeded to make an ideological intervention in the local political scene.

One of the initial difficulties facing the would-be filmmakers was the belief of many of the League's leading personalities that they should maintain a low public profile. They did not want any filmmakers, much less white filmmakers, filming meetings, demonstrations, and factory gate agitation. They feared that workers who were considering joining them would be frightened away. They also felt the film might be useful to the company, police and union in gathering intelligence data about their activities. John Watson, consistently one of the most imaginative and flexible of the leaders of the League, prevailed against the negative response to the prospect of a film by taking personal responsibility for the project. He understood the tremendous outreach a film could provide for organizing workers and he was convinced that his presence in the editing process would eliminate any potentially dangerous footage.

The division over the film was a precursor of the split within the League in 1971. Those who were most dubious about the film were the faction that desired to concentrate on local organizing, on minimizing contact with whites, and avoiding the media spotlight. They would express their uneasiness about the film in many ways. They would not stop nationalist-oriented black workers from running off white camera crews with threats of violence, and they often failed to inform the filmmakers of key public events. Many of the League components under their personal control never appear in the film. This hostility tended to ease somewhat as the film progressed, but it never totally abated. The lack of footage showing violent action or the usual "by any means necessary" rhetoric was a conscious decision, especially influenced by this group which also tended to be the group primarily engaged in day-to-day factory organizing.

The reluctance of these activists to have a film made about them was in marked contrast to the attitude of so many radicals of the time, who often seemed to measure their effectiveness by the number of times they appeared on the nightly news. The League rejected such an approach and was very concerned about the kind of image the Newsreel film would project. Watson was familiar with previous Newsreel efforts and knew their audiences were primarily the white college students who made up most of the "movement." He insisted that the film be conceived with a teaching rather than a reporting orientation and that its Marxism be framed primarily for an audience of black workers. The more usual Newsreel audience was not to be attacked and would benefit from the film, but pleasing that audience was secondary to reaching black workers. Bird, Lichtman, and Gessner were more pleased than upset by this development, but many difficult meetings were required to hammer out specific ideas. Initially Watson wanted to use a lot of heavy terminology and quotations. He was eventually persuaded that it would be more effective to have different leaders speaking informally. Watson, standing in his own living room, surrounded by posters of Mao Zedong, Che Guevara, and Malcolm X, ended up being the dominant figure in the film.

The effective montage history of black labor which opens _Finally Got the News_ was primarily the idea of Stewart Bird, who saw it as a method of presenting complex background material in readily understood images. The filmmakers also came up with the rhythm and blues song, "Please, Mr. Foreman, Slow Down the Assembly Line," which had been written and recorded by Joe L. Carter, a Detroit production-line worker and sometime nightclub performer. Other music was to be provided by Detroit jazz musician Sammie Saunders. Artistic decisions of this kind were worked out in joint meetings with League representatives. Watson generally indicated the overall direction desired and left the Newsreel people to solve the technical problems. Both groups were anxious to have League personnel trained in filmmaking skills. This did not work out as smoothly as it might have, but toward the end of the collaboration blacks were doing some of the camerawork and other technical tasks.

The filmmakers planned to give a theoretical view of how and why the working class was the essential element in creating social change, with most of the actual footage dealing with specific League struggles against racism in the automobile plants. The final form of the film is somewhat awkward due to the deepening disagreement within the League itself on the proper approach to immediate problems confronting the organization.

The first half of the film is the most successful, presenting a clear exposition of the idea that black people in the United States have been and continue to be exploited primarily because they are workers. In an opening section Watson says,

> You get a lot of arguments that black people are not numerous enough in America to revolt, that they will be wiped out. This neglects our economic position.... There are groups that can make the whole system cease functioning. These are auto workers, bus drivers, postal workers, steel workers, and others who play a crucial role in the money flow, the flow of materials, the creation of production. By and large, black people are overwhelmingly in those kinds of jobs.[4]

Scenes within the Detroit factories and interviews with local organizers such as Ron March and Chuck Wooten underscore the more general approach of Watson with specific Detroit experiences of the past year. These sequences emphasize the deteriorating work and safety conditions within the factories. They reach an artistic peak when an off-camera ghetto voice denounces capitalism in a long tirade that can only be described as a prose poem.[5] Against scenes of executives "working" at their desks, the disembodied ghetto voice informs us:

> They give you little bullshit amounts of money--wages and so forth--and then they steal all that shit back from you in terms of the way they have their other thing set up, that old credit-stick-em-up gimmick society--consumer credit--buy shit, buy shit--on credit. He gives you a little bit of money to cool your ass and then steals it all back with shit called interest which is the price of money. They are mother-fucking,

> non-producing, non-existing bastards dealing with paper.... He is in mining! He went to Phillips-Andover-Exeter. He went to Harvard. He went to Yale. He went to the Wharton School of Business. He is in "mining!" It is these mother-fuckers who deal with intangibles who are rewarded by this society. The more abstract and intangible your service, the bigger the reward. What are stocks? A stock certificate is evidence of something which is real. A stock is evidence of ownership. He who owns and controls receives--profit! This man is fucking with shit in Bolivia. He is fucking with shit in Chile. He is Kennicott. He is Anaconda. He is United Fruit. He is in mining! He's in what? He ain't never produced anything his whole life. Investment banker. Stock broker. Insurance man. He don't do nothing. We see that this whole society exists and rests upon workers and this whole mother-fucking society is controlled by this little clique which is parasitic, vulturistic, cannibalistic, and is sucking and destroying the life of workers everywhere and we must stop it because it is--evil!

The shots of interiors of the automobile plants which are seen during parts of this section were done clandestinely, as the auto companies have a long-standing prohibition against any filming on their premises.[6] Part of the resistance to cameras is that the companies claim they are very disruptive to production. Workers have always believed the companies actually are fearful of having their physical plants seen by the general public because of the obviously dangerous conditions. An interesting sidelight in this respect is that the factories where the League had its strongest units were physically demolished and their workforce dispersed when the auto decline of the 1970s set in.

Following the ghetto monologue sequence there is a section which deals with two Ford executives, one black and one white, answering questions posed by the filmmakers. The men are filmed from the far end of a long table and the cutting between the two men's faces establishes that while only the black man speaks, the white is in command. Like some agit-prop player in a vulgar Marxist skit, the white executive chews on a cigar and leers approvingly as the super-dignified black man explains how the company and the union have come together to work for the benefit of the "greater society." This ventriloquist act without wires would have been farcical in a fiction film, but it succeeds admirably as a real-life interview.

The first part of the film concludes with an election at Dodge Main. Rather than the lock-stepped, black-bereted, leather-jacketed Panther units of other films, Finally Got the News shows rather ordinary people becoming very angry with the system. Workers by the busload arrive at a union hall waving clenched fists and shouting, "Drum-Drum-Drum-Drum." A voice belonging to General Baker ("General" is a given name and not a title), one of the key industrial organizers, shouts through a megaphone, "Finally got the news how your dues are being used. Be mad, be mad, be mad, be mad. Can't do nothing if you ain't mad." As the workers, young and old, male and female, black and white, enter the union hall, they have to pass other workers, many of whom are black. These black men wear union caps and stare upon the DRUM forces in the way police stare at peace marchers. The class line is drawn very sharply in terms of psychological identification as well as economics. Some workers have identified with the master and some with the rebel slaves.

Any chance for DRUM to win at the ballot box is foiled by police harassment of DRUM supporters and the secret removal of the ballot boxes from the hall before the final count is made. What becomes most clear in the emotionally charged scenes is that the struggle has transcended a simple plant election. The people we see in motion by the thousands are people who work on the line every day, people who own homes, people who have families, people who drive their own cars, and people who own the proverbial color television set. These same people are very obviously and very enthusiastically supporting an anti-capitalist revolutionary organization. Workers viewing such footage can identify with the kind of people participating and with the kind of activity depicted. They can see that being radical does not necessitate becoming an incredible gun-slinger who defies the police with every breath. An election is one of the lowest levels of mass action, but it is mass, not elite, action, just as the wildcat strike and boycott are mass actions in which the people serve their needs directly.

The second half of Finally Got the News never

regains the sharp ideological and artistic focus which culminates with the Dodge election. There is a valiant attempt to deal with the relationship of white workers to revolutionary blacks, that might have become an entire film of its own. Retired Appalachian-born auto workers are filmed sitting on the porches of their frame houses. They drink beer and play guitars and their denunciations of the company are extremely radical until an old man concludes, "Everyone in this country is almost in revolt. We want to get more money. Everyone else is getting their share. Certain groups are doing good--the colored and the mothers on welfare." Watson's voice cuts in to explain the paradox created by racism,

> The white workers face the same contradictions in production and life as blacks do. If they work harder they think the enemy is "the nigger." If life is worse, the problem is "crime in the streets" ... [George] Wallace raps the money barons and the niggers; and these white workers love to hear it.... Many white workers end up being counter-revolutionary in the face of a daily oppression that should make them the staunchest of revolutionaries.... We are calling for the uplifting of the class as a whole.

Few militants would disagree with Watson's observations, but no solution, not even a transitory one, is suggested. This is less a weakness of the film than of the organization it was trying to serve. Although the League leaders were all oriented to Marxism, the group least accepting of the film had been influenced by black nationalism, which created a mixed ideological signal. Even those who sought to work with whites felt the time required an all-black group that would strike out for immediate gains for blacks whatever the response from white workers.

Genuine concern for reaching action-oriented whites is concentrated in interviews done with students at a working-class community college. They speak poignantly of the hardships and brutalities imposed on families by the industrial system and are very sympathetic to their parents and to the plight of black workers. They argue for an alliance with groups such as the League, but they speak as individuals, not as representatives of groups or movements. These scenes are a brave hope in the future that only underscores the enormous gap then existing between the cutting edge of black liberation movements and the average white worker.

Problematic nuances also surround the treatment of black working women and the role of community organizing. Hurried sequences do little more than register an awareness that these topics need further analysis than is possible within the context of this particular film. The footage showing the funeral of a ten-year-old black boy, accidentally shot to death by the police, is decidedly out of rhythm with the rest of the film in spite of its attempt to link the life of the factory with the violence of everyday life. Ken Cockrel's summation interview suffers because it follows these disconnected and only partially thought-out sections.

The rambling second half of the first film is partly the result of problems that nearly destroyed the entire filmmaking project. While the three Newsreel men already mentioned were busy at work on the film, much of the rest of Detroit Newsreel was doing politics. As part of its program of intervention, Detroit Newsreel organized an anti-repression conference to which it invited Robert Williams, recently returned from China; Emory Douglas of the Black Panther Party; and Ken Cockrel from the executive board of the League. The ideological tensions between the Panthers and the League were very intense at that time, particularly over differing positions regarding inflammatory rhetoric, the role of the lumpen, and local autonomy. At the conference, Cockrel emphasized that as of that time (January, 1970) no one in the Detroit movement had been killed by the police or had lost a trial in the courts. His tone made it clear that he thought League tactics were the major reason for this and that Panther tactics were not needed or wanted in the city of Detroit.[7]

In spite of its lack of a single black member, Detroit Newsreel continued to push the Panther positions as well as maintaining pressure for a Weatherman-style approach among whites. The radical forces within the city, particularly the Motor City Labor League, which was comprised mainly of whites, became increasingly annoyed that a small outside group with no local base and no local experience continued to advocate and work on projects contrary to the wishes and safety of local activists. Sheila Murphy, a radical with a long political background in the city, led the effort to curb Detroit Newsreel.[8] The League joined in the ferment when it learned about the fees and expense money paid to the Panthers by a group which claimed perpetual poverty when it came to donations for local initiatives and groups. The mounting pressure on Newsreel brought about an internal collapse, the majority deciding to leave Detroit and donate their equipment to a cultural group in nearby Ann Arbor, home of the University of Michigan. The League responded by confiscating all the Newsreel equipment, on the legal grounds that it was in lieu of the unpaid speaker fees, and on the revolutionary grounds that the group had raised money for the purpose of making radical films, which was what the League proposed to continue doing. Lichtman, Bird, and Gessner, while not approving of the manner in which the League took the equipment, agreed to continue working on the film as individuals even though Detroit Newsreel had ceased to exist.[9]

The film was finally completed by the League faction headed by John Watson, Ken Cockrel, and Mike Hamlin. They wanted to expand nationally in a formation to be called the Black Workers Congress. A national organization uniting many local black action groups was thought to be essential in dealing with national corporations, national unions, and national repression. Finally Got the News was viewed as an economically efficient and controllable vehicle for mass communication. A Black Star Productions unit under Watson's aegis was formed to make subsequent films. The former Newsreel allies, other whites, and League members made up the staff. One aborted project was to have Jane Fonda star in a film about Rosa Luxemburg.[10] Complementing Watson's Black Star Productions was a Black Star Publications unit under Mike Hamlin. An all-black staff at Black Star Publications published books, newspapers, pamphlets, posters, and other printed materials.[11]

Many rank and file League members considered these projects too ambitious and counter-productive to factory organizing. They argued for greater emphasis on local Detroit groups. Many felt uneasy about working with whites and others were concerned with the kinds of problems the Panthers had encountered in trying to expand nationally from their base in Oakland, California. These criticisms became the background for an organizational schism which resulted in Hamlin, Cockrel, Watson, and their supporters resigning from the League to work full-time for the Black Workers Congress, now an independent organization rather than the national expression of the League. In spite of years of preliminary work, the Black Workers Congress was fated to be stillborn. Of the Detroiters who had elected to work for the BWC, Ken Cockrel became the best known. Upon deciding that the times called for an attempt at electoral politics, in 1972, Cockrel's group successfully ran his white law partner, Justin Ravitz, for a ten-year term on Detroit's criminal court. A few years later Cockrel himself was elected to the nine-seat common council which runs the city of Detroit. Without backtracking on any of the views presented in Finally Got the News, Cockrel remained a favorite of the dominant media and was discussed as a serious contender for the mayoralty.

The group which retained the League name in the split of 1971 soon dissolved, with most of the better known leaders joining the Detroit branch of the Communist Labor Party. Following a year in which there was little public activity, the Communist Labor Party began to organize in the factories and persuaded a majority within the Motor City Labor League to join its ranks. The other major faction of that organization supported the efforts of Justin Ravitz and Ken Cockrel. The Communist Labor Party strove to avoid the label of an irrelevant sectarian group through various public affairs and ran General Baker for elective office in bids that failed.

The ultimate working out of the splits within the League leadership had a disastrous effect on the short-term distribution of Finally Got the News. Those who ultimately joined the Communist Labor Party had originally been against the production and certainly did not want to show a film which spotlighted their political opposition. Consequently, the film was never widely screened among the very Detroit workers for whom it had been made. The forces that worked with the Black Workers Congress used the film throughout the nation for a time, but the schism within the League disheartened workers, who were otherwise inspired by the film's content. Newsreel distributed the film through its usual channels, and individuals such as Stewart Bird and Wilbur Haddock (leader of the United Black Workers at Mahwah, New Jersey, a group similar to DRUM) kept prints in circulation.

Before any of the splits became final, John Watson had had the foresight to take a print to Europe, where he sold segments to German and Italian television. Prints were also made available to a cultural affiliate of the Italian Communist Party and various extra-parliamentary groups then active in Italy. The history of Finally Got the News in Italy is an interesting tale in itself, and the different soundtracks used are of more than academic interest.[12] The version used by the Communist Party toned down the profane language of certain scenes and through discreet translation filtered out the more revolutionary ideology and the critique of established unions. The version circulated by the extra-parliamentary groups emphasized the revolutionary aspects of the film and used creative Italian equivalents for ghetto slang. Italian workers who saw the film identified with the blacks in spite of the enormous cultural differences. They commented on the similarity of working conditions, union bureaucrats, and the nature of capital in cities as distant from each other as Turin and Detroit. Rather than being offended by the swearing, the Italian workers laughed freely and often applauded the most obscene passages and shouted for more.

In spite of the difficulties in its production and distribution, Finally Got the News has proven to be a film which pointed to new directions in radical documentaries. In terms of labor films, Finally Got the News set the tone for other works which investigated the negative role trade unions often play in regard to the demands of women, unskilled workers, and racial or ethnic minorities. Generational differences in radical documentaries are dramatic if one compares the rather naive view of unions found in People of the Cumberland, made in the late 1930s, or The Inheritance, made in the 1950s, with Finally Got the News, Union Maids, or Rosie the Riveter. Finally Got the News also marked a shift away from the highly rhetorical postures of the 1960s to the lower-keyed oral history model most prevalent in the 1970s and 1980s. The insistence that blacks be trained to make their own films was yet another trend that became dominant among minorities, women, and other groups that had traditionally been excluded from filmmaking.

Finally Got the News has been able to survive the organization that gave it birth, because it is ideological in the best sense. It is a film about ideas. Finally Got the News explores a serious perspective for dealing with basic working-class issues. In this sense the film is comparable to Salt of the Earth, the labor classic of the 1950s. Salt of the Earth was made by radical, blacklisted filmmakers determined to record a strike of Mexican-Americans affiliated with a union renowned for its radicalism. The film's perspective was greatly influenced by the workers who played themselves and helped to shape the script. The interaction between artists and workers was so creative that the resulting treatment of sexual, racial, and class problems has remained vibrant for three decades. Finally Got the News allows viewers entry to the fury that black workers felt in the 1960s. The film's raw eloquence deals so vividly with a specific time and place that its terms transcend immediate issues to present articulate themes that must remain relevant as long as working people do not control the basic givens of their everyday lives.

Notes

1 See original version of this essay in Cineaste, Vol. 5, No. 4 (1973).

2 Background to the formation of the League and its achievements can be found in Dan Georgakas and Marvin Surkin, Detroit: I Do Mind Dying (New York: St. Martin's Press, 1975).

3 Morrison served over three years before escaping from an honor farm when he concluded he was not going to be paroled. His present whereabouts are unknown. The screen credits for the film include: "Jim Morrison, political prisoner."

4 All quotes are from a filmscript the author fashioned from a personal print of the film. The script is available at the Tamiment Library, New York University.

5 The voice belongs to Ken Cockrel. The sequence is on the original twenty-two hours of tape made by the first Newsreel unit in Detroit.

6 Years later when Paul Schrader needed interiors for his very non-ideological Blue Collar, he too was turned away. Schrader had to film his production-line sequences at the plant that manufactures Checker cabs. See his discussion in Dan Georgakas and Lenny Rubenstein (editors), The Cineaste Interviews (Chicago: Lake View Press, 1983), pp. 208-209.

7 The text of this speech and other League documents are available in the Black Labor Issue of Radical America; Vol. 15, No. 2 (March/April, 1971).

8 Murphy was a political ally of Ken Cockrel. She served as campaign manager for Ravitz and Cockrel when they ran for political office in the 1970s.

9 When the film was completed, Rene Lichtman remained in Detroit as an activist in a local radical group. Peter Gessner continued to make films, working with Cine Manifest in developing fiction scripts for public television. Stewart Bird's subsequent films include The Wobblies, a documentary on the I. W. W. which premiered at the 1979 New York Film Festival. Of the Newsreel people who went to Ann Arbor, George DePue later became editor of an influential alternative newspaper that appeared weekly for many years.

10 In later years, Fonda would acknowledge a debt to Watson and Cockrel for helping to persuade her that she could do much more for her political ideas through motion picutres than by abandoning her film activities for conventional politics, a course she was then considering. See Georgakas and Rubinstein, The Cineaste Interviews, p. 106.

11 The most ambitious work was James Foreman, The Political Thought of James Foreman (Detroit: Black Star, 1970). Foreman was a national leader in the effort to establish a Black Workers Congress and was a past leader of the Student Non-Violent Coordinating Committee. A copy of this book is available at the Tamiment Library, New York University.

12 The author of this essay was living in Italy at the time, provided some minimal assistance in translating the script into Italian, observed many screenings of the different versions, and interviewed various Italian distributors, exhibitors, and translators of the film.

Chapter 9

FRENCH RADICAL DOCUMENTARY AFTER MAY 1968

Guy Hennebelle*

Of the various years that stand out as crucial turning points in film history--1932, 1945, 1959, 1968, and so on--the last of these is clearly the most significant for the subject of this anthology; and the proliferation of political film discourses set off by that turbulent year was nowhere more dynamic and multifarious than in France. A vivid picture of the prolific decade after May '68 emerges from the 1976 article and interview by Guy Hennebelle presented here. Hennebelle is, of course, the godfather of militant cinema in France. Through his unflagging organizing and publishing acitivites, the most current of which is the review CinémAction, Hennebelle has set the pace for much of the critical discussion about militant cinema (and thus about militant documentary) in that country, and has done more than anyone else to maintain the unique receptivity of French culture to the cinema of the Third World. Hennebelle's article, a combination anatomy lesson, diagnostic and prescription, and his interview with Iskra, the most lively of the post-May '68 collectives, may seem to North American readers to be coming from another planet, as much in the tone of their polemics against the politics and aesthetics of the Old Left as in their indifference to the anti-patriarchal struggle (a gap remedied in part since 1976). Furthermore, many of the films discussed by Hennebelle and Iskra are unknown in the English-speaking world, since their short agitational and topical orientation sentence them to neglect by commercial film importers.

*Translated from the French by Thomas Waugh

Indeed, the few titles we are familiar with tend to be those linked to the superstar auteurs of the French Left, like Godard or Marker, or to the Parisian theory wars popularized by English-language journals like Screen. All the same, the two texts manage to make clear the issues raised even by unknown films, and the rich period flavor, as they say, will no doubt compensate for any Anglo-Saxon disorientation on the part of the reader (who should in any case recognize many of the debates that have occurred in English in slightly different form and that are frequently echoed elsewhere in this volume). In addition, Hennebelle's brief discussion of political applications of video is a good compact introduction to the subject, touched upon in passing elsewhere in Show Us Life but technically outside its scope.

Hennebelle's self-criticism, seven years later, is also very interesting. Though it may bolster Anglo-Saxon stereotypes of the Gallic intellectual world, where repudiations of former positions every leap year are required rituals, its critique of Old Left dogmatism and aesthetic conservatism is ultimately more continuous with the original piece than is immediately apparent. As for Hennebelle's between-the-lines disenchantment with the Chinese (not to mention Iranian) revolution and cinema, spelled out in the intervening years in the texts he mentions, this matches similar trends on the part of North American leftists (who nonetheless are careful to avoid terms that will play into Jeanne Kirkpatrick's hands). At Iskra, however, things are still going strong, with no self-repudiations in sight and with twenty film loans per week and 2000 regular outlets at last count (1982). Whatever, reports have not yet crossed the Atlantic as to the impact of the 1981 elections on the total configuration (in which a party calling themselves socialists came to power), but what is certainly clear is that these two historical documents of the aspirations, achievements, and contradictions of the post-May '68 decade must now be seen as exactly that--history.

I. Taking Stock and Looking Ahead, 1976: A Cinema to Change the World

1983 Foreword

The following article is taken from a dossier called Militant Cinema that I published in 1976 in the journal Cinéma d'aujourd'hui (Nos. 5-6). This dossier of some 200 pages tried to be a "photograph" of different aspects of a current of political cinema born, for the most part, from the May 1968 movement in France (and which had its equivalents elsewhere in the world, as revealed at the "Rencontre pour un nouveau cinéma," organized in Montreal in 1974). The aspirations of this form of cinema, which aimed to "intervene" in social, political and cultural reality instead of only describing it, could be considered to be summarized in the 1967 Argentine manifesto, "Towards a Third Cinema," by Solanas and Getino (authors of the famous Hour of the Furnaces).

But I must say, upon rereading this article in August 1983, I really rubbed my eyes, wondering whether I was indeed the author of these lines and these judgments. While I found my approach realistic in 1976, I now have the tendency rather to judge it, seven years later, mostly ... surrealistic. Since then, many hopes have collapsed and too many "successful revolutions have led to sometimes frightful results (but obviously we must support all liberation movements struggling against all the imperialisms: whether in Nicaragua or Poland, in Afghanistan or El Salvador). It has become clear also that Marxism, if it remains perhaps a good method for analyzing societies, is revealing itself to be inoperational ... at least on the therapeutic level! And its aesthetic conceptions (as Marcuse explained in a small work, The Aesthetic Dimension) are generally deplorable. In 1977-78-79 I organized at Rennes (France) the "Days of Militant Cinema," with all of the concerned groups, to attempt to draw up an evaluation of this current. From this I published a collection of texts entitled Cinéma et politique, including notably a very self-critical reflection on "The Adventures of Political Cinema" (its adventures ... and misadventures).

Be that as it may, that current did exist. It is thus useful to publish testimonies of it, but they must be resituated in their context. I persist in thinking that the inspiration was praiseworthy, but I bitterly deplore that it was incarnated in a vocabulary and style that seem so intolerable to me today.... Enjoy reading this anyway!

1976

What balance-sheet can we draw up on the French militant cinema after eight years of experience?

The French Context

Let's first observe that the initiative of the États-généraux of May 1968, toward bringing the cinema closer to French social, economic and cultural reality, led onto three perceptibly different paths.

The first path consisted of what I have named, following others' example, "la série Z." Mainly represented by Constantin Costa-Gavras and Yves Boisset, this path involved, especially at the beginning, taking over the methods and even grabbing the "strings" of the American action cinema in order to put across the political message with the most chance of being understood by a large audience known to be conditioned by this form of filmmaking. This undertaking was more or less successful, depending on the films. As far as I was concerned, I was at first delighted that the French cinema had finally shown itself capable of dealing with certain political problems; later I tended to be more severe toward this means of advance. I saw therein, in fact, a passive recapitulation of worn-out American dramatic formulae, thus a cultural derivativeness, and, as a corollary, a woeful inadequacy in the progressiveness that I find, rightly or wrongly, characteristic of the Hollywood cinema. Despite certain persistent faults, from both the ideological and aesthetic points of view, films like Dupont-Lajoie and Special Section led me to revise a little my general estimation of the recourse to the "Z effect," which was tending, after all, to get rid of its grossest mannerisms and to refine its aesthetics. Without today being an unconditional fan of this genre, I am cognizant of its evolution and I envy it above all the public success it gets away with, while so many films with popular pretensions never really hook the massive audience they are supposed to reach.

A second path, independently of the respective

political orientation of its films, has consisted of seeking (without ever finding) a foothold in the popular national context without resorting at the same time to the methods of the Hollywood arsenal. We could mention, randomly, Martin Karmitz's Camarades and Coup pour coup, René Vautier's and Nicole Le Garrec's Avoir vingt ans dans les Aurès, and Jean-Louis Comolli's La Cecilia, and still other films such as those of Bertrand Tavernier. This tendency, disparate as much from the formal point of view as the political, seems to have led, toward the end of 1974 and the beginning of 1975, to the series called the "new natural" that, alongside films with a revolutionary tendency such as Lo Païs by Gérard Guérin, also carried with it films marked mainly by individual revolt, such as those by Doillon, Duval, Condroyer, etc.

A third tendency was characterized by films by filmmakers stuck on "deconstruction," for whom the revolution first involved concentrating on the system of forms "perfected by the bourgeoisie." Its best known spokespersons, other than Jean-Luc Godard, are Marguerite Duras, Alain Robbe-Grillet, Jean-Marie Straub, and still others who instead of contributing to the revolution by the cinema prefer to lose themselves in the formalist delicacies of a "cinematic revolution" and to try to set loose "in vitro," as they believed, the elements of a new revolutionary aesthetic. One can consider up to a certain point that the whole current sometimes called "different cinema" or "underground cinema" (in the U.S.) is moving in a parallel direction. I don't expect anything myself from these chamber exercises--at the most, some formal discoveries on the part most notably of Godard; we might be able to make use of them in constructing new aesthetics, but on condition that they be set back on their feet and are used for a clear and coherent expression. Thus, for example, there can be found in Jean-Luc Godard's Victoire, ici et ailleurs, amid a confusion of morbid, absurd and useless considerations, a few relevant reflections on the positive hero and revolutionary romanticism. But in any case, this "different cinema" scarcely deserves in my eyes the label of "avant-garde cinema," unless in the formalist and often decadent sense given to it by Solanas and all those who believe that aesthetic avant-gardes not allied to political avant-gardes which are themselves allied to the masses end up inevitably going up in smoke. Solanas declares,

> The most important issues at stake are not the languages, aesthetics, nor intellectual structures of artistic works, but historical realities of which these elements admittedly are part but in a non-determining way.... A film directed according to a language judged to be outmoded in relation to contemporary cinema can still very well play a more mobilizing and more revolutionary role than certain films called avant-garde, formalist, and aesthetically "original." In fact, what determines the old or new character of a film is its relation with its context.... If the work in question achieves its goal, it's that its ideas, its structure, its language have achieved historically a truly revolutionary and new quality since it has permitted it to expand in a creative way the margin of individual or collective freedom of a group of individuals or of a people. A work is not revolutionary because it is only innovative on the formal level.... All revolutionary cinema is a new cinema but all new cinema is not revolutionary....[1]

The True Avant-Garde of the French Cinema

But the militant cinema, which I put forward as the representative of the true avant-garde in the French cinema, does not constitute a homogeneous whole, far from it.

The overall complex of militant cinema can be analyzed from three different and complementary points of view: from the point of view of its political orientation, from the point of view of its short or long-term objectives, and from the point of view of its styles.

1. FROM THE POINT OF VIEW OF ITS POLITICAL ORIENTATION

On the political level, you may recognize that the grouping of films listed in our index below can be divided into five major tendencies:

a) Communist/revisionist films produced, directed, and distributed by the French "Communist" Party (the P. "C." F.) or by filmmakers who are more or less affiliated with it. As one can imagine, these films undertake to defend and illustrate its arguments and its cause.... In my opinion, it makes sense to distinguish in the Unicité catalogue between films that narrowly support such and such a tactic or strategy of the P. "C." F. (like Les Communistes dans la lutte, for example, devoted to an electoral campaign of Jacques Duclos) and the films of broader scope which could eventually be useful to other groups.

b) Trotskyite films: only a few, these have been produced mostly by the group "Cinéma Rouge." Except for the medium-length film on Trotsky himself, made just before 1968, there don't seem to exist films that illustrate from beginning to end a strategy that is specific to one or other of the groups that currently exist. For example, Le Charme discret de la démocratie bourgeoise, currently distributed by Iskra, incorporated quite a general progressive line.

c) Far left films. This term has tended to designate after 1968 an array of movements and groups extending to the left of the P. "C." F. Using Lenin's meaning of the label, I would classify under this heading the relatively large number of "spontaneist" films, for example. One of the most characteristic of these, in Cinélutte's own opinion (although they don't distribute it anymore) is without a doubt Chaud, chaud, chaud, devoted to the 1973 movement in the "lycées." One can suppose that a certain spontaneity lies below the surface of a good many militant films, for the simple fact of the absence of any large structured far-left organization, or from the powerlessness, to this day, of those groups that exist to lead the struggles that they sometimes initiate. There are also anarchist films: for example, Le Funambule by Serge Poljinski, who in any case no longer fully claims the film.

d) Marxist-Leninist films. Their prototype probably remains Oser lutter, oser vaincre (Dare to Fight, Dare to Win), made in 1968 at Renault-Flins by members of a no-longer-existing group, "Ligne Rouge," who were denouncing in this film the conduct of the Confédération générale du travail (the affiliate trade union of the French Communist Party), at the time in terms that are generally accepted by existing M.-L. groups.

e) Progressive Films: in reality, the majority of the militant films listed here are scarcely classifiable in a predetermined category once and for all. That's why I'm personally inclined to situate under a "progressive" heading, the majority of films that are militating, in the large sense, for the socialist revolution on different fronts and of which it is possible to make different uses.

2. FROM THE POINT OF VIEW OF OBJECTIVES

Militant cinema can exercise four different functions: to arouse spectators' enthusiasm for a given problem; to exhort targeted audiences toward one or more determined actions; to instill in spectators a political culture; to help people unmask the enemy's tricks.

The Question of the Party

These considerations, as well as those preceding them in the first paragraph, imply the famous "problem of the party" which we have encountered several times in this issue. It's a complex question on which I will not endorse a precarious and provisional position here. . . .

Firstly, it seems to me mistaken to say that we must wait for the arrival on the scene of a new truly revolutionary communist party, enjoying an effective and sympathetic hearing within the masses, before making militant films. Not that I believe, however, like certain spontaneists, that it is a question of agitation, and still more agitation, and still even more, and that finally the works will blow up. (Until we know better, I believe, along with Lenin, that "in order to make the Revolution, a revolutionary party is necessary. ")

But this stand, or this feeling, does not prevent me at all from thinking that militant films, even merely "progressive" ones can encourage people to take stands on a whole series of fronts, whether they are primary or (less) secondary (than we sometimes believe). When Yann Le Masson dwells on the limits of his short film, J'ai huit ans, he is too purist, for this film contributed, in its way, to developing at that time, the anti-colonialist awakening of certain Frenchmen. We could easily proliferate examples of this kind.

Secondly, and because of this, a militant film, even if it is not tied directly to a party's strategy, can play the far from negligible role of counter-information, of intervention, and often even of mobilization. Take the case of the films on Larzac [a rural region--ed.] or of Histoires d'A (or on the same subject, Liberté au féminin): beyond the effect of consciousness-raising around their own themes, these films were able also to arouse a more general radicalization on the part of the audience. If I'm not mistaken, it's in one of these films on Larzac, precisely, that you hear a peasant declare, "In 1968, when we saw on television the cops hitting a student, we said to ourselves, 'Serves that long-hair right!' Now that we've seen them at work around here, we think completely otherwise." ... It seems to me that, carefully used, a militant film devoted to a particular subject can instigate, as I said, a similar radicalization: in taking the spectators by the hand to lead them, in a certain way, starting from an apparently isolated event to become aware of the fact that everything is connected and that it's the capitalist system in its entirety that is responsible for the evils that the majority of people are suffering from.

Iskra was right in this sense in thinking that there's nothing wrong with becoming the "loud-speaker of the masses," especially as it is realistic to think that alongside the future party to come, there will always be an important number of progressives who will also have the right to be heard.... A militant film can play an important role in the dialectic of the line of the masses; that is to say, it can also serve to inform the leading elements of a revolutionary party by drawing their attention to a possibly neglected front and to other analogous phenomena.

I will come back a bit further on, from another angle, to this question of the "party" that is so important, but, whatever the case, the "sweeping along" effect of the militant cinema, considered all together, seems to me largely positive at the present time.

Two Kinds of Films

It is appropriate, however, to distinguish militant films that give importance to a single event (a strike, a demonstration, etc.) and those that aim at illustrating or elaborating a more general strategy or analysis. From the point of view of the far left, if there existed a powerful revolutionary party capable of guiding struggles, this distinction between the two types of films would perhaps lose its sharpness, but in the current state of affairs, I don't see how it could be otherwise.

a) Films of Single Events as Exemplary Models: such as for example the Iskra short, Scènes de grève en Vendée (Shirts and Songs) or the videotape from Cent Fleurs entitled Cérisay: elles ont osé, or else René Vautier's film, Transmission d'expérience ouvrière. In the first two, it was a question of publicizing a struggle judged exemplary on several counts, to make an example of it in order to propose some innovative tactics to workers who might end up in the same situation. In the third case, the smelter workers of Hennebont, who had believed the bosses' and the management's promises, warn their comrades at Lip, then in the heat of battle, of their mistake so that they wouldn't make the same one. There's absolutely no need, in such films, to tack on a whole analysis.... It's for discussion leaders to re-situate shorts of this type within the perspective of the class struggle. You can't ask a simple agitation film to do everything.

b) Films of analysis: we also need to have at our disposal at the same time films that articulate the ensemble of a series of facts in a demonstration founded on a more complete political vision. This was the approach, for example, of the authors of the film Attention aux provocateurs, who could avoid only with difficulty giving a lecture to evoke and denounce the chauvinist policy of the P. "C." F. on the Algerian question between 1936 and 1962. The authors of Oser lutter, oser vaincre, already mentioned, use the same approach. I believe that the militant cinema needs at the same time both agit-prop films based on single issues that allow the spread of information and thus the raising of people's consciousness, and more complex films that develop a more global explanation. This is what Video Out explains about Lip: during the struggle, it was enough to show tapes recorded spontaneously on the spot everywhere possible without editing them. Today, however, it would be desirable for a montage to be made of the material shot. It is clear that this could only be done in terms of a general interpretation of the meaning of this conflict. It's the same story for the tape on the prostitutes' revolt, also shot by Video Out. Let's add, in support of this argument, that Joris Ivens did not make explicit reference to a party in his films Spanish Earth and The Four Hundred Million: his job was simply to sensitize world public opinion to the aggressions against Spain and China respectively. It is true, however, that today, we would like to have films that would provide a global analysis of these events....

The Party, Now and Forever...

It remains that in theory one wishes for the option of a powerful and organized communist party, capable by its actions of mobilizing spectators who would have previously been informed by a film. This was the case with La Vie est à nous by Jean Renoir. And it's not by chance if in the French cinema, militant initiatives were always the work, before 1968, of the P. "C." F. or of filmmakers close to it. This tactic was situated directly within the line of Lenin's teachings and of Vertov's and Medvedkin's examples. It was the same in the U. S., members of Frontier Films being close to the American Communist Party.

If, since 1968 in France, most collectives practice a militant cinema outside of the P. "C." F., this fact can be explained to a certain extent by the lightening of equipment and the reduction of costs, but it is also explained by the refusal of the revisionist-reformist deviation on the part of revolutionary militants. As it is difficult for an isolated individual or even for a small group to function as a "collective intellectual" (as Gramsci said), one can understand for example that the far left was not capable of making a comprehensive film on May 1968, leaving the road open for the attempt of Gudie Lawaetz, which is perhaps sympathetic but assuredly insufficient and ambiguous. This fact explains also to a certain extent that it's a conglomerate of minorities (immigrants, the handicapped, etc.) who are the focus of Histoires d'A, which is otherwise excellent. One could point to many analogous examples.

Some people point out that history shows that intellectuals haven't often gotten along very well with communist parties (whether the responsibility lies with the bureaucracy of the latter or the bourgeois heritage of the former). It is reported that Borodin, the Comintern delegate in China before the Second World War, said, "Intellectuals in the face of the Revolution are like a rabbit in front of a cobra. The rabbit knows that the cobra will end up eating it, but continues nonetheless to admire it, fascinated." A comment all the more amusing or sinister, whichever you like, since the same Borodin, if I'm not wrong, was liquidated by Stalin. I don't see how it would be possible to instigate and then to preserve the revolution without a revolutionary party. In La Spirale, Armand Mattelart, Valerie Mayoux and Jacqueline Meppiel, analyzing the Chilean case, demonstrated skillfully the danger for the left of not having a coherent and effective strategy in the face of the maneuvers of a right that is itself powerfully organized.

I offer these embryonic reflections as is. What Lenin or Gramsci will come to propose to us is a vision and a strategy adapted to our situation in developed countries, avoiding at the same time the revisionist quicksand and the temptation of abstract carbon-copy mania for the Chinese-Albanian experiment, of which I naturally do not dispute the value and the attraction (especially since I saw How Yukong Moved the Mountains) but which we cannot graft onto this society, detail for detail? Personally, I haven't got the answer, but I think, as does Cinélutte, that that's no reason for not acting while we're waiting....

All the more since, with regard to fronts sometimes considered secondary, history indicates that the solution to problems situated there has rarely been well handled when it's been postponed until after the revolution. It is important that questions be asked today that we wish to see resolved after the bourgeoisie is overthrown....

The Case of Video

The case of video requires special consideration taking into account the specificity of the medium. In a remarkable study called "Video Groups Up Against the Video-Consensus," Patrice Flichy takes exception first of all to "video-organizing," which J. P. Dubois-Demée has defined in this way: "Any social and cultural organizing that uses the electronic means of closed circuit TV to get things moving in a city or a neighborhood. That implies the will to put people in touch with each other, to help them to discover, to express, to discuss and to resolve the problems they encounter." According to Flichy, this would only have the task of "resolving or at least defusing a certain number of contradictions that appeared with the extension of urban society" and would ultimately only be a "mystification," "a new means of reinforcing the inculcation of the dominant ideology."

The author suggests instead the practice of the video groups interviewed in Chapter 2, which he divides into three tendencies:

Video-action: this consists in creating a dynamic

within an event (the hunger strike of the Huet sisters, the Lip factory occupation, prostitutes' revolt, etc.), recording on location the comments of struggling people in order to give a supplementary breadth to the dynamic. The other side of the coin is that these tapes are difficult to show outside of the context in which they were made.

Video-analysis: This can group together several aspects of a struggle, whether in order to put it in focus in bringing out its principal stages, its stakes and its contradications, or to constitute an information-packet like that on L'école, gare de triage ("schools as sorting depots").

Video-tracts: Like the video analysis, the video tract is made for a larger distribution than the video-action, but by choice it is shorter, more schematic. It must also be put together quickly in order to be able to publicize the struggle while it is going on.

Flichy emphasizes that it is more a question of general themes than of tight categories and shows that video-workers have recourse by choice to different techniques: investigation, subversion of mainstream broadcasts, fiction, parallel editing of sketches and interviews, etc.

It seems that by its flexibility and easy handling, video is suitable for more varied functions than film.

3. FROM THE POINT OF VIEW OF STYLES

Aesthetics remains, to this day, the big weak point of the French (and often foreign) militant cinema. It is true that financial constraints that weigh upon the making of films can to a certain extent explain their under-development, but there are also other factors.

Militant films have access in stylistic terms to four different methods in all:

The filmed lecture on the screen black- (and white-) board: moved by a concern legitimate all the same, to explain, to make the audience understand a certain number of truths, militant filmmakers often tend to adopt a professorial tone and to prop up with a lot of intertitles a veritable filmed demonstration: a plus b equals c. During the years following May 1968, there was a real epidemic of title-itis. That was reinforced at the same time by an excessive and somewhat masochistic reaction against the idea of spectacle. Given that Hollywood and a number of other cinemas had made use of the attractions and the baits of the mechanisms of representation specific to Tinseltown to condition the spectator, we tended to want to "deconstruct" not only these artifices but also the cinema itself, held responsible for these evils. From this tendency arose the use of various tricks like black or white leader instead of images, supposed to permit a better comprehension of the soundtrack, and various other anti-cinematic and inelegant devices whose paternity can often be traced back to Jean-Luc Godard. This tendency leads ultimately to a "scholastic realism" that is particularly boring and overbearing.... The cinema remains and will always remain a spectacle. What is more appropriate to denounce are the manipulations of which it has been the object in a certain commercial cinema. Such is not the danger--far from it--in militant cinema, which suffers on the contrary from too great a formal austerity. From this point of view, Costa-Gavras is right to say, "You don't catch flies with vinegar." We must banish boredom and cultivate the notion of aesthetic pleasure.... In their films, Karmitz and Vautier choose, for example, to replace intertitles by songs, in the manner of Brechtian choruses. We can never say enough how much the French, in the theatre as well as in the cinema, have considerably distorted the concept of distancing, which they have transformed into the fig-leaf of the worst intellectualist pedantry, while the plays of Brecht were conceived also to be warm, funny, and moving. We must combat this deformation and rethink also the systematic refusal of the principle of identification....

No, creating beauty is not reactionary! Jorge Sanjines is right to say that "revolutionary films must be the most beautiful in the world."

The abuse of direct cinema: the crushing majority of militant films are shot in direct. Those that have recourse to the seduction of fiction to explain a concept or to recount an important event are rare; as, for example, La grève d'Apollon by the Italian Ugo Gregoretti, or Soyons tout by the Frenchman Serge Le Peron. This fact suggests once more the reaction against the polish and slickness of the Hollywood cinema and the will to assure oneself a guarantee of authenticity in "letting people speak" who have never had the chance. But if the direct offers these advantages, it can set loose also--and this happens too often--a tedious avalanche of words, a verbal deluge which quickly becomes tiring and which is also frustrating: in effect, it is rarely more interesting to hear someone telling past events than to see with one's own eyes the events themselves, indirect or reconstructed. But it is true that the responsibility for this state of things is due essentially to the meagerness of budgets: for example, the author of Nous sommes une force, Olivier Altman, would have preferred to reconstruct the great miners' strike of northern France of 1941 (as Sanjines did for the Night of Saint John in The Courage of the People), rather than to interview the survivors who, in front of the camera and the recorder, can only offer their memories, depriving us of a visual evocation of their deeds.

As much as the direct has undeniable advantages, it also presents an especially grave disadvantage on certain occasions: in effect, it happens that the people interviewed restore in their speech the clichés of the dominant ideology that have been hammered into them by television and other media. If they are not careful, militant filmmakers can, in spite of themselves, simply wind up rehashing the ideology they are trying to combat! The use of the direct can correspond also in certain cases to an escape from the problems that political analysis inevitably poses. We get back then to the question of the absence of a revolutionary party, evoked several times above. One gets out of it by "letting the masses speak," but in reality one only masks one's incapacity to produce a correct interpretation of the situation, to achieve the "communist decoding of the world" spoken of by Vertov.

Among those films that have avoided the excess of direct cinema, quite numerous all the same, I would mention the shorts of the Cuban Santiago Alvarez, who mixes with much intelligence filmic and other quotations, amusing or amused intertitles, jokes, caricatures, didactic sketches and other devices. I would mention also one more time La spirale, whose authors knew how to achieve a happy balance between interviews and scenes of everyday political life recorded candidly.

And finally, the medium-length film, Changhai au jour le jour by Claude Broyelle and Françoise Chomienne, who had the idea of commenting, directly on the soundtrack, on images brought back from China, as if it were a home movie. This discovery was not used enough, but it is a very effective one. It can be seen also in Vautier's Transmission d'expérience ouvrière.

I can't say often enough how false it is that direct cinema restores reality without deformation of any kind. It is better to admit frankly the manipulation and make it agreeable to the eye and the ear by making use of the whole arsenal of the cinema.

Didactic sketches: it sometimes happens that filmmakers choose to type a situation by having characters function as "ideological puppets" incarnating a position, a tendency, or a role. This is the case for example in Attention aux provocateurs, where the Algerian people, the French bourgeoisie and the communist party are "acted" respectively by three characters whose dialogue summarizes articles from newspapers or official declarations.

A variation of this method consists in having actors, professional or not, play roles that their real authors would never have accepted to perform in front of the camera, and with reason. Thus in Des dettes pour salaire, Guy Chapouille has such actors say lines that were really those of the executives of the Sanders firm that he is denouncing.

This method allows comic effects that can work well but it is clear that the danger of being too schematic looms when it is not handled with care.

Fiction: Fiction is the poor relative of the militant cinema. The rareness of its use can be explained by the eternal money problem but also, in certain cases, by the inexperience of certain filmmakers who still have not mastered the direction of actors. The refusal of fiction is sometimes deliberate: it is thought that direct cinema guarantees, as already mentioned, a greater authenticity. This assertion is verified up to a point by a comparison between Tupamaros, the militant film by the Swede Jan Lindquist, and State of Siege, devoted to the same subject by Costa-Gavras. The first one scarcely permits you to dispute the facts related. But the second has more punch. And I don't know if it is fair, ultimately, to make this comparison. The Tunisian film by Naceur Ktari, Les ambassadeurs, which reconstructs the Djelali affair (the murder of a young Algerian by a hot-tempered Parisian concierge), shows that it is completely possible to attain an impression of authenticity by the detour of mise-en-scène.

Fiction allows one to fix situations in the richness of their complexity. It permits also, better than the direct perhaps, the establishment of active heroes, positive ones if you like, capable of proposing to the audience models of actions for transforming reality. The danger of slipping into hagiography is clearly there. This has so far not yet been the defect of the militant French cinema but the Zhdanovist experience in the U. S. S. R. is there to remind us of the silliness of those characters sculpted in bronze and set against the backdrop of the sky, who seemed to be "born already red" (as Jean Narboni says). I couldn't insist too much, especially with regard to the new Chinese films, on the necessity of not erasing or of not schematizing the contradictions of life for the needs of demonstration. The opposite is true of Western Europe, where we have gone too far on the so-called Brechtian path of the refusal of identification. The contemporary militant cinema has perhaps the job of rediscovering, through a fiction that has been banned too long, the roads of a revolutionary realism of a new kind that avoids both dogmatism and spontaneity, as well as intellectualism and populism, in order to find truly popular forms--following the example of what Dario Fo is doing in Italy with the Troupe de la commune. Or in France, Ariane Mnouchkine with the Théâtre du soleil.

Toward a Far Left Cultural Front

It is impossible as I am writing to foresee the fate of militant cinema in France or in the world. Its financial bases, I've already stated, are precarious and its inspiration depends intimately on the evolution of the political situation. One can think that with time its technique and its aesthetics will improve: the years 1974 and 1975 have seen in this regard some features emerge on a level clearly superior to the previous standard. Independently of their intrinsic value or of their orientation, let's mention as examples _Bonne chance la France_, _Quand tu disais, Valéry_, _Le Ghetto expérimental_, _La Ville est à nous, les prisons aussi_, _L'Olivier_, _Histoires d'A_, _Garderem lo Larzac_, _Quand on aime la vie, on va au cinéma_, and still others that I am forgetting here. Some have finally found a commercial distributor, even if it's limited to a small bastion. The fact is that there exists in any case a vast network of militant distribution in France: through cultural centers, Catholic youth movements, unions, homes for immigrant workers and others, occupied factories, certain politicized film clubs, etc....

I would be happy if this dossier, in its diversity and its contradictions, its questionings also, contributed to reinforcing this sector of the French cinema that one can affirm is its most alive and promising one, if it succeeded in reminding us, despite several previous failures, of the usefulness of establishing a far left cultural front on the basis of the four "anti's": anti-capitalism, anti-imperialism, anti-reformism, and anti-revisionism. We must foster what Gramsci called "the ideological war of the trenches." ...

II. "ISKRA: Militant Cinema Is a Spark..."

Q. ISKRA, FIRST CALLED SLON, WAS FOUNDED BEFORE 1968. UNDER WHAT CONDITIONS?

A. May 1968 certainly gave an important shot in the arm to SLON, but the birth of our group (we became ISKRA in 1974) actually goes back to 1967. In fact, SLON (abbreviation for Service for the Launching of New Works) is the fruit of two experiments: on one side Far from Vietnam, on the other, A bientôt, j'espère. Far from Vietnam was, as you remember, a film against the American aggression in Indochina, composed of several sketches made respectively by Claude Lelouch, Willian Klein, Ruy Guerra, Agnès Varda, Alain Resnais, Michèle Rey and Jean-Luc Godard [and Joris Ivens--ed.]. But in total, there were 150 technicians who united their unpaid efforts around this project. It was a question in a certain way of a first pilot project, but in our opinion it was a failure because the "good intentions" disguised a "bad conscience." Some people participated in this project as if to "clear themselves," without calling into question their style of work and the kind of films they were making in the production-distribution system. Only some technicians stayed active after Far from Vietnam and became part of SLON. The others, especially the spearheaders, returned to make commercial and other kinds of films.

Thus it's especially from the experiment of A bientôt, j'espère that SLON got started. On this date--still in 1967--a big strike had taken place at the Rhodiaceta factory in Besançon (a factory controlled by the French conglomerate Rhône-Poulenc, which employs 3000 workers in that city). This was one of the big pre-1968 strikes, characterized by the occupation of the premises and violent clashes with police. Chris Marker, Mario Marret, Antoine Bonfanti, and others such as Jean-Luc Godard arrived on the spot and participated in the workers' actions. They felt then that there existed a really strong demand for films on workers' struggles, and also a need to make them known by means of the cinema. This was one of the first times since 1945 that filmmakers put foot inside a factory in order to place their cameras at the service of workers. In contrast to Far from Vietnam, the experiment of A bientôt, j'espère turned out to be a positive one. You could say that it gave birth, in one sense, to three groups: the Dziga Vertov group, with Godard and Gorin, no longer in existence today; Dynadia (today become Unicité), through the intermediary Mario Marret; and SLON, through Chris Marker, who was one of the founders.

TWO SPECIFICALLY WORKERS' COLLECTIVES GOT STARTED AS A RESULT OF YOUR EXPERIENCE?

That is true, in a certain way. First of all there was the Medvedkin group, at Besançon, composed of workers from Rhodiaceta who hadn't been completely satisified by A bientôt, j'espère, whose perspective they had found too exterior, even "ethnographic," Chris Marker had then proposed to the workers, taking advantage of the structure of the Centre de culture populaire, that they create a collective and shoot their own films themselves, with SLON's material and technical support. As a result of this were made Classe de lutte (by Pol Cèbe) and three shorts from the Nouvelle société series that we had inaugurated in order to group together films attacking capitalism (the title was a derisory reference to the program of Chaban-Delmas, then Pompidou's prime minister).

The other collective was the "Sochaux group." It was created by a Besançon worker who had gone to work in Sochaux.

But these two collectives have since disappeared.

SLON ALSO CONTRIBUTED TO THE COMMERCIAL RELEASE OF FEATURES LIKE ALEXANDER MEDVEDKIN'S HAPPINESS AND PATRICIO GUZMAN'S THE FIRST YEAR...

Yes, it seemed important to us to make known the admirable film of the great Soviet director Medvedkin because, beyond its aesthetic qualities, it offers many political qualities of the interventionist film. As for The First Year by the Chilean Guzman, it allowed us to focus on the Chilean situation after the first stage of the Popular Unity. It was SLON that arranged the French versions of these films. The former was released accompanied by the short Le Train est en marche (The Train Rolls On) by Chris Marker, who recalled in the film the main aspects of Medvedkin's experience in the Soviet Union in the thirties. We are now thinking of buying a commercial theatre in order to be able to distribute films that seem important to us but are rejected by distributors. We believe that the militant cinema must intervene everywhere it's possible, including the commercial network. If Far from Vietnam was a failure, it was because we were not able to control the distribution.

WHAT TODAY IS ISKRA'S TRADEMARK?

ISKRA is a distribution and production company for political films: we now have eighty in our catalogue. From the first films shot in 1967 until today, each one reflects in its own way one or several aspects of our political choices. Far from Vietnam and A bientôt, j'espère, which were, as already mentioned, the catalysts of our group, established the lines of force that have been followed up to the present, namely militant cinema based on struggles in France and those engaged in the Third World. Within this very large framework of support for the total pattern of confrontations arising from the class struggle and the war against imperialism, we intervene from a progressive point of view.

DO YOU MEAN BY THAT THAT WITHOUT TRYING TO ILLUSTRATE A PARTICULAR POLITICAL LINE, YOU ADOPT AN ESSENTIALLY PRAGMATIC POSITION?

Yes, because of its nature, this definition can only be understood in practice. A recent film illustrates this attitude well: we distribute and are arranging the French version of the film made by Edna Politi, a left zionist: Pour les Palestiniens, une Israelienne témoigne.

We don't exactly share the political convictions of Edna Politi, but for us her film contributes to bringing into focus the convergence of the criticisms of the Israeli Left against the policies of the Israeli state with the Palestinian struggle.

It's the same thing, in our opinion, for our project

on Angola, where only the MPLA is opposing all the united imperialisms. That is enough to justify our support to this organization.

IN SUM, YOU WOULD BE IN AGREEMENT WITH BRECHT, WHO WROTE THAT THE IMPORTANT THING IS TO ASK THE PERTINENT QUESTIONS THAT ALLOW THINGS TO MOVE FORWARD ...

We want in fact to provide a working tool to militants, leaving them the job of criticizing and sensitizing people along the lines that seem most right to them. Chili is a film entirely representative of this desire. Made after the coup d'état of September 11, 1973, its goal was to mobilize people entirely by the montage of newsphotos on the coup and the repression. A silent film (the Chilean Left was itself reduced to silence), it left each spectator, by means of the discourse of the montage alone, the job of drawing conclusions from the Chilean experience.... We believe that if we came across as dogmatic, we would cut ourselves off from a large part of the public, which would be completely contradictory to the goal of militant cinema, which aims for maximum mobilization. At ISKRA, people can find films that, without corresponding rigidly to their line, will serve them in one degree or other of political intervention.

DO YOU ACCOMPANY THE FILMS TO PARTICIPATE IN DISCUSSIONS?

Quite rarely. We are not against this principle, but we do so quite little (in contrast to what we did at the beginning of our existence) and even though we suggested, especially during the first year of distribution, that the director be present during screenings. That can be explained on the one hand because, not being the organ of a party, we don't feel the need to supervise the use of film in the correct direction, and on the other hand, because we think a film should stand on its own. La parcelle, illustrating union action in a rural setting against a land-grabber, Les lignards, which relates the working conditions of workers who lay telephone cables in sewers (safety and health), and P. L. M., which was made during the big strike of postal employees at the end of 1974, in close collaboration with the unskilled postal workers in the Lyons station, for example, are among the films very much in demand because they have exactly this autonomous quality. Of course, they also fulfill a demand coming out of the expansion of the economic crisis and the current strikes.

TO THOSE WHO SAY YOU'RE ONLY THE LOUD-SPEAKER OF THE MASSES: WHAT DO YOU REPLY?

This formulation overwhelms us as much as if we were accused of being a spark! And we're modestly flattered because we still have much to do in the area of amplified sound. We maintain also that this formulation could constitute a satisfactory definition of our progressive role. Do we still need to make it clear that it is not filmmakers, not even militant ones, who make revolution, but workers? It is not for us to create a political line: it's the reality of the political situation that provokes the reality of militant cinema and not vice versa.

ISKRA's political choice is that we have the reality of struggles as a starting point, giving ourselves the tasks of popularizing them, and of intensifying the movements that call into question the system in which we live.... Along these lines, we are witnessing at this moment a great contest against Justice, the soft underbelly of liberalism. We have got into this in three recent films. *L'affaire Huriez* testifies to the reality of the judiciary apparatus in our liberal system. *Pour une poignée de gros sel* uncovers how the regime, by developing the fear of muggers, manages to justify increased police strength and to create an acceptance of repression. And *De qui dépend que l'oppression demeure?* unmasks the most advanced and the most liberal industrialized society of Europe, West Germany, in the repression of the Baader-Meinhoff group, which provides us with an admirable demonstration of the manipulation of public opinion, of inhuman prison conditions, and the staging of a trial in contempt of all democratic forms.

WHAT DO YOU THINK OF THIS SLOGAN, "MILITANT CINEMA EQUALS AWFUL CINEMA," AND HOW DO YOU CONCEIVE OF THE AESTHETIC PROBLEMS OF THE MILITANT CINEMA (DIRECT-FICTION-ABSTRACTION)?

Without having always succeeded at it, we think that a militant film shouldn't be more boring than a "good" western! On this point also, we have a pragmatic attitude. We are not committed to one genre rather than another. Each subject must find the form which suits it. Even if it is true that most of our films are based on direct cinema, we produce and distribute films using all the genres.

Fiction in *Rapport O. M. S.* seemed the best means to address the problem of the vampirization of Latin America by the U. S., in organizing the traffic in human plasma.

For History Book, the Danish film, it was animation--that was the right choice. Conceived in nine independent parts of twenty minutes each, you see a sarcastic little rat walking about from the feudal world to our own, and who, refusing to believe that we arrived at the exploitation of man by man by chance, uses historical materialism to send up the works. As for Mets pas tes doigts dans ton nez: ils sont radio-actifs, it's a film that makes use of all the resources of the titles-stand for denouncing the traps of the nuclear energy solution. Even with the direct, we profit as much as possible from all that lets us get away from "dark and rough" militant films, as Medvedkin said. In Scènes de grève en Vendée (Shirts and Songs), for example, we tried to communicate the dynamism and the joy of this strike by resorting often to drawings, to color, and to popular songs subverted by the women workers to the advantage of their fight.

HOW DO YOU OPERATE? HOW MANY MEMBERS DO YOU HAVE?

Four people assure ISKRA's continuity. In addition to these are some groups or individuals who participate in the shooting or the finishing of the films that they have brought with them. Some of these become part of ISKRA, that is, they participate in technical aid, in discussions, in criticisms, and in the choice of orientations. The director of the film La Machette et le marteau came to ISKRA to finish and make the subtitles. After finishing this document on one of the least known "French" struggles of the present day (he elaborates the real situation, after thirty years of "departmentalization" in this neo-colony of Guadeloupe), he stayed to work with us. In all these cases, it's the participation in a concrete task that is decisive in someone's joining ISKRA. This very flexible mode of operation guarantees the presence of an ever-desirable internal criticism. Lastly, decisions are made by a majority.

Of the eighty films in our catalogue, forty-five are distributed quite regularly. Each week, we rent about twenty programs (and a curious but reassuring thing, they all come back to us!).... Our rentals are the lowest possible, just what allows us to replace a print when a film becomes too worn.

We guess there are about fifty spectators per screening. Half of our customers are directly political groups.

Of our catalogue, three quarters are SLON-ISKRA productions. But we also welcome with pleasure films brought to us by our French and foreign friends that we expect to be valuable and usable in France. When a film is accepted by the ISKRA collective, we can contribute technical material to its making and an actual participation in the work. Still we have to make it clear that this aid remains limited because of our financial situation, which is never very exciting. That explains the time that it sometimes takes us to arrive at a finished product. Maïs vert, for example, is a film on the changes in Portugal and the goals aimed for by the Armed Forces Movement in April 1975. From the fact that we are finishing it only now, with regard to the evolution of Portugal, it could easily see its title changed to Every Revolution That Is Not Won Can Be Considered Lost.

As soon as the film is ready for distribution, we propose to the author a standard contract based on a 50/50 sharing of receipts. One of our main battles, as a political film production company, is to refuse exclusive rights for non-commercial distribution. In effect, in our opinion, if the same film is taken up by several non-commercial distribution groups reaching different publics, its political and practical effectiveness will greatly be expanded. This is also a struggle against the information monopoly. With a minimum of advance notice, filmmakers can take back their films when they want to. Once more, we insist on this point: the political must always take the lead over the commercial.

IN WHAT DIRECTION ARE YOU HEADING IN THE FUTURE?

When you know that 10,000 parallel projection locations exist in France, you notice quite quickly that our "spark" is a little weak....

Note

1 Fernando Solanas, "Pour un jugement critique décolonisé," Cine, cultura y decolonizacion (Buenos Aires, Siglo XXI).

Chapter 10

BRECHT IN BRITAIN: THE NIGHTCLEANERS AND THE INDEPENDENT POLITICAL FILM

Claire Johnston and Paul Willemen

Of the several radical documentaries of the seventies and eighties exemplifying the aesthetic and ideological ideal of "political modernism," guided by Brechtian models and informed by contemporary film theory, The Nightcleaners may not be the most widely seen, but it is one of the best known. The following elaboration and defense of the film was offered at the 1975 Edinburgh Film Festival "Brecht Event," and together with some of the debate that ensued, constitutes a useful summary of the theoretical foundations of one of the most influential streams of political filmmaking of the last decade, as well as an intriguing case study of the contradictions of this intersection of textual activism and political intervention.

... As far as collective political filmmaking is concerned, since 1968 the practice of political cinema has undergone radical changes; along with the politicization of younger filmmakers has gone a highly eclectic aesthetic development. It is worth looking in detail at some of the assumptions behind such developments because only in this context is the unique contribution of The Nightcleaners revealed.

In general terms developments have been intimately linked to a profound ideological reaction to the Hollywood system and to the ownership and control of the television industry, involving a rediscovery of notions of "human nature," "freedom" and "self-expression." This ideological tendency is, I believe, profoundly misleading and has been a major hindrance to the development of the alternative cinema in general. It has led to the adoption of an essentially defensive stance in relation to the whole question of the constitution of the media past and present and even to its own revolutionary potential. This defensive stance has served to mask many of the problems which revolutionary cinema must face, such as the very fact that mere ideological formulae cannot but produce false solutions to political problems. In "Constituents of a Theory of Media" (New Left Review, n. 64. November-December 1970), Enzensberger describes this position as resting on the thesis of manipulation--the idea that the media comprise a concrete entity consciously performing a repressive function in society. This renders possible an idealistic belief that there can be such a thing as pure, unmanipulated "truth" and the posing of a simple solution, ideological in nature, that control of the means of production must of itself serve as some guarantee of revolutionary content. The foremost limitation of the manipulation thesis is that it lacks any adequate theory of what ideology is and how it functions in the film text--how the media as one of the ideological apparatuses of the state inculcate and transmit ideology. Ideology is not a question of conscious ideas circulating in people's heads, but is essentially unconscious in nature, consisting of a system of representations (images, myths, ideas of conceptions about the world)--a structure in which we think and act. In this sense it is inscribed into the very material practices of the cinema; it consists of the totality of the system which makes up the film text.

To make a film is to submit oneself to the rules and meanings generated by classic Hollywood cinema and by television documentary, for it is these dominant cultural modes which have set the standards of visual literacy and readability for us. Thus, in this sense, to work outside the system is still to work in all important respects within its reflection; all artistic production is a struggle within ideology. In his essay on the classic realist text (Screen, v. 15, n. 2. Summer 1974), Colin MacCabe described one of the fundamentally reactionary practices of the classic realist cinema as precisely the petrification of the spectator in a position of pseudo-dominance offered by the metalanguage--a higher degree of abstraction which speaks the truth of the other discourses in the film text. This metalanguage, resolving as it does all contradiction, places the spectator outside the realm of struggle, ultimately outside the realm of meaningful action altogether. The metalanguage offers to the spectator a point of view which is both self-evident and unproblematic and is presented as a sufficient basis for struggle. The dominance of the metalanguage not only characterizes most classic realist film texts made within the system, but most of those made outside it.

In Britain, collective filmmaking practice, despite its achievements (which have been considerable), has been particularly affected not only by the manipulation thesis and the assumptions of the classic realist text, but also by wider political misconceptions about the nature of working-class culture. A persistent limitation has been, on the one hand, a militant economism which sees the control of the means of production as a sufficient guarantee of revolutionary content, and an ultra-leftist idealism which poses the notion of working-class consciousness as the sole basis for struggle. Political cinema has been seen primarily in agit-prop terms--the instrumental means by which the "voice of the people" can be heard. Ideology is seen as a monolith propagated by the bourgeoisie through the media to manipulate and deceive the masses, who are a monolith too. For instance, Cinema Action has concentrated on documenting workers' struggles (UCS, the dockers, etc.) from an essentially workerist perspective; Liberation Films, a community-based group, on the other hand, has concentrated on more populist, grass-roots struggles within local communities, taking up a liberal/social-democratic stance, while the newly-formed Newsreel Collective is developing an ultra-leftist variant of the position. What characterizes all these films is their dependence on cinéma-vérité forms which purport to capture the world as it "really is." The effect of such a form of realism is to convey the impression of a homogeneous world--a false sense of continuity and coherence reinforced by identification: the impression that truth can indeed be manifest out there in the visible world. It embodies a belief in what Christian Metz has called "the innocence of the image, which is somehow mysteriously exempt from connotation." This unproblematic, immediate transparency of the image (discussed by Stephen Heath in relation to the photograph), legitimized by synchronous speech, constitutes a behaviorist strategy aimed at producing the impression that individuals and groups participate in some mythical unity of consciousness. Such a simple reproduction of reality tells us nothing about that reality--the real forces in operation--and yet it produces in the spectator the effect of reality, a reality from which contradiction and struggle have been eliminated.

The best films of this kind--for instance The Miners' Film made by Cinema Action and the London Women's Film Group's Women of the Rhondda--while working within the assumptions of the classic realist text and subscribing to a mythical unity of consciousness, do succeed in a real sense in exploring the strengths of "proletarian positivity" and provide at least some basis for struggle in that they help provide an understanding of the past and set up one central contradiction: between the dominant discourse of the time and that of the film text itself. In this way they are progressive in a limited, short-term sense. At worst, augmented by commentary and glib slogans, films of this kind can deny the reality of contradiction altogether (e.g. the Newsreel Collective's film on abortion) and simply present a view to be consumed by the viewer. The Nightcleaners is a film which radically challenges the assumptions behind this practice of cinema and is undoubtedly the most important political film to have been made in this country.

Before proceeding to a detailed analysis of the film it is worth saying a few words about its relation to the whole question of feminism. Feminism and how one analyzes patriarchy have posed a persistent problem for the vulgar Marxist notion of ideology, and it is significant that it has been in films such as The Nightcleaners and The Amazing Equal Pay Show, made by the London Women's Film Group, which have had to confront the contradiction between sexism and class struggle, that the limitations of the vulgar Marxist position have been transcended from an absolute necessity, as it were. For Marxist-Feminists the nightcleaners' campaign raised fundamental issues of both a theoretical and practical nature, some of which The Nightcleaners examines in detail; most importantly, the relationship between sexual oppression and class exploitation; and in addition, the predominantly middle-class composition of the Women's Liberation Movement and the "socialist tradition," especially the trade-union movement. The feminist intervention redefines what we mean by class struggle, and in this respect, The Nightcleaners offers an important contribution.

II

Our descriptive analysis is divided into two parts, corresponding to the two main subjects of the film: the analysis of a process of struggle and the cinematic presentation of that analysis.

A. First Level of Dialecticization

The first image of the film presents us with an extremely grainy closeup of a woman's face, with the titles diagonally traversing the frame. The image itself has a jerky, stop-motion movement. This opening shot draws attention to the codes associated with mechanical reproduction and iconicity, i. e., to the transforming/productive role of camera and processing techniques at play in the cinematic construction of a film text. One of the basic materials for the construction of a film being precisely iconic images, this opening in effect foregrounds the fact that these images are in no way "nature" or "real," but the product of a work of constructive transformation. Moreover, the graininess, the nature of the closeup and the jerky motion all emphasize that the "recorded" image itself has been worked on: the shot does not "scan the face of a woman," it scans the image of the face of a woman, resulting in a new, different image, setting up a tension between the image obtained through the process of mechanical reproduction (first transformation) and that same image reworked (second transformation), to some extent broken down back into its component elements. In short, the opening shot proposes two elements: the image together with the process of image construction.

This shot is followed by a shot of a clapper board and a woman talking on the telephone, immediately followed by a re-take of that shot. This arrangement, emphasizing discontinuity and repetition, introduces another crucial aspect of text construction: editing. Instead of being drawn into the film by means of "invisible" editing or by a logical succession of shots, the discontinuity and repetition focus attention on the very fact that the sequential arrangement of images is neither accidental nor self-evident, but a strategy involving exclusions and selections.

These same two shots also introduce the notion of the construction of the soundtrack, partly by referring to the function of a clapper board (synchronization of sound and image) and partly by the sudden violent eruption of sound into the silence of the opening. In this instance, the reader is prevented from considering the sound as somehow naturally emanating from the image and the construction of the soundtrack itself is underlined instead. These shots also introduce still another element into the text: they foreground the relation between the image and the pro-filmic event, i. e., between the act of filming and that which is filmed.

It would appear therefore that the first few shots of the film provide a concise but complex (de)construction of the very process of filmmaking.

At this point, a second set of images emerges, relating to the work performed by the nightcleaners and the conditions under which that work is carried out. The analytical-descriptive presentation of this work interacts with the presentation of the cinematic work necessary for the construction of a film text, the co-presence of these two work processes resulting in a mutual transformation: whereas the cinematic process was dominant initially and drew attention to itself only, the meanings produced by the foregrounding of these codes and processes alter when seen in context of the work performed by the cleaners--for example, the discontinuities and repetitions acquire a different connotation when applied to the gestures of the women; but the meanings produced by the images of women at work also change, because they are caught up in a process of cinematic construction/re-presentation--for example, certain aspects of their work, attitudes, etc. are rearranged to bring out their most salient and relevant features. This dual process of transformation constitutes the first level of dialecticization of the film.

Into these sets of images, a new device intervenes: sections of black spacing break up the flow of images. Initially, from a cinematic point of view, the black spacing re-focusses our attention on the editing work, but the alternation between image/black spacing/image, etc. also serves as an analogy for the composition of the image band itself, for this consists of a series of separate images. The "blind spots" between them, normally invisible because both camera and projector are designed to create the illusion of a continuous flow of images, are re-introduced by the marked interruption of groups of images. However, the device has more important functions than this. In the more usual forms of cinema, the filmed world (the diegesis) is presented to us as a coherent, homogeneous whole, precisely because of the apparently uncoded transparent form of text construction relying heavily on the powers of analogical representation. Every corner of the frame is "filled up." There are no gaps or absences in it. This illusion of homogeneity banishes contradiction from the frame, as the frame precisely forms the boundary of a plenitude which is the image. The insertion of black spacing destroys this imaginary plenitude, recreating gaps in the text and shattering the diegetic homogeneity, thus re-introducing contradiction into the frame. Yet another connotation of this particular device is the impression it produces of "obliterated, absent images," perhaps even impossible images, in the sense that there are important aspects of any social process which cannot be filmed. Images never present the reality of a situation, only its phenomenal surface, and even that only in a fragmentary form. In this film, not only is the illusion of a diegetic homogeneity dispelled, but also the idea that reality itself is available in the form of a homogeneous surface waiting to be filmed. Finally, perhaps the most significant aspect of the black spacing is that it allows the reader time and together provides the reader with an incentive to think. Indeed, it seems inevitable that when a reader is suddenly confronted with such inserts, this should produce the questions Why? and Why here? These are in fact the questions the reader must ask and attempt to answer in order to construct the coherence of the film for him or herself. It is therefore also imperative that the black-spacing device be repeated regularly throughout the film, because, as it progresses, there is the ever-present threat or temptation to become immersed in/submerged by the flow of images. This repeated breaking of the flow is one of the most essential aspects of political filmmaking (allowing the reader to construct a critical reading of the text as it unfolds, and not to sweep him or her along on a stream of emotionality). However, although very effective, the insertion of black spacing is by no means the only possible way of achieving this, as is demonstrated by Straub/Huillet's insertion of the car journeys through Rome in History Lessons.

To sum up this first part of the analysis: the initial images of the film present: (a) the fact of cinematic construction (a layer of recurring devices which will run throughout the entire text), and (b) the outline of the socio-political situation of the nightcleaners, i.e., the basis of the struggle. Moreover, the relation between (a) and (b) is also brought to our attention, that is, precisely, the problem of the "representation of a struggle" in cinematic terms.

B. Second Level of Dialecticization

This level depicts the social forces at work in the struggle, and their development during the period covered by the film. It proceeds by orchestrating a series of discourses in struggle: the real object of the film becomes the charting of the shifting relations between these discourses, each representing a political/ideological position within the social formation and caught up within its dynamic. In this context the term "discourse" is being somewhat loosely used to refer to series of signifiers, distributed across various materials of expression which, taken together, outline the space of a particular position outside the discourse. It is the struggle between these positions, the shifting pattern of antagonisms, oppositions and alliances which form the object of the film at this level.

1. The discourse of the nightcleaners

As the film progresses, the mode of inscription of this discourse changes from the spoken enunciation of their initial situation, predominantly presented in the form of sync-sound interviews providing the reader with information, toward images of women listening, their comments on the developments within the issues raised by the struggle being presented in voice-off. The change from immediate expression to learning, listening and drawing conclusions is underlined by means of a change in the mode of inscription, a strategy which introduces the first of the three learning processes which structure the text: the learning process experienced by the women in struggle.

One particular aspect of this discourse, the importance of which cannot be stressed enough, decisively distinguishes this film from more conventional political films. It avoids the trap of presenting the working class as an ideologically homogeneous bloc and focusses on its internal contradictions as well: e.g., the woman who continues to do night work even though it is likely to kill her, not because she cannot afford daycare facilities but because she doesn't trust anybody else with her children (the ideology of the family at work with tragic results).

2. The discourse of women's liberation

This discourse undergoes a linear development, from a position totally divorced from the struggle to a position where it assumes the role of the union (with all the contradictions and problems that such a position entails for a movement which is not--as yet--really geared to fulfill such a function). From isolated voice-off, this discourse gradually draws nearer to the focus of the struggle until finally, after a period of practical involvement, it emerges as the main organizational force. The most important point about this discourse is that it too presents a learning process, developing alongside that of the nightcleaners, converging with it and changing as a function of it.

The first intervention in this series is the voice-over toward the beginning of the film, discussing women's conditioning. However, this statement appears to lack any real connection with the images at that particular point, and intervenes as an intrusion. The second instance of that discourse, discussing women's sexuality, again appears divorced from the reality of the struggle. However, it is immediately followed by images which do establish links: the point about the sexual exploitation of women for the purposes of capitalism is echoed in an image of a nightcleaner, framed in a lit window, forming a frame within a frame and evoking, amongst other things, the aesthetic inscription of the "image" of woman as spectacle. Moreover, this image is followed by a sequence in which two women talk about the destructive results their exhausting working conditions have had on their emotional as well as their sex lives. In this way, the links between the two discourses are suggested, although still in a roundabout way. The next intervention presents the leafleting activities of the women's movement, which is one step closer to the reality of the struggle, although still largely ineffective (as the women point out themselves). Gradually, the representatives of the women's movement become more closely identified with the struggle, a shift in their position underscored by the fact that their discourse is now presented in the form of images with sync-sound, discussing strategy and practical organization, culminating in their assumption of the duties of a trade union, supporting to the best of their ability a full-time officer (May Hobbs).

3. <u>The discourse of the filmmakers</u>

By this we do not mean the discourse of the filmmakers as "authors," but only those interventions which are directly denoted in the film itself. Initially, the filmmakers are present as voice-off, asking basic questions about wages and conditions, i.e., as passive recipients of information. As the film progresses, they appear as more and more involved with the struggle until toward the end of the film they are discussing theoretical issues and aspects of socialism with the nightcleaners.

4. The discourse of the employer

This discourse is carried by a small number of people and changes in the space of the film only from a straightforward authoritarian position to a social-democratic, manipulative one. This change appears to occur under the pressure of the struggle (threat of unionization) and in the context of the requirements of capitalist competition between small employers and big ones: a "good" and "responsible" union may help an employer to eliminate his weaker competitors. It is also interesting to note that there are a series of signifiers distributed across the film denoting the absence or elusiveness of the representatives of the employers (petty officials). The radical separation between employer and worker is not only underlined by "absent" mediators, but also by the fact that the "discourse" of the employer has to be brought to the cleaners in the form of a tape recording!

5. The discourse of the spokeswoman of the nightcleaners

As the struggle develops, the discourse of the nightcleaners splits into two: that of the cleaners themselves and that of their spokeswoman (May Hobbs). She functions as the direct antagonist to the discourse of the employer. Her discourse evolves from a total immersion in a mass struggle (her speech at the Trafalgar Square meeting) toward total isolation from that struggle, as a result of organizational difficulties and a series of other pressures. Toward the end of the film, she is seen sitting alone in the frame, biting her nails, against a blank background. In order to understand how this has come about, it is necessary to chart the progress of the discourse of May Hobbs in relation to that of the unions, that of women's liberation, that of the nightcleaners and of the publicity media.

6. The discourse of the unions

This discourse is inscribed in two forms: one verbal (union representatives talking), the other processional (demonstrations and marches). As far as the nightcleaners' struggle is concerned, both activities appear unhelpful, to say the least. The union is also the main carrier of the discourse of sexism (see below): e.g., the union man paternalistically wagging his finger while laying down the law to a group of women; the two workers dancing together, connoting an explicit exclusion of women from their activities. The issues put forward in this discourse acutely pose the problem of the limitations of Laborism and its relation to the real interests of the working class: e. g. , the women saying they vote Labor because "it is the only Party for the working class. " Whether because of their organizational inertia or because of a strategic unwillingness to support the nightcleaners at that time, the result of the unions' lack of effective support is to create a vacuum filled by the representatives of the women's movement. But as that movement is not really geared for such a function, the cleaners' spokeswoman, May Hobbs, comes to lack a secure base, and in the end finds herself isolated largely because of the nature and the configuration of the discourses surrounding her.

7. There are also isolated interventions by various political figures and other observers such as the bourgeois media. The main function of these interventions, apart from placing the struggle in a wider political context, is to provide one more essential piece of information regarding May Hobbs' situation at the end of the film. The main point about the publicity media is made by the women's movement: the danger that certain aspects of the struggle will be incorporated into the capitalist spectacle: the film shows May Hobbs getting caught up in this process of incorporation, a factor which substantially contributes to her final isolation, as do the interventions by professionals in the arena of "political" spectacles (e. g. , Audrey Wise).

8. All seven of the previous discourses together act as a carrier for the discourse of sexism (particularly evident in the union-discourse), spanning across the entire text, sometimes explicitly, sometimes in the form of an unspoken problem (e. g. , in the employers' discourse). The inscription of the ideology of sexism is diffuse and fragmented because it does not relate exclusively to any single discourse or political/ideological positions, but pervades a large number of them.

9. Throughout the film, a series of other devices punctuate the text. One such element is the repeated return of shots of women working in total isolation, at night, in big empty office blocks, suggesting that, although the struggle is going on and a large number of people are learning valuable political lessons, the cleaners are still working under appalling conditions. A fact which bears repeating. Another consistent feature of the film is its treatment of the individual workers, which one might call Brechtian in the sense that

each worker is shown not only as a member of a class, sharing many characteristics with other members of that class, but also as an individual with more than just class characteristics. Finally, another punctuating device is worth noting: the use of what Brecht called "quotable gestures," such as the (slow motion) gestures of the black woman hoovering an office, the wagging finger of the trade-union representative, etc.

C. 1

None of these discourses in fact contains the truth of any of the others; none stands in a metalinguistic position vis-à-vis the others. On the contrary, each develops as a function of the discourses surrounding it. Moreover, each is tied directly to the concrete situation in which it occurs, to the historical phase of the struggle, and each is determined by the dynamic of that struggle. It is the viewer/reader who has to read the pattern of relations between the discourses and thus produce his or her own critical reading of that struggle. This means that the double learning process inscribed in the film (discourses 1 and 2) must be matched by a learning process in the viewer/reader, i. e., the learning processes forming the focus of the film must be completed by a corresponding learning, cognitive process in the reader.

It appears then that the structuring pattern of the film is provided by a double movement: on the one hand, there is the triple learning process contained within and produced by the interaction of the multiplicity of voices and which is shown to characterize this particular phase of the nightcleaners' struggle; on the other hand, there is the dialectic between the cleaners' work and the filmmakers' work as manifested in the tensions and transformations at play between the filmic and cinematic codes described earlier. The relation between these two processes is itself a dialectical one; there is, as Walter Benjamin pointed out, a "constant dialectic between the action which is shown ... and the attitude of showing an action," which may be transformed to read: there is a constant dialectic between the learning process depicted and the depiction of a learning process.

C. 2

In the present cultural context in Great Britain, The Nightcleaners figures as the most accomplished example of political cinema. But it would be wrong to assume that a mechanical repetition of its procedures is all that is now required. All elements present in the film are directly linked to the specificity of that particular phase of that particular struggle. The presentation of any other struggle would necessarily involve other "discourses" and therefore different relations between discourses, and would not necessarily revolve around the learning processes dramatized in this film. This makes The Nightcleaners a unique text constructed according to the basic principle that historical events must be presented dialectically and that "the point is to change it." It is this very principle which also guided Brecht's theatre practice/theory and which dictated the devices he would use in any given circumstances.

However, I think that in relation to this film, it would be pointless to talk of "Brechtian influences," or of a conscious application of Brechtian devices. By asking the same questions Brecht asked about the mode of representation of a political struggle, the filmmakers are impelled towards a re-invention of certain techniques, procedures and representational devices, pioneered by Brecht.

III

The Nightcleaners raises important issues for the development of political cinema in this country; if we take it seriously, it could provide a basis for a new direction in British filmmaking. At the same time, we think there are enormous problems involved--real barriers to such a development. In the first place, the lack of a critique of ideology and the state has been a persistent shortcoming of British filmmaking since Grierson, as Alan Lovell points out in Studies in Documentary. Grierson's essentially pragmatic stance saw no contradiction involved in making films about social reform within the context of state sponsorship, and one can see how his ideas in many ways affected the development of the "free cinema" movement. On the other hand, attempts at making a radical break with this structure in the 1930's in the work of such people as Ivor Montagu, the Progressive Film Institute and the alternative 16mm distribution network Kino (despite their obvious interest as prototypes for alternative filmmaking practice today) tended to assume a retrograde and moralistic stance toward the whole question of the popular nature of the cinema, seeing the mass audience as drugged by an oppressive, monolithic cultural product into a uniform passivity.

Collective filmmaking groups could offer the possibility of a radical break with the social relations not only of production, but also of consumption, and it is only if these social relations are tackled at one and the same time that the retrograde aspects of the manipulation thesis can be successfully combated. The analysis of film as an ideological product as well as a commodity means that it is necessary to work at the level of the social relations into which the cinema is inscribed in order to achieve a different constitution of the subject in terms of ideology. At the level of production, collective work, as Brecht observed, paves the way for an entirely different notion of artistic production and radically challenges assumptions about the artist in bourgeois society. But as Colin MacCabe pointed out earlier this week, collective work should not be simply defined as groups making democratic decisions, because the code of authorship comprises only one element in the totality of the film text. Brecht, as has been pointed out, did not in fact develop a theory of collective work in relation to independent cinema; nevertheless he did offer us one insight, which is that it can only be really productive in terms of the kind of knowledge it produces. The practice of filmmaking involves, in these terms, not only control of the means of production but a struggle in ideology. At the level of consumption, showings of films in the women's movement and on the Left in general should be orientated much more toward challenging the artificial division between work, which is "productive," and leisure which is seen exclusively in relation to consumption. New social relations of consumption for political cinema would involve creating a situation in which the viewer is not only able to participate, but is required to do so. The act of filming and the act of viewing comprise two moments of equal value, neither having priority over the other; just as the filmmakers produce the film text, so the viewer must work on the film text--to achieve the process of meaning-production which is the film. It is particularly important that this work is carried out on the Left and in the women's movement at the present time, where political film is seen in the most functional and/or philistine terms and where the critique of film as an ideological product is almost totally absent. The kind of accompaniment of film which prevails at present involves using films as an excuse to discuss "political issues." Here it is the film itself which is seen as the "political issue."

A radical change in the social relations of production and of consumption at one and the same time highlights one final, central problem which is, of course, the present very sharp divide between political filmmakers and film theorists. Our present mutual distrust is based on internalized remnants of the good old bourgeois distinction between "doers" and "thinkers"; the notion of the filmmaker and the viewer both having an equal part to play in the process of text production offers some way out of this ideological impasse and moves towards the notion of a generalized activity of reading/writing as a pleasure/knowledge-producing process.

DISCUSSION

Y: Could you clarify how the film was received?

Claire Johnston: On the whole it's been very badly received in the women's movement, especially perhaps by women who were very much involved in the campaign and saw the film originally as a campaign film. It was initially intended to be made in a cinéma-vérité manner (which produces rather interesting formal effects in that it's shot in one way and at the editing stage it was transformed into something else), there was a very close involvement between the filmmakers and women's liberation, and there were expectations that it would be a useful campaign film for the nightcleaners' struggle, but in terms of conventional notions of agit-prop, of course, the film didn't fulfill those needs at all.

Paul Willemen: Most of the real objections came from people not involved in cultural struggle at any level, people who tend to see their actions as interventions in economic struggles: the militant Left in general. I have very little information about the reception in the working class, but there would presumably be ideological difficulties, at least initially.

Y: Who would the campaign film have been shown to if the initial plan had in fact been carried out?

CJ: The purpose of the campaign film was to make money

for the campaign and to generate interest and discussion about the issues within the women's movement and on the Left in general. The idea was to make a film very rapidly in the manner of the Newsreel Collective now, who aim to make about a film a month, and to use that film as the abortion film has been used in the abortion campaign. Such films are seen as having a very short life, and being used for very specific purposes--a very functional, instrumental notion of cinema.

Y: Isn't it possible to combine both processes into one by filming in a cinéma-vérité way for use in a campaign, and then cutting something more culturally meaningful afterwards, using the same material?

CJ: That's a question of the work involved in making even the simplest film. The Berwick Street Collective work full-time at filmmaking, where most of the other groups, the Women's Film Group for example, can only do it in their spare time, and even the Berwick Street Collective have to do commercial work to support their political activities.

PW: But there are also serious ideological problems involved in the cinéma-vérité method with its ideology of transparency. To make a quick film like that might do more harm than good.

Martin Walsh: In your opening remarks about the nature of cinematic discourse itself, you said that in The Nightcleaners we are made aware of it at various levels. I agree that is so in the opening, but it seemed to reach a stasis very quickly, and the freeze-frames and slow motion later in the film seemed to me at least to sentimentalize and romanticize the issues in a manner reminiscent of the German New Objectivity of the 1920s or the Dorothea Lange/Eugene Smith photography of poverty. There's a high-angle closeup of the face of a cleaner in which her eyes gradually close in resignation. It's so emotionally loaded that it begins to eliminate the level that is there in the opening scenes.

PW: First of all, there is, as Claire pointed out, a tension in the film between the humanism and sentimentality involved in shooting cinéma-vérité and its transformation by other cinematic procedures. As for the sentimentality, which I would rather call emotion, in that particular shot, there is nothing inherently evil in having a certain emotion and identification provided it doesn't carry away the rest of the film.

In this case, I don't think it does carry it away precisely because of the formal procedures which have been used to transform this essentially cinéma-vérité shot and the political weight put on it which is that of a contradiction for the working class. The sentiment is generated by the fact that you know she is going to die because of that contradiction.

MW: But there's a lack of any commentary on that when the image occurs, and such images occur at many points. You can't take a photograph and just leave it there, it needs some kind of commentary to clarify the meaning.

PW: I think the commentary on that meaning is precisely its insertion in a continuing series of shifting discourses. Its commentary is its political weight, the political load it carries. The sentimentality or emotion is a surplus. There is a humanist overtone, precisely because the film was shot in a cinéma-vérité style, but that is criticized because the cinéma-vérité has been dismantled.

CJ: That tension has been interpreted rather differently within the women's movement, where that manipulation of the image has been seen as an attempt to objectify women, i. e., as going against identification, towards objectification.

P: You talked about the black spacing between the images as one of the formal structures that criticize this use of the image. But the black spacing throws a great deal of weight on the image it surrounds, emphasizing the absence of commentary. Where I thought this was most crucial was in the use of images of the family and children, which were given great weight as images but went uncriticized.

PW: Who were you expecting to criticize them? Those images of the family do have the connotations of family ideology, and this is linked to the other image we have been discussing, but it is one of the objects of the film to provoke the audience to criticize some of its images, as you are doing now. There are also wrong images in it.

C: The film started out visually as an agit-prop film and then through a radical reorganization and distortion became a kind of theoretical film. Do you see this as a model for future production? Is it possible to conceive of films, perhaps for another kind of audience, that accept the tension between agit-prop and theory, or must theoretical films be made first and political films only later?

PW: In answer to your question I'd like to refer to a film which I would really call theoretical, rather than The Nightcleaners, and that is Penthesilea. That is a film which deals precisely with the theoretical problems of cinematic construction and the ideology of patriarchy. The Nightcleaners does raise theoretical issues when compared with the dominant mode of making political films today, but it is not primarily concerned with those issues. The problem is whether a primarily political film of this type can proceed on these, for want of a better word, avant-garde notions of cinematic construction. I think it's an absolute necessity that it be tried, because at present I do not see any other form within British political filmmaking that counters the ideology of immediacy and transparency which is central to the notion of a coherent working-class ideology, i.e., to workerism. I hope it is the first in a long and fruitful line. But obviously there are all the initial difficulties. Additional information and theory have to be supplied, at least initially, until the form has become a habit. But the primary function of The Nightcleaners is to create political knowledge. As far as I'm concerned I have learnt a lot about the politics of the nightcleaners' struggle from the film.

S: The most significant thing you seem to be saying about the film in the end, though, is that it's made in Britain. A lot of the claims you are making for its formal properties, and even to a certain extent about the way it presents the woman question, can be made for Godard's films. Pravda or Le Gai savoir or Tout va bien contain the techniques you have been discussing and the concern you are articulating; the only significant difference about The Nightcleaners is the fact that it was made in Britain. Isn't that somewhat nationalistic?

CJ: It's not nationalistic. We're making an intervention in British film culture, and the last section of the Brecht Event is about the relevance or not of Brecht in Britain. As Alan pointed out yesterday, there is a tendency to look across the Channel for all one's cultural references. British cinema does present real problems, its conservatism must be confronted, and also the limitations posed by the lack of Marxist theory. The point about Brecht is that he came from a very vital Marxist tradition. You don't have that tradition here.

PW: I would agree that there are a lot of formal procedures

which are very similar to those used by Godard, but it's very striking that some people who had been involved in the nightcleaners' struggle and had adored Godard as a great universal artist violently objected to The Nightcleaners applying those things at home. They were OK so long as they were exotically artistic over the Channel, but not once the point was a concrete analysis of a concrete situation that they were actively involved in and that they had to learn something about. And there is a crucial difference between this film and all Godard's, and that is the very fact that we talk about Godard. Even the Dziga Vertov Group is just a super-auteur; the notion of the individual artist is still at work. In The Nightcleaners, there is no artistic auteur at all....

Z: How is the film in fact being distributed?

Berwick Street Collective: As Claire said earlier, the film doesn't fulfill the messianic functions the organized Left--the Communist Party, the International Socialists, the International Marxist Group, etc.--require of a film. Our struggle is in a sense as much with the Left as it is with the filmmaking tradition we come from. The distribution will largely have to rest with us, for we have to struggle with the Left's notion, for example, of what the working class will understand, what they mean by understanding. If somebody doesn't understand something, and if in the middle of a viewing someone gets up and says, "I'm bored to tears with this," we the filmmakers have to be there to discuss it. The film isn't meant to be shown with everybody unanimously understanding it, it offers itself to be argued with. The film encourages argument, which the Left don't particularly like in a meeting. So we have to fight with them. At the moment it is a losing battle. The short term validity of agitprop films at the moment is the fact that in a period when the revolutionary movement is at an extremely low ebb, you can send them by rail to someone who knows nothing about them but picks them up and shows them that evening to an audience which has no preparation for those particular films, and a certain minimum amount of information is conveyed and enthusiasm generated. The problems presented by a film like The Nightcleaners, which demands so much energy and effort from the people who see it, can't be resolved within the confines of that practice. It presupposes the development of an understanding of film on the part both of the people who are to see it and on that of the people who wish it to be seen. Whether in a few years time this is a film one would want to show is very much open to doubt, but it does pose a question about how films are seen at the moment.

S: But it is in fact distributed like that. I booked the film from the Other Cinema and they just put it on a train addressed to me.

Berwick Street Collective: The question is who are you, how did you hear about the film, and what was it that brought you to the point of asking to see that film? Did you go through the Other Cinema catalogue and decide by the title, well, I shall see that film because I like the subject, or had you heard something about it, or were you involved in the nightcleaners' struggle?

S: I work in a college of education and booked it in the context of studying documentary filmmaking.

Berwick Street Collective: Well, that's a very different notion of looking at films from that of most political audiences or filmmakers.

CJ: That underlines the fact that there is a gulf between radicalism in film criticism, which already at this moment has a place in the educational structures, and radicalism in film practice. Trying to bridge that gulf is a massive problem in its own right. It is at the moment easier to use The Nightcleaners in film education than in any other way. That's not to invalidate talking about Brecht within an educational context, of course, but there remains the problem of bringing that discussion closer to filmmaking. That was one of the aims of an enterprise like this seminar.

Chapter 11

THEORY AND PRACTICE OF THE REALIST DOCUMENTARY FORM IN HARLAN COUNTY, U.S.A.

E. Ann Kaplan

Appearing at about the same time as The Nightcleaners and addressing an apparently similar topic, Harlan County, U.S.A. seemed to be coming from the opposite end of the aesthetic and ideological spectrum from its British counterpart, if not the opposite end of the universe. This most famous of all radical documentaries of the seventies seemed to rise above its sharply etched context by virtue of the timeless classicism of its imagery. E. Ann Kaplan brings both a theoretical and a personal approach to bear on this and other contradictions around Harlan County, the already legendary, exemplary model of the progressive realist documentary form.

Recent film theory, influenced by semiology and structuralism, particularly as articulated by Roland Barthes, Christian Metz and Jacques Derrida,[1] has shown that film of all types, including documentary, makes use of signifying practices, which, structured like a language, are already symbolic. All film is thus ultimately "fiction": images structured in time and space in a series of patterns arranged according to the filmmaker's view of the world, which often reflects the dominant codes through which a culture apprehends "reality."

As Derrida has noted, we have difficulty perceiving

art in this way because the conventional commitment to the voice as the primary means of communication commits us "to a falsifying 'metaphysics of presence,' based on the illusion that we are able ultimately to 'come face to face with objects.'"[2] We cling to the belief that there is "some final, objective, unmediated 'real world' ... about which we can have concrete knowledge," and there will always be kinds of art that "appear to involve an apparently straightforward and stable commitment to an unchanging world 'beyond' themselves."[3] In addition, as Todorov and other structuralist critics have pointed out, art works always depend on those that have preceded them; thus, as an artist begins to work, he/she automatically refers to the signifying practices used by people in similar genres.

In film, of course, the genre that appears most confidently "as a window through which ... [the] world is clearly visible" and where "the signifiers appear to point directly and confidently to the signifieds" is the documentary. Eileen McGarry, summarizing structuralist and semiotic theories, has shown that long before the filmmaker arrives, "reality itself is already coded, first in the infrastructure of the social formation (human economic practice) and secondly by the superstructure of politics and ideology."[4] McGarry calls that "which exists and happens in front of the camera" the pro-filmic event, and claims that even in the case of non-fiction films, this event is coded. "Even if the filmmakers attempt not to control or encode the pro-filmic event," says McGarry, "certain decisions about reality are made: the choice of subject and the location of shooting (not to mention the preconceptions, no matter how minimal, of the filmworkers), all participate in, control and encode the pro-filmic event within the context of the technology of the cinema and the dominant ideology."[5]

It would be interesting to examine political films largely by and about women (like Janie's Janie, Union Maids, With Babies and Banners, Rosie the Riveter) in the light of semiology and structuralism, but Kopple's Harlan County, U. S. A. warrants study particularly since it raises the issues directly. McCall and Tyndall, for instance, have argued that Harlan County, U. S. A. is not politically radical because "the social events were portrayed instead of confronted," the filmmakers failing "to foreground their intervention in the actions they showed." Tyndall and McCall assert that Kopple maintains "the conventional position of the filmmaker as the person with 'knowledge' and the audience as consumers of that knowledge."[6] Although this clearly has some truth, and raises questions that need exploring, it is too monolithic, as we'll see. So, although the film is not at all self-consciously experimental (in the manner, say, of the British documentary The Nightcleaners), it provides an opportunity to explore the differing levels of symbolic communication between what we conventionally call "fiction" and "non-fiction" film.

So far as I am aware, structuralist critics make little distinction between cinematic signifying practices as used with a script and actors, and those used with real people and real events. Yet it is only up to a certain point that things remain the same. The device of pretending to be making a documentary, used by both Mitchell Block and Michelle Citron, reveal how differently placed the spectators are when they believe that they are watching cinéma vérité or watching fiction.[7] While it is true that a documentary is a signifying practice and thus removed from lived experience, it seems to occupy a status differing in some measure from that of signs that are produced in a studio or in a fashion that assumes fiction-proper from the start.

The degree to which a documentary may be said to belong on the level of fictional signifying practices depends on the degree to which it follows routinely the conventions of its particular sub-genre, or perhaps takes off from fictional political films about real events (which of course lie totally within the domain of fictional signifying practices). Harlan County is interesting in working on several levels as a documentary and thus allowing us to see various possibilities for this kind of film.

To begin with the level that McGarry talked about: obviously, the film is no simple recording of any "unmanipulated reality," or a reflection of life as it presents itself, but a highly structured argument about the strike and the union from the miners' point of view. Kopple, of course, makes no attempt to disguise her rhetorical strategy (as for instance classical Hollywood filmmakers do); the point of enunciation (herself and the Union leaders) is at times exposed in the process of filming; and the audience knows that it is being persuaded of the justice of the miners' cause, and the brutality and greed of the bosses.

Kopple's main technique for this rhetorical strategy is careful use of sound and of editing. She makes her points by careful interweaving of several different themes, juxtaposed so as to demonstrate the plight of the miners. (Kopple is here relying on montage very much in Eisenstein's style.) One of the themes is the history of past struggles as narrated by interviews with an old couple and accompanied by newsreel footage of the times being talked about; a second theme is that of the women's lives specifically--their domestic hardships, the problems raising children, the fear for the lives of their husbands on whom they depend; a third theme is that of the history of the United Mine Workers Union, especially its corrupt phase under the leadership of Tony Boyle when the Kentucky miners were involved in democratizing the union; a fourth one is that of the poor medical care given the miners, particularly in relation to black lung disease. These themes are all interwoven with the main event in the present--the strike protesting the company's refusal to let the miners join the UMW instead of being forced to belong to Duke Power, the company union--to which the film returns periodically. The powerful, militant music of a Kentucky miners' group that is on the track for much of the film underscores the strong visual support for the men.

When the structuring becomes extreme, the film works on a second level close to that of fictional reenactments of political events, like Salt of the Earth. At these times, the signifying practices are being used in the self-conscious manner of a classical Hollywood genre that makes the images one further level from actuality, although in fact the people are not actors, the events not scripted in the usual sense. Most documentaries use similar cinematic codes: i.e., the filmmakers interview people, intercut speeches from relevant parties involved, fill in intervening events (either by voice-over or titles), and interpret and comment on what is happening (by voice-over or by editing). Documentary filmmakers generally rely on sound devices and editing to present their points of view since they have little control over mise-en-scène or lighting, and rather little over camera set-ups. These devices are as much conventions of the genre as are those familiar in Westerns or gangster films.

On this level, we begin to get carried away by the narrative of the strike that follows a pattern much like that in Salt of the Earth. The event, of course, is one that lends itself naturally to dramatization: there are picket lines, union meetings, confrontations with the scabs being shipped in, scenes showing the miners' flagging interest in the cause, and discussions of the appalling working conditions and accidents. A lot of these shots seem so familiar from previous strike films that our attention is drawn away from this particular strike. One has the sense one always has in classic Hollywood genre films, of having been through all this before, of knowing how it will end. We become so carried away by the narrative structure that we expect the film to end at certain dramatic moments, e.g., after the funeral of a young man shot on the picket line one morning, or when the miners finally win their right to have a union. We recall the victory at the end of Salt of the Earth and half expect an equally satisfying "ending" in Harlan County, U.S.A.

But the film has all along been working on yet one other level, outside, that is, of what I have called its rhetorical level and its "fictional" genre level. This is the level that can only happen in the documentary (but as I've noted does not necessarily happen) because documentaries deal with real people and real life. At times Kopple breaks through even the codes of the documentary that, as I've noted, are one degree less self-consciously symbolic than codes in fiction films. This happens because of the special situation of the film's making--a situation that gets reflected at certain moments in the film.[8]

For Harlan County, U.S.A. is one of those rare documentaries (The Battle of Chile is another) in which the filmmakers get caught up and intimately involved in the situation that they are filming. Kopple began filming the Miners for Democracy movement, led by Arnold Miller, in 1972. When Tony Boyle was forced out of the leadership and the miners in Harlan County struck for union recognition, Kopple moved to the area to cover it for the next year, and ended up staying three. From her interview with Chuck Kleinhans, it is clear that she quickly became part of the strike in the sense of wanting to help the miners further their cause. She deliberately used her camera to this end: "Because I had a camera in my hand," she says, "I could talk to the union leadership, the coal operators, the gun thugs, the UMW organizers, and the rank and file. It was an incredible influx of information. And then I would communicate and relate that to the people in different courses of the struggle." Thus Kopple is no longer the outsider, observing, filming and arranging her shots; she is rather an involved participant, if not also a kind of organizer, aiming to use her access to information as "filmmaker" for political ends. At one point, she notes, interestingly, that "even if I didn't have any film in the camera it was important for me to be there because having a camera there kept down violence." The experience, she says, "was part of my life. I was there, and I lived there for a long time, and I lived with them, and I wanted to stay."[9]

It is these attitudes, inscribed in the film, that give it its special quality of a unique relation to the struggle that she is filming. For instance, in one sequence, where the Miners are out early on the picket line and suspect that the bosses' henchmen are going to open up fire on them, we know that Kopple and her crew are there, risking their lives along with the picketers, partly because they believe that their presence may prevent the violence, but also to show their solidarity with the cause. A truculent bosses' man drives up and asks Kopple for her press card. Kopple keeps her camera fixed on the man and begins to turn his question back to him, asking him for his papers: how does she know he's got the authority to question her? It's a beautiful moment, one that suddenly makes us recognize Kopple's own presence: we understand the reality of the camera's and Kopple's being there that morning on that line together with the miners, willing and ready, along with them, to take what happens. A second and similar example of such a moment is the time when the women picketers confront the sheriff when he comes to arrest them. They begin to argue with him, trying to shame him because he's playing the bosses' game. We see him wavering, caught off guard, not knowing how to proceed since the women's arguments have some truth: they are asking him to be a real human being and decide for himself what is the responsible thing to do. But he turns out to be a man who can only follow orders and function within a well-defined role. Kopple again catches something spontaneous that reveals exactly where people in authority were.

For me, perhaps the most moving parts of the film on this level are the largely unstructured shots of the women, who, as in Salt of the Earth, move to the center of the action as the film goes on. Kopple managed to create enough trust for them to allow her to be there at meetings, apparently relatively unnoticed, so that we see the various phases that they move through. We see them supporting each other, or divided about how to proceed; we are shown strong, brave women whose dedication never flags and whose pain and suffering make us weep and wonder how they can go on. We see them break down and cry, and yet pick up and begin again. By comparison, the conventions used to express pain in the fictional Salt of the Earth (as for example, in the scene where Ramon's beating by the bosses' henchmen is intercut with his wife's painful childbirth) seem extremely contrived.

How are we to talk about sequences like these? The spectator is clearly in a special relationship to the screen images, given that we are watching real suffering and genuine danger, as against acted suffering and danger. Our voyeurism, necessitated by the mechanism, has a different quality: we cannot simply be passive observers, enjoying vicariously as in a fiction film, the thrill of expected conflict, the comfortable suffering of a struggle we know is not real.[10]

The problematic nature of these images, that arises from the fact that we know we are watching events that actually took place in the natural world, is most clear in the sequence showing a funeral for a young man killed on a picket line. We are caught between a desire to respond on a level different from that in fiction films, and an inability to experience the loss as the miners were feeling it. One has a sense of being asked to be too intimate, of an awkward inadequateness.

So there is an interesting ambiguity about all these sequences; on the one hand, they show a refusal to imitate/reflect the dominant codes through which "reality" is mainly presented to Americans--neither the suffering nor the violence is dramatized, stylized or sensationalized. But on the other hand, the film does fall into the trap of believing that there is "Some final, objective, unmediated 'real world' ... about which we can have concrete knowledge." In Kopple's case, this "real world" is that of a socialist vision; but given her lack of sensitivity to the whole issue of codes, the cinematic apparatus, and signifying practices, she did not strive to make this perhaps strange, and certainly unpopular, notion of "reality" acceptable to people brought up on TV culture and trained to appreciate quite other codings. Students, for instance, often laugh out loud at the images in Kopple's film because the people do not fit the "glamorous" images TV trains us to see as "normal"; or they complain that the film is pure "propaganda," a one-sided ("unfair") depiction of the issues.

It is these responses that give some validity to McCall

and Tyndall's comments about Kopple setting up her film for the most part so that the audience are consumers of a special "knowledge" that she alone has. Paradoxically, this kind of cinematic structure works best with those who already have the "knowledge" that she wants to communicate, although it may also work to stimulate non-unionized workers to press for unionization (i. e. , as an organizing tool--which was, after all, one of her main aims in making the film).

The miners, Kopple and her crew in fact used the film as an organizing tool in the press conference that followed the screening at the Lincoln Center Film Festival in 1976. The projectors went off, the lights came up, and onto the stage stepped the musical group we had heard during the film to continue playing in the flesh. Shortly afterwards, Kopple and her photographer came on stage, along with several of the strikers whom we had also just watched in the film. The discussion that followed focussed not at all on the film _as a film_ but rather on the content, the issues it had raised. People wanted to know what had happened since Kopple stopped filming, and we learned that the most active strikers had been blacklisted, that scabs continued to be brought in, and that the Ku Klux Klan had begun a campaign to divide white and black workers. We also learned that one of the women's husbands, who had been sick with black lung disease, had since died, and the audience were urged to write to Senator Javits to revive legislation in connection with the disease and to help in any other way they could. One left Lincoln Center not thinking much about what sort of film experience one had had, but rather, mulling over the bravery and strength of these men and women, whose daily reality is a continuous struggle for ordinary rights, in a situation where the odds are stacked against them by a company that all but owns them.

We have thus seen that _Harlan County, U. S. A._, because of its very lack of self-consciousness about itself and its signifying practices, provides an opportunity to explore the various levels on which documentaries of this kind function, and the problems caused by the unconscious slipping between levels. Recently, political filmmakers have begun to make films showing an extreme awareness of form and of the cinematic apparatus, refusing to fall into the kinds of traps Kopple gets herself into. While I very much appreciate the kind of formal interventions filmmakers like Sue Clayton and Jonathan Curling, Jan Worth, Jo Ann Elam, etc. are making, I must admit a certain nostalgia particularly for those moments in Kopple's film when spectators are brought right into an intense political struggle as it is actually happening. While it is true that the resulting inspiration for political struggle may last only a few moments, I'm not sure that the new documentaries are any more effective. What is now needed is a careful look at the new formal strategies to see exactly where they take us theoretically and politically.

Meanwhile, it is interesting to note in conclusion how far Kopple got in distributing her film just because its strategies were not experimental. First of all, she was one of the first independent leftist documentary filmmakers to have a film shown at the New York Film Festival; second, she managed to get distribution at Cinema I in New York, where the film played for at least two weeks; and finally, the film received or was considered for several important awards. While most of this success was a result of Kopple's own unflagging energy and drive, she did show that an independent filmmaker could get further with effort than people had hitherto realized. Independent political films now have an established slot in the New York Film Festival, and hitherto independent directors, like Claudia Weill, are getting contracts with major film studios. Perhaps we are finally entering an era when discourses other than the establishment ones can enter the commercial stream, provided, of course, that the cinematic devices remain essentially conventional. We may have to decide how far this kind of success is worth the compromises.

Notes

1 _Cf._ especially Roland Barthes, _Mythologies_ (1957) (London: Paladin, 1973); and _Elements of Semiology_ (1964) (London: Jonathan Cape, 1967); Christian Metz, _Film Language: A Semiotics of the Cinema_, trans. Michael Taylor (New York, 1972); Jacques Derrida, _Of Grammatology_, trans. Gayatri Spivak (Baltimore and London: Johns Hopkins Press, 1976).

2 _Cf._ Derrida, _op. cit._, quoted in Terence Hawkes, _Structuralism and Semiotics_ (London: Methuen, 1977), p. 145.

3 _Ibid._, p. 143.

4 Eileen McGarry, "Documentary Realism and Women's Cinema," _Women and Film_, Vol. 2, No. 7 (Summer 1975), p. 50.

5 Ibid., p. 51.

6 Anthony McCall and Andrew Tyndall, "Sixteen Working Statements," Millenium Film Journal, Vol. 1, No. 2 (Spring/Summer, 1978), p. 36.

7 Spectators typically feel "betrayed," "cheated" when they realize that what had seemed to be "real life" interviews were in fact scripted and acted. This reaction shows that the spectator sets up a different way of attending to screen images, depending on whether they are watching vérité or fiction films.

8 For a full discussion of these issues, see Noel Carroll, "From Real to Reel: Entangled in Nonfiction Film," in Philosophy Looks at Film, ed. Dale Jamieson (New York: Oxford University Press, 1983); I also have a much longer discussion of issues around the realist debate in feminist film criticism in Women and Film: Both Sides of the Camera (London: Methuen, 1983)

9 Chuck Kleinhans, "Interview with Barbara Kopple," Jump Cut, No. 14, pp. 4-6.

10 Semiologists by and large refuse to recognize any possibilities of different "levels" in signification in relation to the "real." This position is clear in a recent article by Noel King, "Recent 'Political' Documentary--Notes on Union Maids and Harlan County, U.S.A.," in Screen, Vol. 22, No. 2 (1981), pp. 7-18. For the moment, I am taking the sort of position that Metz argued for in an interview. Asked if he thought a documentary of a strike could be misleading "insofar as it assumes that knowledge is unproblematic, and on the surface," Metz replies:

> If the film has a very precise political and immediate aim; if the filmmakers shoot a film in order to support a given strike ... what could I say? Of course it's o.k.

Talking specifically about Harlan County, Metz continues:

> It is the kind of film that has nothing really new on the level of primary/secondary identification, but it's a very good film.... It is unfair, in a sense, to call a film into question on terms which are not within the filmmaker's purpose. She intended to support the strike and she did it. It's a marvelous film and I support it.

("The Cinematic Apparatus as Social Institution--An Interview with Christian Metz," in Discourse, No/1 [Fall, 1979], p. 30.)

Chapter 12

FEMINIST DOCUMENTARY: AESTHETICS AND POLITICS[1]

Julia Lesage

The unrivalled doyenne of American feminist film scholarship, Julia Lesage here presents a work that is simultaneously a case study of two exemplary feminist documentaries, a comparison of the two divergent branches of feminist film practice already established by the dialectic of The Nightcleaners and Harlan County, U.S.A., an encyclopedic chronology/evaluation of the first decade of independent feminist filmmaking in the United States, an analysis of the political and theoretical base of feminist media activism, and a political and aesthetic manifesto whose implications range far beyond the borders of the feminist community--all inflected by the author's concrete experience as teacher, activist, and editor.

Feminist documentary filmmaking has developed as a cinematic genre related to a political movement, the contemporary women's movement. One of that movement's key forms of organization is the affinity group. In the late 1960s and early 1970s in the United States, women's consciousness-raising groups, reading groups, and task-oriented groups were emerging from and often superseded the organizations of the anti-war New Left.[2] Women who had learned filmmaking in the anti-war movement and previously "uncommitted" women filmmakers began to make self-consciously feminist films; and other women began to learn filmmaking specifically to contribute to the movement.[3] The films these people made came out of the same ethos as the consciousness-raising groups and had the same goals.

Clearly the cinematic sophistication and quality of political analysis vary from film to film. Here I offer an in-depth discussion of two feminist documentaries which are dissimilar stylistically, and each of which I value politically and cinematically. One, Self Health, follows that artistic tradition in painting, literature, and film that can broadly be characterized as "realist."[4] The other, Rape, comes out of the politically motivated avant-garde, and it can be characterized as an "experimental" film. To consider more works in detail would be beyond the scope of this article. My main concern is to describe the emergence of the feminist documentary as a genre, the aesthetics, use and importance of this genre, and its relation to the movement from which it sprang--a discussion important to any consideration of the aesthetics of political films.

The Realist Films

Many of the first feminist documentaries used a single format to present to (primarily female) audiences the ordinary details of women's lives, thoughts--told directly by the protagonists to the camera--and frustrated but sometimes successful attempts to enter and deal with the public world of work and power. Among these films are Growing Up Female by Julia Reichert and Jim Klein, Janie's Janie by Geri Ashur, and The Woman's Film by the women of San Francisco Newsreel. Other films dealing with women talking about their lives include Kate Millett's Three Lives, Joyce Chopra's Joyce at 34, Donna Deitch's Woman to Woman, and Deborah Schaffer and Bonnie Friedman's Chris and Bernie. Some films deal with pride in the acquisition of skills, such as Bonnie Friedman's film about a girls' track team, The Flashettes, or Michelle Citron's study of her sister learning the concert violin from a woman teacher, Parthenogenesis. Others have more political analysis and are often collective productions; they have provided a feminist analysis of women's experience with the following: (a) prison (Like a Rose by Tomato Productions; We're Alive by California Institute for Women Video and UCLA Women's Film Workshop); (b) the health care system (Self Health by San Francisco Women's Health Collective; Taking our Bodies Back by Margaret Lazarus, Renner Wunderlich, and Joan Fink; The Chicago Maternity Center Story by Kartemquin Films; and Health-caring by Denise Bostrom and Jane Warrenbrand); and (c) rape (Rape by JoAnn Elam).

It is no coincidence that films about working-class women show their subjects as the most confident and militant about their rights in the public sector, and their willingness to fight for those rights. Yet even these films, from Madeline Anderson's I Am Somebody to Barbara Kopple's Harlan County, USA, focus on problems of identity in the private sphere--how one strikeleader's husband views her union organizing unenthusiastically, or how miners' wives reach a new solidarity only by overcoming sexual suspicions and jealousies. As feminist films explicitly demand that a new space be opened up for women in women's terms, the collective and social act of feminist filmmaking has often led to entirely new demands in the areas of health care, welfare, poverty programs, work and law (especially rape), and in the cultural sphere proper in the areas of art, education, and the mass media. And if many feminist filmmakers have deliberately used a traditional "realist" documentary structure, it is because they see making these films as an urgent public act and wish to enter the 16mm circuit of educational films, especially through libraries, schools, churches, unions, and YWCAs, to bring a feminist analysis to many women it might otherwise never reach.

Biography, simplicity, trust between woman filmmaker and woman subject, a linear narrative structure, little self-consciousness about the flexibility of the cinematic medium--these are what characterize the "realist" feminist documentaries of the 1970s. The films' form and their widespread use raise certain questions. Why are they patterned in so similar a way? Why are these films the first ones thought of whenever a group of women decide they want to "start learning something about women" and set up showings in churches, public libraries, high schools, Girl Scout meetings, union caucuses, or rallies? Why do activists in the women's movement use the same films over and over again? What is the films' appeal?

These films often show women in the private sphere getting together to define/redefine their experiences and to elaborate a strategy for making inroads on the public sphere. Either the filmmaker senses that it is socially necessary to name women's experience, or women together within the film do so, or a "strong" woman is filmed who shares her stance with the filmmaker and, by extension, with the women who see the film. Conversations in these films are not merely examples of female introspection; the filmmakers choose not to explore the corners of women's psyches as the hero does in Romantic art. Rather, the women's very redefining of experience is intended to challenge all previously accepted indices of "male superiority" and of women's supposedly "natural" roles. Women's personal explorations establish a structure of social and psychological change. The film-maker's and her subjects' intent is political. Yet the films' very strength, the emphasis on the experiential, can sometimes be a political limitation, especially when the film limits itself to the individual and offers little or no analysis or sense of collective process leading to social change.[5]

Example: Self Health

Among "realist" feminist documentaries, Self Health stands as exemplary in terms of its cinematic style, the knowledge it conveys, and the self-confidence and understanding it gives women about themselves. The film presents women in a group situation, collectively learning to do vaginal self-exams with a speculum, breast exams, and vaginal bimanual exams. Such groups are conducted by women who are part of an informal "self-help" or "self-health" movement in the United States; sometimes their work is connected with the home-birth movement and sometimes with pregnancy testing and abortion referral services. As the health care industry grows like a mushroom under capitalism, the general North American public has become more and more aware of the poor quality of the expensive services offered to them. The women in the self-health movement form part of a large, often informally constituted radical movement to improve health care delivery for the masses of people instead of for an elite.

The place where such a self-health session takes place is usually someone's home or a women's center, rather than a medical clinic. In the film Self Health, the locale is a sunny apartment or informal women's meeting place. Although we see two women giving most of the explanations and demonstrations, no one is distinguished as nurse or doctor. As important to the film as the conveying of anatomical information is the fact that all the women discuss together their feelings about and experiences with their bodies and their sexuality, and that they very naturally look at and feel one another's bodies. To gain knowledge by looking at and feeling each other is acknowledged, perhaps for the first time cinematically, as woman's right.

Such a film attacks both the artistic and the medical tradition of viewing women's bodies. These traditions, as well as the mass media's use of women's image to sell consumer goods, have robbed most women of a real knowledge of both their own and other women's bodies. Furthermore, many women have little personal sense of rightfully possessing their own bodies, little sense of what's "normal" for themselves physically, and little sense of what sexuality on their terms or on women's terms in general might mean.

Doctors, male lovers, photographers, artists, and filmmakers have taken woman's nude body as their "turf," especially as an object of study. John Berger, in his film series and book, Ways of Seeing, has described the tradition of female nudity in oil painting and the presentation of women's bodies in advertising. He understands how the fact that women are "an object of vision, a sight," has affected women's view of themselves: women constantly "survey" themselves to judge how they appear, to try to gain some kind of control over how they might be treated in a circumscribed, patriarchal world.

> In the art-form of the European nude, the painters and spectator-owners were usually men, the persons treated as objects, women.... The essential way of seeing women, the essential use to which images are put, has not changed.[6]

In a sequence in Self Health showing one of the women demonstrating how to do a bimanual exam, the women gathered around her express surprise about the "walnut-size" of the uterus and about its location. Medical textbook drawings have traditionally drawn large the female organs associated with reproduction, demonstrating the ideology of that kind of representational art. They show the uterus as big and near the navel, with large fallopian tubes winding around prominent ovaries. The clitoris, until Masters and Johnson's studies, was not "taught" in medical school as women's organ of sexual sensation. Although I was raised in a doctor's family, I faced similar ignorance, for I learned only three years ago--after having a vaginal cyst cauterized without any local anesthesia--what was to me a startling fact, that the vagina has relatively little sensation because it contains few nerve endings. Why, women are asking, has such ignorance about women's sexuality been promoted in our society--especially since both pornography and modern medicine pretend to be so liberal about sex? That so much of the basic physical information conveyed by the film is very new for women viewers (e.g., the film lets us see the cervix and the os, or the normal sebaceous secretion from the nipple) indicates just how colonized a space women's bodies still are. Self Health goes a long way toward reconquering that space.

Cinematically, the film is characterized by its presentation of women in a collective situation sharing new knowledge about their physical sexuality. About fifteen young women are gathered in a friendly, mundane environment rather than in a clinical white office where the woman patient is completely isolated from her ordinary social context. As the women do breast self-examinations together, they sit around in a circle in what might be a living room; hanging on the wall we see a Toulouse-Lautrec reproduction of a woman. Warm brown-red and pink tones predominate. As the women remove their blouses, we notice them as individuals--some with rings and other jewels, some with glasses, many with different hairstyles. The group is young, they look like students or young working women in flowered peasant blouses and dresses, shirts and jeans. In sum, the colors and the mise-en-scène create a sense of warmth, intimacy, and friendliness.

Even more important to the mise-en-scène is the women's collectivity. Women look at and touch each other; they see their own sexual organs and those of others. They learn the variety of physical types and the range of "normality" in sexual organs in look, color, texture, and feel. For example, they and we notice and let ourselves deliberately look at the variety of women's breasts. The women themselves feel each others' breasts to learn what normal breast tissue is like. Women's breast tissue is fibrous and also varies with the menstrual cycle and the individual; as a result, women often do not know what is normal or what a "lump" might be. A doctor can spot such phenomena from having had the opportunity to feel many women's breasts. Why should such knowledge not be made available to, or seized by, women themselves?

The fact that almost any woman would feel shy and embarrassed about doing such overt exploration is mitigated by these women doing it in a group where everyone feels the same way. The women realize that their fears and doubts about their bodies do not originate from their individual situation as much as from women's physical and psychological colonization. Self Health does not provide an institutional analysis of the health-care industry, as The Chicago Maternity Center Story does. This limits how much this one film can achieve in directly promoting a different kind of health care for women; yet, because of the wide range of discussion and kinds of challenges to the established order it encourages women to formulate, it is useful in a wide range of women's struggles.

Visually and in terms of its overall structure, the film moves as far away as you can get from pornography, yet the cinematography also captures that kind of nervous tension and excitement of discovery which the women themselves undoubtedly felt. The film opens on a close-up of naked skin, the surface moving to the rhythm of a woman's breathing; there is a pan to a breast and a shot of either pubic or axillary hair in close up. As it starts out, the film could be porn. For most women audience members, the initial sequence provides a moment of tension--"Do we dare to or want to look at this?" The voice-over assures us of what we want to hear: "We're learning from our bodies, teaching ourselves and each other how each of us is unique ... and the same.... We see it as reclaiming lost territory that belonged to our doctors, our husbands, everyone but us." As the title comes on, we hear the excited voices of women speaking all at once, a device also used at the end of the film over the credits. The voices of discovery, talking in a simultaneous outburst of sharing observations, needs and experiences--these are the tension-breaking devices, the part of the film that an audience unfamiliar with such a situation first identifies with. And these voices imply an outburst of discussion that cannot be contained, that begs to be continued after the film is seen.

At one point, a high-angle long shot shows three women lying on the floor against pillows and sleeping bags propped up against the wall. Their legs are spread apart and they are all doing vaginal self-exams with speculum, flashlight, and mirror. A pan shot shows the whole group of women on the floor, lined up along the wall, doing the same thing with some women looking at or helping each other. A mixture of voices exclaims and comments on what they see, especially on the variety and uniqueness of the genitalia. This sequence is a first in narrative cinema in the way it presents women's sexuality. Women occupy the whole space of the frame as subjects in a collective act of mutual, tangible self-exploration. As one of my students said of this sequence, "It has none of the 'Wow!' of Candid Camera and none of the distance of medical or so-called sex education films." Particularly in this one section of Self Health, women filmmakers have found a way to show and define women's sexuality on their terms--not with the thrill of possession and not with objectification, but with the excitement of coming to knowledge.

The anatomy lesson, the sharing of feelings, and the learning about others all have equal importance in the film. Close-ups demonstrate specific examination techniques or show individuals talking and listening; long shots convey the sense of a communal experience in the self-health group. No woman is filmed as an object; everyone is a subject who combines and presents physical, emotional, intellectual, and political selves. The women filmed seem amazingly unselfconscious about the camera, particularly given the close range at which the filming was done.

Self-health groups and this film itself both function in an explicitly political way. Reclaiming "the lost territory" of women's bodies and health care is a personal act that has a strong effect on women's identity, emotional life, and sense of control. This film also directly attacks the medical establishment. Women who see the film immediately want to talk about two things--sex education and health care--mainly in terms of what patriarchal society lacks.

In one sense, the film is utopian. It shows a new, collective form of women learning together. It would be an ideal film, for example, to show in high schools. But when I showed the film on the university level to women's studies classes and to film students, both sets of students agreed that the idea of such a collective form of learning about sexuality would have been viewed as "pornography" in their high schools, by the teachers, the school boards, and many of the parents. In cinematic terms, the film's vision of women's sexuality, of their being total subjects to one another and to the audience, is also utopian. Women's very physical presence is defined here in women's terms, collectively. And some might ask, in referring to documentary film alone, why haven't these images and these concepts of women's united physical and intellectual selves been presented by filmmakers before?

Feminist Documentaries and the Consciousness-Raising Group

Cinéma vérité documentary filmmaking had features

that made it an attractive and useful mode of artistic and political expression for women learning filmmaking in the late 1960s. It not only demanded less mastery of the medium than Hollywood or experimental film, but also the very documentary recording of women's real environments and their stories immediately established and valorized a new order of cinematic iconography, connotation, and range of subject matter in the portrayal of women's lives. Furthermore, contemporary feminist filmmakers, often making biographical or autobiographical films, have used cinéma vérité in a new and different way. They often identify personally with their subjects. Their relation to that subject while filming often is collaborative, with both subject and filmmaker sharing the project's political goals. The feminist documentarist uses the film medium to convey a new and heightened sense of women's identity, expressed both through the subject's story and through the tangible details of the subject's milieu.

Yet why do so many feminist filmmakers choose to film the same thing? Film after film shows a woman telling her story to the camera. It is usually a woman struggling to deal with the public world. It seems that these feminist documentarists just plug in different speakers and show a certain variation in milieu--especially in class terms--from the artistocratic home of Nana, Mom And Me by Amalie Rothschild to the union organizers' photos of their younger days in Union Maids by Julia Reichert and Jim Klein. In fact, the feminist documentaries have as a narrative structure a pattern that is as satisfying for activists in the contemporary women's movement to watch as it is for women just wanting to learn more about women. That is, these films evince a consistent organization of narrative materials that functions much like a deep structure, the details of the individual women's lives providing the surface structure of these films.[7]

Such an organization serves a specific social and psychological function at this juncture in history. It is the artistic analogue of the structure and function of the consciousness-raising group. Furthermore, it indicates to the filmmaker a certain reason to be making the film, a certain relation to her subject matter and to the medium, and a certain sense of the function of the film once released. The narrative deep structure sets the filmmaker in a mutual, non-hierarchical relation with her subject (such filming is not seen as the male artist's act of "seizing" the subject and then presenting one's "creation") and indicates what she hopes her relation to her audience will be.[8]

In the consciousness-raising group, self-consciously a group of about a dozen women would reevaluate any and all areas of their past experiences in terms of how that experience defined or illuminated what it meant to be a woman in our culture. It was an act of naming previously unarticulated knowledge, of seeing that knowledge as political (i.e., as a way of beginning to change power relations), and of understanding that the power of this knowledge was that it was arrived at collectively. This collective process served to break down a sense of guilt for one's own problems and provided a sense of mutual support. It was and is a political act carried out in the private sphere.

Often such a group elaborates specific strategies to make inroads on, help its individual members enter, and change power relations in the public sphere. They may, for example, discuss tactics for helping one of their members to say no to making coffee at work, or to demand that the department hire a woman in an executive position. They may strive to get gynecological services at a school clinic. They may help a member of the group insist at work that no more clerical staff be hired and that all women be upgraded, which would mean that everyone in the office do both writing and typing. But consciousness-raising groups cannot be idealized as revolutionary structures. Their problems have been well analyzed by women who have used them and learned how much more organization and economic power is needed to make major changes in the public sphere.[9]

In many ways--for feminists and all the rest of the women in the United States--the private sector of society is uniquely women's space. In that private space, the home, middle-class women of my mother's generation were systematically robbed of their sense of being the possessors of their own bodies. Throughout patriarchy, women have been men's possession and the reflection of men's desires in the sexual act, especially in marriage. Mothers are the child-bearers and self-sacrificers, which is the constant theme of soap operas and domestic melodramas in film. The sense of self for women under capitalism has traditionally had to come from their children, home, and clothes. All the physical, peripheral extensions of themselves that they've been allowed to "possess" have been a mock analog of the real patriarchal possession of themselves, their families, and the sources of economic power that they and their families have had to depend on.[10]

In testimony to the psychological condition of living

out one's life in a state of mental colonization and in a sphere where one's labor is not rewarded socially by either an equitable salary or public power, many women's narratives are about identity, madness, and the fluidity or fragmentation of woman's ego. Yet the very act of writing a diary, of writing poems, or of consulting a neighbor woman about how to get along when times are hard--all these are testimonies to the struggle women wage to create a language, to formulate a stable sense of self, and to survive economic dependency on men or low-paying jobs. Just as women's domestic labor and ways of relating to each other are disdained, so too their forms of resistance in the domestic sphere tend to go unnoticed and unvalorized in a world where the hegemonic male culture, the public culture, has established the socially acknowledged "rules," appropriated women's bodies, and institutionalized the modes of discourse, especially through the Church, education, literature, the medical profession, the law, and the state.

Because women's identity is shaped and sustained in a sphere where men are largely absent, and because girls grow up in an emotional continuum with their mothers and the other women in their intimate environment (unlike a boy's Oedipal development), their emotional ties to other women are deep.[11] Women have traditionally consulted constantly with each other about domestic matters. One of the functions of the consciousness-raising group of the contemporary women's movement is to use in a new way an older form of subcultural resistance, women's conversation. Knowledge is there about domestic life, but it has not necessarily been spoken in uncolonized, women-identified terms. Women's art, especially the feminist documentary films, like consciousness-raising groups, strives to find a new way of speaking about what we have collectively known to be really there in the domestic sphere and to wrest our identity there in our own terms.

A Shift In Iconography

Much has been lost in women's iconography as it has been purveyed in films, advertising, and television. We have, in fact, maintained a rich photographic history of women over the last hundred years, yet this source is not tapped in its richness and variety in patriarchal narrative film. For example, the women that Dorothea Lange photographed do not "speak" to us either visually or verbally in mainstream cinema.

In the United States in the early 1900s, many strikes were led by working women dressed in their best clothes and striding down city streets arm in arm. Why did that iconography get lost?

In the cinematic portrayal of contemporary life, we must question how the details of child-rearing, women's crafts, service work, subsistence agriculture, and women's intellectual endeavors are or are not presented in films, news, or ads. We rarely see media images that match the variety of clothes women wear in daily life, women's varieties of weight and age and tone of voice or accent, and women's varieties of gesture according to their mood and the specific moment in their lives. The patriarchal visual iconography of female figures in film includes the following: mother, child, virago, granny (variant, old maid), ingenue, good wife, and siren. Good wives are blonde, sirens dark-haired; erotically eligible figures of both sexes are slender and not yet old. An occasional comic figure escapes the classification by body type. Women's gestures in cinema are rigidly codified, and women characters, mise-en-scène predetermined by the connotative requirements of previously established narrative conventions.

There are both psychological and economic reasons why the domestic world is devalued in our culture.[12] It is rarely seen or interpreted by hegemonic patriarchal culture for what it is and contains, and its elements are named and defined primarily within the context of a seemingly powerless women's subculture. The domestic sphere, except in melodrama, is rarely depicted in film as an interesting place or the locus of socially significant, multiple, interpersonal relationships. Rather, the domestic sphere is the place where a woman is possessed and a man possesses a woman; a man's castle; a place that the woman runs. Feature films often judge the woman in the home as narrow, as having a stance morally inferior to the male protagonist's commitment to public duty; or home many become the projection backward to the security and presumed moral strength of the mother, which the man regains through his alliance with a good wife. The home lies out of history; cinematic heroes go out into the public sphere to do whatever it is that makes them the hero.

Connotative elements in cinema--here the connotative aspect of film's portrayal of the domestic sphere--are shaped both according to a film's narrative and to what people already know and have seen and experienced.[13] What the elements of the domestic sphere suggest is already conventionalized, already thought about before it gets in a film. But traditional filmmaking has drawn very narrowly even from the pool of conventional knowledge about domestic life.

One of the self-appointed tasks of contemporary feminist art is to articulate, expand, and comment on women's own subcultural codification of the connotations of those visual elements and icons familiar to them in their private sphere. Thus, painter Judy Chicago paints "cunt" flowers, and other artists, notably sculptors, have elaborated sculptures or artifacts of paper crafts, sewing, quilting, feathers, enclosed spaces and cubicles, and family photos, such materials being used for the suggestive value they bear from the domestic sphere.

For feminist writers and filmmakers, autobiography and biography provide an essential tool for looking in a self-conscious way at women's subculture, their subordinate role in or exclusion from the public sphere, their fantasy life, their sense of "embeddedness" in a certain object world. In other words, autobiography and biography become the way both back and forward toward naming and describing what woman really is, in that political and artistic act that Adrienne Rich calls "diving into the wreck."

Feminist films look at familiar women's elements to define them in a new, uncolonized way. Among the connotative elements to which feminist documentaries draw our attention and give an added complexity are the visual cues that define womanliness in film. The women characters' gestures, clothes, age, weight, sexual preference, race, class, and embeddedness in a specific social milieu elicit our reflection on both the specificity of the subjects' lives and our own, and on the difference between these cinematic representations and those of dominant cinema. As a result of these films, a much broader range of and more forceful and complex women characters now engage our interest as cinematic subjects, and they are shown doing a wider range of activities in greater detail than ever before in narrative cinema. The biographical documentary serves as a critique of and antidote to past cinematic depictions of women's lives and women's space.

In the film <u>Self Health</u>, two whole areas of visual imagery are challenged: the portrayal of women's sexuality and nudity, and health care. Domestic space in this film becomes the locus for a collective coming to knowledge about women's bodies and simultaneously the locus for a new kind of health care delivery. The Chicago Maternity Center Story, contrasting home delivery with hospital care, valorizes the same iconic contrasts: health care at home is more "human."

Talking Heads/New Rules Of The Game

The visual portrayal of the women in "realist" feminist documentaries is often criticized for its transparency (film's capturing reality) or for the visual dullness of talking heads. Yet the stories that the filmed women tell are not just "slices of experience." These stories serve a function aesthetically in reorganizing women viewers' expectations derived from patriarchal narratives and in initiating a critique of those narratives. The female figures talking to us on the screen in Janie's Janie, Joyce at 34, Union Maids, Three Lives, The Woman's Film, and We're Alive are not just characters whom we encounter as real-life individuals. Rather, the filmmakers have clearly valorized their subjects' words and edited their discourse. In all the feminist documentaries, the sound track, usually told in the subjects' own words, serves the function of rephrasing, criticizing, or articulating for the first time the rules of the game as they have been and as they should be for women.

The sound track of the feminist documentary film often consists almost entirely of women's self-conscious, heightened, intellectual discussion of role and sexual politics. Received notions about women give way to an outpouring of real desires, contradictions, decisions, and social analyses. After I showed Kate Millett's Three Lives to an introductory film class in 1972, a woman student came up to me gratefully after class and commented, "I'll bet that's the first time a lot of those guys have had to sit and listen uninterruptedly to women talking for ninety minutes. I wonder what it means to them to listen to women without having a chance to butt in and have their say."

More than what it means for men to listen to women's self-consciously told "stories," what has it meant for us women in the course of the contemporary women's movement--what have we learned? We have learned what our sexuality is, how mothers can hate and need and love their children, how we can tell off a boss or a lover or a friend or a sexist fool, how "it's not our fault," and where our personal struggles are located in and contribute to and are supported by the larger forces that define our historical period. These "realist" documentary films both depict and encourage a politicized "conversation" among women; and in these films, the self-conscious act of telling one's story as a woman in a politicized yet personal way gives the older tool of women's subcultural resistance, conversation, a new social force as a tool for liberation.

The Experimental Films

JoAnn Elam's Rape represents perhaps a new trend in feminist documentaries. Coming out of an experimental film tradition, Elam uses both Brechtian intertitles and a symbolic iconography intercut with a video transfer of a conversation she taped with rape victims one night in the apartment of one of the women. The women's conversation forms the sound track of the film, and Elam both heightens and comments wittily on their points by repeating some of their lines in the intertitles. The film is an angry one that elaborates a whole new film style adequate to treating the subject of rape with neither titillation nor pathos. The women filmed are impassioned and intellectual. They are discussing their experiences with the group's support and within the security of domestic space; most of them are political activists in organizations against rape, and all saw the making of the film as an explicitly public act.

Rape rejects voyeurism and pathos. It rejects showing women as powerless. The women dare to speak the unspeakable, to restore to themselves their own identity, and to attack those cultural and economic institutions which make rape likely and those legal institutions which oppress the victim.

The meeting takes place in one woman's living room. It is woman's "turf." Visually, the videotaped milieu conveys a sense of solidarity and security as the women sit around in a circle talking. The videocamera was passed around, and a number of women did the filming, so we cannot identify the filmmaker in that group. There is a sense of warmth and enclosure. The women constantly interact as equals. The filmmaker's relation to her subject is participatory and non-hierarchical. The entire form of the film as well as Elam's participation in that group reveal her identification with and enhancement of the group's analysis rather than the more typical male filmmaker's "domination" of a difficult subject presented as a tour de force to an admiring world.

The Ideology Of Rape

Elam's cinematic technique, her relation to both subject and audience, and her non-voyeuristic depiction of rape all work in an original way to combat what Susan Brownmiller in Against Our Will has called "the ideology of rape."[14] This ideology is a main support of patriarchy, and it is especially visible in cinema.

Usually a "sympathetic" depiction of rape on film presents the victim in terms of pathos, horror, or individual tragedy. In such a case, the audience response may be one of both titillation and catharsis. Both males and females in the audience may respond--for different reasons--with a reaction such as this: "She's dead and beautiful and out there. Lucky it's not me." Either as titillation or catharsis or both, such a response has an adverse social effect in that it serves to limit people's capacity for self-awareness and their impulse to effect social change.

Far worse are the movies where women cry rape or enjoy rape, or movies where a sexual act inflicted by force is ultimately enjoyed. These film portrayals treacherously reinforce the prevalent social myths about rape that are enacted in the legal system of most countries in the world. These myths make the victim the one who must prove that she is not guilty. They include: "All women want to be raped. She asked for it. A woman shouldn't bring up the fact of having been raped as a public statement but should hide it as a shame." Such myths encourage violence against women, indeed make it legal, as in the British Supreme Court decision to free two men who violently raped a woman; in this case, the court ruled that because the woman's husband told the rapists that forceful sexual relations only excited her all the more, the two men could not have known that they were committing an act of rape.

How cinema perpetuates an ideology of rape is far more complicated than the way it depicts actual rapes. An attitude of contempt for women is often inescapably built into a film.[15] This is especially true of a film that shows violence being done to a woman, but it is the case with many other films as well. Woman as victim, woman as object, woman getting fucked, woman getting shot, woman's body as object of public contemplation (only "beautiful" when young, of course)--all these are the staple of narrative cinema and of television as we know it.

Feminist film theorists have currently undertaken the massive task of explaining the mechanisms of how cinema both directly and indirectly oppresses women. Much of this analysis is from a psychoanalytic perspective. Thus, according to Pam Cook and Claire Johnston, women in film, especially fictional film, are generally used as markers in a male fantasy.[16] In their roles, costumes, and ways of being filmed, women in patriarchal narrative film have functioned primarily as fetishized objects of desire, objects that are really feared. According to this psychoanalytic perspective, such a use of the female figure derives from the original male oedipal fear of a lack or castration, an overwhelming Other that may swallow him up, an Other whose traits he must suppress in himself as the locus of power, the male. In his adult life, to possess or desire the woman, not as she is but as he imagines her, guarantees to the man that he is a man.[17] In a similar vein, in a study of the oppressive mechanisms of voyeurism in narrative cinema, Laura Mulvey describes the figure of woman as "an indispensable element of spectacle" in narrative film, where woman functions both "as erotic object for the characters within the screen story and as erotic object for the spectator within the auditorium."[18]

However, the relations of a woman audience member to that voyeurism, to looking at beautiful or suffering women characters in film, is more complex than men's and has not been adequately analyzed.[19] It probably involves a mixture of pleasure, identity, and distance. For example, in watching narrative cinema I can, and in fact usually do, identify with both the male protagonist from whose perspective the story is told and whose values are explored, and also with the beautiful women whom he loves. I can be both Bogart and Bacall. However, although women viewers do not have the same psychological predisposition to view female images as Other as male viewers do, in almost every film they see, women viewers are forced to respond to female images in films, both the minor characters and the "stars," through the filter of patriarchal artistic concerns and conventions.

It is precisely because JoAnn Elam challenges both

patriarchal film content and the conventions with which women and the topic of rape have been filmed that Rape is important, especially to women. In watching this film, viewers must respond in a specifically political way to the facts of women's oppression, and they are also led to reflect on the cinematic treatment of that oppression. In this way, Elam's feminist cinema leads viewers to challenge what they had taken for granted before, especially the treatment of women in film.

Rape

The visual track of Rape consists of three types of footage: a kinescoped videotaped conversation among a group of rape victims and the filmmaker, handwritten intertitles (white on a black background), and symbolic illustrations--filmed in 16mm--of the concepts discussed by the women on the sound track. For the women who met this one time to speak to each other and to make a film, this filmed discussion meant for each of them a coming to knowledge, a healing, a reaffirming of their right to inhabit their own bodies and most intimate selves.

While there is no story line or narrative development in the film, there is a deliberate progression from the women's telling of victimization--by both rapists and the legal system--to an analysis of rape culture, to an indication of possible collective action. For example, the group discusses the ordinary strategies women adopt when going out in the public sphere. These involve paranoia, disguise, and conforming to social expectations about women's roles--e.g., stay at home or go out only with a man or look like you are expecting a man to meet you any minute--none of which has guaranteed women safety. There is also a sensitive discussion of class and racism, as the women (who are all white) respond honestly to these issues in terms of their own lived experience. The group arrives at a political analysis through this one evening's group interaction, which, in fact, is the political analysis of rape that Elam presents in her film.

The visual image of the conversation is that of a grainy video transfer, with foreground and background collapsed. The low resolution of the image plus the "unprofessional" framing as the participants pass the video camera around from one to the other dedramatizes the stories that the women have to tell. Pathos and personality are so minimized that often the viewer cannot remember which person had had which rape experience or took which political stance. The group finally is remembered as speaking with one voice. For political reasons, Elam clearly has eschewed any portrayal of a tragic individual. She films no one with sculpted lighting and shows no acts of rape and no women breaking down in tears. The women's "stories" are experienced only in a situation of collective sharing and protest.

The sound track, the women's conversation, sets the pace of the film. Elam intercuts the video image with symbolic filmed material and Brechtian-style titles which serve to heighten and make memorable what the women say. The viewer must respond to the film politically. There is no other way to deal with the women presented in the film except in the intellectual and analytical way in which they deal with themselves. In particular, the symbolic sequences force an intellectual response. I use the term "symbolic" here to refer to a constructed relation between thing filmed and topic signified in a particular sequence.[20] Elam's visual symbolism is reminiscent of the post-'68 Godard/Gorin films, for it is combined with Brechtian-style intertitles which "explain" or anchor the signification of the concepts expressed explicity on the sound track. As with Brechtian distancing devices, this 16mm filmed material provides an intellectual wit which expands the resonance of the film and also raises our political understanding of what we see and hear. For example, toward the end of the film, Elam inserts an intertitle which lists potential solutions and collective actions that have been taken by women against rape. The intertitle passes by too quickly for it to be absorbed as a worked-out formula to end rape. Rather, it suggests areas for discussion that the film as a whole opens up, indicating ways women <u>might</u> act, rather than ways women <u>must</u> act. The inserted material, both intertitles and symbolic sequences, suggests an analysis but leaves it up to the audience to make the connections for themselves.

Sometimes the cinematic technique has an evocative effect deriving from the simplicity of the image or from the editing and camera movement. Elam's panning across the tops of skyscrapers and court buildings (to represent institutional male power) elicits a sense of paranoia and claustrophobia because of the visceral response it evokes. Other times, Elam uses a vérité-type of on-the-street filming. She combines here a number of shots of women walking, or men's glances, or people walking together. She edits these shots so as to bring out their most salient common feature (i. e., "woman walking down city street"), but she uses a "spontaneous" filming style to demonstrate the real threat women face in public situations and their constant awareness when walking down the street that they could be harassed at any time. You could, the film implies, film scenes like that on any city street on any given day.

To break tension and to make political points in a witty, memorable way, she flashes on at various times a shot of a screw, a pigeon (meaning women are sitting ducks), or columns which are carved into figures of grimacing women (meaning women are the pillars of society). She also uses humorous images of classical painting, showing unhappy or beheaded wives. The images of classical art, especially a painting of the rape of the Sabine women, a statue of a man abducting a woman at sword's point, and a Minerva-type goddess with arms upraised represent a number of concepts--women's traditional roles, the constraints placed on women, and what happens when they confront men or social institutions. These images are used in different combinations with the other symbolic images in a carefully crafted way to evoke the precise kinds of complexities and contradictions that affect or have a bearing on the situation the women are talking about on the sound track in voice-off.

Some of the symbolic sequences are more complex than a one-to-one equation of image with idea. For example, in the children's games, which broadly symbolize "the battle of the sexes," the audience has to attend to the switches in who is chasing whom--the boys or the girls. Certain visual sequences depict an extended metaphor, in particular a hand game where a man's hands hit and grab a woman's hands. Another time we see a hand moving a glass of water around rapidly while a person's hand, with forefinger extended, tries to stick a finger in the glass. Here the women's voices on the sound track discuss how hostile judges have used this very trick to prove to a jury that a woman could never be forced to have sex against her will.

Elam's visual style in both the filmed 16mm inserts and in the video-taped sequences of the women partly derives from a tradition in U. S. experimental filmmaking that is in opposition to mainstream documentary and feature film style. The "home-movie" experimentation of the New

American Cinema movement is characterized not only by spontaneous filming done in the filmmaker's own milieu, but also by a hand-held camera and a seeming lack of concern for the "rules" of narrative cinematography. Thus, in Rape, we often face seemingly erratic camera movement, horizon line askew, or unpredictable kinds of visual repetition. Such a visual style originally functioned as a cheap form of filmmaking and as a protest against the aesthetic structures of commercial film. Even now, because audiences are generally unfamiliar with this type of cinematography, it may be perceived as crude or inept.

Here, in fact, such a style serves a political purpose. Elam has striven to create new cinematic tactics for exploring and explicitly analyzing the topic of rape without being co-opted into using that subject matter for visual voyeuristic pleasure. Furthermore, the intellectual and symbolic nature of her style makes a statement about the women being filmed and makes demands on the audience. The women filmed and the film itself are angry, intellectual, and politically aware. The responses to the visual symbolism must be analytical. The imagery never evokes a feeling, "How tragic!" "How sad!"

The major way in which Elam proceeds from the consciousness-raising filmed conversation to a useful public statement about and attack on rape--to forging a real teaching tool, if you will--is through the intertitles. Some of these are summary statements; they usually follow the mention of a theme or concept by one of the women on the sound track. Often the intertitles define the symbolism of the inserted filmed sequences. More often, they are heavily ironic, underscoring the false consciousness and everyday assumptions that are the major prop of rape ideology. Such assumptions make rape not only a "thinkable" act for the rapist, but for both the rapist and the non-rapist these assumptions reaffirm and institutionalize the notion of men's social and personal right of access to the female body. Some of these titles include the following, the false consciousness of which I hope will be obvious: "say yes and mean no"; "you're so cute when you're mad"; "it's because they like you"; "victim precipitation"; "she claims that she was raped"; "the woman behind the man"; and "it's your burden in society to say no." Other times words such as myth or ravish are used with their dictionary--i.e., patriarchal--definition. There are repeated shots of the Illinois rape statute's definition of rape. Frequently, the intertitles

Intertitles from JoAnn Elam's film, Rape

TERROR--a state of intense fear caused by the systematic use of violent means by a party or faction to maintain itself in power.

Rape is a perfect example of control.
go out and do it again
They think that rape is just a simple screw.
male supremacy
Rapists do not differ from ordinary men.
motivation
women are vulnerable
legal system
consensual intercourse
justified sexual assault
felonious gallantry
assault with failure to please
rape is socially sanctioned
Men think that women want to be raped.
They just do it to be pricks.
They just have a ball.
That's not treating me like a human being.
take it out on someone
You get to a point where you can't stand to live that way.

express women's anger and the resolution expressed in the titles, as well as the political analysis the titles provide, bring great satisfaction to women viewers. I have seen the anger expressed by the titles divide the audience, as Brecht said a good political film should do, along class lines--in this case along feminist lines. Women in the audience usually respond more vehemently and to different issues than male viewers do; and I've had women students call one title "realistic"--"telling it the way it is," while male students characterized the same title as "polemical" or "rhetorical." Elam validates women's anger in this film by raising it to a conceptual level in which that anger becomes part of the most appropriate political response.[21]

The film does not have a beginning, middle or end. There is a process of moving from a personal to an institutional analysis and of ending on a sense (not an answer) of what is to be done and what steps women can take. The film cannot be either received or remembered like a story. There isn't a main point or event that was led up to, no chain of inevitable cause and effect. Women exploring issues of rape--or indeed of the larger, complex subject of their sexuality and their relation to their bodies--need something beyond stories where either something good happens (the woman is "won"; she finds Mr. Right) or something bad (the woman gets raped or shot; woman is vanquished). Elam's film opens on to women's experience in a new way by its very eschewal of a story form. The only "story" is what the group explored in a social act of affirming its members' identity and of fighting rape and the factors that cause rape. After seeing the film, the viewer will remember little about the characters, who are neither cinematically beautiful nor tragic. We will remember snatches of the told experience, some of the titles, and some of the symbolic filmed sequences. The film has forced us to witness women speaking the unspoken, and the film itself is a rare cinematic act in making the unspoken speakable. It shows women in a community of women breaking through guilt, isolation, silence, and alienation from self. The women depicted in the film and the filmmaker's own style create a sense of women as intellectuals and social actors. They are doing--even in the act of conversation--rather than waiting, suffering, and sacrificing, which are patriarchy's notions of women's roles. Elam uses the film to examine and attack oppressive ideological structures and to reinforce women's sense of just outrage and their capacity to act. It is an intellectual film that has a role to play in helping women forge both their own identities and a more equitable world.

Contribution To Public Struggle

The feminist documentaries speak to working women, encourage them in their public struggles, and broaden their horizons to make demands in other spheres as well. To define structures of patriarchy is as important to women workers as to define structures of capitalism. Existential or gut-level militancy becomes refined by a political movement as the movement offers an analysis and provides a way to see both parameters and details within the struggle as a whole. Yet because of male competitiveness, aggressiveness and bluff are not skills women usually learn as children (and many women do not necessarily want to learn these tactics as adults either); the women's movement seeks to create new structures to facilitate women's entry into the public sphere of work and power, and to make that public sphere one they would want to inhabit.

Clearly, the powerless will want power, especially once they define specifically the ways they have systematically been robbed of it. But women also want to imagine what the power would be if executed in a form commensurate with feminist goals. Although it is seemingly filmed in domestic space, Self Health is a powerful public document in the model for sex education and the vision of collective, community control that it presents. And its sense of women together, coming to (creating, seizing) knowledge, is subversive.

The realist feminist documentaries represent a use of, yet a shift in, the aesthetics of cinéma vérité, due to the feminist filmmakers' close identification with their subjects, participation in the women's movement, and sense of the films' intended effect. The structure of the consciousness-raising group becomes the deep structure repeated over and over in these films. Within such a narrative structure, either a single woman tells her story to the filmmaker or a group of women are filmed sharing experiences in a politicized way. They are filmed in domestic space and their words serve to redefine that space in a new, "woman-identified" way. Either the stance of the people filmed or the stance of the film as a whole reflects a commitment to changing the public sphere as well; and for this reason, these filmmakers have used an accessible documentary form. In the "surface structure" of the films, a new iconography of women's bodies and women's space emerges that implicitly challenges the general visual depiction of women in capitalist society, perhaps in many socialist ones, too. The sound tracks have women's voices speaking continuously; and the films' appeal lies not only in having strong women tell about their lives but even more in our hearing and having demonstrated that some women have deliberately altered the rules of the game of sexual politics. All cinéma vérité is not the same, and much of the current discussion of and attack on cinematic realism dismisses the kind of documentary film style that most people are used to.

Both realist and experimental documentary forms have been politicized by feminist filmmakers who see their work as coming out of and having an audience in the women's movement. And in return, the exigencies, methods, and forms of organization within that ongoing political movement have profoundly affected the aesthetics of documentary film.

Notes

1 Portions of this essay appeared as "The Political Aesthetics of Feminist Documentary Film," Quarterly Review of Film Studies, Fall, 1978; and "Disarming Film Rape," Jump Cut, No. 19 (December 1978).

2 For a theoretical discussion of feminist consciousness-raising, see Catherine A. McKinnon, "Feminism, Marxism, Method, and the State: An Agenda for Theory," in Feminist Theory: A Critique of Ideology, ed. Nannerl O. Keohano, Michelle Z. Rosaldo, and Barbara Gelp (Chicago: University of Chicago Press, 1982).

3 Many of the feminist documentaries (I have given only a representative list of them) are described briefly in Linda Artel and Susan Wengraf's Positive Images: Non-Sexist Films for Young People (San Francisco: Booklegger Press, 1976). Interviews with feminist filmmakers often appear alongside reviews of their films in Jump Cut. And Patricia Erens' Sexual Stratagems (New York: Horizon, 1979) contains an extensive filmography of both fictional and documentary films by women.

4 For a discussion of realism in painting, see Realism by Linda Nochlin (Baltimore: Penguin, 1972); for an analysis of these issues in film, see Realism and the Cinema, ed. Christopher Williams (Boston: Routledge & Kegan Paul, 1980).

5 An activist in health care struggles criticizes the political analyses offered in feminist health-care films in Marcia Rothenberg's "Good Vibes vs. Preventive Medicine; Healthcaring from Our End of the Speculum," Jump Cut, No. 17 (April, 1978), p. 3.

6 John Berger, Ways of Seeing (New York: The Viking Press, 1973), pp. 63-64.

7 Such an idea loosely derives from the work of Claude Levi-Strauss in Structural Anthropology, trans. C. Jacobson and B. G. Schoepf (Garden City, N. Y.: Doubleday Anchor, 1967).

8 Cinéma vérité films in the United States made by male filmmakers are characterized precisely by the film's ironic distance from the subject and the filmmaker's presentation of his vision of the subject as his "creation." Films by Frederick Wiseman, Richard Leacock, Don Pennebaker, Tom Palazzolo, and the Maysles brothers fall in this category.

9 For an extended discussion of consciousness-raising groups, see Jo Freeman, The Politics of Women's Liberation (New York: David McKay, 1975).

10 For an overview of the discussion of these issues in Marxist, feminist, and anti-racist terms, see Michelle Barrett, Women's Oppression Today (London: Verso, 1980); and Gloria Joseph and Jill Lewis, Common Differences: Conflicts in Black and White Feminist Perspectives (Garden City, N. Y.: Doubleday Anchor, 1981).

11 Nancy Chodorow, "Mothering, Object-Relations and the Female Oedipal Configuration," Feminist Studies, 4, No. 1, (February 1978); "Family Structure and Feminine Personality," Woman, Culture and Society, Michelle Rosaldo and Louise Lamphere, eds. (Stanford: Stanford University Press, 1974); "Oedipal Asymmetries and Heterosexual Knots," Social Problems, 23, No. 4 (April 1976)

12 Sheila Rowbotham, Woman's Consciousness, Man's World (Baltimore: Penguin, 1973); Eli Zaretsky, Capitalism, the Family, and Personal Life (New York: Harper, 1976); Juliet Mitchell, Woman's Estate (New York: Pantheon, 1971).

13 Lesage, "S/Z and Rules of the Game," Jump Cut, No. 12/13 (1976).

14 Susan Brownmiller, Against Our Will: Men, Women, and Rape (New York: Bantam, 1976). A further analysis of intercourse itself as reflective of the same power relations that Brownmiller sees operating in pornography can be found in Ti-Grace Atkinson's perceptive

and witty essay, "The Institution of Sexual Intercourse," Amazon Odyssey (New York: Link Books, 1971). To quote Atkinson: "The argument goes something like this: man has a sexual instinct, and we know this because men like to have sexual intercourse so much. Since male desire for sexual intercourse is not determined by the recipient, it must be the activity itself which is desired. The activity is defined essentially as the penetration by the penis into the vagina. But the man may have an intense experience, called orgasm, caused by some activity of his own within the particular environment of the vagina. The completion of his experience, or orgasm, is indicated by certain signs, e.g., ejaculation. This experience has been judged by society to be pleasurable [in a similar way for both men and women]." (p. 17)

15 See Barbara Halpern Martineau's "Documenting the Patriarchy: Chinatown" in Women and the Cinema, Eds. Karyn Kay and Gerald Peary (New York: Dutton, 1977); originally in Jump Cut No. 3, September-October 1974. Martineau examines the ideological implications of reviews of Chinatown which ignore the violence done to the female protagonist, ignoring "the fact that while the male star only gets his nose slit open, the female star gets shot through the eye."

16 See especially Pam Cook and Claire Johnston's analysis of Mamie Stover in "The Place of Women in the Cinema of Raoul Walsh," Raoul Walsh, Ed. Phil Harvey (London: Vineyard Press, 1974). Also Claire Johnston, "Women's Cinema as Countercinema," Notes on a Women's Cinema, Screen Pamphlet No. 2, 1974.

17 For a psychoanalytic discussion of these issues see Susan Lurie, "Pornography and the Dread of Women." Take Back the Night, ed. Laura Lederer (New York: William Morrow, 1980); Jessica Benjamin, "The Bonds of Love: Rational Violence and Erotic Domination"; Feminist Studies, 6, No. 1 (Spring 1980); Ethel Spector Person, "Sexuality as the Mainstay of Identity," Signs, 5, No. 4 (1980).

18 Laura Mulvey, "Visual Pleasure and Narrative Cinema," Screen, 16, No. 3 (Fall 1976); reprinted in Women and the Cinema.

19 This paragraph reflects a discussion between feminist literary and film critics in "Women and Film: A

Discussion of Feminist Aesthetics," New German Critique, No. 13 (Winter 1976). For a useful discussion of these issues, see Gertrud Koch, "Why Women Go to the Movies," tr. Marc Silberman, Jump Cut, No. 27 (July 1982); Tania Modleski, Loving with a Vengeance: Mass Produced Fantasies for Women (Hamden, CT: Archon, 1982); Ann Barr Snitow, "Mass Market Romance," Radical History Review, 20 (Spring-Summer, 1979); Linda Williams, "Women in Love: Personal Best," Jump Cut, No. 27 (July 1982); Chris Straayer, "The Lesbian/Feminist Audience and Personal Best," Jump Cut, No. 29 (Fall 1983).

20 I draw here on Peter Wollen's application of Charles Pierce's semiotic categories--icon, index, and symbol--to cinema. "A symbolic sign demands neither resemblance to its object (the definition of icon) nor any existential bond with it (the definition of index). It is conventional and has the force of law." Signs and Meaning in the Cinema. (Bloomington: Indiana University Press, 1972), p. 123.

21 In showing the film I have encountered two types of negative responses, worth mentioning here. Some viewers find the film visually crude, either because they are hostile to the use of video transfer in experimental filmmaking, or because they do not like a film style that differs from TV documentaries. Another negative response, and it is often combined with the above response as a "cover," comes from those who do not want to look at rape in both personal and political terms and who thus reject the type of response insisted on by both the style and the content of Elam's film.

As a friend of the filmmaker and as a critic trying to establish a broader audience for women's films, I have shown Rape in women's studies classes, film classes, and film conferences, and also had it shown to women and police staff working in the area of rape. "Naive" audiences do not seem to have much difficulty with the formal innovations; film students either like its experimental strategies or find it lacking in production values; people in rape-crisis work either accept or argue with its politics. Often this last group is looking for a film that would serve as an organizing tool in a specific anti-rape campaign. Rape's open-ended form and symoblic sequences make it suitable for starting discussions, but it is not prescriptive in terms of strategy and tactics.

Rape may be rented from Canyon Cinema Cooperative, 2325 Third Street, Suite 338. San Francisco, CA 94107 (415/332-1514) or Film-Makers' Co-operative, 175 Lexington Avenue, New York NY 10011 (212/884-3820); in Canada, D. E. C. Films, 121 Avenue Road, Toronto, Ontario, M5R 263 (416/964-6901); in England, The Other Cinema, 12-13 Little Newport Street, London WC2 H7J. Rental charge--$35; Purchase price--$250. For purchase apply to the filmmaker JoAnn Elam, PO Box 41864, Chicago, IL 60641.

Self Health is directed by Catherine Allan, Judy Erola, Allie Light, and Joan Musante. Made in 1974, it's in 16mm, 23 minutes, color. Rental from Multi-Media Resource Center, 1525 Franklin Street, San Francisco, CA 94109 (415/673-5100).

Chapter 13

TALKING ABOUT OUR LIVES AND EXPERIENCES: SOME THOUGHTS ABOUT FEMINISM, DOCUMENTARY AND "TALKING HEADS"

Barbara Halpern Martineau

The following contribution brings to the ongoing debate on feminist documentary activism two additional points of view not yet expressed--from behind the camera, and from within the lesbian community (not to mention from north of the border)--thus succeeding in casting already familiar issues in an entirely new light. Martineau's concluding remarks about her own most recent films, personality-oriented exemplary portraits returning, as Lesage has revealed, to the very sources of feminist filmmaking, testify, among other things, to the continuing need within progressive constituencies for short, low-budget interventions in the domain of morale and ideology, strictly speaking, as well as films analyzing and participating in concrete political struggles--or, as yet another contributor might put it, film-banners and film-poems as well as film-tracts and film-manifestoes.

The first concern of the Movement was simply to put women, recognizable to us as women, in the picture. The first independent women's groups grabbed camera or video and went to talk to women about their lives and experiences. In this context, where what the media offer is

> only misrecognition, the stage of recognition of, and identification with, the category women ... cannot simply be left out in a rush to the total deconstruction of all representation and identification whatsoever.
> --Christine Gledhill, "Whose Choice? Teaching Films About Abortion," Screen Education, no. 24.

> While it is essential for feminist film critics to examine signifying practices carefully in order to understand the way in which women have been constructed in language and in film, it is equally important not to lose sight of the material world in which we live, and in which our oppression takes concrete, often painful forms.
> --E. Ann Kaplan, Women and Film: Both Sides of the Camera, 1983.

As a feminist documentary filmmaker, teacher of film theory, and film critic, I have experienced a widening gap between the practical concerns of making and showing films and the issues addressed by current feminist film theory. It has been a relief to see that other women have also noticed and been concerned by this tendency.[1] Putting the matter as simply as possible, it seems essential to reconcile the facts that: a) film is a two-dimensional, entirely artificial construct heavily laden with ideological import; and b) filmmakers work with real three-dimensional people on both sides of the camera and before and after production, people whose presence has a great deal to do with the effect of the films on their audiences.

I hope to contribute to the process of understanding how a) and b) are in fact continually reconciled in the documentary process, and I propose to do this by looking at some relationships among documentary filmmakers, their subjects, and their audiences, with particular reference to the use of "talking heads." These relationships are the subject of frequent discussion by documentary theorists, as indicated by the widespread (but ill-defined) use of terms such as "advocacy," "balance," "point of view," "representation," and "subjectivity."[2] Every one of these terms is crucially affected by a feminist understanding of power dynamics and media manipulation, yet I observe that feminist film discussions shy away from issues of documentary theory, and documentary discussions avoid feminist analysis.[3]

> ... it was the presence of Kopple and her camera down there in Harlan County, Kentucky, that brought us close to the people and their cause in the unique moments in the film when the camera participates in events rather than trying to record them.... Perhaps this documentary belongs in some category of its own, representing a series of screen images that complement lived experience rather than images that stand completely on their own....
> --E. Ann Kaplan, "Harlan County, USA: The Documentary Form," Jump Cut, 15.

The "category of its own" which Kaplan suggests for Harlan County can in fact accommodate many of the films called "radical," "committed," or "advocacy" documents. I think any radical documentarian would be insulted by the suggestion that her/his films did not "complement lived experience." And, although Kaplan was amazed that the audience at the New York Film Festival talked solely about the subject matter of Harlan County, apart from the rarefied atmosphere of film festivals and film studies classrooms, social-issue documentarists, radical or not, are accustomed to audience discussions which focus on the issues raised by the film, rather than on formal filmic issues. (Only rarely are social and formal issues combined constructively in North American documentaries, but when this happens it is very exciting for both audiences and filmmakers.)

The aspect of Harlan County which evoked interest and perplexity from Ann Kaplan was the demonstrable, on-screen relationship between the film crew and the events they were filming, a relationship which can also be observed in militant films from Latin America.[4] This committed relationship between filmmaker and subject is often present less dramatically in feminist documentaries made apart from conditions of armed struggle, where the risk taken is not an immediate physical risk, but rather one of a life lived openly against conventional pressures, as expressed by one's filmmaking. Most lesbian documentaries represent such risk-taking on the part of filmmakers and subjects.[5] The relationship of commitment between filmmaker and film subject, and between these two and the audience, provides a little-discussed dimension to the issue of how women are "represented" in documentaries.

It is now widely accepted that all documentation is subjective, that "objectivity" is as much a fallacy for human observation as it is for subatomic physics. The act of observation affects what is observed, and the process of recording the observation further interprets the originally subjective observation. The use of semiological analysis is a valuable tool in discovering and describing how the subjectivity of the filmmaker is ideologically influenced, and how this emerges in the film. I don't know if attention to film codes is sufficient to discover whether a given film approaches its protagonists and its audience as subjects or as objects. This is a question of direct import to feminists, since women are so often objectified by film. If the protagonists are treated as subjects, i.e., as centers of consciousness with accessible points of view, how is this rendered by the film? If treated as objects, i.e., their images manipulated to illustrate certain ideas or attitudes alienated from their own consciousness, in whose interest is this manipulation carried out? How is it rendered, or disguised, filmically? What are the possibilities of response open to viewers? Is the audience expected to consume objectified images, or is there a possibility of dialogue and subjective response? What can be gleaned from watching a film about the filmmaker's stance towards the film subjects, the subject matter, and the audience? Whose interests are represented by a given film, and whose interests are served by it? Are these interests identical or different? Is advocacy necessarily opposed to investigation, or can they coexist? What is just representation, or is it just exploitation? Is balanced programming a boon for independent producers, or is it a balancing act to distract attention from the status quo?

Rather than constructing theoretical answers to these questions which would then be illustrated by appropriate filmic examples, I propose to approach theory by way of practice, looking at various ways the much-maligned "talking head" has been used, in some films which have influenced my work, and in my own films.

A Subjective Sketch of the Development of Talking Heads

When the first close-up appeared on the silver screen, so one story goes, audiences were shocked--a disembodied head! (Memories of heads on pikes, the Terror, the Cheshire Cat....) Roland Barthes wrote of "that moment in cinema when capturing the human face still plunged audiences into the deepest ecstasy," referring to the impact of Garbo, Valentino, Chaplin. He remarks, but does not explore, the implications of androgyny in these masklike, disembodied faces, nor does he consider the effect of silence, which is crucial to the famous last close-up of Garbo in the talking film Queen Christina.[6] Early documentaries used close-ups for similar dramatic effect--Vertov's stunning editing sequences in Man with the Movie Camera use frames of candid close-ups to move between screen illusion and cutting room manipulation.[7]

The introduction of synchronized sound, revealing another source of fascination with the sight of lips moving and the sound of words emerging in perfect synchronicity, had an impact on film design which has still not been examined in depth by film critics. In documentary, Grierson and others immediately used the new dimension of sound creatively; the commentary of Industrial Britain (1933) valorized and patronized Flaherty's lyric portraits of British working men, increasing the myth-bearing potential of the close-up; Housing Problems (1935) offers both interpretive voice-of-God narration and an early experiment in direct cinema, when a slum dweller tells her story of an encounter with a rat, not so much to the camera as in front of it. Although the woman's story is so placed in the film, framed by a traditional use of visuals illustrating her situation and strong upper-class male commentary interpreting it, that she tends to become a piece of local color, something else remains. Unlike Roland Barthes' example of the black soldier saluting the French flag, this woman has an individual spirit which comes across very strongly. This remarkable representation of an English working-class woman telling her own story is generally credited to Ruby Grierson, listed in the credits as "assistant."[8]

Housing Problems was unusual in its time. Location interviews were very cumbersome affairs, requiring massive invasions by crews and equipment; the results were usually equally cumbersome. The typical talking head scene started as a long or medium shot of a professional white man in a suit behind a desk, announcing official policy, imparting official information, or expressing an official attitude, which is rendered official precisely by the office setting of the shot. Informality is connoted by having the man lean against the desk instead of sitting behind it. A standardized technique of changing the length and size of the shot and shooting cutaways was developed to allow editors room to play with the length and pacing of the interview.

Lightweight, portable sound equipment enabled two or three (strong) people to dash around catching sound as well as picture on the run. Transparency became a tempting trap for the documentarist, and interviews were out of fashion--instead, people were caught in "candid" conversations, and their casual conversation was then edited to represent whatever was required on film. There were still talking heads, but they moved about more, as did the camera, which roamed in search of interesting cutaways and climactic moments. Occasionally, as in Allen King's Warrendale (Canada, 1967), a subject would turn to address one of the crew, and King would leave the moment in the finished film. Other filmmakers did not. Just as early voice-over narration and interviewed authority figures interpreted visual material, now sync sound and picture were shaped and recontextualized, so that images of people were strongly coded by camera style and editing.[9] Just as earlier audiences tended to accept the narrated documentary as simple truth, so audiences now hailed vérité filming as being even more truthful. Little attention was paid in the U. S. or English Canada to the remarkable work of Jean Rouch, which made the role of the filmmaker highly visible in relation to interviews as well as to other kinds of footage. Interestingly enough, it was mainly in the work of women avant-garde filmmakers that the truth of vérité was first questioned: Shirley Clarke's Portrait of Jason (USA, 1967), Agnes Varda's Lion's Love (USA, 1969), and Joyce Wieland's Reason Over Passion (Canada, 1967-1969) all specifically questioned the candor of "candid" filming, and all three rang ironic changes on the motif of the talking head.

By the mid-1970s, when I began working as a documentary filmmaker, "talking heads," to be seen every time a TV set was turned on or an "educational documentary" shown, had become a term of dreary opprobrium among "hip" film people. And yet liberation cinema, as developed by feminists and third-world activists, had already invigorated and transformed the use of talking heads in documentaries. The featureless head of a Tupamaro guerrilla, silhouetted against a vivid banner of national liberation, speaking concretely about the conditions in his country which led him to resistance, and intercut with clandestine footage of those conditions, had a very different effect from the official talking heads of presidents and psychologists. The Tupamaro guerrilla (Tupamaros, Jan Lindquist, Uruguay/Sweden, 1973) functions as a visual symbol of oppression and resistance, and, speaking as he does from personal experience, he represents himself, and empowers himself and his colleagues by so giving voice to a perspective which had previously gone unrepresented.

By the late 1970s, even the dreary standard interview with an authoritative business suit was transformed by California Newsreel's Controlling Interest (USA, 1978), where we see executives of multinational corporations speak with disarming candor to solemnly suited Newsreel interviewers about the need for steadily increasing profits, intercut with location footage and voice-over narration which shows the results of "development" for the majority of workers, both in the U. S. and in "developing" countries.

Early women's liberation cinema used images of women talking in close-up to validate the concept of self-expression, a crucial concept for women used to being objectified, interpreted, eroticized and generally discounted by the mass media; examples of some liberating talking head films are Janie's Janie (Geri Ashur, USA, 1971); Women Talking (Midge Mackenzie, U. K. , 1970); and Three Lives (Kate Millett, USA, 1971). Although the way in which these talking heads are filmed and used has a great deal to do with their effect, very little attention has been paid to such distinctions by critics. In a groundbreaking article which brings feminist analysis to bear on some documentary practices, Julia Lesage remarks that many early feminist documentaries "used a simple format to present to audiences ... a picture of the ordinary details of women's lives, their thoughts--told directly by the protagonists to the camera."[10] She lists a number of films as examples, and I note that in most of them most of the women do not in fact address the camera directly--instead, they speak to an off-screen interviewer, or to someone seen by the viewer as the back of a head and a shoulder, or they are filmed in candid discussion with one or more women. When the protagonist does address the camera directly, as Robin Mide does in Three Lives, there is a considerable difference in the effect on the viewer--Mide immediately takes on more apparent responsibility for her presentation in the film.[11]

The decision about whether or not to ask a documentary subject to address the camera directly is one which depends on many factors, such as the desired effect on the audience, the subject's personality, the filming situation, the subject matter to be discussed, the filmic context for the shot. There are physical considerations, such as lighting, the comfort of the subject, the kind of lens being used, the amount of film stock available; and there are other considerations, harder to define, concerning the rapport between filmmaker(s) and subject(s), motivations, understanding on each side of the camera of how the pro-filmic situation relates to the subject's milieu, the filmmaker's milieu, the milieu in which the film will be seen. Clearly these factors operate differently in documentary situations than in feature filming; I think they are also different for filmmakers who bring a feminist approach to documentation, that is, an approach which is anti-sexist and which is sensitive to power dynamics among filmmaker, subject, and audience.

Some Theory Begins to Emerge from Observation

It should be clear by now that synchronized sound close-ups, or "talking heads," can be used in different ways to achieve very different results. It seems useful at this point to make a general distinction between the use of talking heads to represent some official or authoritative position, and the use of talking heads of people who are telling their own stories. Another, more formal three-part distinction can be made among: 1) interviews where the subject addresses someone who is either off-screen or on; 2) candid or informal discussions filmed in close-up; and 3) direct address to the camera, where the subject appears to be talking to the audience. Each of these approaches has quite different implications in terms of shooting, editing, and final result.

Examples of all the above uses of talking heads can be found in feminist documentary films, sometimes in ways which challenge dominant coding, sometimes, unintentionally I think, in ways which reinforce dominant, therefore sexist/racist, assumptions. I have several times been in screening situations where the women in the audience groaned and jeered to see a male doctor or psychiatrist used as an authority on subjects such as rape, pornography, or sex-role stereotyping.[12] Sometimes the use of a female doctor, judge, or other professional as an authority works as a refreshing reversal; but it can also function to invalidate the self-definition of non-professional women. Close-ups filmed during group discussions can be used to show the power of women working together, as in <u>Self Health</u> (Lighthouse Films, USA, 1974) and <u>Rape</u> (JoAnn Elam, USA, 1976); depending on the context they can also be used to focus attention on personalities and divert it from relevant issues of class, race, age, etc. A problematic film in this respect is Nana, Mom and Me (Amalie Rothschild, USA, 1974), where the protagonists speak about their lives in a personal context, but omit references to their considerable wealth and social status, which obviously had a lot to do with the nature and outcome of their personal struggles.

Sometimes it is important, in analyzing a feminist documentary, to recognize other priorities than those involved in challenging dominant coding--for example, In the Best Interest of the Children (Iris Films, USA, 1977), a film designed to be used as an educational tool to help lesbian mothers fight court custody battles, deliberately stresses the expertise of various women who testify as authority figures, at the same time that it validates the ability of lesbian mothers and their children to speak clearly for themselves. The film also emphasizes the nurturing qualities of the women, and avoids issues of interest to the lesbian community which might easily have come up in the interviews (e.g., separatism, community responsibility for childcare) but which might adversely affect the audience for whom the film is primarily intended: social workers, judges, lawyers, legislators.[13]

Given the constantly changing parameters of documentation, I find prescriptive theorizing about what feminist documentarians should or shouldn't do worse than useless. What is helpful to me as a filmmaker and teacher is analysis of different approaches which have been used by other filmmakers in terms of their effects and further potential.

Three Contemporary Documentaries Which Use Talking Heads in Thought-Provoking Ways

A strong documentary which uses a conventional authority figure in an unconventional way is the anti-nuclear film Dark Circle (Judy Irving, Chris Beaver, Ruth Landy, USA, 1982), a feminist film about the effects of plutonium on the environment, and about the efforts of people, three women in particular, to stop the operation of nuclear reactors which produce plutonium. One of the interviews in the film is with the architect who designed a housing project in Rocky Flats, Colorado, built, without his knowledge, on plutonium-contaminated soil. The architect tells his own story--his young daughter died of cancer, which he believes to have been caused by plutonium poisoning. Speaking at first to an offscreen interviewer, his image intercut with photos of his daughter, the architect later addresses the camera directly when he suggests the "authorities" would have a different attitude towards nuclear hazards if they were to consider that it is their own children's lives at risk. Clearly he has undergone that precise transformation of attitude.

Another example of how interviews with professional people can be used to raise questions about traditional authority is As If It Were Yesterday (Miriam Abramowicz, Esther Hoffenberg, Belgium, 1982), a documentary about Belgians who hid Jewish children from the Nazis during the Occupation. One of the main figures in the film, an elderly doctor, tells of how she and others in her hospital falsified records to save Jews. Responding matter-of-factly to a question, she says, "We never obeyed German laws. Why should we? Just because they put a piece of paper on the wall... ?" This woman, like most others interviewed in the film, was concerned that she and her colleagues should not be seen as heroes. The filmmakers, themselves daughters of Jews who were hidden during the war, were able to get most of the interviews because of their personal connection to the events discussed, because they also wanted to stress the ordinary, everyday qualities of the Resistance, and because the people interviewed "are very conscious about the uprising of fascism today, because they feel war is imminent again."

The interviews in As If It Were Yesterday are carefully selected and honed--the filmmakers, aided in making their first film by the advice of Resnais' editor, Henri Colpi, learned the difficult lesson of discarding material by "someone who had done extraordinary things but who didn't know how to express it."[14] The subjects are shown in their homes or offices, in a street café, in a park, always a familiar environment. In each interview the framing and use of background was determined according to the individual situation--Dr. Hendrick, described above, is first shown in her office in a long shot, which includes one of the filmmakers. This follows an extended close-up from the preceding interview and "gives some air," as director Miriam Abramowicz explained in a recent interview. Then the camera moves in to a medium close-up--Hendrick addresses the filmmaker seen with her earlier. The dramatic and often problematic extreme close-up (ECU) is used only once in the film--when a woman who was hidden as a child speaks about her difficulty in being appropriately grateful to the adults who hid her. The shot is suited to the feeling of the interview and also practical, as the setting is a street café, and an extreme close-up allows the microphone to be held close to the subject's mouth without appearing in the shot. The woman's face has a well-defined bone structure, and "takes" the ECU well, not distorting as some faces do. (Abramowicz's background as a photographer stood her in good stead here.)

In an interview the filmmakers spoke to me about their concern to achieve "a certain quality of light, a life-like manner of presenting people, a sensitive climate," not to intrude on or violate people's homes. They also spoke about the fact that, unlike Marcel Ophuls' interview documentary on the French Resistance, so many of their subjects were women. Women were very active in the Belgian Resistance (as they were in France); women, on the whole more than men, have learned to express feelings directly rather than to be abstract and impersonal; and, as women themselves, the filmmakers found women more open to talking with them. These last two points are not new to feminists; they are central to an understanding of talking heads in feminist documentary.

Like As If It Were Yesterday, Dark Circle is a film in which women played strong creative roles on both sides of the camera, a feminist film about an issue not specifically defined as feminist, to which the filmmakers have a clearly articulated personal commitment. It is this commitment, rather than their technological presence, which is consciously inscribed into the film. At one point in Dark Circle, where a housewife is interviewed about her painful decision to sell her Rocky Flats house to another couple with young children (she is moving because of her fears about plutonium poisoning for her own children), one of the directors is heard, voice over a shot of the house before the final interview. She says, "I wondered what I would do in her situation." In this way the filmmaker urges the viewer, by her own example, to consider the situation and its implications, rather than passing a moral judgment on the woman. This is also a good example of a situation where an informal close-up is at once essential and insufficient, requiring additional commentary--the woman is seen in the process of moving, clearly upset about her decision and unwilling to go into details. (In earlier scenes, when she was working to organize the neighbors, and was much more hopeful, she cooperated fully with the film crew.) Had the film simply showed her moving, vérité style, without comment, and showed the new family moving in, the crucial analysis of the heavy forces at work might have been lost.

Both *As If It Were Yesterday* and *Dark Circle* are advocacy films designed to inspire a specific reaction, popular resistance to situations seen as threatening people's lives today. Both films use talking heads as empowering devices, representing people who represent themselves, and thereby suggesting that we are all capable of representing ourselves, of interpreting and acting upon our own interpretations of reality. By the simple fact that both films use numerous experiential interviews and other kinds of footage, the audience, by now sensitized to issues of editorial manipulation, is aware that an argument is being constructed. Unlike the vérité films of Wiseman or King, these films invite a questioning, critical stance towards the subjective attitudes they represent; unlike government or corporate propaganda, they represent a challenge to traditional authority. By empowering ordinary people to speak as experts, they question a basic assumption of dominant ideology, that only those already in power, those who have a stake in defending the status quo, are entitled to speak as if they know something. By ensuring that a range of attitudes and actions is presented by their subjects, these films avoid the "extraordinary portrait" syndrome so dear to the hearts of tokenists and beloved of the National Film Bored, whereby a welfare mother of six studies welding all night and works to feed her children all day for a year, finally triumphing and becoming an example to the undeserving masses of less energetic welfare mothers in the land (*Pretend You're Wearing a Barrel*, Jan Martell, Canada, 1978).

Les Servantes du Bon Dieu ([*The Handmaidens of God*], Diane Létourneau, Quebec, 1979) is not an advocacy film, and its use of talking heads is more traditional than in either of the two films discussed above. Designed as a group portrait of an order of nuns based in Quebec whose primary role is to serve priests, the film includes interviews with priests and male doctors, as well as with the nuns themselves; also observational footage of the nuns at work and in their mother convent, with voice-over narration by a female commentator and by the nuns. Typically, an interview in which the subject speaks to an off-camera interviewer, presumably the director, is intercut with footage of the subject at work, if a nun, or in a situation related to the nuns, if a priest or doctor. There is no question but that the filmmaker's attitude to the material is used to shape the material implicitly--for instance, an interview with a priest who praises the work of the nuns is intercut with a scene where the same priest is shown at dinner with his colleagues, being served silently by a nun who is not directly addressed even though the topic of conversation is her order.

As might be expected, the film reveals a good deal about sex-role stereotyping within the Catholic Church, and the way theology is used to justify the exploitation of women's labor. However, something else is also revealed by the film, which raises even more interesting issues. The nuns are clearly happy and self-fulfilled, and not mindlessly so at all. Coming, for the most part, from large, not well-off Quebec families, faced with the choice of traditional marriage, traditional spinsterhood, or the Church, many of these women embraced the order as their only chance for a relatively decent existence. As nuns serving priests they get formal appreciation for work which would be dismissed as mere housework were they secular wives. They are fed, clothed, housed, and very well cared for in their old age. They are not beaten nor sexually abused nor forced to bear many children. They have strong friendships with each other, satisfying work relationships, the chance to learn non-traditional skills (e.g., car mechanics, appliance repair, printing) if they are interested, and they can develop creative interests (music, painting). Compared to their contemporaries (most are over sixty and the order is not attracting younger women), a comparison not made explicitly by the film but rather inferred by the commentary and the women's own remarks, these women are doing unusually well.

Having viewed the film with several different classes of students of different ages and backgrounds, the consensus has been invariable, that the film works to change the viewer's preconceptions, whatever they were originally. I think that no amount of commentary over visuals or expert testimony would have made this impression; and certainly a cinéma-vérité portrait of these nuns, who work mainly in silence, or singing quietly to themselves, would have fallen far short of the effect achieved here. It is the cumulative effect of the nuns themselves, each speaking, with considerable humor, wit and some profound reflection, of her own history, which challenges whatever stereotypical judgment the viewer may have brought to the film.

Direct Address, In Which I Speak of My Own Films

Although the subjects in the films discussed above tend to evoke an impression of directness, they do not actually address the camera directly. Having inadvertently stumbled on the device of direct address in my first independently produced film, Good Day Care: One out of Ten (Martineau and Lorna Rasmussen, Canada, 1978), I have found direct address increasingly important as a way of setting up dialogue with the audience, as well as collaboration with the film subject, marked for the audience as such by the device itself.

Pat, who runs a day care center for children of immigrants, was nervous and stilted when we interviewed her, and none of her normal energy or lucidity was coming across. It was Martin Duckworth, our cameraman, who said to me later, while we were shooting some candid footage of Pat playing with the children, "Why don't you ask her those questions now?" I was standing behind Martin, and I shouted my questions to Pat, who shouted back over and through the excited children. The resulting footage was wonderful--Pat appears to be speaking straight to the audience. Years later, people who saw the film once still remember Pat vividly and, more importantly, they remember what she said, mainly a rather complex argument about the inaccessibility of day-care subsidy for most working-class parents, and the need for all children to have the best possible day care in an environment scaled to the needs of the child.

We used the device again in Good Day Care when we filmed two parents from a cooperative center. That's when I realized the economy of the device: we were running out of footage and money, and the direct interview material ended up being used on a ratio of $1\frac{1}{2}$ to 1, compared to 12:1 for the rest of the film. Discussing the material with the parents ahead of time, knowing, because we were already well into the editing process, almost exactly what we needed, we had unusual control while shooting. In the finished film I found that the direct interviews, which appear in the latter part of the film, help to balance the voice-over commentary used earlier to convey historical and factual information. People involved in the field are seen to articulate their sense of how it works in a way which is experienced by the audience as sharing. In a film intended for use as an organizing tool for parents and day-care workers, this is an important effect, used sparingly.

Similar thinking led me to use direct address in my next film, Tales of Tomorrow: Our Elders (Canada, 1982). That film, concerned with the issue of choice for lucid seniors, interweaves two stories: Alex Kielish has moved into Baycrest Jewish Home for the Aged to obtain chronic care for his wife, Helen, who has Alzheimer's Disease. Sarah Binns, confined to a wheelchair for forty-five years with rheumatoid arthritis, moved into and out of a home for the aged, and explains her choice to live in an apartment by herself at the age of 80. The film shows some footage of the lives of each person, supplemented by photos, and there are two crucial talking heads scenes, filmed differently. In Alex's case, we filmed a discussion in his humanities group, where he talks about his grief over his wife's illness and engages in dialogue with other group members. He was aware of our purpose in filming and was eager to cooperate, but we did not ask him to address the camera. I had found in doing audio interviews that direct address, even to a microphone, made Alex self-conscious, that he rambled and tended to lose focus. In the familiar setting of his group he relaxed and accepted the camera as part of the group. This was appropriate to another function of the scene in the film, which is to show the kind of emotional support Alex receives at Baycrest. He cries in the scene, and argues about the inevitability of his wife's decline. Audiences usually respond to Alex's emotion with sympathy, pleasure in recognizing a validation of a man's expression of emotion, and an intellectual, critical response to the role of the group leader in terms of her approach to Alex.

In the case of Sarah, immediately following the printed title which introduces Sarah Binns, 80, labor organizer, wheelchair activist (identical in style to the title introducing the Kielishes), Sarah speaks briefly on screen, directly to the camera. The effect is very strong, as Sarah is lucid, charming, humorous, and also evidently old and very crippled. From this point on, Sarah's voice is used as commentary over visuals of her life and some scenes from Baycrest. Very different from the conventional authority figure, Sarah's direct address serves to underline her point, that she is sane, determined, and entirely capable of making appropriate decisions about her life and needs.

After making two social-issue documentaries designed to stimulate change on topics I considered important, but which concerned people close to me rather than my own lived experience, and in which I used footage of people to illustrate ideas and issues, I wanted to do work that felt closer to me. Both Good Day Care and Tales of Tomorrow, while modestly budgeted by any commercial standards, were still expensive enough to require outside funding, which took an enormous percentage of my own time and energy. At the end of five years, three of which were spent fundraising to produce two films, I wanted to try making a film much more cheaply, much faster, and more joyfully!

Talking heads--what more unlikely choice for a joyful documentary? But I had noticed over and over that the effect of talking heads depends on who is talking about what and how. I resolved to make a cheap, entertaining talking heads film, one in which the subjects would be collaborators. The topic was at hand--a friend had given me an article in the Village Voice by Jane Lazarre about her course at CCNY, "The Woman as Hero." She applied the mythic pattern of the hero to the poor black and Hispanic women in her course, and found that these women were heroes in the sense that they had survived potentially crushing life experiences and survived to tell the tale. I made a film called Heroes about three women I know: Sarah Binns, the octogenarian protagonist of Tales of Tomorrow: Olga Lamb, a music student from Trinidad, 75 years old, who was in my film class at York University; and Martha Keaner, 46, photographer, carpentry student, and my partner. I shot half the film myself, with borrowed equipment, and edited it myself--both personal firsts. I designed the film to suit my limited skills and tiny budget, and depended heavily on my friends in front of and behind the camera. Direct address was a key element in my design for the film. (See photos, p. 268.)

I asked each woman three questions, designed according to the heroic archetype described by Lazarre (which I believe she derived from Joseph Campbell):[15] What was the most difficult time in your life? (the ordeal of the hero); How did you get through that time? (the heroic character and response); What is the most important thing you've learned that you can share with other people? (the hero's gift for the world). Each woman had time to think about the questions and formulate her answers (at least a few days before filming). We filmed each woman in her home, with some candid footage, worked out with each subject, to establish her context. I chose extremely simple

"Talking heads" in Heroes: top to bottom, Sarah Binns, Olga Lamb and Martha Keaner address the camera. (Photos: Barbara Halpern Martineau)

backgrounds: a colored wall, a rocking chair, a brick wall, focusing attention on the woman herself. Lighting was bounced and we used fast color negative to avoid direct light, which is uncomfortable and distracting. (In Sarah's case, as her eyes are extremely sensitive to light, it was particularly important to light her indirectly.)

In the finished film there is an introductory section which is a musical essay on the concept of woman as hero. I appear briefly in two scenes as a filmmaker making a film about women who are heroes. We see each of the three women, filmed in a working situation, then the rest of the film consists of the responses to the three questions. Each response is used uncut, and candid footage of the women is used between the responses.

For most of the film the audience is watching sync sound close-ups of women talking directly to the camera, pausing, considering, listening to a question, hesitating, smiling, finishing, being silent. The subject of each woman's discourse is her own life, interpreted in collaboration with the filmmaker as part of a heroic pattern. Martha, the youngest woman in the film at forty-six, describes herself as being in the midst of her own heroic process. In coming out as a lesbian to the camera, which requires a deep breath, she continues the process, on film, which she has been describing as part of her life.

Because the three women are very different from each other, and because they are all very different from the women we are accustomed to seeing valorized by the mass media, they offer a wide range of comparison/identification to the audience. The most common response I have heard from women in the audience is: "That means I am a hero, too," or, "That means I can be a hero." Because one or more of the women are often present when the film is shown, and because I appear in the film, audiences have explicitly commented on the sense of collaboration they feel while watching Heroes.

As I was finishing post-production on Heroes, the opportunity arose to make a short film I'd been planning for several months, and I was able to take the process of collaboration one step further. Several years before, on a canoeing outing, my friend Keltie had told me and another friend the story of why she wears a beard, which is hereditary from women in her father's family. We found her story both moving and transforming--our stereotyped responses to a bearded women were permanently altered. It finally occurred to me that we could share this experience with many other women if we made a film of Keltie's story. Keltie agreed--the problem was then to find the time. There was one afternoon in May when Keltie was in town and we had film equipment on loan. I had one 400' roll of film, and some sound tapes. We rehearsed the story four times, on video, each time looking at what we'd done and discussing how it worked and how to pare it down a bit more. Finally we felt ready--there was a thunderstorm, and we just prayed it wouldn't thunder while we were shooting. I knew Keltie had done some acting, and I counted on her to improve with practice, instead of going stale. I wanted her to tell her story in the most creative, communicative way possible.

I had asked Keltie from the start to address the camera. During the first two video shoots she found this difficult, but when she saw the results and we talked about it, she agreed that a direct gaze was important. She also took off her tinted glasses. We, and a lot of subsequent viewers, discovered that Keltie has beautiful blue eyes, and the combination of her beard, her blue eyes and shiny brown hair, and a few bright daffodils in the frame with a background of old wood, coupled with Keltie's ability to tell her story clearly, with humor and warmth, is now working to alter many stereotyped responses to the sight of a bearded woman. Audiences discuss their own facial hair, the standardization and cosmeticization of female beauty in our culture, stereotypes of lesbian women, divisions within feminist/lesbian communities, ideas of women as spectacle, Keltie's storytelling prowess, the process of making the film ... (encouraged to this last point by a rather comic initial frame including Keltie, Martha with a clapper board, and me recording sound).

It is true that a finished film consists of two-dimensional images which are projected on a screen and accompanied by electronically recorded, transferred, processed, amplified sound. It is many removes from the original filming situation, which is itself removed from the experiences that situation has been set up to express. With all this, there are many degrees of correspondence between the film as seen and the original experience. Just as in our daily lives we present fragments of our experience to each other, filtered and shaped by our presentation, so we do in film, with many more technical tools, which are aids or impediments depending on their use. The sound and sight of a woman's talking head can function in many ways. I have delineated a few of the ways such an image can be used to challenge stereotypes, establish degrees of commitment, and set up the preconditions for useful dialogue--and action--towards social change.

Notes

1 Christine Gledhill, "Whose Choice"; Julia Lesage, Judith Mayne, B. Ruby Rich et alia in "Women and Film: A Discussion of Feminist Aesthetics," New German Critique, special issue on Women and Film, No. 13 (Winter 1976); E. Ann Kaplan, Women and Film, forthcoming, but see my forthcoming review in Jump Cut for some skepticism about the follow-through on Kaplan's expressed concerns.

2 During a recent conference on independent documentary, co-sponsored by the American Film Institute and Public Broadcasting, in the course of an argument about whether or not a forthcoming PBS series on the Vietnam war represents a "balanced" approach, a producer in the audience remarked that the North Vietnamese were consistently referred to by the series narrator as "the enemy." He remembered working on a New England newspaper which ran a picture of Lyndon Johnson with the caption "Enemy Bombs Hanoi."

3 At a conference on feminist film criticism held at Northwestern University in 1980, mine was the only paper of about forty presented concerning documentary film criticism. This lack of critical attention to documentaries has been characteristic of conferences, periodical publications since the demise of Women & Film, anthologies, course curricula, and scholarly work by feminists; on the other hand, women's film festivals, especially those organized on a local level, are often showcases for documentaries, and those programs are often very well attended. In the documentary milieu, conversely, while women are generally acknowledged, or at least seen to play increasingly strong and influential roles as filmmakers, feminist analysis is seldom brought to bear on controversial questions. This was true at the AFI/PBS

conference; it holds in terms of books on documentary theory (except for this one), and it seems to be the case at documentary seminars, such as the Grierson in Canada. Seth Feldman's three-part series for CBC Radio's "Ideas," on documentary film, managed to write women and feminism out of documentary film history once again.

4 Some examples are: El Salvador: The People Will Win (El Salvador, 1981); The Brickmakers (Colombia, 1973); To the People of the World (Chile, 1975).

5 See my article, "Out of Sight, Out of Mind, Out of Pocket: Lesbian Representation in Documentary Film," Resources in Feminist Research, forthcoming.

6 Compare the final close-up of Viva in Agnes Varda's Lions Love, a shot shortly preceded by a still of Garbo. Viva, like Garbo, is silent, but we hear not only her breathing, but the recurrent question of Varda behind the camera: "How much longer?" (Viva has just said to the camera that she wants to just breathe for one minute.) The final flash frame on the shot is left in. Due to these interventions it is difficult, if not impossible, to lose oneself in Viva's face.

7 There is no information available to us about the people whose close-ups are used so freely by Vertov--what remains of them is pure mythology in the midst of Vertov's process of exposing the making of mythology.

8 Ruby Grierson and Evelyn Spice Cherry were described by Paul Rotha as "women directors" who "handled their characters with greater sympathy than is found in other documentaries of the Grierson group." Documentary Film (London, 1935; 3rd ed., 1952), p. 150.

9 Eileen McGarry, "Documentary Realism and Women's Cinema," Women & Film, 2:7, is the oft-quoted standard article on this subject. What neither McGarry nor Claire Johnston, whom she cites, examine in their calls for a "counter-cinema," is the possibility that "realism" as a style can be used to challenge dominant coding rather than to reinforce it. Christine Gledhill and Julia Lesage (see below) both raise this possibility.

10 "The Political Aesthetics of the Feminist Documentary Film," Quarterly Review of Film Studies (Fall, 1978), incorporated into Lesage's "Feminist Documentary: Aesthetics and Politics" included in this volume.

11 I think it is this same notion of apparent responsibility which draws first-time viewers into accepting the women in Michelle Citron's Daughter-Rite (USA, 1978) as documentary subjects, and which often leads to a feeling of betrayal when they discover the women are actors using a script. Rather than invalidating the feminist documentary, I think Daughter Rite raises questions about the relationship of trust between feminists on each side of the camera.

12 An unfortunate example is Bonnie Kreps' early and otherwise progressive film, After the Vote (Canada, 1969), which uses a standard interview with a male psychiatrist; another, more recent example is Not a Love Story (Canada, 1981), where both women and men as professional authority figures are contrasted with Linda Lee Tracy, the "subject"--who is patronized and objectified by her contextualization in the film.

13 See Cathy Cade et alia, "Interview with Iris Films," Jump Cut, no. 19.

14 See my review/interview in Broadside (Toronto), Oct/Nov. 1980.

15 The Hero with a Thousand Faces, 1949-68.

Chapter 14

SHINSUKE OGAWA'S PEASANTS OF THE SECOND FORTRESS: GUERRILLA DOCUMENTARY IN JAPAN

Joan Braderman

Committed documentary from Japan is sadly neglected in the West, with Peasants of the Second Fortress still remaining the best-known example of a very dynamic tradition, more than a decade after its release (the other representative with some exposure in the West has been The Minimata Trilogy, Noriaki Tsuchimoto, 1974). The airport that was the focus of Ogawa's peasants' struggles was ultimately built, but its siege still continues and the peasants' mobilization has long since encompassed other issues.

The most remarkable aspect of Peasants of the Second Fortress is the degree to which aesthetic decisions affecting its shape and content have been systematically rendered as political decisions. Not only the structure of the film itself has been determined by a concrete political context and ideology, but the way this film was made and shown throughout Japan to hundreds of thousands of people represents a virtual model for political filmmakers, East and West. It is a model not necessarily in terms of the correctness of its political line (a kind of ultra-left Maoism) nor even the "perfection" of the film as an art object for consumption. It is a model precisely because of the attempt of the filmmakers, themselves working collectively, to make a commitment to a desperate and violent political struggle, and to produce a partisan document of that struggle. And this partisanship is never suppressed in the interests of false objectivity. The "side" taken by the camera is as out front as the decision of a community of Japanese peasant farmers to resist being run off their land by the government-supported Narita Airport Corporation.

The militant and protracted fight of this group of peasants, aided by workers and members of Zengakuren, the radical student left of Japan, against the usurping of their land by Japanese monopoly capitalists, is a phenomenon largely unknown to Americans. It began in 1966 at Sanrizuka, a district of Narita designed by the government for the construction of a large, new airport. It continued for over five years. The characteristically limited perspective of American journalism is itself dramatized when we in America see the bloody confrontations which Peasants of the Second Fortress documents. However, there are several important elements in the process of its making and distribution which should be clarified for Western viewers in order to better understand the film within its own historical context.

First, the two-and-a-half-hour film is, in fact, a relatively small segment of a longer "open" or ongoing film. What we see here is but a portion of an unstaged, virtual serial. After editing, apparently at a ratio of about 2:1 (footage shot to footage used), the Ogawa group produced about 16 hours of film in a series of two- to four-hour formats.[1] The filmmakers did not just "shoot and run," as is often the case with such projects. They have attempted to give a continuing, multiple series of reports on the events at Narita. This two-and-a-half-hour segment begins in the middle of the struggle, as indeed all so-called documentaries begin with the personal decisions of filmmakers in the midst of complex historical processes. It ends in the tunnels under Sanrizuka, to which the peasants retreat between overt "dramatic" battles above ground.

In view of this overall open design, the assumptions behind the temporal structure of this film may become clearer. For the first part of the film describes battle: discussions of battle strategy, the wait for the moment of confrontation, the battle itself. The intrinsic excitement of that battle, punctuated by sequences of more personalized discussions among the members of "our side," play on our conditioned responses to the romantic, idealized excitement of war and movies about war. The fact that this is sync sound and imagery from what we are told is a "real" war may even intensify that excitement. But the film ends with an extremely long sequence shot within the labyrinthine tunnels where nothing--at least according to standard dramatic-psychological conventions--happens.

Digging in "underground," below the land that represents their traditional way of life and only livelihood, the peasants make their ultimate stand. In a sense it is a symbolic stand, but it is also a significant strategic one in that holding the tunnels meant forcing the tactical hand of the government-backed construction corporation and its military arm--the police--in evicting the peasants. Pushing back poorly-armed students and peasants and knocking down their jerry-built fortresses is one thing. Crushing intransigent human beings under the earth would be quite another.

Obviously, the tunnels are constructed and maintained meticulously, but under great duress. Perhaps less obviously, what prompts the filmmakers, I believe, to include this lengthy sequence below ground, is an attempt to reproduce an experience analogous to that of the people inside. It is a visual experience of darkness, constriction, and ritualized repetition. The long static shots and obsessive interview commentary, in effect, have a direct expressive relation to the quality of the lived experience. The length of temporal scale of this sequence, then, proposes filmically a representation of the importance of the tunnels to the peasant campaign. This directly expressive impulse accounts for the overall shooting and editing style of this film.

Just as the second fortress we see destroyed here is the second of seven, so the inconclusive, a-dramatic structure of this film inscribes in its long meandering form the ongoing process through which the peasants take an initial step, then gradually become politicized over five years of direct experience of repression by the Japanese ruling class. There is, by the way, a precedent for "long movies" in Japan: witness the extreme example of Kobayashi's nine-hour version of The Human Condition. But the necessarily long process of struggle and political awakening for the peasants is recapitulated here by the filmmakers' long-term commitment to making images from behind the barricades at Sanrizuka. For us, the length of the tunnel sequence and the film itself--in its parts and across its segments--constitutes a kind of attack on accepted conventions of Western commercial cinema. The serial strategy also allows the filmmakers to give an extended, explicitly counter-establishment voice to the peasants doing battle in this small but intensive war with corporate Japan. The view, over time, from their adopted position with the people under attack behind the fortresses, carries the ideological clarity that this physical position, almost by definition, represents. The camera sees, we the viewers see--from and only from this position of commitment.

The Ogawa group makes a related attack on established forms of film distribution. With Tsuchimoto, the other major independent left documentarist currently working in Japan (on a series of films-in-process about the struggles around the disastrous effects of mercury-poisoned fish in Minimata), Ogawa and group are creating an alternate screening context for these films. The films themselves were made on an astoundingly low budget. Then, renting at minimal fees the municipal halls in townships all over Japan, the filmmakers involved each city's left base in mobilizing around publicity for and showing of the films. Thereby, they are able to create contemporary agit-prop situations outside of the aesthetic parentheses of movie houses. The stranglehold of monopolistic film distributors is cannily circumvented. Moreover, the films-in-process about the coming to political consciousness through process (of continued struggle and oppression) engage their audiences themselves in a qualitatively different process of film viewing. It takes place outside of the bracketed theaters of art or entertainment and inside a context of political discourse and political action on each home ground.

The trust established between filmworkers and farmworkers here is evidenced in a number of ways. The camera people are subject to the same tensions and dangers as those engaged in active fighting. The camera therefore shakes and wavers in confrontation sequences. This crew is plunged into the midst of action. As we watch, say, the Women's Action Committee and other groups in the Sanrizuka community engaged in discussion of defense tactics, the hand-held camera "presence" has clearly been accepted as an ally. This camera is tolerated as it records long continuous sequences at extremely close range. It roves from face to face over quieter as well as more vocal group members. It will often rest on non-speakers while we hear the voice of a speaker on the soundtrack. The number of such sequences and this "democracy" of shooting style emphasizes the filmmakers' investment in the collective process as a central ideological axis for both themselves and the peasants. It is clear then, that getting the word out about the dynamic of the Narita struggle is a shared goal.

The fact that we see what is accessible only from one "side" of the action also puts forward formally what underwrites the film ideologically. The typical long establishing shots of movie battle sequences (intercut with salient details) suggest some invisible, objective third-person narrator behind the camera. Here, on the other hand, the few long shots "establishing" the location of approaching police in relation to militants are made from a hillock on land occupied by the peasants. Indeed we see them on this hill in the same space the shots were made. The camera stays close and tight on women and children chaining themselves to the trees on their land. It doesn't "look away" from scenes of brutality or from the faces and bodies of screaming victims. This camera is committed to staying physically where its operators are politically: unblinkingly facing the bitter realities of state oppression.

But given this rigorously one-sided view of events, we, as viewers, are in fact in a better position for thinking about the views of the other side. It is of course this "other side" which controls a near monopoly on the means of information production in Japanese as well as our own culture. Toward demystifying this notion of information or "documentary" material as being produced objectively by any person, interest group, state, etc., the Ogawa group offers a biased account of real events but systematically renders its bias visible. As the Narita struggle itself served as a brutal catalyst for the political consciousness of the people who lived there, so such films as this can become consciousness-raising tools for others. To look unremittingly for nearly three hours (or better, 16, over a series of showings) at the armed front of a corporate state overtly protecting its interests, and to look at this from the perspective of the directly endangered, is to see these interests laid out more clearly than they may generally appear.

An interesting final note on the way consciousness spread from the experience of this group to others in Japan: on last word from the area, though construction was under way on the airport and the people we see in this film were (temporarily) defeated, peasants on the other end of Narita were resisting the implacement of airport pipelines under their lands. This must needs be seen as a small provocation given the powers they were up against. But it can certainly be read as a show of solidarity with ideas bitterly learned in Sanrizuka and the many other struggles for self-determination throughout the world. (1976)

Note

1 For background material on the making of this film, I have relied heavily on the research and generous consultation of Noel Burch.

Chapter 15

COMMITTED DOCUMENTARY IN QUEBEC: A STILL-BIRTH?

Réal La Rochelle*

The trajectory of the committed documentary in Quebec provides a fascinating case study of the vicissitudes of a small national cinema constructed around one of the most eloquent and most unjustly neglected (even on its own turf) bodies of political documentary in the world. La Rochelle's study of its unique context (now threatened, whence this article's tone of urgency) and its contradictions (impassioned militant documentary nurtured within the apparatus of the bourgeois state!) and his critique of some of its nationalist and sectarian tendencies are relevant to cinemas caught up everywhere in resistance to the Star Wars empire, First World, Second, and Third.

For Gilles Groulx

The Québécois cinema is barely twenty years old. It only appeared at the beginning of the sixties, as part of the international emergence of young national cinemas and "new waves." Defined for the first time as "Québécois" as opposed to French-Canadian, this new cinema profited from the cultural and economic momentum of the Quiet Revolution (a period of rapid change set off by the modernizing reforms of Jean Lesage's Liberal government, 1960-1966).

*Translated from the French by Mark Leslie and Thomas Waugh.

In large part, Québécois cinema is documentary, in the current sense of the term. Many of these documentaries, moreover, may be categorized as tools of analysis and social intervention. So much so that the international reputation of Québécois cinema--through names like Gilles Groulx, Pierre Perrault, Michel Brault, Arthur Lamothe, Jean-Claude Labrecque, Anne-Claire Poirier, Claude Jutra, etc.--is largely based on our cinema's unique relationship with the historical trends of the social documentary.

I am going to attempt to review briefly these twenty years of Québécois documentary. I will concentrate on a few significant films, and in particular on the most committed ones, representative of certain intellectual or ideological tendencies. By "committed," I mean films critical of Quebec's past and present social fabric, films which question economic, political and cultural realities, films which are politically involved with social changes and transformations, as well as with democratic rights; films in which popular content, both cultural and social, is clear.

> ... in Quebec, the cinema that questions has disappeared. It's too demanding. --Gilles Groulx (1980), in A vos risques et périls.

The Québécois cinema is not aging well. It is going through a crisis which is shaking its very foundations. It could be christened by the title of a documentary by Alain Corneau, La première chance (ou peut-être la dernière?) (The First Chance--or Maybe the Last?). That is, the Québécois cinema's first chance, which made it grow on and off, like a delinquent, until it was twenty years old, will perhaps not take it beyond adolescence. Jeunesse année zéro (Youth, year zero) was how Louis Portuguais entitled his 1964 portrait of the new generation disappointed and revolted by the Quiet Revolution. It could be said that today we are at the same point in relation to the youth of the Québécois cinema.

One of the most revealing aspects of this crisis is precisely the radical systematic questioning of the Québécois documentary. The commercial Québécois fiction cinema, which so badly wants to consolidate itself, does not appear to be able or to want to do so except by sacrificing the social documentary. We destroy what we love. Director

Claude Jutra recently let it be known "that he is not of the militant type, and that he no longer believes in the construction of a national Québécois cinema," and director Fernand Dansereau, making his first fiction feature after an entire career of documentary, explains, "At the beginning we wanted to make fiction, but it was the social climate which pushed us towards the documentary." Similar comments have been made in the last two years by other filmmakers as well.

Thus the shadows of Dziga Vertov, Robert Flaherty, Jean Vigo, Renoir (of La vie est à nous), Richard Leacock, Joris Ivens ... no longer look down on the Québécois cinema. And are we still aware today that one of the most circulated films in Quebec in the seventies was Biberman's The Salt of the Earth?

The weakening of the social documentary in Quebec is the weakening of the entire Québécois cinema. A number of signs have reflected this situation in the last few months:

--the Institut québécois du cinéma, the provincial funding body, no longer subsidizes documentaries in any meaningful way;

--Ottawa's Applebaum-Hébert Commission on Canadian culture has recommended that the federal government shut down the National Film Board and assign its film production activities to the private sector, and the same for the Canadian Broadcasting Corporation. This aims at the very heart of the documentary, and even of the Québécois cinema as defined so far, with waves being felt as far as the commercial fiction cinema.[1]

--Since the creation of Ottawa's Canadian Film Development Corporation in 1968 and new tax incentives for film production in 1975, federal aid to the Canadian film industry not only has helped set up a few mini-monopolies around generally banal commercial features, such as Porky's (thus eliminating financial aid to the documentary), but has also caused Québécois filmmakers, in view of national and international competition from Hollywood, to produce in English such "Québécois" films as Quest for Fire, City on Fire, Visiting Hours, and Atlantic City.

--the arrival of Pay TV is politically supported by the Canadian government with the same logic; the only

Québécois film model likely to survive is that of the big-budget nostalgic national epic, The Plouffe Family.

If we link up these political/economic factors with the intellectual crisis of many filmmakers and the cultural chaos into which Quebec has plunged since the defeat of the referendum on independence in 1980 and the 1982 proclamation of the new Canadian Constitution, there is nothing surprising about the funereal tone of recent debates on the Québécois cinema and the future of Quebec. Just when Quebec is timidly trying to retain its cultural autonomy in the areas of film and television, the federal government is actively preparing its new laws in these areas, consolidating the industry networks while ignoring Quebec absolutely.

In this context, the proposal of a General Bill on Quebec cinema, coming out of the recommendation of the Fournier Report and presented by the governing Parti québécois (the PQ) in December 1982, is properly entitled A Question of Survival. We shall soon see if this is not simply, in this cultural sector, the negation of the Quiet Revolution and the capitulation to Ottawa's policies.[2]

Let's look then at the short history of the committed documentary in Quebec. We can distinguish three fairly separate periods in its evolution: 1) from the end of the fifties up until about 1968, the emergence of the Quiet Revolution and of the new Québécois cinema; 2) from 1968 to 1975, the apogee and radicalization of the social documentary; 3) from 1975 to the present, crisis, renewal and prospects for the future.

1. "Maîtres chez nous" in Our Neighbor's House[3]

At the beginning of the sixties, the new Québécois cinema inherited the "Candid Eye" movement, and took over as the leader of direct cinema.[4] Three factors combined to produce this result:

--the consolidation of government production and distribution, principally by the NFB and the CBC on the federal level and secondarily by the Office du film du Québec on the provincial level;

--the cultural capabilities for filmmakers and technicians to work in homogeneous, continuous teams, without an overly technical or hierarchical division of labor (already present in the NFB's Les raquetteurs [The Snowshoers] in 1958);

--their ingenuity also in technical tinkering, for example, their modifications to the Arriflex 16mm camera.

Thus, supported by government budgets, Québécois filmmakers and technicians, who regrouped as the "équipe française" (French team) at the NFB, dived into an explosive cultural film adventure, which very early on, for many, would take a stand in the areas of national and social liberation struggles. In the space of, at most, four years there appeared documentaries like Golden Gloves (Gilles Groulx, 1961), Les bûcherons de la Manouane (Manouane River Lumberjacks, Arthur Lamothe, 1962), Pour la suite du monde (Moontrap, Pierre Perrault and Michel Brault, 1963), and Le Chat dans le sac (Cat in the Bag, Gilles Groulx, 1964), a work of fiction but a highly documented kind of fiction.

It would long remain one of the most contradictory historical facts that this boisterous birth of a "national" Québécois cinema occurred inside a Canadian government apparatus, which never intended it and always renounced it. The NFB would never manage to throw out this baby with the bathwater, water no doubt considered fairly polluted since, a few years later, when NFB Commissioner Sydney Newman suppressed On est au coton, he angrily explained to the press that "the NFB is at the service of capitalism and Canadian unity."

The Board's technocracy certainly tried everything to inhibit the consolidation of this cinema: through project refusals; administrative snags; censorship, involving both cuts (already in 1959, the NFB bowdlerized Gilles Groulx's Normétal to the point where he refused to have his name in the credits) and outright bans; and disclaimers to the public via the distribution service. If we add to this the self-censoring habits practiced more or less consciously by filmmakers at the Board, it isn't surprising that the innovative character of the Québécois cinema and documentary goes far beyond the films' context and formal aspects. To make Quebec films which asserted their own distinctive national character was already a form of subversion within the federal apparatus, and even outside of it. If this were not enough, these contradictions also set off serious splits among the filmmakers themselves, which were far deeper than the conventional distance between documentarists and proponents of fiction: contradictions between French and English production studios, but also between two different types of French production. NFB producer Jacques Bobet wrote in 1966 that "[at the NFB] ... there have been cries of anarchy, socialism, and revolution, but all told, the French filmmakers feel at home, tackling the problems they know best and which inspire the best cinema."

Thus, on one side, we see a Pierre Perrault assert himself, and with his trilogy on the isolated St. Lawrence island community of Ile-aux-Coudres (Pour la suite du monde, 1963; Le règne du jour [The Reign of Time, 1966]; Les voitures d'eau [River Schooners, 1968], establish the prototype of a Québécois cinema based on the "nature" of Québécois man ["the essence of Québécitude"]), on the values of his past and traditions, the search for his country and ancestors. One of the positive aspects of these films, other than that they are about ordinary people, is their historical reappropriation of the lives and livelihoods of some Québécois fishermen and farmers, their presentation of a "spoken image" of an authentically popular culture. "Family album," and "finding one's own voice" have been used to describe these films. True, but by being oriented only towards the past, by systematically ignoring the present of Ile-aux-Coudres, Perrault started the embryo of what he would soon develop into extreme ethnocentricity, calling out for a Nation-State Protector, and for artists to take over from the politicians, to be the conscience for masses atrophied by history. It had to lead up to films like Un pays sans bon sens (Wake up, Mes Bons Amis!, 1970) and Les gens d'Abitibi (People of Abitibi, 1979) in the seventies. For all these reasons, I consider the films of Perrault and his students to be subversive, without a doubt, because of their "political-cultural autonomism" (as with the Parti Québécois on the Canadian scene), but their contemplative and nostalgic character does not make them progressive. They are not part of a fusion of national liberation and social change since the social basis for these films can be summed up at the Folklore Museum.

On another, opposing, side, however, films such as Golden Gloves and Les bûcherons de la Manouane, while also demonstrating a marked national character, are founded on social analysis which goes beyond a strictly ethnic framework. The first describes how young men from the working-class Montreal neighborhood of St. Henri risk their lives in amateur boxing tournaments, dreaming of trophies and championships to escape from unemployment and welfare. The protagonist of the film is a black Anglophone who has learned Québécois French, and who shares the same fate as other Québécois. Arthur Lamothe, for his part, in describing the life of Québécois lumberjacks from the Mauricie region, gives many examples of their exploitation as workers, but he doesn't forget to emphasize that the "Tête-de-boule" Native People, living next door, are even more marginal and exploited than the lumberjacks.

Thus, in these two poles of the Québécois cinema at its birth, already there appeared the important split which would come to the surface in the seventies. We see, therefore, especially in the first half of the decade, the marked development of the social documentary but also its profound ideological division. The first tendency, shown for example in the ultra-nationlist La visite du Général de Gaulle au Québec (Jean-Claude Labrecque, 1968) would first continue in the "macramé cinema" of Québécois folklore, then in political films, openly pro-PQ (around and after the PQ's election in November 1976).[5]

The other tendency in a few years was to produce the finest hour of radical cinema, the beating heart of Quebec cinema, our most significant explosion of political films and video-tapes, the most important of which would be banned by political censorship, and which would touch upon practically all aspects of workers', community and cultural struggles, and those of nearly all social marginalities. This tendency would be in a certain sense the films of the October Crisis of 1970 and its consequences, a cinema of a slightly less quiet Revolution, foreshadowed by the sparks of Gilles Groulx's Chat dans le sac (1964).[6]

2. "...the most obvious mistake: we believed that the revolution would be soon." --Pierre Maheu

Already in 1968, the Quebec social documentary expressed its function not only as a witness (even of a revolutionary reality), but as a tool of social intervention. Michel Brault and Pierre Perrault reported back to us the Francophone students' strikes from Moncton, and a stunning portrait of the Anglophone chauvinism of the Loyalist New Brunswickers: this film would become L'Acadie, l'Acadie (Acadia, Acadia, 1971). In the entire Québécois cinema there is not a more angry film, sadder or more desperate, than this portrait of the unceasingly humiliated children of the Acadian Dispersion; the comparison with Quebec therein became strengthened unbearably.

For his part, Fernand Dansereau, with *Saint-Jerôme* (1968), placed a camera in a working-class environment in a Montreal suburb, a camera which intervened in the direction of a discourse of social reform--Christian humanist on the left--and which would also come to its conclusion a few years later in PQ nationalism. Dansereau's achievement was to have removed cinema from its descriptive function, and progressively, not only to place it at the service of working-class, popular, and intellectual speech, but also to try to give it back to the protagonists themselves, so that the camera could work to express their reality and their fantasies.

These two films were still being made at the NFB in 1968. The year 1968 also marked the first political cinema series in Quebec, which popularized foreign films like *Hour of the Furnaces* and *Now!* But the vise would tighten up again, so much so that political films to come would all be subject to censorship, whether drastic or not so drastic. *On est au coton* (Denys Arcand, 1970) was formally banned by its producers, the NFB, in 1970, as was *24 Heures ou plus* (24 Hours or More, Gilles Groulx) two years later. As for Arcand's *Québec: Duplessis et après* (*Quebec: Duplessis and After*, 1972), this film was subjected to a number of cuts before its release.

It was thus outside the NFB that the social and political documentary would most come into its own. Arthur Lamothe began filming newsreels about students' and workers' struggles, and in 1970 directed an outstanding film for the trade-union umbrella organization, the CSN. Called *Le mépris n'aura qu'un temps* (*Hell No Longer*, or more literally, "Contempt will last only for a time"), the title itself became a kind of rallying cry for radical trade-unionism and the revolutionary political movements then in gestation.

Lamothe constructed a bitter mosaic of news documents about workers and unions, with long, fluid direct-cinema sequences literally at the service of workers' voices, and others exploring an unemployed worker's cramped apartment or following him on his hopeless job hunting; in summary, *Le mépris n'aura qu'un temps* was a condemnation of on-the-job accidents in the construction industry, calling them the "murders of capitalism," and heralded the upheaval of

Direct cinema at the service of workers' voices: unemployed construction workers argue bitterly over beer in Le mépris n'aura qu'un temps. (Photo by Yves Sauvageau; Cinémathèque Québécoise)

the system. (See photo above.) It was the most important film of the beginning of the seventies, the era of the October Crisis, of factory occupations, of road blocks, of the radicalization of the student movement, of the bloody strike at the Montreal daily, La Presse, of the general strike in 1972, leading as far as the total occupation of the city of Sept-Iles by workers. This was Quebec's May 1968 with jet lag. There was also a rediscovery of the struggles and strikes of Duplessis's time, the forties and fifties, by veteran activist Madeleine Parent (On est au coton); there appeared the first signs of a bridge between the progressive and communist militancies of that period and a newly arising Marxist-Leninist movement.

On est au coton, by also using interviews and direct investigation of working and living environments, confirmed a good part of these links with the deep dark past, and also showed the extreme exploitation of textile workers in the Eastern Townships. If it was not as direct a denunciation as Le Mépris, it was no less corrosive, because its portrait of capitalism was merciless. The film would only be "liberated" from its release ban in 1977--with amputations. But meanwhile video had arrived, and copies of On est au coton were pirated from the original, sleeping in the vaults of the NFB. It was to become one of the most widely distributed, screened and studied NFB films. Counter-information worked perfectly with this film, and the NFB, from time to time, took out advertising in the press to remind us that those who defied the ban were liable to prosecution.

But the process of radicalization had not yet used up all its ammunition. On a raison de se révolter (We Are Right to Revolt, 1973), a working-class investigation and a collective project, brought together past and present struggles in even sharper focus. Using extensive interviews, archival insertions, and direct-cinema accounts of factory occupations, picket-line police violence, and union meetings and debates, it was a striking portrait of different kinds of workers' struggles at the beginning of the seventies, and thus became the first feature of its kind in Quebec. (See photos page 290.) Above all, this film called for the unification of these struggles in a revolutionary workers' and people's organization. Even this film's promotional material made bitter political distinctions (whose sectarianism is evident) within the committed documentary current:

> The only "political" films produced to date by our Québécois filmmakers support ideas that are either trade-unionist (Les gars de LaPalme [The LaPalme Boys, Arthur Lamothe, 1972]), pro-PQ (La Richesse des autres [Other People's Wealth, Maurice Bulbulian, 1973]), humanist (Le mépris n'aura qu'un temps), or fatalist (On est au coton). We therefore wanted to make a film which will act as a propaganda tool, spotlighting the most combative workers' struggles, from which we can take political lessons for the entire working class.... It seemed important to us to give a voice to "the most advanced" workers.

The voice of the Quebec documentary was no longer that of a vague "Québécitude" or of the "uncertain country." It became that of the radical intellectuals and workers who would

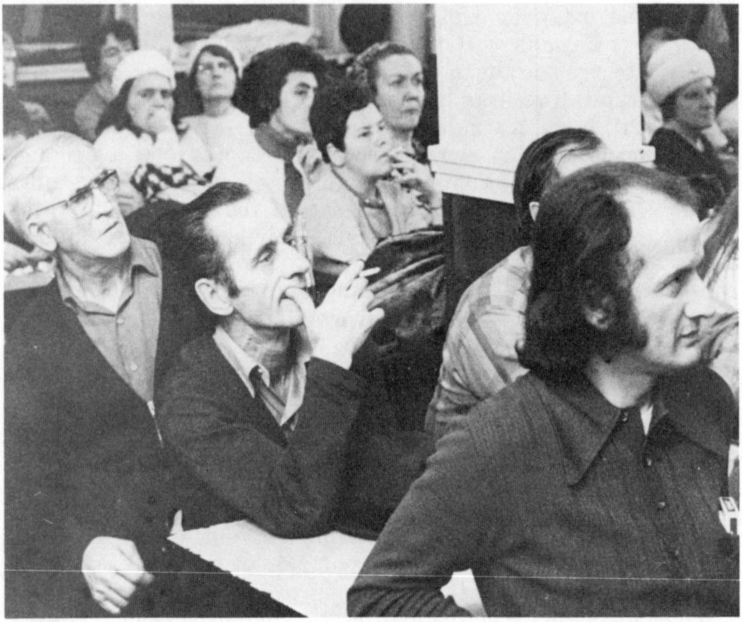

In On a raison de se révolter, direct cinema is a witness both to workers' voices (a union meeting, top), and to their actions (a factory occupation, bottom), but the film's "program" is too "complete." (Photos: Cinémathèque Québécoise)

soon appear with "complete" revolutionary "programs," agitation and propaganda outfits, and structured and disciplined organizations.

Outside of this organized movement, 24 Heures ou plus, its release delayed by the NFB for five years until 1977, testified in its own way to this anchoring of the documentary in political discourse. A dazzling fresco-reportage on the hot autumn of 1972 in Quebec, its editing is literally framed by the didactic texts of Gilles Groulx and Jean-Marc Piotte, read to spectators in the manner of the driest lecture. Revolutionary political didacticism triumphed. This does not lessen the interest of many sequences in the film, such as, for example, the calm testimony of the woman whose husband had one day been fired and, in return, had coldly assassinated three of his bosses at the Montreal Dupont plant. Other highly interesting sequences include: the case of censorship and the strike at La Presse, the October Crisis in 1970, the ideological bombardment of the mass media, youth dropouts, Native rights, Fred Hampton's murder in the USA, the recognition of Quebec's right to self-determination, the denunciation of the Québécois national bourgeoisie allied to Ottawa, all punctuated with haunting, tragically overtoned confrontations with urban landscapes, with schoolchildren, with caged animals....

In this context, The October Crisis did not itself find an explicit cinematic expression right away. A few Québécois filmmakers produced some documentary material, which passed into the Anglo-Québécois director Robin Spry's hands for the 1974 NFB compilation, Action. As a result of censorship or of self-protection tactics the Québécois cinema was thus deprived of its documentary film on this key event. Action was nevertheless fair compensation, just like Les ordres (Orders), directed by Michel Brault in the same year. This feature, while made within the framework and style of commercial fiction, was all the same based on actual documentary research drawn directly from a number of victims of the War Measures Act.

This avoidance or hesitation regarding the October Crisis, as I see it, was the first element of a rupture in the Québécois documentary of the beginning of the seventies, the other being the coming to political power of the PQ in 1976, which tied one part of the progressive cinema securely to state nationalism. But the spirit of combat did not die out so easily, though the poles shifted somewhat. At the NFB, the Société Nouvelle and Vidéographe projects became sites for channelling the social intervention documentary, harassed and censored somewhat here as well.

In the private sector, it was still Arthur Lamothe who was innovating and would produce and direct, little by little, in twelve feature films, what now appears to be the greatest achievement of the committed Québécois documentary: La chronique des Indiens du nord-est du Québec (1973-79). The traditional culture of the Montagnais nation was revealed in all its fullness in this series of films, part ethnographic and part combative, and Native political demands were shown in all their complexity and justice. In addition, the racism felt by Quebec's Native People, above all from pro-PQ nationalists, provoked an unprecedented self-laceration among the majority of Quebec progressives and certain PQ supporters. Through his films, Lamothe demonstrated, beyond any doubt, the pernicious character of narrow-minded nationalism, of ethnocentrism, by letting the Indians express themselves fully: the Quebec people can never be free, Chronique seemed to say, if it oppresses other people, and on "its" own soil. On the other hand, these films established for one of the aboriginal nations of Quebec the archives and memory of its own culture. For once, both political and cultural voices came together in the committed cinema. (See photos, p. 293.)

More recently, Maurice Bulbulian has succeeded in the same feat, for the dissident Inuits of northern Quebec in the NFB film, Debout sur leurs terres (Standing on their Lands, 1982). If we add to this the films of the Canada-Mexico co-production, involving the NFB and the SEP (Mexico), concerning Indians within the Mexican peasantry--Tierra y Libertad, Bulbulian, 1978; Les Délaissés (The Forsaken Ones), Bulbulian, 1978; Première question sur le bonheur (First Question on Happiness), Groulx, 1977--it would appear that the Québécois committed documentary has made a significant contribution to Native Peoples' reviving struggles.

3. Changing the Documentary Without Shortchanging It

If the seventies saw a fiery explosion of the radical, even revolutionary, political documentary, its second wind was snuffed out no less rapidly. This outcome corresponded to the evolution of Marxist-Leninist schemas or points of view, which turned straight into propagandist didacticism,

La chronique des Indiens du nord-est du Québec, "the greatest achievement of the committed Québécoise documentary," brings together both political voices (a blockade of Native land, above) and cultural voices (a recital of cultural memory, below.) (Photos: Cinémathèque Québécoise; photo below by Guy Borremans)

"workerist" simplifications, and a reduction of its conceptualization exclusively to terms of "class struggle." But other questions appeared, as well as other ways of witnessing to and analyzing problems. The feminist movement was the motor of this renewal and the entrance of women into the Québécois documentary is one of its richest and most promising recent elements.

The seed of this renewal was found in the NFB's Société Nouvelle (the French parallel to "Challenge for Change"), whose most striking production was the series of six films, En tant que femmes (Speaking as Women, 1973-74). Elsewhere, another project initiated by the NFB, the Vidéographe, which would inaugurate and consolidate the practice of portable video in Quebec, today finds its extension in the very active group, Vidéo-Femmes. Thus the contradiction of the sixties recurs. Projects initiated within the federal state apparatus for governmental information and promotion have been subverted by the social documentary of struggle and intervention, and this time primarily at the service of women's reforms and revolts.

Repercussions, however, were not late in appearing, and it is outside the NFB that we now find the most interesting feminist productions. Luce Guilbeault's 1978 D'Abord ménagères (Housewives First of All) portrays the daily, "non-sensationalist" violence of Québécois women's housework. Le grand remue-ménage (The Clean Sweep, Sylvie Groulx and Francine Allaire, 1978) exposed, in its apparently banal and inoffensive everyday-ness, male sexism and its contemptuous manifestations, in children as much as in adults.

Such films, through their content and their construction, innovate on various levels: first they demonstrate that violence, social inequality, and contempt are realities not only for trade unions or in the general political sense; they are scourges with which human beings, and women above all, have been living on a continuous, daily basis for a long time. The sublime egalitarian dream of the classless society, to follow the masses' overthrow of the exploitative minority, had hidden this fact which was staring us in the face, and which we end up living with, almost apathetically. For the documentary cinema, then, these kinds of feminist films have shown that filmmakers can do without dogmatic commentaries with every i dotted, pointing their finger at "analyses" we must extricate, and at the "solution" for the future. In other words, a point of view can be relayed while remaining non-propagandist. Finally, such films have a modesty of approach and of audio-visual communication which gives a different creative sensibility to direct cinema, to the social documentary. Personal feeling plays a front-stage role. By feeling their way and experimenting, the feminist filmmakers often uncover the "never before seen," which also happens to be the social configuration of women's condition.

Recently, Une histoire de femmes (A Wives' Tale, Joyce Rock, Sophie Bissonette, Martin Duckworth, 1980) reached a mastery of these innovations, of this renewal. The film follows the action of the wives of striking miners at Inco, Sudbury's huge nickel mine; from this event arises an awakened consciousness among the women, of their situation, of an historical link woven with the original women settlers of Northern Ontario. The originality of the film lies in its capacity to allow the women and the events to speak for themselves, to unmask contradictions without having to dub them over with commentary. This is a feature film of very great sensitivity in its look and sound, very much alive and moving.

Elsewhere, it is to Tahani Rached that we owe the best film on immigration in Quebec, Les voleurs de jobs (Where Money Grows on Trees, 1980); her denunciation of the "cheap labor" market in unorganized immigrant women in Montreal sweat-shops is an eloquent podium, like the Sudbury film as well, for women subjects no one had ever listened to before.

The sudden disintegration of a "party-line" political framework for the committed documentary has caused the appearance of many such treatments of nearly all imaginable social subjects, as much on the national Québécoise level as international.

At the NFB, in 1979, La fiction nucléaire (Nuclear Fiction, Jean Chabot) is a ruthless attack on nuclear development, but one situated in the larger framework of the exploitation of Quebec natural resources by political interests, both Canadian/Québécois and American multi-national. Through past and present newsfilms, Jean Chabot and his crew trace a startling objective portrait of the Quebec political economy, bordering on a "theatre of horror," without neglecting to introduce to it personal feelings and frustrations, fear amongst others, a fear fed by facts, statistics, Geiger counters, computer programs, political speeches, and nightmarish landscapes.

In the cultural arena, A vos risques et périls (At Your Own Risk, 1980), puts together the first systematic montage of historical cultural resistance in Quebec, from the "Refus global" of the pioneering abstract painter Paul-Emile Borduas and the Automatistes in 1948, up to the International Counter-culture Week in Montreal in 1975. Between these two events, the film lays out, in its willfully anarchic and spontaneous form of collage, all of the important struggles on the Québécois cultural front. Gilles Groulx--who has always acknowledged his debt to Borduas--makes an appearance, as do the poets Claude Peloquin and Raoul Duguay, Allen Ginsberg and William Burroughs, Québécois handicrafts and "ti-pop" (populist Kitsch), the march from the NFB on Ottawa in 1968 ("Open up the NFB!"), the first Common Front of Creators in 1972-73, the Culture Tribunal of 1975, the demonstration against the Montreal World Film Festival in 1979 for the survival of independent cinema, etc.

Moreover, the cultural struggles are linked to diverse forms of social commitment: fighting against both the pillage of Quebec's natural resources by monopolies and discrimination against Native People, solidarity with political prisoners, feminists, youth against the schools, the Quebec Liberation Front, and so on. The smoky and spiritualist counter-culture is immersed therein as well, but what emerges in particular is the will for a liberation of Quebec, for a struggle of the anti-bourgeois classes (references to Marx, Brecht, Allende, Guevara); aside from a jam session which concentrates for a moment on the "Internationale," the film nevertheless serves to draw the line unequivocally at Stalinist Marxist-Leninism, since "proletarian revolution cannot be taken on by intellectuals in this society." (See photo, p. 297.)

Film-poem, film-banner, feature-length manifesto, A vos risques et périls is without a doubt the only cultural documentary of struggle by an intellectual left which depicts itself openly as consisting of intellectuals and not workers, which sees itself admittedly as very divided, but which gathers up steam, loads its barrels, and, without stopping, renews its combat for the national liberation of Quebec, its will for radical cultural survival.

A vos risques et périls: the question of the role of cultural workers in revolutionary social change. This improvised jam session of the "Internationale" is not the answer. (Photo: Cinémathèque Québécoise)

4. The Cinema in Our Two Houses

Last fall, the "Autumn Rendez-Vous of Quebec Cinema" was reborn, after a disappointing absence of nearly two years, on the ashes of eight previous annual festivals. At the previous one, the filmmakers had declared, all out of breath and in some disarray, "It's no longer enough to be against American cinema or its substitutes, we must be for a national cinema!"

We feared the worst--the disappearance of our national cinema--and with reason. But this most recent autumn Rendez-vous has given us back a certain confidence that has lasted after the excitement of those reunions. For the committed documentary above all, the Rendez-vous was a revelation as three films in particular stood out clearly on the program, full of promise for the future: Albédo (Jacques

Leduc, 1982), Souvenirs de guerre (Memories of War, Pierre Hébert, 1982), and Le futur intérieur (Yolaine Rouleau and Jean Chabot, 1982). They are films with shared characteristics, striking human and social theses (deterioration of the urban fabric, children and wars, and the history of feminism), but also a renewal of form, mixtures of filmic modes and styles. These films are already concrete indications that the Quebec radical documentary is coming out of its impasse.

Albédo treats the industrial degradation of the Montreal neighborhood of Griffintown, as well as the suicide of David Marvin, one of its historians, a photographer and archivist. Leduc's film mixes and connects fiction, documented fiction, and documentary, and if its construction is a little too complex, the film effectively plays with the rich possibilities of re-aligning content with the image and sound tracks, of which the spectators have to make a synthesis, as with a collage.

Souvenirs de guerre goes still further, using two types of animation (scratching on film, and cut-out papers), experimenting with new colors on the optical printer, and inserting real shots from documentaries within and around the animated images. This film is a violent and outraged poem on the future of children in a context where war and militarization are growing on all sides. From time to time, an old folk lament asks, "Will we ever have liberty?"

Le futur intérieur, for its part, dares--for the first time in Quebec no doubt--to place the international and Québécois histories of feminism in their relationship to politics in the broad sense, a politics which still is based after all on war. The film links general social violence to that which women live everyday, the "violence in the kitchen," as one of them says in a broken voice.

Le futur intérieur is an important film, a transitional film for the Québécois committed documentary of the eighties. It takes on the look of a veritable manifesto, emphasized by its citation from Virginia Woolf's Three Guineas:

> ... the public and the private worlds are inseparably connected; the tyrannies and servilities of the one are the tyrannies and servilities of the other.... For such will be our ruin if you, in the immensity of your public abstractions forget the private figure, or if we in the intensity of our private emotions forget the public world. Both

houses will be ruined, the public and the private, the material and the spiritual, for they are inseparably connected.

The committed Québécois documentary is now actually brought to this turning point. Of course, it can no longer be as it was, and so much the better. But it doesn't have to start at the beginning. The Québécois cinema has accumulated its experiences and its failures, it has achieved its independence and affirmed its cultural sovereignty. It has mapped out for the most part the contours of its commitment which ally it to other international currents. The outline of the route is traced, though the ground is fragile and precarious.[7]

In order for it to survive, a few conditions seem to be necessary: we must maintain the NFB and the support of the State; at the same time, however, we must not ignore recourse to all kinds of non-governmental collective financing (union, popular, cultural, etc.); filmmakers need to maintain the independence of their thinking and work, in spite of the contradictions encountered (in this respect, the lesson of political and cultural dependence on the PQ, to which too many filmmakers submitted, should serve as a warning); and finally, to avoid the pitfalls of being closed in by ethnocentrism and chauvinistic nationalism, we must continue to work on national subjects of international relevance, or on international subjects. As the Breton filmmaker Réné Vautier demonstrated in Le dur désir de dire (Alain D'Aix, 1982), a progressive national cinema does not necessarily need a nation-state to affirm itself and survive.

Recently [Jan. 1983], on the editing tables of the NFB, we have seen a team working on a film about the refugee camps in Beirut. On this team we find an immigrant Québécois woman, director Tahani Rached; an old hand on the first NFB French crew, editor Pierre Bernier; and a director-operator of the second generation, Jacques Leduc....

When the committed Québécois documentary moves ahead in this way, we can continue to keep our hopes up. Because, banned or not, there is a cinema that must be made. And, as was chanted in Paris in May 1968, if possible, do it in 35mm; if not, in 16mm; if not, in Super 8, on video, on slides, with polaroids--or without a camera, if necessary, with scratch-pen or paint-brush for working right on celluloid....

Bibliographical Note

Some recent English-language sources on Quebec political documentary are:

Pierre Véronneau and Piers Handling, eds. Self Portrait: Essays on the Canadian and Quebec Cinemas. Ottawa: Canadian Film Institute, 1980.

Malcolm Dean. Censored! Only in Canada. The History of Film Censorship--the Scandal off the Screen. Toronto: Phenomena, 1981.

Seth Feldman and Joyce Nelson, eds. Canadian Film Reader. Toronto: PMA, 1977.

D. B. Jones. Movies and Memoranda: An Interpretative History of the National Film Board of Canada. Ottawa: Canadian Film Institute, 1981.

Réal La Rochelle. "Is There a Future for a Quebec National Cinema?" Cinema Canada, Film and the Future, special supplement to No. 97 (June 1983).

and the following issues of film periodicals which contain special dossiers on Quebec political or documentary film:

Cineaste, Vol. V., No. 3; Jump Cut, No. 22; Ciné-tracts (Montreal) Vol. 3, No. 2, and Vol. 4, No. 4.

Notes

1 The magnitude of this threat to close down the NFB can be conveyed by the statistic that more than half of the films cited in this article were produced at this government studio.

2 The two reports, the federal one headed by Louis Applebaum and Jacques Hébert, and the provincial one by Guy Fournier, are entitled respectively Report of the Federal Cultural Policy Review Committee, 1982 and Le Cinéma. Une question de survie et d'excellence. Rapport de la commission d'étude sur le cinéma et l'audiovisuel, 1982.

3 "Maîtres chez nous," a campaign slogan of the Quiet Revolution, means "Masters in our own house."

4 The "Candid Eye" movement, comprised primarily but not entirely of Anglophone filmmakers at the NFB

during the mid- and late-fifties, pioneered the techniques and the aesthetics of direct cinema/cinéma-vérité; it was named for a 1958-59 Canadian television series to which the NFB contributed.

5 In the "macramé cinema," there are also different levels of nationalism. For example, in La Veillée des veillées (Bernard Gosselin, 1976) or Le Son des Français d'Amérique (Michel Brault and André Gladu, 1979), there are several elements of Québécois popular culture, but also Acadian, Louisianan, Breton, etc. These elements are not however re-situated in the present nor, in certain cases, in their context of social life and struggles. Other films on traditional crafts are more directly "museological" and passive.

For its part, the unconditionally pro-PQ political cinema has above all given us films like 15 novembre (Hugues Mignault, 1977) or Gens d'Abitibi (Perrault, 1980).

6 "October Crisis" refers to the political crisis of 1970, set off by the FLQ's politically motivated kidnappings, in which Ottawa imposed the War Measures Act, suspended due process and jailed hundreds of Québécois without trial.

Le Chat dans le sac presents the revolt of a young Québécois student, Claude, who breaks off with his girlfriend, Barbara, a Jewish Anglophone artist, as well as with the journalistic and intellectual milieu he finds not radical enough. The general portrait of this Québécois and of Quebec, colonized by Capital, finds its ultimate expression in a symbolic tableau of the armed revolts of the FLQ (Quebec Liberation Front), the detonators of the October Crisis.

7 Since the writing of this article, three new films have appeared that confirm the trend towards an experimentation with mixed modes, documentary and fiction: Un journal inachevé (Marilu Mallet), La Mémoire battante (Arthur Lamothe) and Pas fou comme on le pense (Jacqueline Levitin).

Chapter 16

THE CHALLENGE OF RADICAL FILM DISTRIBUTION: CONVERSATIONS WITH TORONTO'S DEC FILMS COLLECTIVE

Margaret Cooper

Radical film activists have come to a much more realistic awareness in recent years of the central importance of the link between filmmaker and spectator. In fact, one sometimes gets the impression that distribution is all filmmakers talk about anymore; it is much less common in these days of dried-up funding for radical films to be thrown out into the marketplace without a concrete distribution strategy or political base, than it was, say, in the early and mid-seventies. Nevertheless, there is still much to be shared and learned about the dynamics of distribution, exhibition and audience reception, and the following discussion with political activists who are also film distributors, and vice versa, makes an important advance in the discussion of the complex interface between these two domains.

A unique Canadian phenomenon, DEC Films grew out of the Development Education Centre, an independent, non-profit collective formed in 1971 by New Left activists and researchers to provide alternative educational perspectives on Canada, the Third World and a wide range of contemporary issues. As an integral part of the Toronto-based Centre which houses a reference library and bookstore and produces books, radio programs, slide-tape shows and community workshops, DEC Films has become the leading distributor of progressive films in English-speaking Canada. Over the years since its founding in 1974 it has upheld a commitment to distribute films about social and political struggles throughout the world, while also accommodating the legitimate needs of filmmaking which critically documents and analyzes Canadian reality.

The following conversation between three members of the DEC collective and film programmer Margaret Cooper took place over a two-year period between 1979-81. It was undertaken as an ongoing dialogue about the work of DEC Films, its role in English-speaking Canada and its responsibilities toward independent Left filmmaking. The collective's current members are Ferne Cristall, Barbara Emanuel, Jonathan Forbes, Peter Steven, and Margaret Watson.

Margaret Cooper: When you compare DEC Films to most independent distributors, your beginnings seem exceptional. Film acquisition certainly wasn't your primary concern, was it?

Jonathan Forbes: Hardly. As a resource collective, DEC had been surveying books and pamphlets and doing research on Canada's relationship with Third World countries. In 1974, no Canadian film distributors handled the kind of Third World materials we needed. For our work, we had to import Third World films from the States. We had a great deal of difficulty in getting these films into Canada and found shipping and customs costs prohibitive. To have the films at our disposal, we were actually forced into becoming distributors.

Ferne Cristall: DEC Films started out with a small grant for Third World films from the Canadian International Development Agency, which had money for educational work on developing nations. After that initial seed money, we became self-supporting. We don't, we can't, rely on grants for funding.

MC: Even commercial distributors who are free of U.S. affiliation have a rough time in Canada. How has it been possible for you to keep going for seven years?

JF: The Centre had already developed a network with its educational work and its distribution of printed material. We also filled a real need for films, since universities and political or community groups were tired of having to go to the States for them. We started our collection slowly and developed it film by film. For every film we got, we mapped out where it could be used and how we would distribute it.

MC: Who were your users at the outset?

Glen Richards: Basically the same as now, with a division between institutions and community groups. We can distribute regularly in institutions because certain sectors in schools and universities, for example, have a continuing interest in our kind of films. Outside this area, people often use films for educational work in a particular community, or for different kinds of public screenings. In DEC Films' early years, some public screenings first interested people in our collection. One major series providing us with a local base was organized in '75 at the University of Toronto by the Toronto Committee for the Liberation of Southern Africa. It showed many of our films for the first time here. Then word spread that we had films. In a sense, the network built on itself.

JF: The network also developed beyond Toronto as we did teacher workshops in northern Ontario, mostly high school level but also for some community colleges. We'd have, for example, a two-day workshop for our films and written materials. We'd also provide a speaker and show teachers the available resources. At the time we developed these Northern Workshops, Toronto seemed well served by different groups; nobody ever went to the smaller cities in the north. These places had no contact with a resource center, so we'd go up, help develop curriculum and show our films. Also, teachers would invite outside community people to our screenings.

FC: Our distribution grew with a strong educational orientation--which it still has.

MC: But you're more focused than other educational distributors. And you do outreach work which actively responds to the needs of different communities and groups.

GR: Right. We contact community groups and trade unions as a regular part of our workshops and trips outside Toronto. Sometimes we hook up with community activists for a trip. A few years ago, a collective member and a person who worked with Native Canadians went across the country with a car and a projector, stopping in small communities for screenings where they encouraged people to use our material and showed how it could be used. To a lot of people they met, using a film differently in a community setting--not just in classrooms or in cinemas--seemed unusual in the mid-'70s in isolated parts of Canada. Since then, there have been some marked changes. Now community groups from all over use our films fairly regularly. Furthermore, they used to look for something to suit a specific interest but now they're drawing from other subject areas which raise social and cultural questions we'd like to see presented in a clearer context. People are still learning how to use the material, but with choices broadened.

MC: To what extent have you influenced their receptivity to a broader selection of films?

JF: A lot. And out of necessity, because there still aren't enough films specific to Canada. We draw analogies between a group's particular situation and the material we have.

MC: For example, you'd encourage a women's caucus from a particular Canadian union to use Rosie the Riveter or Babies and Banners for historical examinations of women's role in the work force.

GR: Yes. Or someone interested in a particular industry--let's say, potash in Saskatchewan--might not find anything available on the subject but could use Controlling Interest, which explores international and domestic relations in a major industry and shows how large companies control huge markets and offer workers low wages.

FC: A good speaker in the right setting can draw specific connections for Canadian users. Our role as distributors makes us facilitators as well.

MC: How do you decide which films to pick up, especially foreign films?

JF: We argue a lot. Every time a film comes in, we argue on the basis of its usefulness and cost. We're still too marginal to be able to spend much.

GR: Some films take precedence over others because of the subject's need or accessibility. Years ago we picked up the Swedish film, Tupamaros, partly to combat local press reports about Tupamaros as bloodthirsty terrorists. Yet sometime later we didn't take a film on East Timor, even though the Canadian media also distorted that liberation struggle. The film was just of too poor quality, not very informative and with only a limited application. Taking on that kind of film would have been a luxury.

FC: When we acquire films, content plays a prime role. But we want creatively made films which say something about issues through their form. Of course, we also have to make choices on the basis of available money.

GR: On the one hand, we have a definite need to do something; on the other hand, we know our financial responsibilities and liabilities. If the two are incompatible, we could not do the things we really need to do and would do a disservice to the people we're trying to support--whether they're involved in liberation struggles abroad or whether they're doing things here.

FC: We place a priority on producer reports and sending money back to producers. Most of our contract agreements stipulate producers receive 50% of net income. That was a political choice for us. Just as we're distributors working in adverse conditions, so are most of the filmmakers we work with, or who use us as their Canadian distributor. We know they need some income to continue doing what they're doing. So we keep our other costs down. Salaries--we all draw the same--stay pretty low, and we do our catalogues as economically as possible.

GR: We're a small collective, twelve people, operating on many levels, all collectively, and cannot do what other people have to do, such as form support groups for liberation struggles. We are out to make the most of resources which can raise consciousness.

JF: For example, we've started working with INCINE in Nicaragua and COMU-NICA in New York to do English versions of some Nicaraguan newsreels and documentaries.

MC: So you acquire films to fill already existing needs.

GR: And to move into areas which the groups and communities we service have not fully explored, such as cultural questions. Over the past two years, we've been getting films in this area, such as the West German film, John Heartfield--Photomontagist.

FC: *Heartfield* represented a conscious decision to break into new territory.

GR: As we tried to define areas in which to expand, we felt the need to deal with the cultural aspect of people's lives. A film like *Heartfield* counters the Hitler nostalgia vogue with little known information about an anti-fascist artist and his work. At the same time, it explores the process of his art. Since getting *Heartfield*, we've moved into features like *Northern Lights* and *Wobblies* as well as culturally based shorts which deal with social and political problems, like *Dread Beat an' Blood*, the British film about Reggae poet Linton Kwesi Johnson.

MC: As part of a collective, you have to consider DEC as a whole in your decisions--such as moving into features or cultural subjects. Does the entire collective influence and participate in the film section's activities?

JF: Obviously, other members use the films, quite often in educationals. That's the most direct contact.

GR: Also, people from the rest of the collective sit on the acquisitions committee to select films.

FC: That's a working committee, not just for decision-making.

GR: It tries to call in as many people as possible to test reactions to a film we're thinking of picking up, including people outside the collective who have an interest in the film's subject. For a film about Jamaica, let's say, we'll invite people from Toronto's Jamaican community as well as knowledgeable non-Jamaicans to a screening to discuss the film's potential use.

JF: We also get tips about films as people in the extended collective and people outside DEC come across something they think would be appropriate for us.

GR: Once a week we all meet to discuss what we're doing on a day-to-day and long-term basis, so there's a dynamic relationship with the entire collective. To some extent the collective's activities are integrated, to some extent they're separate. All the administrative work with the film collection--cleaning, shipping, booking, accounting--that's our responsibility. But everybody has the responsibility to do the Centre's work. Each of us spends a week at a time doing front desk, answering the phone and opening mail. If one of us goes to another province, that person will check out radio stations to see if any of our books interest people there. There's a give and take all the way. With the films, the collective takes a serious look at what we propose and then participates in the general discussion.

MC: You distribute many films which aren't available elsewhere in Canada. Do you try to make sure that people don't book films and then use them in ways that are diametrically opposed to your goals and the purpose of the films?

GR: In one case, a military institute wanted to book a Latin American film. Obviously, we didn't give it to them. The thing is, we're trying to provide a certain kind of education but we can't maintain total control over it. What if someone buys a print, let's say, of The Triple A, the anti-junta film about the effects of the '76 coup in Argentina, and uses it as an example of a leftist propaganda film?

FC: I think misuse like that rarely happens. Remember, we know our network and we're talking about a pretty small market within a small population. Canada is geographically huge, but there are only about 17 million English-speaking Canadians.

GR: With some of the recent acquisitions, of course, there's less danger of misuse. Also, films like Rosie the Riveter or Heartfield speak for themselves. You can disagree with what they say but you can't dismiss them. Users will have different approaches to our material but I can't overemphasize the fact that we don't have films you can eat. You can try, but they'll give you indigestion.

MC: I know that you encourage open, active screenings for your films whenever possible. Do you also encourage an active demystification of film and filmmaking in these situations?

FC: We've considered it an important role to teach some of our users film technology, even at the most primitive level, such as how to handle a print or what to do when the film breaks. In some cases, with community groups, we've been able to get into what makes a particular film work and how it does what it does.

GR: We have different backgrounds in relation to film. But

we've grown to put our differences together--to put filmmakers in touch with the people who use their films and vice versa; to present a film and discuss what is in the film and how such a film is made. You know, the whole thing: what the filmmaker wanted to do, what happened to the film afterwards, or how to creatively present ideas through certain forms. For example, in Film Forums we helped sponsor in Toronto in 1975, we started out with local filmmakers and invited them to participate in discussions with the audience. The next year, when we had access to some Chilean films for a weekend festival which took place at a downtown repertory house, we got Chileans who'd been involved with film work to take part in the discussions. At that time we were part of a network which André Paquet had helped set up from Montreal, with tours for foreign filmmakers from Third World countries. So we manged to work with films not yet in Canadian distribution.

MC: Since the mid-'70s Toronto seems to have had a consistently good audience for public screenings of Latin American films--mainly because of the impact of Latin American refugees on the city's activists and its politicized Left. The same hasn't been true for domestic-issue films, such as films about organized labor and Canadian workers. Was this the case with your Forums involving labor films?

JF: Yes. The program oriented toward unions and working people were the least well attended.

FC: Also, when our film section started in '74 and began the Forums, we were pretty inexperienced in our contacts with unions. Only a few years later, after we'd really developed our collection of films on labor and work, did unions begin using our films and become aware of the extent of our resources. Trying to do educationals within the context of organized labor has also helped us increase union access.

JF: It's taken time to build this part of our network. Much of the labor movement in English-speaking Canada has been tied to the New Democratic Party, a minority opposition party with a Social Democrat orientation, and we're not affiliated with the NDP, or with any party. Unions mistrusted us at the beginning because we couldn't be placed. We weren't affiliated, but an independent group.

MC: Some of your films also criticize business union

practices and U. S. domination of Canadian industrial unions, so I don't suppose they go over too well in certain sectors of organized labor. But as a trade unionist, I can certainly see a real need for some of these films among indigenous Canadian unions and among the reform groups in other unions.

FC: That kind of interest is really picking up now and should become stronger as we develop this part of our collection.

JF: Ten years ago, compared to Europe, Canada was quite wealthy. Although that's not true now, people still assume there's lots of money here. We have to explain that we have a small market scattered across an immense area and that for most of the films, shipping charges use up half the rental. We do try to develop a good relationship with our filmmakers, who can tell other filmmakers that we've done well by them over the years but that we can't pay a lot of money for films.

FC: Another problem is getting English-language films. Arrangements with American and British and Australian distributors take time. It's also tough to initiate acquisitions when we find a film we'd like to have which isn't in an English-language version. Here we're stuck; we have to contact people outside Canada, usually in the States.

GR: In getting films through the U. S., you're also talking about a lot of Third World films. The U. S. distributors have internegatives which we can draw on, whereas in Europe you have to buy into an interneg. So there it costs maybe twice as much to start--and the cost is prohibitive. TV sales are where Europeans may make money back on a film. In Canada, it's next to impossible for the kind of films we get.

MC: That's a real obstacle. Outside of print sales to schools and public libraries, you don't have access to some of the sales areas that would help expand the audience for your films while also bringing in money. English-language networks outside the Canadian Broadcasting Corporation, for example, program few Canadian films and rely heavily on U. S. features. The CBC sees itself well served by government-produced films--whether it's a case of airing its own productions or work from the National Film Board.

FC: The NFB is well respected in many countries because it subsidizes filmmakers. But what's not realized is the NFB's strong bias. And it creates serious problems for independents and totally cuts out people trying to work like we do. The NFB sells its films for the cost required to make the print, so people rent or buy NFB films because of the low rates. Some libraries even have to buy a certain number of NFB films to meet a quota.

JF: People phone us up and say, "Why should I pay $50 to rent such-and-such film when I can get one just like it for free from the Film Board?"

GR: Only it isn't "just like it." Distinctions become blurred because of people's financial concerns. A school board can acquire fifty films from the NFB for the same price that they can get twenty from us, so they expand the collection from the Film Board, a state-run monopoly.

JF: You're also talking about co-opting of young filmmakers who go to the Board for steady work, where nine out of the ten films they'll make are specifically for government agencies or private corporations which subsidize the NFB budget. To top it all off, the NFB has a ready-made distribution network, with offices across Canada and abroad which can carry on circulation of the films.

FC: The NFB does subsidize some filmmakers doing independent work, but the percentage is extremely small.

MC: What about the reputation built up by the now-defunct Challenge for Change program? That was supposed to bring filmmaking to the people.

GR: Its "radically innovative approach" duplicated early work done in the Soviet Union with the Kino train. In reality, it addressed itself largely to middle-class concerns, even though it sometimes dealt with isolated examples of working-class individuals or people on welfare. It went, for example, to small towns and showed that people had no sewer system. Middle-class people got together, made a videotape and pressured a government agency so that the town got a sewer system. But Challenge for Change wouldn't deal with the social reality of issues like massive unemployment in the Maritimes.

JF: The NFB won't even do a historical film like Union

Maids, which is analytical and critical and open-ended. It never will, but it will keep the people who would busy with other projects.

FC: It gets those people attuned to a seamless style of social documentary, a style that pervades English-language production at the Board, even in the best films. The English productions travel most. The French section at the NFB has a very different history and quite often does rather different work, so it doesn't really figure here.

GR: The NFB has done some good films--there's no doubt about it. But it's been despite the Film Board, which even at the start had a social democratic position on the working class. It allied itself completely with whatever government happened to be in power in this country.

To get back to Challenge for Change, look at Things I Cannot Change, one of the earliest films in the program. It's about a Montreal welfare recipient who couldn't make ends meet. When the film was shown abroad, audiences thought it was wonderful that a state-run institution would make a film about poverty, but in fact, when you use the film in Canadian context, all you create is a sense of pessimism.

This is a complicated issue. We don't have a real solution but we know that for a long time the NFB has been taking Canadian filmmakers who might be making the kind of films we can distribute and turning them into uncritical creators of seamless films.

MC: You've just brought up a most pressing issue for Canadian distributors: developing an independent film tradition with a progressive orientation in English-speaking Canada.

GR: It has something to do with the state of the Canadian Left. The fact that social democracy is stronger here than, let's say, in the United States actually creates more problems for us than it solves.

MC: Isn't it also connected with a tendency to breed "grant junkies?" Federal grants for independent filmmakers through the Canada Council and arts council grants in each province have been a big help, even if there is less money now than there was a few years ago. But they can also work to disadvantage and breed a kind of "grant-itis" which isn't always compatible with work promoting social change.

JF: We're not sustained by grants, and few of the Canadians whose films we distribute have been able to depend on them exclusively.

MC: As "mavericks," how do you view your role in helping to promote or develop independent Left filmmaking? Do you think that money could be generated independently for the kind of films we've been talking about?

FC: That depends. If you decide, for example, to make a film on work, it's not likely that a union will offer support unless you make the film for a union. At least, not in the same way that U.S. independents have managed to get union money for some of their films.

JF: What about A Wives' Tale?

FC: One of the most interesting things about that film was the way in which organized labor, women's groups and individuals across the country worked together to help its productions.

MC: What A Wives' Tale had going for it from the start, I think, was a subject which touched a lot of people. The 1978 International Nickel Company's strike was one of the most important labor struggles in recent history and it raised issues which became well known across the country.

JF: That's why we made it one of our projects and spent time working with the filmmakers to reach different community groups and individuals to fund the film.

MC: Here's a perfect demonstration of active collaboration between distributors and filmmakers to promote what needs to be done.

FC: We've wanted to do that, and A Wives' Tale gave us the opportunity. Obviously, we got involved because we'd already been involved with the Sudbury, Ontario community where the strike took place. DEC published a book written by a collective member about INCO's involvement in Sudbury called The Big Nickel. DEC also helped produce a videotape about Sudbury and the strike called Winding Down, and had done workshops on the strike. We knew the filmmakers. It seemed a logical extension to help with the film.

GR: It's also very close to our hearts at DEC because it

challenges fixed notions on the Left and in the trade unions from a socialist-feminist perspective.

FC: Helping to promote the film in Toronto meant arranging for one of the filmmakers to come and work with us at a salary while doing the premiere showings here. We also involved local women's organizations who'd supported the making of the film so that they'd incorporate the film in their work.

GR: In fact, the activity with A Wives' Tale gave us our first taste of a different kind of public exhibition and provided insight into new ways to promote our films and involve community groups in public exhibition. The people who ran a downtown cinema made their theater available for four screenings over a two-week period. The first week the film played to pretty skimpy audiences. But by the second week, people lined up outside the theater. We now feel confident that more of our films can have the same effect if we actively involve our audience.

MC: Without an independently run, centrally located cinema, I don't think you'd have done as well. Also, a theater like the one you used can't really afford to depart too much from its regular art house programming. It's caught up in its own struggle bucking American chains and block-bookings of U. S. product.

JF: You're right. Having access to a screen and getting good projection in a theater space for public exhibition on an ongoing basis present real problems for us.

GR: Ideally, we'd like a community cultural center.

FC: That's how we envision DEC in the future. We have a library, a bookstore and videotape facilities. Having a small cinema nearby or on the premises would be a natural development.

GR: Especially since we're planning to do more public screenings on the order of what we started last winter with our "Reel to Real" series.

JF: That grew out of our experience with A Wives' Tale.

FC: When we started thinking of "Reel to Real" as a new cinema of solidarity project, we thought it would be exciting.

We chose the films from new acquisitions, things we felt deserved theatrical presentation, and approached the same cinema we'd used for A Wives' Tale about renting the theater for ten Sunday afternoons. Then we went to groups which we thought would have specific interests in the films: an alternative cultural magazine, a left community newspaper, a Native Canadian school, the International Women's Day Committee, an inner city Black activist band and a research group which publishes material on Latin America. All of the groups became really keen on the project. We met regularly to plan the series and then promoted it collectively and individually. DEC did a newsprint flyer for the entire series and each group did a separate flyer for its program, with probably 15,000 promotional flyers circulating around Toronto as dropoffs and mailings.

MC: How effectively were the films presented as sponsored programs?

GR: A good example would be the Blacks Britannica and Dread Beat an' Blood screening. It was a mixed media presentation because the sponsoring group, the Guyap Rhythm Drummers, performed as well. Then the Guyap talked about the problems presently facing Toronto's Black and West Indian communities.

JF: As a cultural event, it had a real political focus. The films deal with the oppression of Blacks in Britain, and the Drummers had recently been harassed and raided by the city police.

FC: There were other developments from our work with the Guyap which had positive results. The two publications which sponsored other screenings in the series came into contact with the Guyap at one of our planning sessions and eventually did feature stories on their problems with the police.

MC: So the series brought together some common interest groups who may have been previously working in isolation from each other.

GR: And it developed more community contacts for us. The spinoff is the number of people who have seen the films in the cinema setting and then have gone on to use some of the films themselves in other public settings. Other groups who don't have financial resources are starting to pressure public libraries to purchase prints from us. That will mean that free library prints will be accessible to people we can't serve because we have to charge rentals.

MC: What about the economics of "Reel to Real?" Did the series pay for itself?

FC: The theater rental and fees for house manager and projectionist came to $300 each Sunday. One half of that amount came off the top of the gate. From what remained, 50% went to the sponsoring group. With the rest, DEC paid its own film rentals, the other half of the cinema rental and covered the production of the series flyer.

MC: Did the series break even?

GR: Not completely, if you consider that we eventually lost about $340. The sponsoring groups did pretty well, however, when you consider they didn't have any cash outlay.

MC: What about your own labor? How did that figure in?

FC: We put a hell of a lot of time and energy into "Reel to Real" and didn't get any financial return on it. So in a sense, none of our labor costs were covered, and the amount of time we put into the series did make our other distribution work suffer. During the winter, for example, we received a number of new films which we weren't able to promote as well as we'd have wanted.

GR: The problem with "Reel to Real" was the same problem which has often come up with similar short-term projects. It was difficult to get a coordinating committee to carry out the work we could do because of our experience. For one thing, the sponsoring groups did not usually work full-time as groups, and their members had jobs outside. Or else the groups were volunteer ad hoc committees. It was right for us as facilitators to do what we did. But financially, over a four-month period the additional work load became a real burden.

MC: When you do this kind of program again, will you consider getting paid for your labor?

GR: Yes. Now that something like "Reel to Real" has shown it can work, sponsoring organizations may be willing to share the finances. As it was, some of the groups involved had absolutely no money, and they were uneasy about raising, let's say, $150 because the whole thing might go bust and nobody come. None of us knew what was going to happen.

JF: Remember, we conceived "Reel to Real" and started organizing it not more than eight weeks before the series started.

MC: We were talking earlier about ways of promoting a critical Left tradition in Canadian independent film. To my way of thinking, "Reel to Real" was a good way of getting film users to support the screenings and films fairly creatively. That kind of support should encourage filmmakers in their work.

GR: There was a much tighter integration of users, distributors and, in the case of some locally produced films, the filmmakers themselves. It may even have implications for some institutional film users across the country whose financial resources are starting to dry up. Maybe they should consider going directly to the people who want to see films.

JF: DEC wants to work with people across the country who can get communities to support these films in public exhibition. When that's at the integrated level, as in "Reel to Real," audience response can't help but encourage more filmmaking activity.

FC: Especially if the filmmakers build into this network, like the people who made A Wives' Tale. Actually, for DEC, this is really just a new twist on what we started out doing years ago. Our collection has grown, our users have increased and diversified, and we've gone through a number of changes. It's a process that's ongoing, but with a basic consistency to what we do and how we do it. It will be exciting to see what happens next.

Chapter 17

FORMS, POLITICS, MAKERS, AND CONTEXTS: BASIC ISSUES FOR A THEORY OF RADICAL POLITICAL DOCUMENTARY

Chuck Kleinhans

This manifesto of pragmatic, ideological and aesthetic considerations for radical media workers is a fitting conclusion to and summation of this section of eleven articles on contemporary committed documentary in the West. Based on the author's experiences within a community and movement of artists and activists, and on both his exemplary self-awareness and unflinching criticism of a variety of examples of recent work, this piece of theory-in-progress (as all theory must be) presents no small challenge to readers of this volume, both media-makers and media-users.

Radical film/video makers today, if they are to make genuinely liberating work, films and tapes that contribute to fundamental change, must examine their own taken-for-granted ideas and behavior: about society, about politics, about their medium and its techniques. About everything, because they need critical awareness as a vital part of media that can deal with the dynamics of personal and institutional change. Makers have to think like political organizers--with both intensity and distance, attention to the immediate and the long range, to the tactical and the strategic, and to the individual and the group--in other words to the complexity and richness of the immediate historical moment and its potentials and possibilities.

But today we're a long way from that point. Most politically engaged documentaries are made because the people making them have been strongly committed to the project, doing it as a hopefully socially significant and personally rewarding task. All too often, films and tapes are made primarily for reasons of individual commitment and are not accompanied by other, more complex political reasoning. It often seems that only a distinct minority of makers have analyzed political forces, examined changing conditions, considered various analyses, thought about who the audiences are for their work, what the practical need for it is, how people might use it, the most cost-/ and time-efficient medium and format, what distribution and exhibition channels are available, and how those considerations could and should shape their work. At the same time, for more than a decade we've seen hot debates by theorists and critics and copious examples by film/video makers around matters of a radical documentary practice. For both documentarists and theorists today, in the Reagan-Thatcher era, I think it's necessary to survey the field less dogmatically and to rethink some basic questions.

Any adequate theory of radical political documentary must have a dynamic relation to media practice and political activism in its own historical moment. Theory never emerges as a pure timeless abstraction but always in relation to changing political, social, and communication concerns and situations. With time and changing conditions, theoretical emphases shift and different issues become the center of concern. In the late '60s and early '70s some key questions about documentary were posed differently. Then both critics and documentarists raised questions about production technology, especially about portable sync sound film and video, as well as matters of group organization (collective, hierarchical, etc.) and arguments about genius (variously interpreted and shaded as the discussants varied in or referred to others' commitment, sincerity, personal vision, experience, celebrity, inspiration, etc.). Today these matters seem less relevant and secondary to issues of forms, politics, makers and contexts.[1]

To have genuinely radical political documentary activity today, we have to work on four basic issues. First, we have to interrogate film and video form and its use in documentary work. In particular we must question the tendency to formalism--of both the left and the right varieties. This tendency assumes that one kind of correct form exists and that it will solve other problems. Second, we have to consider the variety of ways in which a documentary can present politics, and we must be alert to the problems of how a documentary can avoid hard issues through reformism or simplify the question into ultraradicalism. Third, we have to consider the maker's position--political, personal, historical, social, and institutional. Fourth, we have to think about the film/video work's context--the historical moment in which it is produced, distributed, and exhibited, and the audience it reaches. Keeping such interrelated issues in mind, we can then construct a theory of radical documentary on a more sophisticated basis and enact a more effective film/video practice.

Radical documentary in all its media--still and moving image, audio, verbal and written, etc.--has always had at least two basic inescapable functions. Some examples and documentary genres almost exclusively use these two functions: witnessing and affecting. To witness is to say this happened, look at this--this was a concentration camp, these people are demonstrating for their rights, this is what napalm does to children, these are American cluster bombs being used against noncombatant civilians, etc. Given the overt censorship, the covert self-censorship, and the deliberate lies propagated by the dominant order, clearly the simple use of images as witness is itself often radical. To affect is to move: let this touch you, let this shock you or surprise you, make you weep or scream with anger, let this affect your heart, your emotions, your unconsciousness, your body, let this move you to act, to resist, and to change. This is always the other function of documentary, even when presented in a deliberately cool or rational style.

These functions of documentary always operate to some extent, but the films and tapes I want to discuss here go a step further because they interpret and analyze as well. They elaborate the "here is...," and they shape the viewers' response in a deliberate direction. Yet we need to go even further for a truly radical documentary. We need to teach people how to analyze things themselves in order to give them more power to act in their own future. As Julia Lesage has put it, we have to produce a radical media which deals with structure--with how things are and the underlying forces which make them that way--and with contradiction--with the differences and oppositions within a situation which indicate how change might take place.[2] To witness, move, and interpret is not enough. We must also produce radical documentaries which deal with why things are the way they are and how they might change and be changed.

Form

Formalism is the most seductive mistake in political documentary. By placing form over content, meaning, and actual effect on an audience, formalists try to escape from the problems of politics, their own relation to their work, and their work's context and reception. By assuming that they can solve these problems simply through using the correct form, they find a quick, easy, and almost always badly misguided solution to what are at heart political questions.

One kind of formalism often goes unrecognized. This is the formalism of documentary makers who tend to use old forms, well-known and accepted styles, which in fact have become tired clichés. Again and again we see political documentary following the typical network TV format in structural organization: opening dramatic example, quick discursive presentation of issue, mini-history, conflict-oriented presentation around a central figure or between two sides, appeal to "experts," and final indication of solution through legislation or change of heart. Specific techniques accompany this structure which vary only slightly from network to network and country to country. Such techniques include the use of authoritative narrator, maps and charts, talking-head interviews, "neutral" point of view shooting and editing, etc. In many ways this form is guided by pre-production considerations such as initial and continued financing, the hope for PBS or educational or art-house-circuit distribution, the maker and crew's previous formal and on-the-job training, and the taken-for-granted assumption of industry standards both in equipment and in the use of it. Films and tapes in the dominant culture have to be "smooth" and "perfect" precisely because they have to cover over social cracks and contradictions. In fetishizing what already exists, this contemporary "realistic" documentary form echoes the already known.

Usually, makers and producers justify this by saying you have to use familiar forms to reach a large audience and that more experimental forms cannot be used because people do not understand them. It's a Lawrence Welk approach that ignores the actual nature of visual literacy in our Atari culture. A four-year-old with access to television comes to symbolic consciousness both visually and verbally while immersed in complex image/sound combinations; the child does so while watching commercials as well as many of the animated and documentary segments of children's shows. To make films that will reach people "where they are at," in media culture now means to use familiar forms such as rapid montage editing, nontraditional cutting, layered sound and images, and metaphoric and symbolic images. For better or worse, Music Television represents the audiovisual norm of most adolescents today.

Most political film and video makers lag sadly behind the times in terms of communication techniques. As a result their work is often dull, static, boring, and even insulting to the audience. Their work succeeds often in spite of the form, not because of it. In order to change, political documentarists must study other kinds of film and video work and learn from these how to make more imaginative, creative, and exciting work.

While a more exploratory documentary practice appears in the avant-garde, often, on closer examination, specific cases turn out to be reversed from the dominant ideology but still symmetrical with it. Experimental formalism rests on the belief in a content-free area, a world of pure forms that determine how audiences will receive the work. From this perspective, just change the form and you automatically arrive in a new place. This argument has gained force in the last decade by the arguments of theorists who have pointed out the weakness of traditional and new realist forms. For example, Eileen McGarry's essay, "Documentary Realism and Women's Cinema,"[3] exposes the central fallacies of cinéma vérité in political filmmaking. Slipping into the easy assumption that a self-reflexive form contradicts naive political realism, some makers and theorists look to the highly self-conscious art of the high culture marketplace as providing the only way out. In contrast, a number of critics and theorists argue for a more sophisticated understanding of formal options and their use. Julia Lesage discusses how some feminist filmmakers use the already-existing political form of the consciousness-raising group to create a new cinematic discourse. Bill Nichols analyzes forms of documentary address or voice--the way the work speaks to its audience--to point out a newly emergent heterogeneity in radical documentary. In specific historical and critical studies, other writers have similarly argued for a variety of innovative forms appropriate to new political realities.[4]

The issue of form often becomes oversimplified, treated with expediency rather than deliberation. If we remain aware of the ideological nature of forms, be they realist or avant-garde, we can expand our options to embrace a variety of forms which depend on context, audience, intention, and other concerns for effect. We can also be open to using new forms, mixing and creating forms appropriate to new political forces, and new voices within the progressive coalition.

Politics

Politics in documentary work certainly remains an intractable question, as evidenced by the number of neurotic responses to challenges on this issue. As I have argued, political arguments are often displaced onto the question of form and then disposed of by invoking a formula. Another frequent strategy, often favored by makers, is to simply answer a challenge by evoking the maker's good intentions or to denounce the bad intentions others may have deduced from the work itself; the maker may also defend her/himself by appealing to membership in or sympathy for this or that organization or lifestyle. But these in fact evade the central issue. That can be brought forward only by asking directly: what are the politics of the work? Does it accurately present those politics? And are those good politics?

Two major problems face today's radical media person, and both of these have to do with the nature of the radical movement in our time: first, understanding and presenting the complex interrelation of issues, and second, finding a place between co-optable reformism and ultraradical purism.

On the level of content, many political documentaries underestimate their audience by soft-pedalling their message and sanitizing its radical content, even when those films take on a supposedly militant subject matter. In opposition to this, I argue that not only can people understand more than radical media typically present, but also that if radical media are to play a leading role in the movement, they must deal with political questions in much greater detail and complexity.

The standards for a good radical film and video documentary should be the same as those for good political journalism. This includes a thorough investigation, an understanding of the history and development of the matter being documented, and an honesty in presenting the living complexity of the situation and its politics. Clearly, the standards for a short agitational film or tape made to provoke discussion, emphasize an issue, or move people to a specific decision or action will be different than those for a long analytic work. Yet often extended radical works present simplistic and sanitized versions of their subject. For example, the popular "oral history" interview films--Union Maids, With Babies and Banners, and Rosie the Riveter--erase their interviewees' connections with and sometimes actual membership in the Communist Party and other left organizations. By reproducing anti-communist ideology, such works easily become co-opted, and their widespread use makes it that much harder to get audiences to remember facts that even conservative mainstream historians acknowledge--for example, that the initial CIO organizing drive was led by Communist organizers.[5]

While historical documentaries can be faulted for inaccuracy and distortion compared with other historical accounts and interpretations, the current-reportage documentary often escapes criticism because it assumes an authority in a vacuum. Yet without fuller and deeper analysis, such films often date instantly. A particular pertinent example is Finally Got the News, a report on one organization in the militant Black labor and community movement in Detroit in the early '70s.[6] By the time the film was distributed the organization had split; yet the film never gave any indication of different forces and positions to begin with. Of course, documentary makers cannot be clairvoyant, but if they have in fact observed well, done their research and investigation ("Without investigation no right to speak"--Mao), and tried to understand the phenomenon in its entirety, the resulting work should be relevant and informative long after original events pass. We need only to think of such films as Borinage or How Yukong Moved the Mountain by Joris Ivens, or Kino-Pravda or Three Songs of Lenin by Dziga Vertov, or 79 Springtimes of Ho Chi Minh by Santiago Alvarez to see this is possible.

But to follow the standards of good radical reporting

in journalism, we must get beyond the conventions of the dominant documentary. Today's conventional film/video documentary has several typical characteristics which reinforce its general ideological function. First, it is usually constructed around a single protagonist, a set of related people, or several individuals. The emphasis is on the individual at present rather than collective history. This individual is depicted either as typical or sometimes as unusual (but then, implicitly or explicitly revealing of the typical, the odd ball remains framed by the dominant order). The documentary stresses such an emphasis through a number of style choices, including the following: framing which concentrates on the protagonist (often using a zoom lens to isolate or emphasize the character), the presentation of "significant" actions used to reveal personality; the use of "seeing" shots which give a general approximation of the protagonist's point of view; and the subjective use of sync sound which privileges what the protagonist says or hears. The documentary also often uses authorities, whom it frequently privileges as stars or to whom it gives narrational dominance. Editing and other elements tend to remain secondary or invisible compared to the focus on the main figure(s).

Other key elements of conventional documentary derive from the effort to maintain a conflict structure in the action; this is maintained by a unity of space or location and seeking after an interest-grabbing concern, i.e., the unusual or sensational. Further conventional elements coalesce into a code of "quality"--the one already well known and established in commercial work. Similarly a code of "objectivity" is evoked; two opposing sides must be put forward, with the film being somehow "outside of" or "above" the conflict.

Because the political situation is always changing, no single universal political criterion can apply to radical documentary. However, any fully revolutionary analysis within such work must answer two questions. First, what is the situation? Second, how can it change? In other words, the documentary must deal with structure and contradiction. These require distinctly different approaches from the usual "problem and solution" expository pattern so frequently used. Typically, problem, solution narrative organization removes the problem from its larger political, economic, and social framework and presents it on its most empirically observable level. To take an example from today's television news: a man comes to the rescue of a "bag lady" who is being assaulted while sleeping in a public park. Problem: it's hard for homeless people to find safe places to sleep. The news offers no analysis of why the United States contains two million or so homeless people like her. In contrast, a radical documentary such as Jim Klein and Julia Reichert's Methadone: An American Way of Dealing offers a specific case study as well as a comprehensive analysis of heroin addiction and methadone maintenance as paired aspects of a larger system of social control of a segment of the population.

Radical documentary needs to get beyond the most immediate level of emotional involvement--isn't this shocking, deplorable, unjust, etc.?--and give viewers a way of understanding why this condition exists in the first place, the underlying causes for it, and its relation to other parts of the society. Without such a fuller conception, the immediate emotional response is easily turned toward a simple solution: change of heart, charity, or legislative reform. And the documentary then leaves the ongoing causes of the problem unexamined.

People often forget that the oppositional movement and its politics largely respond to the configuration of the dominant order and that as the established system changes, so will the resistance to it. Since World War II, the distinctive feature of successful radical movements has been their ability to link different kinds and aspects of oppression. This linking has come neither easily nor automatically, of course, but taking a long view of it, we can see a distinct difference between the Old Left's raising of class issues, defined in fairly strictly conceived economic terms, and a still-evolving contemporary radicalism which stresses the fundamental interrelation of class, race, and gender oppression within the context of an anti-imperialist consciousness and an insistence on social and cultural issues as well as economic ones. In fact, the most lively and effective left politics of our time emerges from coalitions which represent a range of interlocking concerns. In this context the substance and style of radical documentary must change to become more capable of working within a changing and evolving coalition. And makers, as well, need to be more flexible and able to work in a variety of ways, to fit different situations and possibilities.

The issues of form and politics which I've discussed so far can be considered in greater detail by discussing some specific works. The War At Home (Barry Brown and Glenn Silber) works in a familiar recent genre--the radical nostalgia film. It combines footage of past events with contemporary interviews with participants. The film appeared at the same time as legislation to reinstate peacetime draft registration, and it found ready use in campus anti-draft organizing as well as getting some theatrical attention. As a documentary about the protest movement in Madison, Wisconsin from the mid-'60s to mid-'70s The War At Home exhibits many typical intermeshed form and content problems. The interviews are shot in a visually uncompelling TV style which in turn visually heightens the historical footage. That footage largely comes from TV news coverage of the most public and "newsworthy" events, newsworthy according to broadcast journalism standards, which the film doesn't question. In this way, The War At Home unreflectively presents two levels of discourse. One level evokes the past by recalling--"what I thought then, what it felt like then,"--rather than critical memory--"what I think now of what we did then." The other discourse documents what TV news typically shows--the immediate and empirical. Thus we see confrontation, but not the planning and discussion that precedes it; tactics, but not the strategy; we see the results of bombing the Army Math Research Center building, but not the years of organizing and education that went on around that institution. As a result, the film produces one overwhelming interpretation of the past: we demonstrated, then the police attacked, so next time we got tougher. And in the absence of any other information, this seems to constitute an organizing strategy. In fact, it is a method which boils down to men escalating violent confrontation, which may go too far--i.e., inadvertently killing someone in the bombing. But at least, the film seems to conclude, you can elect a progressive hip mayor and get an ex-radical to head a government social control agency (VISTA).

The film signals such an attitude, with 1963 newsreel footage depicting Madison as "the All-American town." This setup makes the ensuing demonstration seem even more dramatic--protest just springing up like mushrooms after a shower. But even in this opening detail lies a major distortion. The state of Wisconsin has a long tradition of populism and founded the Progressive movement; industrial Milwaukee had socialist mayors for most of the 20th century; Madison was a haven for radicals of all stripes during the McCarthy period; and the campus was a favorite of East Coast red diaper babies. In the late '50s and '60s a progressive campus ministry supported eating cooperatives, free university courses on social issues, avant-garde theatre, civil rights activism, and anti-nuke protest. (I speak from personal experience. As an undergrad at UW from '60-'64, I met ministers who had worked in San Francisco's gay community and been on civil rights demonstrations in the South, academics who had traveled to post-revolutionary Cuba, Old Leftists' children who visited the USSR and took supplies to striking miners in Harlan County, grad students putting out the early New Left intellectual journal Studies on the Left, and SNCC organizers fundraising for voter registration drives.)

Madison was anything but typical. But the film distorts this and in representing history actually drops out a good deal. What is left out or misrepresented reveals the film's weakness. The film repeats the same kind of confusion of image and truth which one of its interviewees expresses as he recalls how the sudden appearance of 25 black guys in berets and army jackets seemed to mean the revolution was at hand. Much of the movement disappears. The film drops out or gives token recognition to women, Native Americans, workers, gays, groups other than SDS, and radicals working in culture and arts. One of the most insulting examples comes with the film's only reference to feminism--a quick shot of a "Sisterhood Is Powerful" banner in the final credit roll. Similarly, the film never deals with capitalism (though it carefully includes a Businessman for Peace) and it misses the evolution of protest from predominantly pacifist anti-war to distinctly anti-imperialist. In this framework the film never examines the bizarre (and perhaps agent-inspired) tactics of Karl Armstrong's New Year's Gang, debates over strategy and tactics on the left, or associated organizing on and off campus--such as the remarkable growth of the nation's first Teaching Assistants Association to gain collective bargaining (one of its prime movers, Henry Haslach, is interviewed, but only as a former SDS figure).

In contrast, Mifflin Street (Howard Monath), a short documentary which covers the same period, comes much closer to capturing the fluid complexity of the Madison scene. By using heavily manipulated, optically printed images; multiple layers of sound, including music and overlaid voices; home movies footage mixed with dramatic reenactment, as well as interviews, it shows the student and counter-culture resistance from within. As in The War At Home, mayor Paul Soglin is interviewed, but in a patently crude set-up which avoids the slick style of the feature documentary. The overall result establishes a kind of psychedelic history. In its negative aspects, at times it uncritically celebrates male fantasy and sexuality and sometimes disguises counter-culture elitism, as in repeated shots of people trying to overturn a bus. (Actually the bus had been rented by welfare mothers protesting cutbacks at the nearby state capitol. On their return they found this trashed vehicle for which they were financially liable.) My point is not that Mifflin Street is an exemplary film for all occasions, but that despite its limits, in comparison with The War At Home it underlines the latter's limits in form and politics. The War At Home presents a cleaned-up history in a flawless form. In the process it ignores the complications and complexity of the movement. The War At Home shows us Karl Armstrong in jail and his father reflecting on how he, the father, didn't realize that the government and media were lying about the war. But Mifflin Street gives the feeling of the frenetic community base of the movement, the context in which Armstrong could feel that bombing was appropriate, the people's lives--people who knew all along from street hassles, drug busts, tear gas in their neighborhood, and cops at their door that the government was an oppressive force and that the established media distorted events.

Makers

The social, political, institutional, personal, and historical positions of specific film and video makers affect radical documentary, although many ignore the question. Perhaps in response to Romantic theories of the artist, genius, and inspiration and to the actual obnoxious behavior of certain makers, in the past decade or so many critics have concentrated on the film/tape itself and not dealt with the actual producer and production situation.[7] Yet for the documentarist, the issue doesn't go away; and among critics the net result in many cases has been to produce a criticism which does not and cannot say anything significant to makers.

The concrete situation of individual makers is something they must come to terms with precisely because building a contemporary radical movement depends on understanding the interrelation of race, gender, and class oppression. Minority media activists have constantly stressed the necessity of white radicals' coming to terms with racism and their own privilege. Feminists have criticized men for not dealing with sexism in their behavior and in their documentaries. Because those issues have played such a central role in recent criticism and discussion about radical documentary--particularly in the wake of the Alternative Cinema Conference in 1979--I want to stress a related issue which is often not raised: that of class position and class politics.

Whatever their sex, race, and class origins, almost all documentary makers belong to a specific class--the petty bourgeoisie in Marxist terms--and a stratum of that class--intellectuals, in the broad sense, those whose training and work is centrally concerned with the production and dissemination of ideas, images, information and analyses. Intellectuals' work consists largely of manipulating things or information without consciousness of a larger context, without reflecting on whose interests are served. (Upper-level managers who hire them are usually quite consciously cognizant of those matters.) The key defining feature of the petty bourgeoisie as a class is its position in between: in between the capitalist class which owns the means of production and the working class which has its labor power to sell. As members of the in-between class, petty bourgeois media people like to think of themselves as "free professionals"--an attitude which matches their class interests. Precisely their class interest is to waver and not commit themselves, or if they do, to be free to reverse at a later point.

The ability to generate, manipulate and distribute sound and moving image material in a modern industrial culture is very specialized and typically requires large amounts of capital. It usually demands considerable means of production. To master the means of production, in turn, demands considerable technical skill and knowledge, including specialized skills in organizing the labor of the project as well as decision making in shaping and executing the product. The very attainment of these skills for someone in the working class raises them out of their class in significant ways. Often attainment of skills, as in the health profession, is class-stratified. Most typically, the training of working class media people gives them access only to restricted technical jobs, which, given the severe division of labor, does not grant them access to major decision making.

Typically the training phase of media work concentrates almost exclusively on production. In this way it fits in with the logic of capitalist social relations. Very few film and video makers encounter a wide range of work and ideas in their training. The increasing, and increasingly destructive, split between production, on the one hand, and history, criticism, and theory on the other fuels the problem. The extreme division into specialties and areas of knowledge, craft, and methodology accentuates the difficulty. Most ways of learning production skills, from apprenticeship to formal academic training, involve learning only one way or a few similar ways of doing things. Without any further critical reflection or thoughtful historical understanding or comparison with other and different ways of making documentary, people learn certain technologies, procedures, ways of organization and working which are themselves ideological, though presented as "this is the way it's always done..." or "this is the norm in the industry..." or "this is the right way to do it." And while this is most obvious in university and technical school classes with a formulaic industry-oriented emphasis, in a more subtle but just as ideological way it permeates art schools. Here film courses take individual expression as the norm, but implicitly limit that initiative when teachers assume that other kinds of work are off-limits and show across-the-country-work from a remarkably similar set of examples.

Students who want to make radical documentary have to break consciously with often ruthlessly imposed norms of film practice. To do so, they must make a point of learning from other forms of documentary than those they are most familiar with. They must seek out a broader range of films and tapes to view, works from around the world and from the history of documentary practice. An ongoing process of self-education is an essential corrective if documentarists are not simply to repeat the assumptions of the status quo. It's the necessary foundation for their continuous renewal of vision and their reference from which to construct a genuinely new documentary practice as they engage in new realities.

The very nature of film and video work makes considerable economic demands on makers in terms of buying, renting, or getting access to equipment, paying for film and supplies and lab costs, etc. which emphasize its class-restrictive nature. When conducted in a deliberately "poor" way, as with Super 8 or ½" or ¼" video, the built-in prejudice of the system is to conclude that thrifty means aesthetically poor.

Having learned how to make effective media, the committed documentarist faces a basic dilemma ... it doesn't go away. Media makers have to make a living unless they have unearned income or are supported by someone else. They want to use their skills and they want to make politically significant work. All these factors are only rarely compatible. It is virtually impossible to do politically radical work within the existing system such as with the networks, National Endowment grants, or PBS, particularly under a conservative government. So you can choose to make a living elsewhere and then be free to pursue your art and politics, but you only have your "free" time to do so. Or you can work in the industry and maintain your skills but probably have to work on projects which you find more or less ridiculous or even reprehensible.

Many people try to work in the media and build some kind of a career within it. But this puts certain constraints on what you can do. You have to accommodate yourself to the already existing system. Younger people starting out feel the pressure to get established, to have some kind of stability in what is a typically project-oriented field. Established people have acquired responsibilities, dependents, etc. which often act as a conservative drag on career decisions. And we are all painfully aware of the figure of the radical who, through "practical compromise," gets to the position of having some control over what he/she is doing, only to have sold out. Even the very rare reverse figure falls within a similar structural situation--what do you do when your film/tape on behalf of a cause suddenly nets you half a million dollars?

The key element here is precisely a class phenomenon--the extreme individualism of the petty bourgeoisie. Much more than the capitalist or working class person, the petty bourgeoisie holds to self-interested notions of autonomy, freedom, and self-determination. (And I speak here as a petty bourgeois intellectual.) Radical intellectuals' need for autonomy creates deep ambiguity in relation to the movement which supports them directly or indirectly, especially if they are radicals trying to make a living off of movement work. Most media work actually removes people from direct contact with the masses of people.

Once established in the media world, you are in the position of selling either a specific product--this film/tape--and are put in the position of being a small business entrepreneur; or you are selling your reputation in order to get the chance to do more work, or another grant. Or sometimes you take up one role and then the other. The situation itself contributes to reinforcing sentimental politics. You see yourself meeting responsibilities simply by doing what you're doing. Or you react with cynicism and reckon with compromise, accepting it over principle or political judgment. Furthermore, once established, even alternative institutions become less likely to take risks. And even within an alternative you need capital and have to earn your own way, prove yourself, and justify your project.

The left, the "movement," is not able to deal with this very well. It is dominated by people who don't understand the use of visual media and who either see visual media as simply instrumental or reduce them to some verbal component. Yet only in establishing a relation with the left, in becoming politicized, can petty bourgeois media people break with the logical outcome of their class position and develop a class politics that gets beyond their immediate interests. Just as men can develop an understanding of individual and institutional sexism and contribute to the fight against it, just as whites can come to terms with racism and work to eradicate it, documentary film and video makers can understand class issues and make media which contributes to advancing the working class and combatting imperialism.

To make documentaries with strong working-class politics does not simply entail attaching some worn political formulae to working-class subject matter and using a conventional form. That will only produce left-wing hackwork. Radical media makers need new forms of collaboration in the making of the work and new ways of articulating class issues. Several recent documentaries are especially successful in showing what can be done. The Chicago filmmaking collective Kartemquin's Winnie Wright, Age 11 and Now We Live on Clifton are half-hour vérité-style documentaries which present working-class family life and community concerns from children's point of view--a perspective seldom given attention. The kids articulate class issues in a very concrete form, such as living in an interracial neighborhood and having to move because of gentrification. At the same time, the films provide recognition of the everyday, as when we see Winnie Wright disinterestedly doing homework while watching television. These films' strength lies in their ability to present working-class life without condescension or idealization. The contradictions stand clear, as seen in a shot of Winnie Wright, poised between childhood and adulthood, wearing two buttons--Smile and Boycott Lettuce.

Michelle Citron's What You Take For Granted compares and contrasts the experiences of women working in traditionally male jobs. The film emphasizes the differences between working-class and professional jobs by using both formal interviews and a fictional narrative showing the developing friendship between a doctor and a truck driver. Citron's research involved interviewing dozens of women, both professionals and women in the trades; she used these interviews to learn the conditions they faced and to distinguish the idiosyncratic from the common. Her decision to synthesize the material into scripted interviews--the public--and to combine that with fictional narration--the private--reflects Citron's desire to show the personal, everyday, and intimate (something documentary does well only by moving away from the representative) as well as the public. The film is carefully calculated to allow a very complex audience projection, which works on identification (with the truck driver and/or the physician as well as with the interviewees). The film then painfully complicates identification by showing the flaws and problems in each character.

Similarly, JoAnn Elam's Everyday People (in progress) portrays the work of letter carriers. The film constantly pivots around what workers find interesting, important, and rewarding about the job, and how management tries to control the worker. The soundtrack uses interviews, pop music hits, and a voice-over narrator explaining the official policy. The visual track consists of hand-held documentary footage of postal work, often edited in-camera with a rapid montage. The total effect is to provide an analysis which doubtlessly provides the best film documentary example of Harry Braverman's contemporary Marxist classic, Labor and Monopoly Capital. This analysis is framed within a context of frequent humor and obvious love for the job and for the letter carriers depicted.

One of the most important innovations brought by cinéma vérité was its ability to portray the extraordinary texture of events and life by showing detail and gestures, as with Jackie Kennedy's hands in Primary and the facial expression of physical weariness of the Bible salesman in Salesman. Kartemquin, Citron, and Elam take that motive of documenting the everyday further by providing intimacy as well. This intimacy comes from knowing the subjects over a period of time, developing the material in collaboration with others, and, more profoundly, seeing the personal not merely as interesting but as fundamentally political.

Louis Hock's videowork, Criminal Tales, shows the power of such intimacy. Made over a period of years by an Anglo film/video maker in San Diego about his neighbors, who are almost all illegal Mexican immigrants, the tape serves as an overture to a longer project, The Mexican Tapes (in progress). The neighbors relate stories of U.S. immigration officers' picking people up and how the Mexicans crossed back, of exploitation and racism by local whites, of the neighbors' hopes and fears. Two women discuss a case of devil possession (a movie plot? a tale retold?) and subtitles tell us one of them returned to Mexico and died in childbirth. Hock captures the unwritten history of these people's lives, presenting both their oppression and their resistance, seen in the story-telling that preserves and creates their knowledge and memory. The easy informality, metaphoric richness, and firm concreteness of working-class conversation emerge again and again, testifying to the subjects' total ease with the presence of the camera and trust in Hock's intentions.

The works I've just described fall distinctly outside the clenched fist, red flag, battle-with-police type of documentary about workers. But I think these works are no less valid. What they offer is a complex view of working-class life and resistance, and in particular, insight into the sources of workers' strength and will. What these works show radical documentarists is that it is possible to make films and tapes which go beyond establishing workers as mouthpieces for correct lines or as abstractions who propel history forward. These works provide exemplary answers to the question of how media people can relate to the working class.

Contexts

Theoretical-critical work on radical documentary and on makers' actual practice grows increasingly sensitive to questions of context. Formalism and an emphasis on production without thinking of distribution and exhibition have marked the past. Today, seeing the documentary in a process encompassing production and distribution-exhibition, and as having its own history within a set of changing expectations and situations, gives makers a more sophisticated view. Rather than being audio-visual illustrations of this or that political issue, today documentaries help the very cognition of political reality and have a crucial place as part of the ongoing discourse of the movement.

What You Take For Granted is constructed to both draw in and distance the audience by stressing the contradictions in working women's lives. The film becomes a topic of conversation, an active social phenomenon, as viewers work out for themselves after the screening their relation to the characters, the issues, and the questions presented. The film enters the lives of women and the feminist movement, not as a report on the politically correct line but as an investigation of the structured oppression of women and the contradictions within and between women.

To see documentary in this way--as an intervention, a provocation for discussion, a necessarily incomplete statement--restores to analytical documentary work the immediacy of reportage and the bold emotions of agitational film and video without letting the film/tape fall into rhetorical posturing, condescension to the audience, or ironic dryness. Understanding documentary as "complete" only when seen and reacted to shifts the maker's goals from producing a perfect, whole, comprehensive work to producing a work with new values and new designs, which will make it viable, interesting, and educational for a longer time. From this perspective, we can have no "One Size Fits All" correct form for documentary, because each work will have its own exhibition itinerary intersecting with its makers' goals and abilities. Nor is there simply a choice between wimpy reformism and heavy-rhetoric militancy. Rather, the political dimension of documentary becomes a process of educating the audience about the complexity of the subject matter, about the structures and contradictions of this situation so that they might grasp the situation's evolution when they see it at a later time. In other words, the documentary does not simply present the correct analysis but rather helps people to analyze their own and other situations. When a film/tape does this, it, in turn, changes the very nature and role of the maker who becomes less of an authority and more of a teacher.

In the process, the maker's own position in relation

to the events depicted becomes part of the heart of the work. Every documentary reveals, if nothing else, the relation between the maker and the people documented. In this way, ethnocentrism becomes a crucial issue; the filmmaker's class, race, and gender position (always present) becomes acute when dealing with different groups. At times this position becomes reflected directly, as in Louis Hock's initially introducing his community and neighbors and later taping while the "Migra" police are asking who he is in the middle of a roundup. At other times it appears indirectly, as in the intimacy of Everyday People's showing work procedures and the letter carrier's relation to the social and climatic environment on his/her route.

The importance of context for the political documentary is dramatized by the example of Los Hijos de Sandino (Sandino's Children; Kimberly Safford and Fred Barney Taylor). Shot in Super 8 and optically printed and manipulated in the step-up to 16mm, it shows daily life and festivals in and around Managua during the first anniversary in July 1980 of the Nicaraguan revolution. A Spanish-language soundtrack of local music, the radio, and location non-sync sound adds to the film's density. With exquisitely framed shots, rich in color and deliberately long, often slowed as if to savor the moment, as well as "exotic" (to U. S. ears) soundtrack, the film can be seen on one level as an arty travelogue--an avant-garde filmmakers' trip to Nicaragua, heavy on local color. Indeed, the makers even thought of calling it "Tourists of the Revolution" to mark their own position in relation to their subject. But that label does not convey the film's only level.

In the same way that a Gestalt psychology foreground/background figure demands an alteration of views, Los Hijos de Sandino has another dimension, especially for anyone familiar with Latin American life. Depending on the context and the audience's knowledge and expectation, the film changes. It has been widely screened in conjunction with Nicaragua support work in Mexico, where it is understood as a vibrant portrait of the Nicaraguan people and the Sandinist movement. Similarly, shown to Latino audiences in the U. S., the film finds a warm reception for its strongly emotional moments (Fidel Castro's addressing the crowd, military units passing in review, boys diving into water while a male voice-over describes how as a child he was afraid of the National Guard and ran from them, how he went off to join the rebels, and was captured and tortured). In fact, the current major re-injection of open emotion into recent radical documentary must be linked in part to the explosion of media work about Central America and the Latin insistence on speaking from the heart as well as the head. And music and radio, as primary radical forms in Latin America, are now contributing to our new understanding of the political use of sound in media.

Shown in Nicaragua, Los Hijos de Sandino elicited enthusiastic audience response for its lyrical beauty and emotional resonance; dissent came only from politicos who complained that the film wasn't political enough and didn't explain enough. I think this is a case where the people are smarter than their leaders. The film presents the poetry of the revolution; that is part of the total picture never captured in maps, charts, and official talking-head interviews with officials. Instead, the film is constantly transforming its own images. The standard tourist shot of a group of youths pushing each other and posing for the camera becomes something totally different when it is held for a long time and one fellow in military fatigues begins putting his beret at a more rakish angle and pulling up his collar in a preening gesture. (See photo, p. 339.) Here, the others laugh at him, he smiles too, and the exchange of glances back and forth to the camera (and its obviously present operator) turns the moment into something shared, mutually enacted, and mutually recognized.

To help develop a new context for this film the makers encourage screening it following John Chapman's dramatic reportage of the last weeks of Somoza's overthrow, Nicaragua: Scenes from the Revolution, also shot in Super 8. Chapman provides background information and links it to astonishing action of children on the barricades and in the streets. Safford and Taylor provide the cultural, social and everyday moments that let us into the rich, complex dimension of a new revolutionary society, as in a sequence where we hear revolutionary commercials for using the bus and women vending fruit to bus passengers. At the end of the film, after seeing marching columns passing in review at the Independence Day celebration--columns containing men and women, children and adults, and old veterans of Sandino's original army--the official ceremony ends, and suddenly a thunderstorm breaks out. The rain becomes a metaphor of transformation, as rain-soaked militiamen jump up and down in slow-motion celebration. Moving from formality and order to spontaneous joy this sequence encapsulates much of the

Los Hijos de Sandino is a film constantly transforming its own images. The standard tourist shot of youths posing for the camera, held for a long time, becomes a moment mutually shared, enacted and recognized by filmmakers and subjects.

film's form as well as the film's political significance. The tourist camera and tape recorder pay attention to the official, but the film constantly recognizes the human and everyday. People stare back at the camera, at the audience, changing who and what is the subject. Certainly Los Hijos de Sandino is not analytical in the sense of providing a summary of conditions, causes and results, yet it analyzes an experienced human reality--the Nicaraguan revolution as that revolution looks to people on the streets--and transforms the tourist-travelogue film in the process.

Many radical documentarists have accepted a familiar form or reproduced an established politics and aimed at the existing distribution-exhibition system. The new documentary work I have discussed does not fit easily into conventional categories. We live in a time of rapid political and cultural change. New groupings are emerging which do not fit traditional Left thought and new coalitions form around new issues. At the same time the media are undergoing vast technological change and this is transforming financing, production, distribution, and reception. Few generalizations remain valid in such a period. Everything, old and new, must be examined, questioned and tested. We must deduce our aesthetics, like our politics, from understanding our situation and responding to our movement's needs.

Notes

1 My central reference for this discussion is the U.S. in the mid-80s. These issues would doubtless have a different priority elsewhere. In addition, matters of financing, distribution, and exhibition are essential. This essay reflects lessons from practice, particularly my films The Jerry Lewis Labor Day Telethon (with Liz Schillinger), The Ten Million Dollar Bash, Men Men Men, and Rising Expectations (in progress). On other occasions I've written about political documentaries by people I did not know; because these issues are so central to my current creative and intellectual work, here I chose to concentrate on work by people I know well and have worked with: Michelle Citron, JoAnn Elam, Kimberly Safford and Fred Barney Taylor. I first presented some of these ideas at the Alternative Cinema Conference in 1979 and they have been shaped by many people since then, especially in discussions with John Hess and Julia Lesage. I hope this stresses the collaborative nature of current theoretical-practical work in political documentary. I also had the opportunity to discuss their work with the Kartemquin filmmakers, and Louis Hock and Howard Monath.

2 In addition to her essay on Self Health and Rape in this volume, see Lesage, "One Way Or Another: Dialectical Filmmaking in a Post-Revolutionary Society," Jump Cut, no. 20 (1979) and "For Our Urgent Use: Films on Central America," Jump Cut, no. 27 (1982).

3 Eileen McGarry, "Documentary, Realism and Women's Cinema," Women & Film, 2:7 (1975).

4 Bill Nichols, Ideology and the Image (Bloomington: Indiana U. Press, 1981), pp. 170-284, and Nichols, "The Voice of Documentary," Film Quarterly, 36:3 (Spring, 1983). Examples of recent discussion of these issues:

Jeffrey Youdelman, "Narration, Invention, & History: A Documentary Dilemma," Cineaste, 12:2 (1982); John Hess, "Notes on U.S. Radical Film, 1967-80," Jump Cut, no. 21 (1979); B. Ruby Rich and Linda Williams, "The Right of Re-vision: Michelle Citron's Daughter Rite," Film Quarterly, 35 (Fall, 1981). Although dealing largely with still photography, two important contributions to radical documentary theory are: Martha Rosler, "In, Around, and Afterthoughts (On Documentary Photography)" in Rosler, Three Works (Halifax: Press of the Nova Scotia College of Art and Design, 1981) and Allan Sekula, "Dismantling Modernism, Reinventing Documentary (Notes on The Politics of Representation)," Massachusetts Review, 19:4 (Winter 1978). In addition to Cineaste and Jump Cut, I frequently find important discussions of documentary in Afterimage (US), The Independent (US), Fuse (Canada), Film News (Australia) and Camerawork (UK).

5 Historians have been especially perceptive in discussing the wave of radical history films. See, for example, Sonya Michel, "Feminism, Film and Public History," Radical History Review, no. 25 (1981); Michael H. Frisch, "The Memory of History," Radical History Review, no. 25 (1981); John Demeter, "Independent Film & Working Class History: A Review of Northern Lights and The Wobblies," Radical America, 14:1 (1980); Linda Gordon, "Union Maids: Working Class Heroines," Jump Cut, no. 14 (1977); Sue Davenport, "The Life and Times of Rosie the Riveter: Invisible Working Women," Jump Cut, no. 28 (1983).

6 The background and events as well as the film are analyzed in the exemplary study by Marvin Surkin and Dan Georgakas, Detroit: I Do Mind Dying (New York: St. Martin's Press, 1975).

7 I am not trying to argue the meaning, validity, or value of works on the basis of the maker's intentions. I am saying that the documentarist's goals and anticipated circulation and use of the work must be considered. Pure formalist analysis, dealing with none of this, has a very limited usefulness for film and video makers. It is interesting to notice in this regard that the most formalist media work produced cannot be understood alone. It depends on personal appearances, interviews, manifestoes, critical

articles based on discussions with the maker, and current critical-theoretical fads, fashions, and posturings.

PART III

CONTEMPORARIES: THE THIRD WORLD

Chapter 18

DEMOCRATIZING DOCUMENTARY: MODES OF ADDRESS IN THE LATIN AMERICAN CINEMA, 1958-72

Julianne Burton

Much of the most exciting recent work in documentary studies has focused on the relations of sound and image, or more precisely, on that of the narrational voice (or its absence) to visual diegesis. Julianne Burton, foremost American authority on Latin American cinema, takes up the terms of this discussion and applies them to liberating impulses in Latin American social documentary in the first fifteen years or so of the vérité period, locating a democratizing trajectory of shifting voices. The next step beyond this groundbreaking but definitive apperception of a much neglected area will be to integrate that trajectory with the evolution of its technological base over the same period, and to situate it with regard to the economic and political problematic of the state film industries, most notably of course as pertaining to the Cuban examples under study.

Deposing the Authoritarian Narrator

From the inception of the social documentary movement in the mid- to late- fifties,[1] Latin American filmmakers began experimenting with a broad range of strategies designed to eliminate, supplant or subvert the standard documentary mode of address: the anonymous, omniscient, ahistorical "Voice of God." These social issue filmmakers were determined to challenge what they perceived as the authoritarian characteristics of this particular mode of address, since they equated it with an unjust, hierarchical, closed socio-political order which they were equally determined to expose and combat. Long before the technological innovations in sound recording associated with "direct cinema" and "cinéma vérité" were widely available in the region, Latin American filmmakers explored indirect and observational modes in an attempt to pluralize and democratize modes of documentary address.

In their drive to subvert or eliminate the authoritarian narrator, some filmmakers substituted intertitles: others went so far as to completely extirpate the logos--aural and graphic--in films whose "vanguard" practice resuscitated formal strategies of the silent era. When not totally eliminated, voice-of-God narration often had to cede aural space to folk lyrics, the on-camera and/or on-microphone presence of the filmmakers or their surrogates, and the self-presentation of social actors. Other films utilized a participant or social actor as a kind of "meta-narrator" who appears on camera to perform and explicate simultaneously. Two Uruguayan filmmakers imitated the more "detached" approach of North American cinéma vérité, though not without elements of irony or even parody. As the following chronological survey will reveal, Latin America's militant filmmakers retained the authoritarian narrative voice only with reluctance, deferring it beyond the point of unselfconscious expectation, diluting or relativizing it in a composite of other modes of address, devalidating it through the manipulation of the image track.

In this process, both simultaneous and concerted, Latin American filmmakers constantly forced the expansion of the concept of documentary by favoring investigation over exposition, hypothesis over prescription, "process" over "analysis,"[2] poeticized over "purely" factual discourse. They produced films which were not only "imperfect" but also "impure" or hybridized in their mixture of modes of address and in their recourse to narrativity and devices conventionally associated with fictional or experimental modalities. The drive to democratize modes of address, which foregrounded issues of organization and access to power in the larger society as a political-economic system, was often accompanied by a parallel impulse to foreground issues of formal organization within the film itself as a signifying system (a conjunction which will be discussed in more detail in the conclusion to this essay). The films

Direct and Indirect Modes of Verbal Address:
Original Paradigm by Bill Nichols

DIRECT ADDRESS (EXPOSITORY CINEMA)

	sync	non-sync
narrators	voice of authority	voice of God images of illustration
characters	interview	voice of witness images of illustration

INDIRECT ADDRESS (OBSERVATIONAL CINEMA)

	sync	non-sync
narrators		
characters	cinéma vérité (voice and image of social actors)	voice of social actors images of illustration

Expanded Paradigm:

DIRECT ADDRESS (EXPOSITORY CINEMA)

	sync	non-sync
narrators	voice of authority	voice of God images of illustration
filmmaker	voice of filmmaker image of filmmaker	voice of filmmaker images of illustration
character	integral interview (filmmaker/narrator and character on screen)	voice of conversant(s) images of illustration or observation
	off-screen interview (filmmaker/narrator off-screen; character on screen. Variations: filmmaker/narrator occupies contiguous space; or non-contiguous space of the same diegetic order; or is represented non-spatially, through graphics)	
	pseudo-monologue (image of character; visual and aural absence of film- maker/narrator)	voice of character images of illustration or observation

INDIRECT ADDRESS (OBSERVATIONAL CINEMA)

	sync	non-sync
narrators		
filmmaker	participant-conversation (implicit or explicit meta-communication)	voices of conversants images of conversants (observation) or illus- tration
character	cinéma vérité or direct cinema	voice of social actor images of observation

which demonstrate this dual impulse utilize self-reflexivity to acknowledge the interrelationship between politics in the society and politics in the text.

Four recent essays on documentary, converging, helped to constitute the theoretical and methodological point of departure for this inquiry. They are: Bill Nichols' "The Documentary Film and Principles of Exposition," Annette Kuhn's "The Camera I: Observations on Documentary," Jeffrey Youdelman's "Narration, Invention and History: A Documentary Dilemma," and Michael Chanan's "Considerations on Cuban Documentary."[3] From the first I have taken--and, in collaboration with its author, expanded--the paradigm of direct and indirect modes of verbal address (see page 346). In response to the second, I have tried to take into consideration as well modes of visual address, though here the question of systematicity is much more problematic. Chanan's article surveys the various documentary typologies offered by Latin American filmmakers themselves in their attempts to classify their documentary production. He argues for the centrality of intentionality (how the filmmakers themselves define the purpose of their films) and reconstructs some of the historical-philosophical-ideological underpinning of such a stance, calling in his conclusion for a more systematic study of how the films define "the position which the viewer occupies in relation to the film's mode of address." Youdelman's article provides a partial model. Before veering off onto a discussion of historical accuracy and political affiliation, he offers an (incomplete) survey of non-authoritarian forms of direct verbal address in the "older tradition" of (Euro-American) documentary filmmaking.

What I propose to do here is to trace variations in modes of verbal and visual address through fifteen years of Latin American social documentary production in hopes of adding to the current historical and theoretical work on documentary a whole new range of (substantiating or contradictory) "evidence" from an extensive and important film tradition which is insufficiently recognized outside its own geo-linguistic parameters and inadequately studied within them. In addition to examining modes of verbal address (synchronous or non-synchronous, direct or indirect, expository or observational) and modes of visual address (fully frontal "eye-to-eye"; subject looking away from the camera; subject in intermediate posture, looking toward but not directly at the camera), I will also consider issues of formal structuration, narrative and experimental modalities, self-reflexive devices, and in several cases, genesis and modes of filmic production. The fifteen films analyzed here represent six countries: Argentina, Cuba, Bolivia, Brazil, Uruguay and Colombia. Individually, and as a group, they exemplify the most significant and influential documentary shorts produced in Latin America in the period under study. *

TIRE DIÉ: The "First Latin American Social Survey Film"

Fernando Birri's Tire Dié (Toss Me a Dime, 1958) begins with an aerial shot of the provincial city of Santa Fe, Argentina. The association of voice-of-God narration with perspective-of-God images only reveals the full extent of its parodistic intent as the narration progresses and conventional descriptive data (geographical location, founding dates, population, etc.) give way to the less conventional (statistics concerning the number of street lamps and hairdressers, of loaves of bread consumed monthly, cows slaughtered daily, and erasers purchased yearly for government offices). As the houses give way to shanties, the narrator declares, "Upon reaching the edge of the city proper (la ciudad organizada) statistics become uncertain.... This is where, between four and five in the afternoon ... during 1956, 1957 and 1958, the following social survey film was shot."[4]

The railroad bridge which the aerial camera surveys just prior to the credits is the site of the first post-credit

*Story of a Battle (40 minutes), Cyclone (25 minutes) and Now (5 minutes) are available from San Francisco Newsreel, 630 Natoma Street, San Francisco, CA 94103. Memories of the Cangaco (25 minutes) is distributed by New Yorker Films, 16 W. 61st Street, New York, NY 10023. For the First Time (12 minutes) and The Brickmakers (41 minutes) may be obtained from The Cinema Guild, 1697 Broadway, #802, New York, NY 10019. Finally, Hombres de mal Tiempo, Hablando del punto cubano, Tire Dié, Revolución, Viramundo, Carlos, Elecciones, Me gustan los estudiantes, and Vida y muerte en El Morillo are not currently in U.S. distribution.

sequence. From God's vantage point, the camera has descended to the eye-level of the children who congregate there every afternoon. In the first post-credit shot, a little boy in close-up stares directly at the camera, then turns and runs out of frame. Other children appear in close-up, looking and speaking at the camera in direct address. Their barely audible voices are overlaid with the studied dramatic diction of two adult narrators, male and female, who repeat what the children are saying, adding identifying tags like "... one of the boys told us," "... said another." This initial sequence ends as the camera follows one of the boys home and "introduces" his mother in direct visual and verbal address, followed by her voice-over (soon compounded by the overlay of the mediating narrators) and images of observation and illustration. This "chain" sequence, where one social actor (usually a child) provides visual linkage with another (usually an adult) continues throughout the film.

The primary expectation, deferred and eventually fulfilled by the film's intricate structuration, is the arrival of the long and anxiously awaited train to Buenos Aires. The interviews in which local residents discuss their economic plight are repeatedly intercut with shots back to the tracks and the growing number of children keeping their restless vigil there. The eventual climax of expectation (subjects' and viewers') has the bravest and fleetest of the children running alongside the passing train. As they balance precariously on the narrow, elevated bridge, their hands straining upward to catch any coin the passengers might toss in their direction, childrens' voices on the soundtrack chant hoarsely, "Tire dié! Tire dié!" ("Toss me a dime!").[5] (See photo, p. 350.)

The first product of the first Latin American documentary film school (the Escuela Documental de Santa Fe, founded by Birri in 1956 upon his return from Rome's Centro Sperimentale), Tire Dié was a collaborative effort whose evolution and ethos suggest a more observational than expository motivation. After selecting this particular theme and locale from preliminary photo-reportages, Birri divided his 59 students into various groups, each of which was to concentrate on a particular personage from the community under study:

> We went there every afternoon for two years, to get to know these people, to exchange ideas, to spend time with them; but we ended up sharing

Children run along the railroad trestle begging small change from passengers on a train, in Fernando Birri's Tire Dié.

> their lives. We never concealed the fact that we were making a film, but neither did we emphasize it. The film was clearly secondary to the human relationships which we established.[6]

Despite severe financial and technical limitations, the group sought the synchronous self-presentation of social actors. Interventions by the authoritarian narrator cease after the initial pre-credit sequence. The filmmakers deleted their own presence from the interviews with riverbed residents, neither appearing on screen nor retaining their questions on the soundtrack. Generally, though not always, the film introduces social actors in direct visual and verbal address, followed by a montage of images of illustration and observation which are unified by the social actors' voice-over commentary.

Given this apparent commitment to direct verbal address, the persistent intervention of the anonymous male and female mediator-narrators, speaking over the voice of the social actors, is unexpected and disconcerting. Investigation into the film's mode of production reveals that this expedient derives not from prior design but from deficiencies in the original sound recording. Faced with the inadequate technical quality of the recordings made during the filming, Birri and his students had to compromise their original conception:

> We approached two well-known actors ... and asked them to re-record the original soundtrack, not dubbing the film but rather serving as intermediaries between the protagonists and the public. This re-recording is what appears in the "foreground" of the soundtrack, but beneath it we retained the original track.... Even though at first glance this voiced-over "professional" soundtrack seems contradictory to our approach, it was an unavoidable necessity.

This overdubbing technique is quite common today in foreign-language documentaries when the filmmakers wish to retain the "flavor" of the actual social actor's speech, but here it plays quite an opposite role, signaling the locus of contradiction and branding this early and seminal attempt to democratize documentary discourse with the unwanted stamp of residual authoritarian anonymity.

STORY OF A BATTLE: Voice-of-God as Voice-of-the-People

Manuel Octavio Gómez structures Historia de una Batalla (Story of a Battle, 1962) around the parallel intercutting of two separate sequences of events, a device that other filmmakers will later adopt to somewhat different effect. In Gómez' case, although both "lines" are factual, only one is expository in the conventional sense; the other shades off into a more narrative mode. The expository line uses primarily archival images of illustration to chronicle the major events in and concerning Cuba in the year 1961. These include nationalizations of U. S.-owned firms, acts of terrorism and sabotage by those opposed to the new regime, the Bay of Pigs invasion, and Fidel's speech declaring the Marxist-Leninist orientation of the revolution. The second line chronicles the national literacy campaign, electing to do so by means of more observational, subjectivizing techniques.

The pre-credit sequence belongs to the latter category; shots of an expectant crowd are intercut with shots of a train overflowing with animated young people singing, clapping, craning to see their destination approach. As the train arrives, parents anxiously scan the disembarking crowds for a glimpse of their offspring. The film ends with a montage of home-site reunions whose intense emotional impact is due in large part to the observational style in which they were filmed.[7] This second sequence of events functions not as information but as evocation, transporting the film beyond the conventional confines of compilation documentary. Its multiple and anonymous protagonists constitute the locus of a generalized, symbolic diegesis which frames the year's public events and anchors them in subjective human experience.

These two foci--the literacy campaign, and the other events of national importance, whose presentation is subordinated to the former--are united by a single narrative voice: omniscient, anonymous, male. Yet Gómez' voice-of-God narrator deviates in significant ways from the authoritarian model. His diction is poetic and evocative rather than dryly "objective." He uses first and second person forms of address (the familiar, singular "you" [tú] and the first-person plural [nosotros] rather than the more detached third person), shifting between the personae of the literacy teachers, their peasant pupils, and the national collectivity. These variations, coupled with the simulation of synchronous sound (singing and chanting among the returning literacy workers, Fidel's speeches and the crowds' response to them), indicate an attempt to democratize an authoritarian mode of address by converting the voice-of-God into a surrogate for the demos. Such a strategy assumes an experience universally and monolithically shared within the nation.

REVOLUCION: Atavism or Vanguard Practice?

Jorge Sanjinés' Revolución (Revolution, 1963) suggests a reversion to the silent era: a controlled and intricate agit-prop montage of images of underdevelopment and of opposition to the dominant powers; a kind of Bolivian Potemkin in which the only commentary is musical. Sanjinés made the film without access to the kind of equipment which would allow for sound recording. In this case the technological rearguard coincided with the artistic vanguard. If Sanjinés' film referred backwards in time to Eisenstein, it also pointed forward to the most formally innovative of the Latin American documentarists, Santiago Alvarez.

CICLON and NOW: Banishing the Logos

The same year, Alvarez, a musical archivist who had been put in charge of the weekly Cuban newsreel, would make the first of a number of autonomous shorts destined to bring him international acclaim. Ciclón (Hurricane, 1963) surveys Hurricane Flora's damage to the island and Cubans' response to the devastation without either narration or the graphically innovative intertitles which would soon characterize his style. Aside from an animated map which illustrates how the hurricane swept over the island and repeatedly circled back to cut a new angle of destruction, the film contains no graphic display. It is as if the logos has been excised from the films as superfluous to the momentous eloquence of the images. To ensure that the absence of the word does not escape the viewer's notice, however, the film includes one brief shot of a newspaper headline (Storm Now Lashes Camaguey Province) superimposed over a shot of the storm's devastating force, as well as an occasional destination written above the windshield of a bus. The very rarity of these designations intensifies one's awareness of the absence of the written and spoken word.

The images are primarily observational. Except for Fidel and his brother Raúl, the social actors in the film are anonymous. None is identified in any way; their eye movements (except for Fidel's) do not acknowledge the camera; and though we occasionally watch them talk, we never hear what they say, either first- or second-hand. Words are superfluous here. Alvarez, though proceeding quite differently from Gómez in Story of a Battle, communicates a similar conviction: the essential universality of national experience.

If the films by Birri and Manuel Octavio Gómez shade from the expository into the narrative realm, Alvarez' work veers toward the experimental while still continuing to function as reportage. Now! (1965) is constructed from "found" footage around a kind of "found narration": Lena Horne singing the homonymous black liberation song to the music of the Hebrew folksong "Hava Nagila." No attempt is made to "translate" the lyrics of the song for Alvarez' Spanish-speaking audience. This visual collage of news photos and secondary footage of racial tension, violence and abuse in the United States functions on the more visceral plane of agit-prop, with the rhythms of the song reinforcing the rhythms of the editing and the dynamization of the still images through the movement of the camera. Lena Horne supplants the narratorial function, serving instead as a kind of enlisted evoker/invoker. Again, graphic language only appears incidentally, e.g., the world "Police" on the side of a squad car. (See photo, p. 355.) Only at the end does the (written) word replace the image as simulated bullet marks spell out the word "NOW!"

VIRAMUNDO and MEMORIAS DO CANGAÇO: Multiple Modes of Address

In 1963, due to political pressure from a newly installed military government, Fernando Birri, his wife Carmen and three associates--producer Edgardo Pallero and filmmakers Dolly Pussi and Manuel Horacio Giménez, all former students at the Escuela Documental--left Argentina semi-clandestinely, taking prints of their films with them. Seeing themselves as a kind of "scouting expedition,"[8] the group went to São Paulo where former students Vladimir Herzog and Maurice Capovilla arranged a retrospective of their work at the Museum of Modern Art and put them in contact with producer Thomaz Farkas and a group of aspiring documentarists.

A "found" image of graphic brutality in Santiago Alvarez' compilation documentary on racial violence in the U. S., Now.

Though the Cinema Novo movement had already begun with the decade, it was concentrated around Rio, with some early activity in Bahia and elsewhere. The presence of the Escuela Documental group catalyzed the first important documentary production in Sao Paulo, a series of four simultaneously and cooperatively produced films: Geraldo Sarno's Viramundo, Paulo Gil Soares' Memorias do Cangaço (Memories of the Cangaço), Manuel Horacio Giménez' Nossa Escola do Samba (Our Samba School), and Maurice Capovilla's Subterraneos do Futebol (Soccer Underground).

Though Birri moved on to Rio and, after the coup d'état of April 1964, to Mexico, later to Cuba and finally to Italy where he remained until 1979, the rest of the group stayed in São Paulo for several years. The dozens of documentaries financed by Thomaz Farkas, many made with Pallero as executive producer, attempt a systematic survey of Brazilian society and culture, particularly in the disadvantaged Northeast. As an integrated body of work, they are unique in Brazilian and in Latin American film history.

Both Viramundo and Memorias do Cangaço use synchronous sound recorded with synchronous equipment, though neither uses this approach exclusively, preferring instead a kind of composite address which charts the gamut of narratorial possibilities.[9] Viramundo explores the experience of peasants from the drought-stricken Northeast who migrate to São Paulo in search of work, juxtaposing their voiced expectations to the actual prospects awaiting them in the metropolis. Memorias do Cangaço's subject is more historical: the legendary bandits of the Northeast, the cangaceiros.

Both documentaries present themselves as a kind of investigation-in-progress. Each begins with a voice-of-God narrator who quickly cedes his privilege to more democratized modes of address. Viramundo uses the on-screen (integral) interview, where both interviewer and interviewee appear in the frame and both question and answer are heard on the synchronous soundtrack. It also gives us a kind of "pseudo monologue" where the visual and aural presence of the interlocutor has been deleted in favor of the "pure" response of the social actor, who either presents himself to the camera (sync) or comments over images of illustration. Finally, Sarno uses a kind of montage interview, intercutting fragments of responses by various interviewees as if to suggest a conversation between them. Viramundo is a prototype of "interventionist" documentary style characteristic of

Brazilian documentary in the sixties, in contrast to a more "detached" or "minimalist" approach common to the seventies.[10] One Brazilian critic claims that, from the inception of the interviews which make up the bulk of the film's narration, "Viramundo is organized like a dialogue."[11] His observation on the lyrics and music which composer Caetano Veloso wrote for the film are particularly suggestive:

> The music enters with evident sonority at the beginning, the end, and in the middle of the narrative to separate two blocks of interviews. This sung poetry ... functions as a text for the analysis of the situation, for despite its being written in the third person (as if it were another immigrant being interviewed) it provides a general vision of the problem of northeastern migration to São Paulo, presenting a global understanding that transcends many of the partial depositions. The music acts, qualifies, completes, dialogues and interferes in the spoken text.[12]

This strategy constitutes a fifth mode of address, a kind of anonymous meta-voice, surrogate both for the filmmaker and for the social actors and a bridge between the two.

Soares' Memorias do Cangaço proceeds in similar fashion, beginning with a voice-of-God which inquires, "Who were the cangaceiros?" and continues, "We pose the question to a professor of the Department of Legal Medicine." An on-camera authority proceeds to offer a technical discourse on the morphology of physical types, insisting that cangaceiros are exclusively ectomorphic types because "only thin men hold a grudge." Such preposterous testimony from an "expert witness" sets the viewer up for a more convincing answer to the question originally posed by the anonymous narrator. The subsequent on-screen interview with a cangaceiro, in medium long shot, is framed to include the interviewer holding a microphone, his back to the camera. The authoritarian narrator returns again to offer an account of the "real" causes behind this semi-organized banditry. His explanation is followed by another synchronous interview with a matador de cangaceiros (cangaceiro killer-for-hire, prototype of the protagonist of Glauber Rocha's Antonio das Mortes, 1968) whose voice then continues over images of illustration: archival footage of Lampião, the most famous of the cangaceiros, who died in 1938. The soundtrack retains the interviewer's questions, though he does not appear on camera during this sequence. The matador's voice-over "introduces" the next interviewee, a former cangaceiro who has gone straight. Period footage of Lampião's woman is accompanied on the soundtrack by spoken lyrics of folk songs about her, the anonymous narrator here functioning not as the voice-of-God but as the "voice of the people," a folk surrogate. The final shot in a montage of freeze frames resumes movement as Lampião's woman refuses to be interviewed, "Don't come to me with tape recorders! I was his woman." Her refusal adds another dimension to the pluralization of modes of documentary address: the right of the social actors to refuse the platform which the filmmakers offer them.

CARLOS and ELECCIONES: "Cinéma Vérité" in Uruguay

The work of the two foremost Uruguayan filmmakers was inspired in the changing international film scene--in new experimental forms and particularly the direct cinema and cinéma vérité techniques pioneered in France by Chris Marker and Jean Rouch, and in the United States by Richard Leacock and Don Pennebaker. Mario Handler returned from film study in Germany, Holland, and Czechoslovakia to assume the directorship of the Film Institute at the University of the Republic, ready to assemble the infrastructure which would finally make national film production feasible. He had to reconcile himself not only to a chronic lack of equipment and resources, but also to resignation, disinterest or outright opposition on the part of his superiors. The discovery of some unused film stock donated years before by UNESCO launched him on a film project which he conceived as a reaction against all his advanced technical training--simultaneously a protest against and a reckoning with the artisanal conditions under which he was condemned to work if he was to make films at all.

The resulting 30-minute film, Carlos: Cine-Retrato de un Caminante (Carlos: Cine-Portrait of a Walker [Vagabond], 1965) is the closest approximation to observational cinema to come out of the New Latin American Cinema movement in the period under study. Clearly, neither the filming nor the subsequent taping which would be edited to form the soundtrack were incidental to Carlos' life, but both were done in such a way as to minimize the intervention of the technical apparatus and the fact of being the object of an inquiry which would eventually be converted into a cultural artifact. Handler maintains that instrumentality was subordinated to human interaction, to the process of inquiry into the life of the other which constitutes a simultaneous inquiry into the self and the large society. He recalls,

> Carlos and I spent a great deal of time together, just getting to know each other. We would drink beer and talk, or we would walk for hours on end without saying a word. Gradually I got him accustomed to the camera. The shooting was slow, exhausting work.
>
> I didn't tape the audio part until after the shooting was complete. In a session which lasted three hours, I asked him questions about life, education, society, himself--sometimes cajoling him and other times treating him quite forcefully.[13]
>
> Because there was no moviola in Uruguay at the time, I did the editing with a viewfinder and a projector, making all the cuts on the original negative because I had no money to pay for a workprint. The approach I used in this film meant that the research and the creative process were one and the same. It was a painstaking method, a brutal apprenticeship. I would never lavish so much time on a film again.[14]

The vagabond's voice-over commentary, accompanied at times by instrumental music, is the only aural accompaniment to the images of observation and occasionally illustration which reproduce his environment and activities. No other narrative voice intervenes. The filmmaker does not acknowledge his own presence either visually or aurally.

Throughout the film, there is an impulse toward poeticization of the material followed by the refusal of that impulse. Certain visual themes emerge: the dichotomy of indoor-outdoor, particularly marked for a homeless wanderer who generally sleeps in the open air; the "voyeurs" who gaze outward from the security of a private interior space; the repeated compositional device of close-ups of Carlos with another figure remote upon the horizon line, an individual isolated but never totally removed from a larger social context; the motif of the <u>cosas tiradas</u> (discarded objects) intercut toward the end like ironic still lifes suggesting Carlos' comparable status as a persona tirada. These clusterings testify to the interventionist stance of the film-maker, for whom exposition merges with narrative and observation inevitably entails interpretation.

Despite the relative "purity" of its observational form, Carlos shades back into direct address for another reason as well: the particular style of speech which the protagonist spontaneously employs. He constantly interjects confirmational queries--"Isn't that so?", "Don't you agree?", "Do you understand?"--and almost as frequently confronts his interlocutor with an even more direct question, e.g., "What would you have done if your woman deceived you?" As a social actor in a documentary film, Carlos is the most consistently self-representational personage in all the Latin American documentaries surveyed here. The film thus stands as the foremost example of one means of democratizing the documentary modes of address, by giving voice to one individual whom society had condemned to be voiceless, by giving visibility to someone society prefers to keep invisible.

Later that same year, Handler collaborated with Ugo Ulive on a film called Elecciones (Elections, 1965), which combines an essentially observational approach with a very fluid, modernist shooting style that hones in on the telling detail of gesture or expression by means of "choker" close-ups, rack focus, extreme angles, and the fragmentation of the image. The editing style is equally aggressive. Through its treatment of two candidates for minor political office, Elecciones satirically calls into question the then much-vaunted tradición democrática uruguaya.

No authoritarian narrator intervenes to impose an analysis on the assembled visual evidence. Instead, social actors stand condemned by their own self-serving bombast, in "post-synched" or contrapuntal sequences. In one of the latter, the female candidate, flanked by photographers and admirers, is shown distributing gifts in a hospital maternity ward while she expounds in voice-over upon the anonymity and spontaneity of her gesture. Though the candidates never acknowledge the camera, some members of the crowds do look directly at it, raising the issue of viewer complicity by this form of direct--if "incidental"--visual address.

ME GUSTAN LOS ESTUDIANTES: Selective Denial

Me Gustan los Estudiantes (I Like Students, 1968), also by Handler, represents a reversion to even more primitive, artisanal conditions than his first film. Its agitational, experimental style is more evocative than expository. Like Historia de una Batalla, the film is structured by intercutting two independent sequential lines. Unlike the Cuban film, there is no voice-over narration, and none of the people photographed--Latin American heads of state conferring at Punta del Este, and Uruguayan students battling police as they take to the streets to protest Lyndon Johnson's attendance at that meeting--are granted the opportunity to speak either on or off screen. The conference sequences, somewhat hazy from intentional over-exposure, are denied any sound whatever, while the student sequences, in normal exposure, carry the voiced-over musical accompaniment of popular Uruguayan singer Daniel Viglietti singing a march which he composed for the film and a Violetta Parra song which gave title to a film Handler had intended to call "Violence in Montevideo." The impact of this 10-minute film, like that of Santiago Alvarez' Now, comes from the careful synchronization of musical and imagistic rhythms and is intensified in this case by the additional strategy of alternating denial and conferral of musical accompaniment.[15] Like Alvarez' Now, Me Gustan los Estudiantes illustrates a strategy which might be called "diffusion" of the mode of narrative address, relinquished in this case to a popular performing artist.

POR PRIMERA VEZ: The Interview and the Last Word

Octavio Cortázar, whose national reputation as a documentarist was for years secondary only to that of Santiago Alvarez, was the first Cuban filmmaker to construct his films around synchronous interview footage. Por Primera Vez (For the First Time, 1967) begins with the posing of a question through graphic rather than aural means. Word by word, in telegraphic style, the following question appears on the screen: "Qué labor realiza un cine móvil?" (What does a mobile cinema do?).

Two uniformed men appear on camera in the first shot of the film, lounging on the fender of a truck while another man, in shadow, makes some adjustments under the hood. (The casualness suggested by the posture of the social actors and the general composition of the shot is belied by the precise way in which the letters ICAIC [acronym for the Cuban Film Institute] are framed between the bodies of the two men facing the camera.) In sync, one begins to explain that the mobile cinema units bring films and projection facilities to remote areas. His voice continues to describe the electrical equipment and interior furnishings of the truck over images of illustration in which another technician handles the equipment referred to. A cut back to the original shot has the second technician talking in sync about the work schedule. Over a close-up of the first technician, with a microphone visible in the extreme left of the frame, an off-screen voice (Cortázar's own) inquires, "Do you know some place around here where people still have not seen movies?" The technician faces leftward at a 3/4 angle as he answers in the affirmative, ending the pre-credit sequence.

The initial use of a graphic rather than an aural question allows Cortázar to circumvent the need for an anonymous voice-of-God narrator whose relationship to the film and its characters is never defined. When his own voice intervenes, it is that of a participant-investigator. This pair of sequential pre-credit questions lead to a third which determines the structure of the body of the film: "What is a movie like?" This interrogatory series leads the viewer from the realm of factual information to the experiential, phenomenological realm of first discovery. Viewer identification shifts from the outsider (first question and response) to the participant-agent (second question and response) to the participant-subject (third question and multiple responses--of which, on a "meta" level, the film itself is one).

Por Primera Vez unfolds through the telling of a simple story in which the resolution of the enigma equals the (happy) end of innocence-cum-ignorance. With the exception of a few cutaways, generally to other members of the speaker's family, the responses to Cortázar's questions about expectations involve the coincidence of voice and image of the social actors. His own questions are often, though not always, heard from off-screen, and respondents generally face the direction from which the question comes instead of directly facing the camera.

With the preparations for the open-air evening screening, the film moves from the realm of conjectural concepts ("A movie must be like a party, ... a dance, ... a large town, ... something with lots of pretty girls, weddings, cavalry and war, and everything ... ") to the realm of subjective experience as reflected in body postures and facial expressions. In these montages of spectator response to the mechanical feeder sequence from Charlie Chaplin's Modern Times, Cortázar constructs a microcosm of life stages--childhood, adolescent romance, nursing motherhood, old age--while capturing all the rapt and radiant expressiveness of a highly animated people.

Por Primera Vez sounds a deep chord because it so compellingly recreates the subjective discovery of the magic of the movies. Watching it, each viewer recapitulates her/his own initiation into that realm of the marvelous by looking into the "mirror" from which Cortázar's captivated and captivating faces shine. Great reward for a simple quest. The gratification Cortázar provides is all the more genuine because he does not end his film at the emotional summit of discovery, but instead continues to monitor the audience's mounting fatigue and waning attention. As with a classic bedtime story, not only is the ending happily predictable and predictably happy, but the inducement to surrender to satisfied sleep is inscribed within the tale itself. (One need only follow, for example, a character like Dervis who inserts her fingers in her mouth and curls up on her girlfriend's lap.)

Cortázar here democratizes the documentary voice through his concentration on the most marginalized within the marginalized. (His interviews are with women and children; the only man interviewed appears only to rectify his young daughter's confusion.) Cortázar also democratizes the documentary gaze, not only through presenting the range of people he interviews in direct visual address, but also, and much more intricately, in the film viewing sequence where the shot-reverse shots set up a complex "mirroring" dynamic. The ultimate democratization lies of course on the film's meta-cinematic level: the people of Los Mulos are now incorporated into and represented by a medium which they had never known.

In symmetrical relationship to the film's opening, its final statement is (tele)graphically rendered on the screen: "Thus/on April 12, 1967/in Los Mulos/in the mountains of Baracoa/more than one hundred people/saw a movie/for the first time." The screen behind the initial motivating question was blank. The final "answer" is superimposed on a long shot of the darkened village, identifiable only by the concentration of a few lights. A coda gives one of the social actors the last word as a fragment of her interview is heard again in voice-over: "A movie is ... something very beautiful and of importance."

HOMBRES DE MAL TIEMPO: Handicapping the Voice-of-God

Hombres de Mal Tiempo (Men of Mal Tiempo, 1968), filmed in Cuba by resident Argentine filmmaker Alejandro Saderman, is a meditation on the representation of history. Five veterans of the Battle of Mal Tiempo, fought during Cuba's war for independence from Spain, are assembled to share their memories and instruct film actors and technicians in recreating that experience on film.

The pre-credit sequence begins as if in medias res, cutting repeatedly between shots on on-site preparation and the assembling, transport, and reception of the five centenarians. These shots are fragmentary, snatches of a larger picture fleetingly captured by a camera as restive as it is inquisitive. Period engravings of battle scenes, animated by puffs of smoke, provide a background for the credits. The "film proper" begins with a montage of still photos, a kind of reprise in a different key, since these "snapshots" recount the same process of preparation, transit, and assembly from different angles that the original moving footage, and with a very different "feel." An anonymous narrator offers a disquisition on time, heroism and history which culminates in a bald declaration of (poetic) intent:

> The life of the hero, according to what we are told, is simple: it moves in a straight line, like an arrow, toward its end. But heroes themselves seldom have the right to recount it, and when they do, that line begins to weave, to tremble, to disperse on a hazy horizon because it is contaminated by dreams, by truth, by lived experience.
>
> We are going to play with time. They will retell in the present what for history is part of the past, because memory is beyond time, beyond history: memory is a reason for being.
>
> This is not a historical documentary; it is a fiesta of memory.

The association of anonymous voice-over narration with still photographs and freeze-frames--arrested motion, congealed time--is not incidental; it is marked by its systematic persistence. Five times the film cuts to still photographs of the assembled group, tracking in and then holding on a particular veteran as the narrator provides his name and background. Each time, the voice of the social actor, supplanting the narrator's, sets the film in motion again. Through the repeated association of the authoritarian narrative voice with stasis, and the complementary association of the voices of the social actors with the resumption of movement, Hombres de Mal Tiempo alludes to some of the ideological and artistic limitations of the former mode of address while continuing to utilize it.

If Por Primera Vez was structured like a bedtime story, Hombres de Mal Tiempo has a symphonic structuration which is, predictably, much more complex. The piece begins slowly, sedately with the introduction and assemblage of the various character-performers. It rises in intensity as, after recounting individual recollections, the centenarians begin to reenact their memories, and then to interact with one another and with the professional actors who are eager to assimilate and replicate their retrieved experience. The use of the machete as a weapon, ritual dances, a military ambush, a mock execution are demonstrated by the original historical actors and then reenacted by the professionals. The culminating movement consists of the fully orchestrated reconstruction of the battle, complemented by solarized, intermittent-motion sequences which represent the distance between reenactment and subjective memory of the original event. Descending from this crescendo of movement and participation, the original combatants turn from the field in a series of still dissolves until their images fade away.

In the case of Hombres de Mal Tiempo, the authoritarian narrative voice has been transformed into a self-limiting, self-referential authorial voice, one which, in attempting to conserve voices from the past, defers to them without abdicating its responsibility to insert them into a meaningful context. In addition, the film proposes the inadequacy of a purely aural representation of the voice of historical experience or memory, just as it declines a purely "realistic" mode of visual representation of that experience. Saderman's film is one of the most suggestive and artistically satisfying results of the practice of generic self-reflexivity which characterized Cuban filmmaking from the

The conjunction of documentary and fictional techniques in Alejandro Saderman's Hombres de Mal Tiempo: runaway slave and independence fighter Esteban Montejo recounts his experience to actors from ICAIC who proceed to reenact them.

late sixties through the mid-seventies, a compelling example of what theorist and filmmaker Julio García Espinosa believes is the impossibility of questioning a given reality "without questioning the particular genre you select or inherit to depict that reality."[16] Saderman's "fiesta of memory" may not prove the "impossibility" of unreflexive uses of genre, but it certainly exemplifies the virtues and artistic rewards of a more self-conscious approach. (See photo, above.)

CHIRCALES: Hierarchical Modes of Address

Like several films already discussed, Chircales (The Brickmakers, 1968/1972), by the Colombian team Jorge Silva and Marta Rodriguez, also aspires to an observational mode. For over a year, before bringing in even a light meter, Silva and Rodríquez virtually lived in the brickyards on the outskirts of Bogotá, returning to the city only to sleep. Hundreds of hours of taped interviews constituted the first practical phase of their work; still photography the second. By the time a movie camera was eventually introduced, the filmmakers claim that community familiarity and trust was such that no one was inordinately disconcerted by its presence.[17] From the first sociology assignment which led Rodríguez to that community, to the final mixing, Chircales was six years in the making. This delay, caused by lack of funds and equipment, turned out to be boon as well as bane. The intricate structuration of the final film--the product of extended deliberation between filmmakers, social actors, and the community at large--might not have been generated under a tighter production schedule.

In its mode of aural address, Chircales offers a hierarchy of predominantly non-synchronous voices. (There is only the most "incidental" simulation of synchronous sound: the paterfamilias goads the mule with shouts of "E-va! Arre!" in a sequence shot from a distance and angle which make it difficult to discern any movement of his lips; a voice-over dialogue of initially mysterious provenance is "explained" when the camera pans briefly to a transistor radio; "source noise" of shovels or falling water occasionally punctuates otherwise silent sequences.) A collage of anonymous voice-overs accompanies the pre-credit sequence, and continues briefly after the credits. Bombastic political speeches are contrasted to a more personal monologue which can only retroactively be identified with one of the film's protagonists. Several members of the brickmaking family are visually introduced while engaged in the preliminary stages of their labor process in a sequence whose silence rings loud. (See photo, p. 368.)

Only then, six minutes and 45 seconds into this 41-minute film, does a voice-of-God narration begin: "Colombia. The family of Alfredo and María Castañeda and their twelve children live this reality which is concealed, denied...." The deferral of this omniscient voice helps make the audience conscious of its intervention. Throughout approximately half of the film, the images "speak" for themselves, often in silence, occasionally with source noise and/or musical accompaniment. The voices of the social actors--Alfredo, Maria, their eldest daughter and son--heard over images of observation and illustration, generously supplement but never altogether displace the voice of the anonymous narrator who frames their personal experience within

For the Castañeda children in Jorge Silva and Marta Rodriguez's Chircales, the number of bricks they carry is an index of their age.

a larger analytical context. Within the body of the film, this authoritarian narrator has the first word and the last, relegating the voices of the family members to a secondary rung of importance.

Other voices from the socio-cultural context also "address" the viewer, often less directly: priests, politicians, radio announcers hawking products, soap opera characters. The importance of these "tertiary" voices derives from the influence they have had in shaping the voices (consciousness, world-view) of the protagonists. A fourth category consists of analogous voices visually linked to their sources very loosely if at all. These only intervene toward the end of the film, around a funeral sequence which is more metaphoric than "real"; they are the voices of a bereaved widow, her children, and her female neighbors who, having endured what she now faces for the first time, comment upon her suffering, its causes, their shared predicament. Finally, María's discourse often includes direct quotes from authority figures who have an (adverse) impact on the family's life: a doctor who condemns her for "bringing more beggars into the world" without offering any alternative; el compadre Germán, intermediary between the owner of the brickyards and the tenant brickmakers, who eventually evicts them. Ironically, these hostile voices have to be "heard" through María's soft, rancorless tones.

If some more incidental "characters" in the film have voices without any physical presence, several of its visually predominant protagonists are conceded no voice at all. Each of the characters thus confined to modes of visual address is female; each is associated with a more metaphoric or symbolic mode of representation which seems to be enhanced by their silence. Leonor, the Castañedas' second daughter, dressed in her white communion gown and veil, wanders from her present into her "future" in an atypical sequence which elides communion, marriage, and widowhood. An unidentified mother and daughter who work and live in the same brickyard constitute another axis of cumulative poignancy and pathos. The mother is grave, taciturn, gnarled from her unceasing labor. Her three- or four-year-old daughter is delicate and hauntingly lovely. It is she who, in contrast to her mother and to all the other characters, engages in direct visual address. Throughout the film, cutaways to her in various postures and dress coalesce into a kind of compelling refrain which directly challenges the passive voyeurism of the viewer and transports the film from the sociological register to the symbolic.

VIDA Y MUERTE EN EL MORILLO: Historical Reenactment and Self-Reflexivity

In Vida y Muerte en El Morillo (Life and Death in El Morillo, 1971), Cuban filmmaker Oscar Valdés reconstructs an incident of intrigue and heroism from the days of underground opposition to Batista. In the absence of archival footage, the director opts for on-site dramatic reenactment with professional actors in period costume, using third-person narration to comment upon the re-presentation of the incident. What is notable about this use of anonymous narration is that it is doubly synchronous: not only do the voice and image of authority coincide, but this on-screen narrator offers his account from the foreground of the frame, while behind him, on a second plane, we view the simultaneous reenactment of the events he describes. In his modes of representation, Valdés has thus found an objective correlative for the fact of mediation. Like the play within a play, this device carries the potential for "infinite" regressions of aural and visual overlap (e.g., the filmmaker's appearance in the foreground, pushing the narrator into the middleground and the professional actors into a third plane of remoteness from the viewer) but the single meta-level is sufficient to acknowledge the relativity of questions of objectivity, facticity, and representation. (See photo, p. 371.)

HABLANDO DEL PUNTO CUBANO: Towards the Unification of Substance and Form

Hablando del Punto Cubano (Talking About the Punto Cubano, 1972), a tribute to a particular tradition of rural music, begins in characteristic Cortázar style with an informal group interview. (In contrast to the modes of verbal address used by Gómez and Alvarez earlier in the decade, predicated upon the experiential and ideological unity of their Cuban spectatorship, Cortázar's approach is built upon an acknowledgment of difference and potential disagreement.) Ignoring the filmmakers whose off-camera questions have sparked their debate, workers at a Havana bus factory argue heatedly about the nature and appeal of the punto cubano style. The spectrum of their opinions--from enthusiasm through ignorance to outspoken disinterest and skepticism--anticipates the spectrum of audience attitudes to the film's subject, thus providing a bridge between viewers and participant-actors. The preparatory testimony of these casual witnesses is supplemented by expert testimony (a

Superimposed planes of presentation and re-presentation in Oscar Valdés' Vida y Muerte en El Morillo: the narrator narrates in the foreground what the actors re-enact in the background.

female musicologist) and the comments of various performers. More than inform, however, the musicians demonstrate, illustrating varieties of the punto cubano through their performances.

These threads are tied together by the multidimensional performance of another punto cubano singer, the most famous practitioner of the style, recruited to serve simultaneously as performer, narrator, social actor, and emblem of creole culture. Joseíto Fernández punctuates the film like a lyric refrain, singing his commentary in the improvisational, self-referential style typical of the punto cubano, to the tune of "Guantanamera." The exposition he provides is thus simultaneously exemplification.

His appearances occur in different settings, but the mise-en-scène is always highly "creolized." This tall, lanky, heavily-mustached mulatto--decked out in immaculate white cottons, topped by white straw hat, and puffing a

Hablando del Punto Cubano: Joseíto Fernández as a visual and aural icon of a Cuban musical tradition and recruited in the film also as narrator, social actor, and performer.

large cigar--leans against arched latticework amid lush tropical vegetation, or lounges on a lacy wrought-iron bench in front of a stuccoed wall, grilled windows, and an arching palm tree. (See photo, above.)

His final appearance, which closes the film, involves the reversal of the stylistic conventions used in his prior presentation, in which the camera would track in progressively closer from increasingly close-range establishing shots. The final sequence begins with him walking away from the camera, increasing rather than diminishing the distance between camera and subject. Joseíto's visual address here ceases to be direct. The stationary subject has resumed his mobility; the (social) actor who posed and composed himself for the camera now appears indifferent to it. Previously photographed in relatively enclosed spaces (patios, archways, a textile factory), Fernández now strolls down a city street filled with cars and pedestrians. Five jump cuts accelerate his passage. His concluding comments are not sung in sync (impossible from such long range) but in voice-over. With the final syllable of the final word of the final refrain of "Guantanamera," the frame freezes, allowing the viewer to scan the descending street for a last glimpse of the performer who has immersed himself "in the sea of the people" from which he originally emerged.

The formal self-consciousness of this remarkable film extends to yet another level. I have alluded to literary and musical structuration with reference to a number of the preceding documentaries; here the structure of the film is poetic in a very literal sense. Hablando del Punto Cubano replicates the structure of the Spanish décima which provides the basis for the variants elaborated in the punto cubano tradition. A classical décima (ten-line poem of eight syllables per line) might have the following rhyme scheme: abba/ac/cddc. The pie forzado is one of the variants demonstrated most self-reflexively in the film--in a synchronous, on-camera improvisation by one of the performers-cum-informants in response to a question from the filmmakers:

Nuestra décima cubana	(a)
con sus notas harmoniosas	(b)
ya difunde muchas cosas	(b)
de nuestra patria cubana.	(a)
Y es algo que nos engalana	(a)
en la típica faceta	(c)
que en la obra y en la meta	(c)
llevados de la misma afán	(d)
hay muchos niños que están	(d)
aprendiendo a ser poeta. *	(c)

Cortázar structures his film like a décima, "rhyming" sequences of similar length in varying patterns and rhythms, playing with different combinations of six different types:

(a) interviewee/casual witness (social actor as audience surrogate)
(b) (meta-) participant-narrator (Joseíto Fernández)
(c) expert witness

*"Our Cuban décima/with its harmonious notes/conveys many facets/of our Cuban homeland. /And it adorns us with riches/in the graceful cut of each gem/that in the quality of their workmanship and their purpose/motivated by the same desire/there are many children/who are learning to be poets."

(d) performers performing
(e) performers as informants
(f) images of (supplementary) illustration: montages of still photos.

Following the same scanning procedure as above, the "rhyme structure" of the film begins abcdedabdd. The pattern becomes less sharply defined in the remainder: dbcfcfdeefeceddfabb, but does return, as the classical décima and its variants often do, to a final repetition of the first syllabic rhyme-sounds. In its use of content to explain form, and of form to illustrate content, Hablando del Punto Cubano achieves a perfect unity of substance and form.

Conclusion: The Social Documentary and the Quest for "National Reality"

"The revolutionary function of the social documentary in Latin America," according to Fernando Birri's 1963 assessment, is to present "an image of the people" which rectifies "the false image presented by traditional cinema." This documentary image "offers reality just as it is; it cannot do otherwise.... Irrefutably, it shows things as they are--not as we might like them to be or as others ... would have us believe they are."[18] Birri thus posits a double function for the documentary: to negate false representations of reality, and to present reality as it really is. His willingness to compromise the mode of address in Tire Dié through the overlaying of voices of lived experience with voices of dramatic artifice testifies to a naive faith in the direct and incorruptible communicability of a pure and passive truth which merely awaits capture by the right agency. There is a double essentialism at work here: an assumption that the essence of the nation can be apprehended with camera and tape recorder, and a related belief that what is seen (and heard) is the essence of what is, and of what is knowable about what is.

Inspired by Birri's example and by the Italian neorealist cinema which inspired him, or simply motivated by a similar political philosophy, Latin American social documentarists began as self-appointed ethnographers in search of the "true face" of their people, of the true custodians of national culture, of the true exemplars of national identity. Because they are intimately tied to the conscious and systematic search for Brazilian-ness, Argentine-ness, Latin

American social documentarists began as self-appointed ethnographers in search of the "true face" of their people, of the true custodians of national culture, of the true exemplars of national identity. Because they are intimately tied to the conscious and systematic search for Brazilian-ness, Argentineness, Latin American-ness, the themes, forms, and trajectory of the Latin American social documentary movement cannot be understood independent of the history of the concept of nationality in Latin American societies.

National boundaries in Latin America are recent and arbitrary, the result of prolonged and traumatic wars for independence from European powers which, once won, often required equally brutal and prolonged civil wars to quell lingering internal opposition and help legitimate the new regimes. The more tenuous the basis of national cohesion, the more urgent an ideological cement to hold together the fragments of the new nation-state. Throughout the nineteenth century, the formulation of the national project was the province of the creole oligarchs. This new leadership class, which had expelled the colonialists only to embrace the neocolonialists, zealously preserved a self-serving split between rhetorical representations and actual practices. Their ideologues molded their concept of national identity in the European image, viewing all non-European components of national life as obstacles to civilization and progress.

Such a monolithic class perspective could not survive the growing self-assertion of the working and peasant classes, or the crisis of economic and political systems inaugurated with the 1930s. The rise of Marxist-inflected ideologies in Latin America prescribed a dual quest: for a less stratified socio-economic system, and for authentic, autonomous, culturally specific forms of expression. The prevailing disparagement of non-westernized elements as extraneous, impure and generally detrimental produced, in reaction, a counter-tendency to hypostatize these same components as no longer the source of but rather the solution to all the problems facing the nation.

The politically committed Latin American filmmakers who came of age in the 1950s participated in an essentially Manichaean view of society: the world at large, and specific countries within it, were clearly divided into haves and have-nots. Purity and authenticity resided only in the latter. Those strata and institutions which exhibited Western traits were inherently corrupted by them. Cultural colonization was just as pervasive as political and economic varieties, but much more insidious. The decolonization of national culture, the discovery of authentic rather than falsified national reality, required a rejection of the privileged and a concomitant privileging of the marginalized.

In their search for subjects, these militant filmmakers opted for misery over opulence, rural over urban, primitive over modern, artisanal over industrial, indigenous and/or African-derived over European, pre-literate over literate and folk over elite. The key to la realidad nacional was thought to reside in a simple operation of inversion: turning the official version of nationhood and national culture on its head in order to reveal what had previously been unseen, unheard, unseemly. Before Brazilian Paulo Freire developed his "pedagogy of the oppressed" to combat the "culture of silence," social documentarists from throughout Latin America were using the film medium to expose and combat the culture of invisibility and inaudibility. Style became another arena for the expression of the filmmakers' anti-colonialist stance. An imperfect, artisanal, technically limited cinema defiantly turned scarcity itself into a signifier.

The Manichaeanism apparent in Birri's early formulation of the social documentary project--the emphasis on presentation over representation, as if the former could exist any more independently of the latter in oppositional than in traditional filmmaking--was shared by a number of Latin American filmmakers, as was the belief that a camera and a tape recorder were sufficient tools for the apprehension of "national reality." Gradually, social documentarists--and fictional filmmakers as well--began to question these assumptions, demonstrating an increased awareness of the complexity of "national reality" and of the relationship between textual and civic politics which led them to a more self-conscious acknowledgment of their own processes of meaning production. What was originally the equivalent of an ethnographic project--with all the problems and limitations historically inherent in that kind of undertaking--was thus transformed into a kind of auto-ethnography.

The ethnographic filmmaker is imperialism's heir, perpetuating a legacy of cultural chauvinism. The ethnographer's culture constitutes the unquestioned norm against which the culture under study is to be measured and assessed. The authority of the ethnographic filmmaker is established by the mere fact of his/her presence within the domain of the Other; possession of the tools of recording is merely a further demonstration of an empowerment which was, to begin with, beyond question. Observer and observed exist in different worlds. The attempt to capture the world of the "primitive" Other and turn it into a product for consumption by the culturally "normative" assumes a transparency and a privileged access which are, ultimately, nonexistent. Unless the attempt at cross-cultural representation is reciprocal--unless there is an explicit acknowledgment of the investment of the self in the other and the other in the self, and of the degree to which the act of observation transforms both observer and observed--the result is condemned to being incomplete, distorted, profoundly and self-defeatingly tendentious.[19]

Latin American filmmakers may have subscribed to an over-simplified notion of reality, but never to a static one. Their mission to capture la realidad national was part of a larger mission: the transformation of that reality. They were simultaneously creators and transformers, artists and activists, observers and participants, aware of themselves as social actors on the same national-historical stage as their subjects. Their project necessarily exceeded the renovation of film content and film form. Beginning with Birri, they not only undertook to transform the existing structures and relations of film production, but also the ways films were used in society.[20] The most significant, though the least critically accessible, achievement of the New Latin American Cinema is this unremitting transformation of the modes of filmic production, diffusion and reception.[21]

To trace the history of social documentary production over the fifteen years surveyed in this essay is to trace the problematization of a series of concepts which have undergone a metamorphosis from obviousness to complexity: realism, objectivity, history, culture, national reality, documentary itself as a form and as a practice. During this period, the re-vision of social stratification (Tire Dié, Viramundo, Brickmakers), racial and ethnic difference, (Revolución, Now), national institutions (Elecciones, Me Gustan los Estudiantes), past and present history (Historia de una Batalla, Hombres de Mal Tiempo, Muerte y Vida en El Morillo), the endangered heterogeneity of folk cultural forms (Hablando del Punto Cubano) has invoked a convergence within an essentially expository genre of ethnographic, experimental and narrative approaches and an increasing tendency towards a politicized self-reflexivity. The attempt to democratize documentary modes of address stands as a prime example of the repositioning of the spectator, the social actor, and the filmmaker, while at the same time testifying to the exuberant proliferation of forms, styles, and approaches which characterized the entire New Latin American Cinema during those years. Without an account of the way these films were reinserted into the reality they aspired to depict and transform, this survey remains fragmentary.

Yet this does not diminish the eloquence of the fragments, singly and as a composite constellation. Such films are the product of a rare conjunction of energies and commitments in which the search for underrepresented aspects and underrealized potentials of national-cultural identity coincides with the search for underrepresented aspects and underrealized potentials of the self; in which the production and circulation of images cease to perpetuate expropriation and exploitation in order to function instead as reciprocal revelation and emancipation, as a joint investment in more enhancing forms of social organization and cultural expression.

Notes

1 Fernando Birri's Tire Dié (Toss Me a Dime), begun in 1956 and completed in 1958 (second version, 1960) is generally considered to mark the inception of social documentary filmmaking in Latin America. Birri is credited with catalyzing a movement which achieved a certain coherence--often more circumstantial than formal or organizational--despite formidable geographical, political and economic obstacles which impeded communication and contact between filmmakers. Other important films from the early period which will not be discussed in this article because I have not been able to see them are: Margot Benacerraf's Araya (Venezuela, 1958), Alberto Miller's Cantegriles (Uruguay, 1958), Linduarte Noronha's Aruanda (Brazil, 1959), Ugo Ulive's Como el Uruguay no hay (There's No Place Like Uruguay, 1960) and Sergio Bravo's La marcha al carbón (Coal March, Chile, 1960).

2 In his influential essay, "For an Imperfect Cinema," Julio García Espinosa distinguishes between "analysis" and "process." The former, he argues, is the result of prior operations which are not visible on the screen; the latter--more a joint exploration than a foregone conclusion--performs its operations in

conjunction with the spectator. (See my translation of this essay in Jump Cut: A Review of Contemporary Cinema, Number 20 [May, 1979], p. 26.)

3 Bill Nichols, "The Documentary Film and Principles of Exposition," Ideology and the Image (Bloomington: University of Indiana) 1981, pp. 170-207; Annette Kuhn, "The Camera I: Observations on Documentary," Screen, Vol. 19 (1978-79), pp. 71-83; Jeffrey Youdelman, "Narration, Invention, & History: A Documentary Dilemma," Cineaste Vol. XII, Number 2 (1982), pp. 8-15; and Michael Chanan, "Considerations on Cuban Documentary," excerpted from The Cuban Image: Cinema, Cultural Politics and the Process of the Cuban Revolution, work-in-progress, courtesy of the author.

4 See Fernando Birri, La Escuela Documental de Santa Fe (Santa Fe, Argentina: Universidad Nacional del Litoral, Cuadernos de Cine, 1964) for a full account of the film and the process of its production, including portions of the scripts

5 Part I of Fernando Solanas' and Octavio Getino's three-part documentary The Hour of the Furnaces "quotes" one of these sequences from Tire Dié.

6 This and other direct quotes from my interview with the filmmaker, published in Italian as "Fernando Birri: Pioniere e Pellegrino," in Lino Micciché, ed., Fernando Birri e la Escuela Documental de Santa Fe (Pesaro, Italy: XVII Mostra Internazionale del Nuovo Cinema), June 1981, pp. 2-13.

7 An interview with Manuel Octavio Gómez gives some background on the genesis of the approach he used in the film. Disappointed by the dearth of archival footage on the Literacy Campaign, which he considered the most significant event of the year 1961, Gómez decided to take advantage of the imminent return of the literacy brigades from their months in the countryside:

> I decided that this homecoming would provide the overriding structure of the film, the framing for the archival footage.
>
> The day arrived and I went with my crew to the train station to begin shooting. Thousands of

parents and children were being reunited.... It was incredibly moving. There was such a wealth of material that we couldn't possibly record it all, and many good scenes were being lost. I decided that it was necessary to lend a guiding hand to all this spontaneity.

I began following those arriving volunteers whose families were unable to meet them at the station. We would offer them a ride home.... Since I knew that to drive up to their house in an official Film Institute car would certainly break the mood, I'd stop about a block away and ask them if they didn't mind walking the remaining distance. They were much too excited to wonder at this strange request. We then followed them on foot, which is how we were able to capture those tearful and joyous homecomings....

Making Story of a Battle taught me that preparation can enchance spontaneity instead of negating it. Above all, it gave me a perspective on the expressive potential of the documentary mode. I learned how a filmmaker could confront an actual situation and--without either violating it or totally subordinating himself to it--interact with existing circumstances to the best advantage of his own creative purpose.

From Julianne Burton, "Popular Culture and Perpetual Quest: An Interview with Manuel Octavio Gómez," Jump Cut: A Review of Contemporary Cinema, Number 20, (May 1979), p. 19.

8 From the Birri interview, op. cit.

9 O homen de couro (Man of Leather, 1969, unavailable in the U.S.)--a slightly later example of the Farkas group's work in the Brazilian Northeast--offers an even more systematic catalogue of modes of address. The opening minutes constitute a survey of possible voices and attitudes. The voice-over narrator exercises a dual function here: as voice-of-God and as surrogate for the mythic voice of the social actors. When he recites folk songs and tales, it is without "marking" the different source and nature of his words through changes in tone or rhythm or intonation.

Though not distinct enough to merit separate treatment, this film is also notable for its use of synchronous self-presentation of its social actors, particularly the "unreliable" self-representation of the cowboy's wife. Her obvious discomfort at finding herself in front of a camera, coupled with the rote, almost sing-song quality of her recitation, suggest to the viewer that her actual attitudes are quite the opposite of those she espouses before the camera.

10 Jose Carlos Avellar notes this historical dichotomy without using these particular terms in his essay on Brazilian documentary in Randal Johnson and Robert Stam, eds., Brazilian Cinema (New Brunswick, New Jersey: Associated University Presses) 1982, p. 331.

11 Ibid., p. 329

12 Ibid., pp. 331-332

13 The full text of Carlos' narration appeared in 1965 in an issue of the Uruguayan weekly Marcha under the title "Habla el propio Carlos."

14 This and subsequent quotes from my unpublished interview with the filmmaker recorded in Havana in December of 1979 and 1980.

15 In our interview, Handler described the genesis, mode of production, and reception of the film in detail:

> ... In 1967, Uruguayans were faced with a burgeoning bureaucracy, a rapidly deteriorating economic situation, and increasing political polarization. I was desperately searching for the means to finance a film on the Conference of American Heads of State at Punta del Este scheduled for April....
>
> Montevideo erupted with student demonstrations in response to the conference, and I took to the streets to film them with my Bolex until one day I was attacked by a policeman who wrecked my camera. For the sequences shot in Punta del Este, I had no choice but to use a borrowed camera, which would have been notably inferior to the Bolex even without the leaky diaphragm.

There was quite a discrepancy in technical quality between the student footage and that of the heads of state.

Since I had no money for editing or processing, that footage just sat around for several months. Every once in a while I'd work on the editing a bit by hand, intercutting scenes of students and police in the streets with shots of politicans meeting in sedate luxury behind closed doors.... I was working without funding or assistance, so I really had to economize. I drew the title by hand right on the negative, one syllable per frame. I decided to do without commentary and just use music. There was already a tremendous disparity between the two kinds of footage, so I decided to exaggerate that contrast by adding music to the student sequences and leaving the footage of the heads of state silent....

Without proper equipment, the synchronization process was a nightmare.... Since the film was so technically crude, I assumed it would not be very well received, and had only one optical-sound print made.... At the premiere, the members of the audience were so indignant at the visual proof of violent repression by official agencies in their enlightened, democratic country that they rushed out of the theater and staged a spontaneous demonstration in the Plaza de la Libertad. The event became famous as a classic case of agitación directa. It was just after May, 1968 and student activism was a burning issue around the world....

Me Gustan los Estudiantes enjoyed enormous success at home and abroad. It opened in Paris with the Bolivian feature Blood of the Condor. Several European countries showed it on television. It was the first Latin American film requested by the Vietnamese. We kept sending off more and more prints, though in many places people just pirated copies of their own--an expedient which seemed perfectly in keeping with the way the film was made.

16 See Julianne Burton, "Theory and Practice of Film and Popular Culture in Cuba: A Conversation with Julio

García Espinosa," Quarterly Review of Film Studies Vol. VII, Number 4, fall 1982, pp. 345.

17 See Andrés Caicedo and Luis Ospina's interview with Silva and Rodríguez in Ojo al Cine # 1 (Cali, Colombia), pp. 1-10.

18 Fernando Birri, La Escuela Documental...., op. cit., p. 13.

19 For a particularly compelling account of a field experience which forced one group of filmmakers to come to terms with their own unconscious complicity in imposing exploitative, westernized expectations on indigenous peoples, see Jorge Sanjinés' "Cine revolucionario: La experiencia boliviana," Cine cubano # 76/77 (1972), pp. 1-15.

20 The students at the Escuela Documental distributed Tire Dié and subsequent films throughout the province with a primitive "mobile cinema" which consisted of a truck and a projector. This first sustained experiment in establishing "parallel" structures of distribution and exhibition anticipated the much more ambitious mobile cinema project instituted by the Cubans and demonstrated in Cortázar's Por Primera Vez. This is but a single example of numerous strategies used by Latin American filmmakers to democratize modes of diffusion and reception.

21 See Julianne Burton, "Film Artisans and Film Industries in Latin America, 1956-1980: Theoretical and Critical Implications of Variations in Modes of Filmic Production and Consumption," Latin American Program Working Paper # 102, Michael Grow, coordinator (Washington, D.C.: Woodrow Wilson International Center for Scholars), October, 1981, 20 pp.

Chapter 19

SANTIAGO ALVAREZ: CINE-AGITATOR FOR THE CUBAN REVOLUTION AND THE THIRD WORLD

John Hess

The twenty-five years of Cuban revolutionary film production have been built far more directly on a base of documentary culture than might be assumed from the most visible fictional features circulating abroad. Numerically speaking, ICAIC's production has been overwhelming documentary in orientation, for economic, historic and ideological reasons. It is fitting that Santiago Alvarez should represent Cuban documentary for the purpose of this anthology, not only because he is the most famous artist working within this current, but also because compilation, the documentary method that Alvarez has elevated to new artistic heights and political acuity, has been, along with historical reconstruction, the most innovative and dynamic branch of the Cuban documentary. There are, of course, economic, historic and ideological reasons for this importance of compilation, too, which John Hess weighs as he catalogues and analyzes the procedures behind Alvarez's exemplary achievement.

> Isn't a documentary perhaps a testimony re-elaborated starting from the ideological view of the director? He records the testimony and then transforms it and projects it into the film. I can't separate journalism from documentarism. [1]
>
> We [Cuban filmmakers] start from the basis that

> we belong to the social reality of our country, we are not foreigners, we are part of the people and our films grow out of a shared reality. If we thought we were a privileged group above the people, then we would probably make films that communicated only with a minority or an elite group. But we are not a group of poets producing abstract or bizarre poetry. One can only be a revolutionary artist by being with the people and by communicating with them.[2]

> The greatest pornographer of the U. S. was Richard Nixon--he was more dangerous as a moral example for North American youth than any scene in any film shown on 42nd Street.[3]

Introduction

Mourners file by Ho Chi Minh's open coffin. The close and medium range shots of the lines: the anguished, tear-streaked faces; and the shuffling, sandaled feet are step printed and in slow motion. This combination of avant-garde techniques produces an effect which flows smoothly while paradoxically expressing great fragmentation and abruptness. The sound track? Iron Butterfly's "Inna Godda Da Vida"--North American flower and drug rock used in a eulogy to Ho Chi Minh. It is inappropriate, outrageous, and absolutely perfect.

For me, this extremely moving, even heartrending, section of The 79 Springtimes of Ho Chi Minh (1969) sums up Alvarez's work--the use of highly innovative music and film techniques and often seemingly inappropriate materials to express his emotional and political outrage against the violence and brutality of imperialism. Like the collagists and photomontagists of the European avant-garde, Alvarez juxtaposes images and sounds to surprise, shock, and create new ideas. As a Marxist, however, he also does it to uncover underlying political realities.

Using Iron Butterfly's music to eulogize Ho Chi Minh draws out the connections between the North American counter culture and the Vietnamese people. It helps make the point (made elsewhere in the film and in many Alvarez films) that the U. S. government and not the North American people are Vietnam's enemy. In the U. S. there is another culture, a culture of liberation, that supports the Vietnamese people and opposes the war.

In this short article I can only scratch the surface of this filmmaker's 24-year career. After giving some brief introductory information on Alvarez's career and on the Cuban film industry, I want to analyze closely one film, Now, to show how Alvarez works and then critique the overall ethical/political argument Alvarez constructs and promotes in his films. In both parts I will comment on other films, especially on other short agitational documentaries he made in the 1960s and early '70s. Although more recently Alvarez has also made documentary features, using footage he and his crew shot on location, I will not include these films in my discussion. I don't find them as good or as useful. Also, most of us don't have access to them. I believe that most of what I say here can also be applied to those films, but that is mostly speculation on my part.[4]

Soon after the triumph of the Cuban Revolution in Jan. 1959, Santiago Alvarez began making Newsreels for the newly formed Instituto Cubano de Arte y Industria (ICAIC).[5] He's been in charge of the weekly newsreels, Noticieros Latinoamericanos, as well as ICAIC's documentary film section ever since. Because documentary production for theatrical distribution has been ICAIC's most important function, and since most Cuban filmmakers receive their initial training working on documentaries, Alvarez occupies a very important position in the Cuban film industry. Better known world-wide, of course, are his films themselves, and his extensive influence on young filmmakers around the world is an index of this.

Alvarez was born in Havana on March 8, 1919, child of Spanish immigrants to Cuba. His father, an anarchist storekeeper, spent some time in jail during Alvarez's youth. At 15 Alvarez went to work in a print shop and then began taking night courses at the University, where he became involved in its volatile and violent student politics. He also worked in radio during these years.

At 20 Alvarez went North to inspect what Jose Marti called the "Belly of the beast." Riding the bus, working in Pennsylvania mines and New York kitchens, and briefly attending Columbia University, Alvarez got a first-hand view of North American life. Back in Cuba he quickly joined the Partido Socialista Popular (Cuban Communist Party) and became involved in the anti-Batista underground.

During the 1950s he worked as a music archivist for a TV station and with the PSP-associated cultural society, Nuestro Tiempo (Our Time), which included a film club. With other future ICAIC founders--Alfredo Guevara (long-time head of ICAIC), Julio Garcia Espinosa, Tomas Gutierrez Alea, and Manuel Octavio Gomez--he screened and discussed classic films and recruited other artists and intellectuals into the struggle against the U. S. -supported Batista dictatorship.

In his excellent annotated filmography, Michael Chanan lists 62 films made between 1960 and 1980, excluding most of the weekly newsreels Alvarez has been responsible for. These films range in length from Now's six minutes to 195 minutes for I Am a Son of America ... And I Am Indebted to It (1972). The films range from low-budget agitational films constructed from found materials to expensive color spectaculars about Fidel's trips to Chile, Angola, and Eastern Europe. Nearing 65, Alvarez remains a vital and important contributor to Cuban and World Cinema.

NOW: The Political Aesthetics of Alvarez's Montage

> ... I had committed myself to do a benefit at Carnegie Hall for SNCC.... So I asked Jule [Styne] if he could do something special for that concert. He mulled it over and said, "Hey--how about putting some lyrics--just the way you talk and the things you talk about--to the Jewish song called 'Hava Nagillah.'" He got Betty Comden and Adolph Green to do the lyrics and the song was called "Now" and it became a cause célèbre, when the networks refused to allow the recording I made of it to be played.[6] -- Lena Horne

> American imperialism is the greatest promoter of communism in the world. In fact, it was my experiences here [in the USA] that form the roots of Now.... It all came back to me one day when I was listening to a song called "Now" sung by Lena Horne.... When I started work on the film at ICAIC ... I used all the hate I had felt against discrimination and brutality.[7] --Santiago Alvarez

Santiago Alvarez produced Now in 1965. In this powerful six-minute film on racial discrimination and black protest in the USA he combines mostly still images of racial confrontation with Lena Horne singing "Now." Early travelers to Cuba's new revolution smuggled copies of Now into the country and it saw yeoman service on the underground circuit in the mid- and late-1960s.

The film, along with a few other available Alvarez films influenced U.S. filmmakers, especially those who formed Newsreel in late 1967 in New York. In fact, the distinctive Newsreel logo--the flashing title "Newsreel" with machine gun fire on the sound track--comes from Now's end title, "NOW!" spelled out with machine gun bullet holes on a white background.

Before the credit sequence, Now opens with a live image of troops lined up across a street at screen right, facing on-coming demonstrators. This familiar image of late '60s confrontations--an icon of the period--sets the film's tone which the credit sequence elaborates. This sequence continues the notion of confrontation and also adds a sense of fragmentation by dividing the screen into three independent vertical sections. "ICAIC (written out) presenta" dissolves to the figures of Martin Luther King and a subordinate in the center panel facing right. The image has been photographically altered so that the figures are nearly silhouettes; there are no dividing lines between the panels and the background is white. After the song credits come and go in the left panel, LBJ appears in the right-hand panel looking left. This entire image is from the famous confrontation between LBJ and civil rights leaders in the oval office. Amidst this basic confrontation, the film's credits appear scattered among the three panels and the fragmented images.

Alvarez develops this graphic use of letters and words in his later films. Here the credits appear at different places on the screen and relate to the images. They fill out empty spaces and balance the composition. Later, the letters and words become graphic elements by themselves--as in concrete poetry. (See photo, p. 389.) In 79 Springtimes lines of poetry appear at different places on the screen relating to directional cues in the poetry. For example, a reference to feet appears at the bottom of the screen. Alvarez zooms in on "Pueblo" (people) and then cuts to Ho Chi Minh surrounded by admiring people. Take Off at 18:00 (1969) is a veritable catalogue of things you can do with words. They come out at you, slide by you in all directions, appear as parts of other graphic elements. In The Tiger Leaps and Kills but It Will Die (1973), Alvarez's eulogy to the murdered Chilean folk singer, Victor Jara,

An intertitle ("May the division in the socialist camp not cloud the future") in Santiago Alvarez's The 79 Springtimes of Ho Chi Minh, with words and letters becoming part of a graphic composition.

words scatter all over the screen, forming graphic designs. Here it is truly concrete poetry in motion.

With his credit montage in Now Alvarez has set the confrontational tone of the film and indicated the black-white, people-government nature of the civil rights movement. It is a struggle which reaches from armed conflict in the streets to the highest levels of the government. By placing the troops and LBJ on one side, blocking the demonstrators' and the black leaders' progress, Alvarez characterizes the struggle and takes sides himself.

After the last of the credits fades to black, the same image of Lena Horne appears in rapid sequence in the right, center, and left panels. It too is under-exposed to create a graphic rather than a photographic impression. This alteration creates a stark, monumental image. (In 79 Springtimes Alvarez uses negative images of Ho Chi Minh in much the same way.) As the third image appears, Lena Horne begins to sing, departing from the very percussive instrumental music of the credit sequence. Alvarez replaces this first image, nearly in profile, with one showing Lena Horne turned slightly toward the audience. This tripled image quickly gives way to one that is even more turned toward us. Perhaps she too has been watching the credit sequence. Since she will be our narrator (through the lyrics of her song), a position between us and the film, but slightly off to the side, seems appropriate.

The presentations over, the film proper begins with an important montage sequence which I will analyze in detail. It presents not only an important thesis statement for the film, but it also typifies the way Alvarez works a few rather simple images up into a complex ethical and political statement. This sequence has only six images connected by two cuts, two dissolves, and a fade to black. Four zooms, two pans, and a tricky special effect multiply the imagery.

Here is how it goes. In the first image, two black women, a white woman, and three black children are sitting outside on the steps holding American flags and some signs demanding voting rights for blacks and an end to police brutality. They are watching or pausing during some sort of civil rights demonstration. Though poor, they are exercising their rights as citizens. They are tired, but militant. The camera zooms in to a small boy in the lower right hand corner. The camera movement thus anticipates and prepares the dissolve to the next image by moving with our eyes to the right and isolating the small boy, the subject of the following image.[8]

In the next image we see a cop, belly to knees, night stick drawn, apprehending a small black boy and taking what looks to be flags or signs from him. Though it is clearly a different image from the first, Alvarez builds a narrative of police repression of peaceful, legal protest by young children. The camera zooms in to intensify the action here and Alvarez cuts to two black boys under arrest at the Los Angeles Sheriff's Department. One child holds a number in front of his chest, while the younger child looks on. The shot, from the point of view of the police photographer, completes the idea of police repression of protest.

The first narrative movement, from innocent exercise of rights to repression, is over. The next image maintains the black child imagery, but opens it out to a more public and national scope. A black woman in mourning comforts a child. Alvarez pans across and down to center on the child. When he zooms out, we see that it is a Life magazine cover. A headline reads, "A Martyr--and the Negro presses on." This is Medgar Evers' wife and child mourning his death at the hands of white racists. An additional headline on the magazine cover adds another dimension--not altogether serious--to the image: "Soviet space girl makes U. S. men sound stupid." Whatever Life's original intent, the second headline suggests both a connection between U. S. stupidity and racism, and an alternative way of thinking about and dealing with the race issue.

From this national, public image of mourning Alvarez dissolves to a close-up of a black boy's forehead, eyes, and nose. Though simple enough, this image has multiple, complex connotations in the present context. First, it continues the boy-child imagery with its connotations of innocence, of learning for future action. The sex bias of this imagery is obvious in retrospect. Mixing boys and girls in these images would have made an even stronger point. Fortunately, Lena Horne's song and some strong female "characters" later in the film redress this omission.

Next, the focus on eyes connotes witness. The whole world is watching the United States and its racial problems; "it's there for all to see," as the song says. Finally, this very private image suggests what might be the effects of this racism on a young person's inner thoughts and feelings. In 1965 few things were more important to Cubans than their children, whom they saw as the future of the revolution. Alvarez would be very sensitive to this aspect of U. S. racism--the waste of young people's lives.

So far Alvarez has moved from very specific events to raise more general ethical questions. Now, he transcends this complex imagery with special effects. Out of the child's eyes, moving up and toward the middle of the image, come two identical images of Abe Lincoln's head. As the heads meet and become one, the rest of the image fades to black. Under the head appears the rest of Lincoln's statue at the Lincoln Memorial in Washington, D. C. The camera pulls out to reveal the whole statue, then pans down to the pedestal across which "Now" is scratched. The national, public scope of the Life cover has been expanded to take in U. S. history, particularly as it relates to the black struggle.

Yet there is a further, very specific political connotation to this reference to Lincoln. Lena Horne's song begins by invoking Jefferson, Washington, and Lincoln. Basically, the song, and through it Alvarez, argues that the U. S. was once a revolutionary country which then lost its way. To solve our contemporary problems--for example racism--we must reclaim our revolutionary past. This argument was very popular with the U. S. Communist Party in the late 1930s and early 1940s (see Native Land, Leo Hurwitz et al., 1942). During this period Alvarez coincidentally studied at the CPUSA's Jefferson School in New York and most likely learned the Party's racial politics. It is noteworthy that Alvarez reinforces this political argument in the song with specific imagery, because by 1965 it was anachronistic. In the era of Martin Luther King, Malcolm X, and SNCC, civil rights activists were well aware of and publicized the long history of racism and racist violence in the USA (which Alvarez refers to later in the film with a very graphic lynching sequence). There was little desire to point back to a good-old-days of peace and progress in race relations.

The scrawled "Now" on the pedestal updates Lincoln's image with the connotations of urban graffiti: big city ghetto, youth gangs, poor and oppressed minorities finding a way to express themselves. Also the image of the word coincides with the song's exhortation to "put these words [Washington's, Jefferson's, and Lincoln's ideas about freedom] into action, and we mean action now."

In this short prefatory montage sequence Alvarez uses six simple images cut from magazines and newspapers to build up an expressive narrative sequence. It moves from innocence, through harsh repression to defiance. It moves from the simple to the complex. By beginning with the oppression of women and children, Alvarez invites audience involvement, perhaps even outrage. The rest of the film repeatedly recapitulates this dialectical alteration between repression and resistance, both escalating in intensity up to the defiant conclusion. Alvarez makes a comparison between the KKK and the German Nazis: he also constructs a dramatic and moving lynching sequence. Also, as the film progresses, an increasing number of blacks and some whites join protest demonstrations.

Alvarez also continues to dynamize images as he did with the Lena Horne stills that turned toward the audience.

He also uses quick zooms and cuts to bring figures to life, to make them move. In a very effective series he shows a young woman reacting to a scene of violence. She is in profile and her head is thrown back in anguish. Alvarez cuts to a somewhat closer shot of the same image which has been tilted backwards a bit, making it seem as if the woman has thrown her head back more. A third image follows which is tilted back even more. These two cuts are timed to the song, the first coming at the end of "for all to see" (meaning people's rights in the constitution) and the second on "now." This series creates an intense feeling of violence and vulnerability.

Through the film Alvarez builds short narrative sequences out of urban rebellion stills--cops with clubs, pistols, and shotguns; and national guardsmen with rifles and fixed bayonets restrain, cuff, beat, hold at gunpoint, and shoot a variety of black men and women. Alvarez activates these already dramatic images with pans and zooms, and constructs short narrative sequences of oppression. He then juxtaposes these sequences with ones showing some form of resistance: demonstrations, street fighting, a clenched fist salute, a young woman's defiant shout.

Much of the image editing in Now is narrative in intent--that is to say, two images are placed together in order to construct a narrative sequence of events: this happened and then this happened; this action resulted from that action. To do this he follows the standard conventions of Hollywood editing: he uses eye-line matches and cuts on objects and movement; he observes the conventions of screen direction. He uses reaction shots of anonymous witnesses to increase a sense of documentary realism. Further, he uses pans and zooms both to increase the sense of movement and depth, and also to create narrative. For example, from a close-up of an anguished face, he zooms out to reveal a cop beating a man. He will also pan across a panoramic image to slowly reveal its full impact. In one case he pans across three different horizontal images of demonstrations to increase the sense of numbers and strength. He cuts from a raised club to a man defending himself.

All this editing is applied to still images. (See photo, p. 394.) Alvarez and his French contemporary Chris Marker are inventors of this photomontagist form of documentary filmmaking, and the radical filmmakers gathered in Newsreel, facing no doubt similar budgetary constraints, picked

A still photograph in The 79 Springtimes of Ho Chi Minh, "dynamized" by Alvarez's editing.

it up from them. This mode of filmmaking, which goes back to Eisenstein and the German Communist Party photomontagist of the twenties and thirties, John Heartfield, runs counter to the prevailing positivist, empiricist cinéma vérité approach to documentary which dominated the 1960s.

And true to this montage tradition, much of Alvarez's montage work can be called intellectual montage. The point being made lies in neither image, only in their juxtaposition. In 79 Springtimes, for example, we see a popular Cuban singer performing in a studio or club. Alvarez cuts to Vietnamese children and Ho Chi Minh clapping their hands and then back to the singer. With this brief montage he connects the Cuban and Vietnamese people in a very profound way. In LBJ (1968), Alvarez's most innovative film, he cuts from an image of John F. Kennedy in his car in Dallas with superimposed cross hairs to a medieval crossbowman hiding behind a tree. The film is about the corruption and brutality of U.S. society and Alvarez uses many such intellectual montages to make this point. (See photo, p. 395.)

A "photomontagist" construction from Santiago Alvarez's LBJ (1968): a medieval crossbowman created out of still photographs in the artist's "most innovative" film.

The most creative part of Now, perhaps, is the sound-image montage. From the start Alvarez establishes and then maintains a bitingly ironic tension between the song's lyrics and the image track. In general, he contrasts our society's professed notions of freedom, justice, equality, and humanity with stark examples of racial injustice and violence. The song's opening verse imagines what would happen if Jefferson, Washington, and Lincoln came back and Walter Cronkite put them on TV. They would, of course, chastise us for quoting them so much rather than putting their ideas into action. Then follows a long chorus, parts of which are repeated throughout the film.

> Now is the moment, now is the moment
> Come on, we've put it off long enough
> Now, no more waitin', no more hesitatin'
> Now, now, come on, let's get some of that stuff
> It's there for you and me, for every he and she
> Just want to do what's right constitutionally
> I went to take a look in my old history book
> It's all there in black and white for all to see

Now, now, now, now, now, now
Everyone should love his brother
People all should love each other
Just don't take it literal mister
No one wants to grab your sister
Now is the time, now is the time.

Many of the sound-image juxtapositions are straightforward; one illustrates or expands on the other. Under the exhortation, "No more waitin'," Alvarez places the kind of police brutality blacks have had enough of. He accompanies "people should all love each other" with protest images--a literal example of love in action. But Alvarez accompanies certain key words and phrases with particularly striking images in order to set up ironic displacements which alert and challenge the audience to think about what is going on. For example, he combines "for all to see," with its connotations of freedom of expression, openness of society, and proclaimed equal rights, with an image of a cop holding his hand over the camera lens.

At the same time, it seems to me, he questions some of the naive assumptions of the song itself. He doesn't believe it is all there to see, all lying there on the surface. He knows we need to do more than go back to the old history book. By contrasting the viciousness of racial violence in our society with a militant but rather naive expression of hope, he critiques notions about social change which do not take into consideration the truly vicious and systematic nature of a class- and race-stratified society.

Alvarez also uses humor in the film. To "no one wants to grab your sister" he juxtaposes live footage of cops dragging a black woman off a speaker's platform. The imagery reverses conventional expectations. It is also humorous because the woman puts up a good fight and the cops look silly.

The song talks a lot about the constitution and Alvarez connects very heavy images with these references. The first time the constitution is mentioned, he uses an image of a group of well-dressed blacks walking out of church. One man carries the inert body of a young woman. She might be dead, or perhaps she fainted in a stuffy church. Whatever the actual event, the image's powerful connotation of repression magnifies the already implied irony of "just want to do what's right constitutionally." Later in the film Alvarez juxtaposes a reference to the constitution with an image of storm troopers marching past a reviewing stand which displays both a German Nazi flag and an American one. We had Nazis too. They used the same symbols and styles as their German counterparts and, one assumes, held similar views about racial questions. In *Now*, this brief scene is soon followed by references to the KKK and cross-burnings, and finally by a grisly lynching sequence, primarily using images from the 1930s. This sequence ends with an image of a black man tied to a cross on top of a burning pyre. Then the image itself burns--"free and equal now."

But these lyrics are drawn out over the cut to a live action image of black men and women, arms chained together, walking down a street towards us. This cut to live action protest is powerful--"Now" is repeated five times. Then there is a series of protest images, gaining in visual power--"people should all love each other"--"come on let's share our rhythm with 'em"--"now is the time." The film ends with a zoom into a woman's defiant shout and Lena Horne's long-held "Now."

Film and Politics

Santiago Alvarez makes films about struggle, not class struggle in the classical Marxist sense, but rather the struggle of third world people against U. S. imperialism and against the major manifestation of imperialism--underdevelopment. Even films about natural disasters, such as *Hurricane* (1963) and *Stone Upon Stone* (1970, about an earthquake in Peru), are really about underdevelopment.

Most of his films are responses (sometimes very quick ones: 48 hours for *Always Until Victory*, 1967, prepared for a mass eulogy for Che) to foreign events or to attacks on Cuba by U. S. imperialism. *Eleven-Nil* (1970) is about the kidnapping of 11 Cuban fishermen by anti-Castro exiles. *To Die for Your Country Is to Live* (1976) is about the C. I. A. bombing of a Cuban airliner on a flight from Venezuela to Cuba. The dead included the Cuban fencing team and Alvarez's wife, who worked as a stewardess.

Commonly his films begin with ordinary life, focusing on production and a sense of community. *Hanoi, Tuesday* the 13th (1967) opens with color images of Vietnamese art work. But then an erupting volcano and a birthing cow announces the grotesque birth of Lyndon Johnson in 1908. The film goes back to tranquil images of peasants working in the fields. The arrival of U. S. bombers interrupts this tranquil, communal scene. 79 Springtimes opens with the slow, time-lapse unfolding of flowers. This dissolves to images of bombs, whose fins resemble the flowers' petals, falling onto the countryside.

Other films begin with disruption: the troops at the beginning of Now and explosions at the beginning of The Tiger. Either way, Alvarez goes on to elaborate the basic opposition between tranquility and disruption. Tranquility is associated with work, third world people, socialism, peace, community. Disruption is associated with chaos, violence, war, capitalism, imperialism, the U. S. , fascism, the KKK, racism, corruption, Lyndon Johnson, and assorted dictators.

Alvarez sets up a complex Manichaean world--good versus evil, third world versus U. S. , socialism versus capitalism. He works by analogy and opposition. Socialism is tranquility; capitalism is corruption. And they oppose each other. At one level this is as clear as could be. It enables Alvarez to create powerful moral, ethical, and emotional responses to the coup in Chile, the Vietnam war, racism in the U. S.

Yet analogy can be very ambiguous, too. When Alvarez sets up the analogy in Now among Nazis, the KKK, the U. S. government, the police and guardsmen (this was before Kent State), white racists, and LBJ, what is he trying to indicate? Is he arguing that they are all Nazis, that politically the U. S. is a fascist state (as some leftists argued in the 1960s and some still do today)? Or is the basis of the analogy their racial theories, the belief that some groups of people (blacks or Jews) are inferior, nonhumans who should be eliminated. Or is he saying that all these men--Klansmen, storm troopers, cops and racists--serve the same function within their respective societies: they repress disenfranchised people?

I can't answer this question, and think that this ambiguity, which works well on an emotional level, is also Alvarez's greatest weakness as a filmmaker. In Now Alvarez offers the feel of racist violence and reacts with justified rage, yet he doesn't explain racism or its deep roots and important functions in our society. It is not a moral issue, as liberals tend to claim, but a political problem requiring radical social and political change. References to Lincoln and Jefferson or some past revolutionary spirit don't explain anything. Leftist filmmakers have a responsibility to explain things, to increase our knowledge and capacity to understand reality.

I recognize the need for and the importance of short, emotional, agitational films made to contribute to moments of heightened struggle--like Newsreel's films in the late 1960s and Alvarez's own films. And I would be less critical of Alvarez if I thought the problem had to do with mode or style of film rather than with politics. What is most striking to me is the contrast between the subtle politics of many Cuban fiction films, such as Memories of Underdevelopment, Lucia III, One Way or Another, A Man, a Woman, a City, and Alvarez's films (short and long).

We must remember that Alvarez is an official spokesperson of the Cuban Revolution. In the Noticieros and in his own documentaries he expresses the official position of the state. There is no room for hedging, for doubts, for questioning. By the time he goes to work the decisions (however difficult and painful they may have been) have been made. Once we understand this, we can better understand his failings--but also his greatness. Where else has any state spokesperson made such imaginative, creative films over a more than 20-year period? What we're looking at is a terrible contradiction between the tremendous analytical power of Marxism and the real political needs of a small, struggling socialist island under constant economic, ideological, and even physical attack by the most powerful country in the world. How Alvarez operates as a propagandist and artist within this contradiction is what we need to work out in great detail.[9]

Having made a necessary detour, we are ready to look at Now with fresh eyes. Alvarez made Now, like the rest of his films, for a Cuban audience first, then for a Latin American audience. Although I am sure he would have wanted a U.S. audience for the film, given the Bay of Pigs invasion in 1961 and the blockade of Cuba by our government, he could not made made the film with that audience in mind. Two aspects of the Cuban reality help explain the film's politics and make the film's ambiguities seem less ambiguous within the context of Cuba's life and death struggle with the U.S. government.

First, Cuba had just liberated itself from a particularly brutal dictatorship. Batista's U. S. -supported regime used all forms of repression: imprisonment, torture, disappearance, repression of parties and censorship of publications. Since the early 1930s, even before Batista came to power, street fighting of the kind we see in Now was common in Cuba. Thus the struggle represented in Now visually reproduces the Cuban struggle against a series of repressive governments, struggles that Alvarez saw all around him and participated in as a young militant in the 1940s and '50s. To some extent Alvarez has imposed his reality on us. The irony is of course, that by visually reproducing his own struggle against a repressive regime, he has uncovered the real nature of our reality.[10] Second, the issue of racial conflict was very important in racially mixed Cuba. Ethnically, Cubans are a mixture of the African slaves brought over to work in the sugar plantations and the Spanish seamen, traders, adventurers, aristrocrats, and prostitutes who came there to make a fortune. Cuba was always a race-stratified society, with the Africans on the bottom and the Spanish aristrocrats on the top. The Cuban Revolution set out to end racial inequality, and films such as Simparele, Memories of Underdevelopment, Lucia, The Other Francisco, and Sergio Giral's films on the period of slavery, are all part of that struggle. So is Now.

Alvarez's film had three functions in 1965. First, it was topical, it portrayed what was going on in the U. S. and thus served the journalistic purpose of ICAIC's documentary section. Second, it functioned as a weapon in the ideological struggle with the U. S. in Cuba and in the rest of Latin America. It visually characterized the U. S. government in terms immediately understandable by and emotionally potent for Latin Americans who have suffered so much at the hands of U. S. -imposed dictators. Finally, Alvarez suggested a comparison between how race relations were handled in the U. S. and in Cuba. Looked at from a Cuban perspective, we can see Now as a potent, partisan contribution to Cuba's struggle for survival against U. S. efforts to destabilize it.[11]

Conclusion

While Alvarez and his work have been very well-known and influential abroad, they have remained relatively obscure here (this is the first substantive article to appear on Alvarez in North America). Just as Cuban films began to come into the U.S. legally in the early 1970s, U.S. progressive filmmakers and critics turned against the militant, montage-oriented filmmaking of Newsreel--based partly on Alvarez. Instead, they favored a modified cinéma vérité, TV-style "talking-heads" documentary. At the same time, "progressive" and "social change" replaced "militant" and "political" as self-definitions. The mass movement of the 1960s faded, forcing the many politically conscious filmmakers it produced to depend on government and corporate handouts to continue working.

Now, however, opposition to the Reagan administration increases daily and, at the same time, the $100,000 budgets are out for progressive filmmakers. They will have to become less progressive or learn to make cheaper films for immediate use. To these filmmakers Santiago Alvarez has an enormous amount to teach. He has shown how to turn poverty into wealth by using all manner of found materials to make highly expressive and creative films--films which teach and please. And since U.S. leftist filmmakers are not caught in the same contradictions Alvarez is, they should be able to bring our 20-year experience with the black, feminist, gay male and lesbian movements and what we are learning from more recently activated anti-nuke, ecology, and trade union movements to what Alvarez has already taught us: to make truly wonderful and useful films--films Santiago Alvarez would love to see.

Notes

1 From Michael Chanan, "Introduction (in the Style of Santiago Alvarez)," BFI Dossier, No. 2: Santiago Alvarez (London: British Film Institute, 1980), p. 8.

2 " '5 Frames are 5 Frames, Not 6, but 5': An Interview with Santiago Alvarez," Cineaste, Vol. 6, No. 4 (1975), p. 20.

3 Ibid.

4 See Chanan's annotated filmography in the BFI Dossier where he argues strongly for these feature documentaries.

5 See Julianne Burton's Introduction to the first special

section on Cuban Cinema in Jump Cut, No. 19 (December, 1978), pp. 17-20, for a good discussion of ICAIC.

6 Lena Horne and Richard Schickel, Lena (Garden City: Doubleday, 1965), p. 289.

7 Cineaste interview, p. 17.

8 Many people today dispute this notion that we read images from left to right. But because it has become such a convention in filmmaking, it has become true in most cases.

9 Chanan begins this work in his filmography.

10 This is a good example of how truth resides more consistently in revolutionary struggles than in counterrevolution. The North Vietnamese and Viet Cong told the truth, while the U. S. government consistently lied about the war in Indochina. Today, the best assessment of what is happening in Central America comes from Nicaragua and the Salvadoran revolutionaries, not from Jeane Kirkpatrick, Ronald Reagan, or our mass media. Our government tries to cut off the flow of information and ideas from Cuba and Nicaragua because it also understands this.

11 Shortly after finishing this essay, I saw a newly struck 35mm print of Now as part of the "A Decade of Cuban Documentary Film" program which is touring the U. S. The opening imagery is much more elaborate than in the 16mm prints I have seen. This included several newsreel shots of urban riot footage ending with the image I describe.

The several new Alvarez films shown, My Brother Fidel (1977), The Challenge (1979) and A River of Enraged People (1980) were based on extensive primary footage, much of it in cinéma vérité style. Alvarez and his crew don't seem entirely comfortable with this kind of filmmaking, yet the bite and power remain strong and clear. 79 Springtimes and Now rounded out the Alvarez program. Interestingly, Now produced the most audience reaction.

Chapter 20

DOCUMENTARY AS PARTICIPATION: THE BATTLE OF CHILE

Victor Wallis and John D. Barlow

The Battle of Chile was the Third World Harlan County of the seventies, the political epic film that succeeded in reaching beyond the ghetto of political and art cinema, even as far as, most famously, Pauline Kael. More than any other film, it was able to mobilize liberal and mainstream support in the West for the Chilean cause, as well as providing radical post-mortems and continuing resistance with sharp analytic tools. Victor Wallis and John Barlow provide, on the tenth anniversary of the coup d'état and alongside renewed public resistance in the streets of Santiago, an assessment of the political and aesthetic strategies of this unique testimony from exile.

Imagine a live, prime-time TV debate between a left-wing student leader and a conservative senator. No commercial interruptions; plenty of rapid-fire exchanges; above all, a nationwide audience overwhelmingly polarized behind one or other of the speakers. This is just one episode of The Battle of Chile, with the debate scene shot straight off the flickering tube. It epitomizes, however, the dramatic quality of the raw material which has made possible a documentary of extraordinary power and impact.[1]

The film's main actor is the Chilean working class--the "people without arms" of the subtitle. The subject is the life-and-death struggle in which they find themselves after the two years of heightened mobilization made possible with the election of a Socialist president (Salvador Allende) in 1970.[2] What Allende's election meant was above all a call to action for the working class. Allende himself could not move much. The presidency was far from being the only institution of power, and the remaining ones--the economy, Congress, courts, bureaucracy, and armed forces--remained overwhelmingly in the hands of his enemies. Those who were inspired by Allende's platform had to act largely for themselves, in the face of obstruction which by late 1972 had reached fever-pitch.

This political setting had no real precedent anywhere. It attracted a degree of worldwide interest which the protagonists could not fail to recognize. A movement with revolutionary goals had gained an important element of power through strictly legal means; everything that it might do with this advantage was in the nature of an experiment. Creativity was at a premium.

At least in some respects, the Chilean left was well prepared to rise to its challenge. Its electoral triumph was the culmination of a long growth-process, punctuated by Allenda candidacies every six years since 1952. By 1970, the left's base consisted not just of a large electoral and trade-union following; it included also an overwhelming popular sentiment favoring the nationalization of Chile's major raw materials, and it showed itself more specifically in a great proliferation of study/action groups and/or campaign committees designing alternatives to a wide range of current practices.

Chile's filmmakers were thoroughly caught up in this process. During the 1970 campaign, the Unidad Popular[3] Cinema Committee drew up a manifesto that uniquely combined political commitment and respect for the creative process (see Appendix to this article). Patricio Guzmán, returning to Chile after Allende's victory (from a period of film-study in Madrid), found that his ideas for fiction films "were completely outstripped by reality."[4] A number of enthusiastic documentaries were produced during the first two years of the UP government.

By the third year, however, the element of joy at new-found possibilities had given way to a recognition that the easy victories were over. The power of capital had not yet been overcome. Some on the left expected a violent showdown; others thought that concessions might stave off a clash. But it was clear in either case that difficult moments were in store.

The new level of crisis heightened the challenge in revolutionary filmmakers. They could no longer content themselves with recording the people's achievements. Though the achievements themselves might become even more impressive, they could no longer be understood apart from the constant threat that faced the left, and from the resultant uncertainty and hence divisions within its ranks. Agitational films had had their day; what was now needed, as Patricio Guzmán would put it, was "a great analytic film."[5] This was the task that the Equipo Tercer Año (the Third Year Team) set itself.

The Battle of Chile lasts $4\frac{1}{2}$ hours. Parts I and II incorporate a thoroughly detailed narrative of the UP government's last seven months, from the March 1973 congressional elections through the September coup. Along the way, we are shown the multiplicity of forces on both sides of the basic conflict, with special attention to the debates within the left. Part III, conceived as a tribute to the Chilean workers, includes a retrospective look at the October 1972 crisis--a key moment whose resolution set the limits within which subsequent struggles would be fought out.

In sum, the film provides some of the major elements needed for discussing why the Allende experiment turned out the way it did. It is in this sense a demanding film; it stimulates informed debate about alternative strategies. But at the same time, it is a film of great excitement. The most interesting critical question is how it manages to combine these two attributes.

We have already stressed the dramatic nature of the political raw material. The circumstances in question were special, however, not only for the scenes they offered, but also for the film-artists they produced. The "people without arms" were a people discovering and applying their abilities for the first time; the six-member Tercer Año group, except for Guzmán himself, consisted entirely of novices to filmmaking. But what they lacked in prior technical knowledge was more than made up for by the depth of their political commitment. Techniques could be learned as they were needed; political commitment was a precondition for seeing what was going on.

In their political vision as in the level of their technical capacity, the filmmakers resembled their primary subjects. Like the Chilean workers, the filmmakers differed among themselves over specific questions of political strategy, but both groups--in contrast to some of the party leaderships--were ready to limit the scope of such difference in favor of a common approach to practical tasks.

For the task of making "a great analytic film," it was essential that the filmmakers be clear and open about their subject. On the one hand, the film would have to be unambiguous in reflecting their commitment to the side of the workers. But on the other hand, it would have to give full play to whatever internal divisions arose in their own movement. They would have to avoid omitting anything that might prove to be important in understanding the Allende experience. If nothing else, the film would have to be comprehensive, at least in terms of the points of view that it showed.[6]

The political understanding of the filmmakers was also shown in several other decisions that were crucial to carrying out their work. First, during the whole period of filming, they never made their project public. Their caution in this regard went so far that when the police ransacked Patricio Guzmán's apartment after the coup, they did not even discover that he was a filmmaker. In addition, each day's footage was hidden in a different place, with only Guzmán and his compañera having a record of its whereabouts. Thirdly, the filmmakers used different credentials to gain access to different protagonists. In effect, they gained the trust of those who were anxious to be understood (for example, workers debating the government's strategy), while using subterfuge against those who had something to hide (for example, a bourgeois household, which they entered posing as representatives of the conservative TV network).

Beyond determining the film's basic outline and guiding the film-team's interaction with the public, the political insight of participants was crucial to the countless immediate decisions that had to be made in the course of filming and editing. After all, most of The Battle of Chile was made with only one camera and one sound recorder. It was therefore necessary to be at the right place at the right time and to be prepared in advance for the moment when the twenty hours of hidden footage were finally collected in one place (Cuba), to be assembled into a whole that showed how each force in the battle affected and was affected by the others.

Underlying all these elements of method, however, is a commitment based on the idea that the filmmakers themselves are an integral part of the struggles they are filming. In The Battle of Chile, this commitment is embodied in a special sequence placed at the end of Part I and repeated at the beginning of Part II; it consists of the frames taken by an Argentine TV camera operator, during the June 29 coup-attempt, as he filmed his own death from the gunfire of a Chilean army officer. (See photo, p. 408.)

The Battle of Chile is both committed to the workers' struggle and open about the possible shortcomings of its strategies. This combination of commitment and openness translates into a tension between involvement and detachment in the viewer. The tension is maintained throughout the film, but is particularly acute in Parts I and II.

The element of detachment is immediately suggested in the way the film's title is shown: the reference to an unarmed people, in stark block letters on a blank background, accompanied by the sound of jet fighters and gunfire. The opening camera-shots show the destruction of the presidential palace, the final enactment of a threat which remains present throughout the film, and which gives all the popular struggles the aspect of a race against death. The army footage used in showing the attack on the presidential palace dramatizes the brutality of the Chilean bourgeoisie in destroying precisely what their slogans will claim they are defending: legitimate, representative, democratic government.

From the burning palace, the scene shifts quickly back in time to place us in the middle of a marching crowd. The first shot, 45 seconds long, comes directly from the demonstrators, as the hand-held camera bounces along with an almost amateur energy and excitement, picking up the faces, the chants, and the placards that surround each participant. During the sequence of shots that follows, the filmmakers call attention to themselves and their involvement by tapping their microphone before starting an interview and by recording themselves shouting the instruction to cut. These self-reflexive gestures occur only during the first five minutes of The Battle of Chile and present an

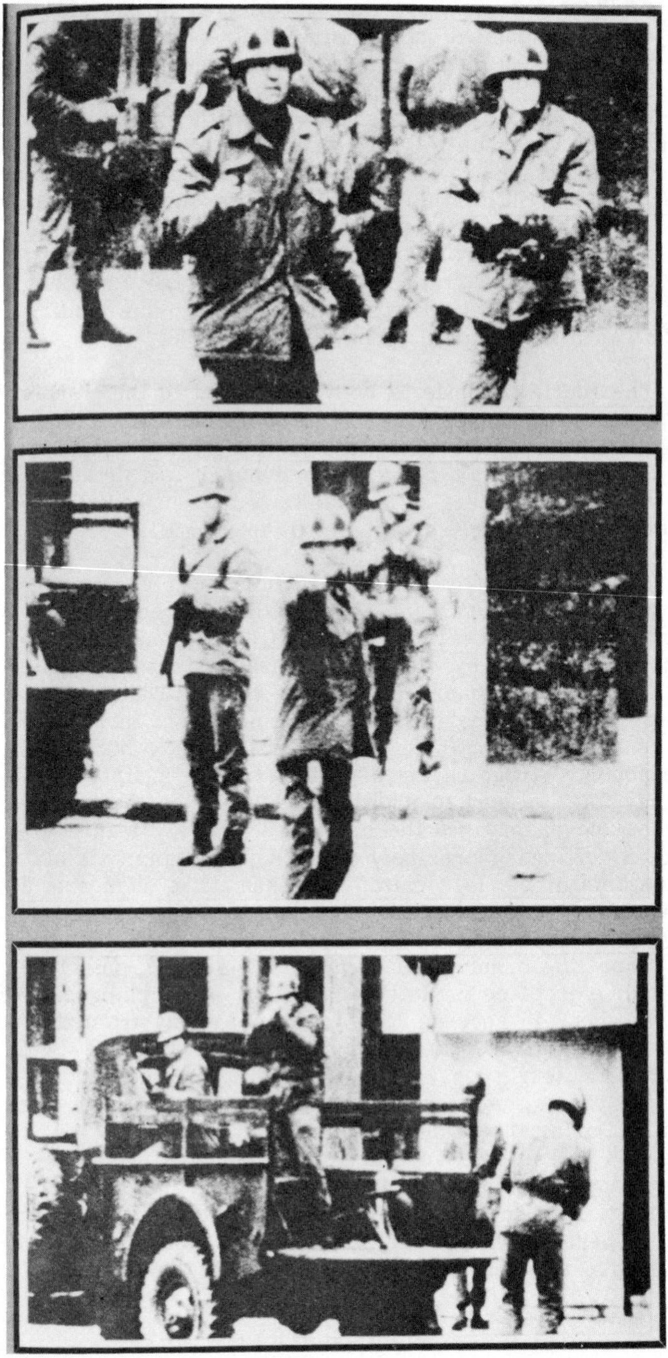

obvious contrast to the preceding shots of the coolly functioning military jets impersonally bombing the presidential palace. The filmmakers, by making themselves personally visible among the events they are filming, establish thereby their commitment to avoid the slick manipulative devices of commercial newsmaking, and make it clear to us as viewers where they stand in the conflict between the people and the bourgeoisie.

With their presence on the screen, the filmmakers channel our involvement through themselves. We are made consciously aware of ourselves as viewers. This awareness frustrates the kind of passive emotional identification with participants that is so dear to the "human interest" newsreel. To further encourage our active involvement, the filmmakers often call attention to their editing. Transitions are sometimes deliberately inelegant, as, for example, in the treatment given at one point to a strike-meeting held in a stadium. The camera shifts from the speakers' stand to a segment of the audience by zipping up into the sky and then back down into the crowd. The roughness of this pan, as opposed to a cut, removes any doubt as to the immediacy of the connection between what was happening in two separate parts of the stadium.

Despite such rough edges, however, the events of Parts I and II unfold with a high level of excitement. This reflects several components of the filmmakers' approach. First, images of political struggle encompass the full range of people's lives--not just parliament, press conferences, speeches, and demonstrations, but also scenes at work, in government offices, in neighborhoods, and in living rooms. Second, even where the focus is on public figures, they are almost always shown candidly, without glorification or special attention, whether giving speeches, attending ceremonies, or issuing orders. (See photo, p. 410.) Use of interviews is for the most part limited to bringing out the unrehearsed responses of ordinary people on both sides of the confrontation. Third, tension is heightened by shifting the focus back and forth between different kinds of action and between opposed forces.

Opposite: Battle of Chile: an Argentine camera operator films his own execution, images symbolic of the filmmakers' commitment to be part of the struggle they were filming. (Photo: Equipo tercer año)

A political platform image from The Battle of Chile, with Allende visible to the right of photo center. When the focus is on public figures they are usually shown candidly, without glorification or special attention. (Photo: Equipo tercer año)

Given the complexity of the interaction between the various protagonists, it is remarkable how little the film depends on voice-over narration. What there is, however, at least in the English-language version, sometimes deprives events of their impact by belaboring a point that is eloquently clear in the image itself. For example, when the Argentine camera operator records his own death, the viewers are told that this is the "naked face of fascism." Not only is this liable to patronize the viewer, but it suggests that the film-makers are uncertain about the significance of what they are doing, which almost the entire visual material of the rest of the film belies. [7]

The director, Patricio Guzmán, has said, "[The Battle of Chile] is not a sensuous film. It makes no concessions to the viewer. It offers little relief. It is really a filmed essay."[8] To this end, music, extreme close-ups, and unusual camera angles are used sparingly. The film's emotional appeal lies above all in its presentation of the Chilean

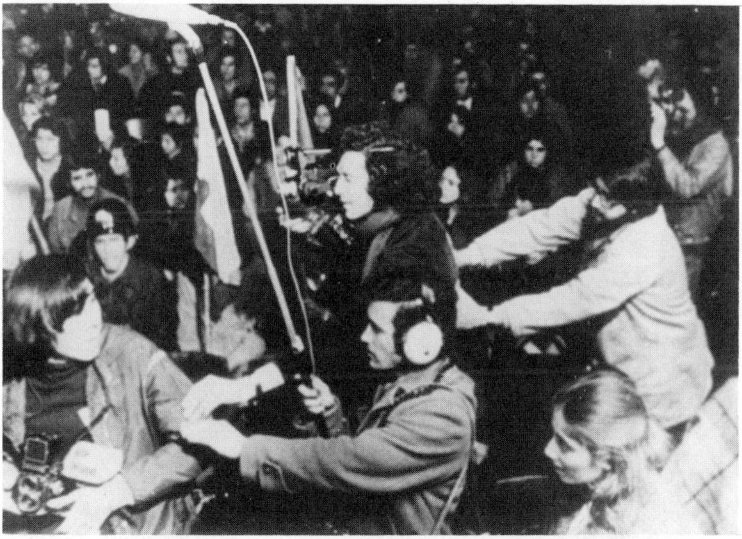

Operator Jorge Müller, "disappeared" and presumed dead after the 1973 coup, shown filming a nighttime demonstration in The Battle of Chile, steadied by director Patricio Guzmán. (Photo: Equipo tercer año)

workers and their movements from within. (See photo, above). It is not for the consumption of merely interested, uninvolved spectators. It does not respond to the demand for entertainment, for the easy edification of the evening news, or for a Hollywood portrayal of the forces of liberty opposing those of tyranny. We see the left in its weakness as well as its strength, all without the slightest adornment.

Occasionally, however, the filmmakers seem to slip from their detachment when photographing elements of the right--a fascist rally, generals at a military funeral, a middle-aged momia venting her fury at having her class privileges challenged. This is most noticeable at the military funeral, where the camera wanders around among the generals, caressing their uniforms and insignia, in an effort to demonstrate the cold contempt for the people that lurks behind such symbols. (See photo, p. 412.)

It is these right-wing elements that appear to have

The military funeral sequence from The Battle of Chile: slipping from its customary detachment, the camera wanders among the generals, caressing their uniforms and insignia, demonstrating the contempt behind these symbols. (Photo: Equipo tercer año)

triumphed at the end of Part II. With the bloody coup of September 11, 1973, the film's dramatic component has played itself out. That event brought an end to the filming, but it is not the end of the film. Nor is it the end of the struggle; there is more to what went on before the coup than the coup itself can terminate.

Part III of The Battle of Chile has the character of a full-scale flashback. It gives us the opportunity to meet again, under more relaxed conditions, some of the individual workers who spoke to us in the context of the accelerated factory-takeovers that were carried out during Part II (i. e., after the June 29 coup-attempt). It also takes us back to the turning point of October 1972, at which time the workers showed their power in the most decisive way, occupying and running factories whose owners had declared a lockout "with pay" in hopes of bringing down the government.

All the events of Parts I and II had taken place in the shadow of the final outcome of that October crisis. Allende, who feared losing the trappings of legality more than he feared demobilizing the workers, reached an agreement with the Armed Forces not long after the October takeovers; he would order the factories returned to their former owners, while the head of the Armed Forces (the constitutionalist General Prats) would enter the Cabinet and would guarantee the holding of the March elections. Prats was true to his word, but the advance of the workers was halted and an easier path was cleared for the plottings of General Pinochet.

Although this judgment of Allende's concessions is not made explicitly in Part III (they are attributed simply to economic requirements), the very fact of focusing on the October events gives a particular thrust to the film's retrospective view of the intra-left debates of the first two parts. The issue throughout was whether Allende should water down his program in order to avoid provoking the right, or whether he should assume that a right-wing onslaught was inevitable, and therefore give priority to mobilizing the left's bases while there was still time.

The debate over this question is undoubtedly what will remain as the key issue in the discusssions that are integral to the experience of viewing The Battle of Chile. As a document, the film provides materials for both sides of the argument. Though it does not glorify Allende, it is careful to present his own statement of the reasons for his actions. It does not record his weakest moments--as for example when he publicly denounced rank-and-file sailors who had been organizing to defend his government against their pro-coup officers. But by showing the insufficiently tapped militance of the Chilean workers, it gives us some sense of the depth of the UP's missed opportunity.

Only four years after the completion of Part III, Chile's workers have begun to show an organized defiance of the Pinochet dictatorship. What they have yet to recover, though, is bitterly suggested in the following exchange with the 29-year-old leader of the June 1983 protest:[9]

Q: What is your image of Allende?

A: None. For me he was a president, elected democratically, who was killed by those who are presently the dictators of this country. But it didn't give me any lessons. On the contrary, the thousand days of the Popular Unity was a very bitter period for the country. It began well and ended badly, and in the end it cost Allende his life and our country its democracy.

Throughout Western Europe and parts of the Americas, The Battle of Chile has stirred audiences with what it shows of the creative potential of revolutionary workers. Its great test will be the task of restoring the collective memory of the Chilean working class itself.

APPENDIX

Los Cineastas y el Gobierno Popular
(Filmmakers and the Popular Government)

Declaration of principles of the Comité de Unidad Popular del Cine, 1970 (preamble omitted)

1. Before being filmmakers, we are individuals committed to the political and social life of our people and to its great task: building socialism.

2. Film is an art.

3. Chilean film has the historic obligation to be a revolutionary art. * (See page 415.)

4. Revolutionary art is art which is born of the joint work of the artist and the people, united for a common goal: liberation. The people (el pueblo) is the moving force and the true creator; the filmmaker is its instrument of communication.

5. The revolutionary credentials of films cannot be imposed by decree. We therefore do not advocate any single approach to filmmaking, but rather as many approaches as may become necessary in the unfolding of the struggle.

6. However, we believe that a cinema removed from the masses inevitably becomes an article of consumption for the petty bourgeois elite which is incapable of being the moving force of history....

7. We reject as sectarian the mechanical application of the above principles, or the imposition of official formal criteria of cinematographic method.

8. We affirm that the traditional forms of production are a bone of contention for young filmmakers and that they imply a clear cultural dependence, given their origin in aesthetic principles foreign to the idiosyncrasy of our peoples.

To a technique without meaning we counterpose the will to seek a language of our own, based on the immersion of the filmmaker in the class struggle, a confrontation which generates its own cultural forms.

9. We believe that a cinema with these objectives necessarily implies a distinct type of criticism; we affirm that the great critic of revolutionary film is the people to which it is directed and which does not need "mediators to explain and defend it."

10. No films are revolutionary in themselves. They earn this label through the contact of the film with its audience and above all through its impact as a catalyst of revolutionary action.

11. Access to cinema is a right of the people; ways must therefore be found to bring it to all Chileans.

12. All workers in film must have equal access to the means of production. With the people's government, expression will not be the privilege of the few, but rather the irrevocable right of a people that has taken the path of its independence.

13. A people that has culture is a people that struggles, resists, and liberates itself.

(translated by Victor Wallis)

*(Translator's note:) The following passage from the preamble suggests the thinking behind this statement: "Contradictions should not be swept away; rather, they should be developed, in order to find the way to build a lucid and liberating culture. The long struggle of our people for its emancipation shows us the way."

Notes

1 The Battle of Chile: The Struggle of a People Without Arms, made by the Equipo Tercer Año; director, Patricio Guzmán. Part I ("The Insurrection of the Bourgeoisie") and Part II ("The Coup d'Etat") completed in 1976; Part III ("People's Power") completed in 1979. U.S. distributor: Unifilm, New York.
This article complements an earlier review of Victor Wallis, in Jump Cut # 19 (1979) which focused prim rily on the specifics of the Chilean political setting.

2 For a useful bibliography on the Allende period, see the Appendix to Dale L. Johnson, "Chile: Before and During," Science and Society XLVI, 4 (Winter, 1982-83), 461-476.

3 Unidad Popular (Popular Unity) was the coalition of parties that Allende represented.

4 Interview with Julianne Burton, in Socialist Revolution # 35 (September-October, 1977), p. 50. All our information about the actual work of the filmmakers is based on this interview.

5 Ibid., p. 52.

6 For a listing of aspects of the Allende period not treated in the film, see Dennis West, "Documenting the End of the Chilean Road to Socialism: La Batalla de Chile," The American Hispanist (February, 1978), p. 14.

7 Cf. Pauline Kael's review in The New Yorker (January 23, 1978), p. 82.

8 Interview with Julianne Burton, p. 48.

9 Interview of Rodolfo Seguel by John Dinges, In These Times (July 13-26, 1983), p. 22.

Chapter 21

CHILDREN OF VERTOV IN THE LAND OF BRECHT

Pierre Véronneau*

Of all film genres, documentary has been the least distinguished performer on the film scene in Eastern Europe and the Soviet Union since the war. It is perhaps as symptomatic as it is tragic that things have come to such a pass in the society that provided the first heroic crucible for radical documentary (as described in the first part of this anthology), and whose newsreel cinematographers equalled if not surpassed their Western allies in courage and commitment during World War II. Nevertheless, in two distinct subgenres, the work of the children of Vertov is rivaled by few: archival compilation, and the globe-trotting trouble-shooting subgenre of international solidarity, both areas in which the East Germans have proven to be leaders (a few pockets of interesting work in another subgenre, direct-cinema analysis of domestic social problematics, most notably in Hungary, must not be overlooked either). In compilation, the Thorndikes began making important strides towards historiographical analysis in the fifties, and Joris Ivens contributed the great but little-seen Song of the Rivers, an epic of trade-union fraternity and Third World resistance, in 1953. As for globe-trotting, the Soviets offered one of the most important pioneers in the person of Roman Karmen, whose career spanned from the twenties to the seventies, taking him to every world front of revolutionary struggle from Spain to Vietnam, from Stalingrad to Santiago. But since 1965, it has been the Berlin duo, Heynowski and Scheumann, who have been taking

*Translated from the French by Thomas Waugh.

up where Karmen left off. Pierre Véronneau's sympathetic appraisal briefly surveys their early work on the resurgence of the Right in Europe, and on two major events of the seventies, victory in Vietnam and defeat in Chile, the latter highlighted in extracts from H & S's working journals that follow. Since Véronneau's 1979 text, H & S's work has been concentrated chiefly in Kampuchea. The reader will be at no loss to explain the scandalous neglect in the English-speaking world of these two important committed artists, honored in 29 major retrospectives around the world since 1974.

I

In 1924, the great Soviet documentarist Dziga Vertov declared:

> Cinema-eye: the possibility of making visible the invisible, of illuminating obscurity of laying bare what is masked, or rendering not-acted that which is acted, of changing falsehood into truth. Cinema-eye, the juncture of science and actuality towards the goal of fighting for the communist decoding of the world; an attempt to show truth on the screen by Film-truth (Kinopravda).

A few years later, presenting A propos de Nice, Jean Vigo proclaimed:

> Moving towards the social documentary would be consenting to exploit a whole mine of subjects that the current situation would endlessly keep renewing....
>
> This would mean avoiding the too artistic subtlety of a pure cinema and the super-vision of a super-navel seen from one angle, then from another angle, then yet another angle: technique for technique's sake....
>
> Moving towards the social documentary is thus assuring the cinema of a subject that arouses interest: of a subject that eats meat.
>
> But I would like to take up with you a social

> cinema that is even more defined and one I'm closer to: the social documentary, or, more precisely, the documented point of view....
>
> This social documentary distinguishes itself from the mere documentary and from the weekly newsreel by the point of view that the author openly defends in it. This documentary forces you to take a stand, for it dots the "i's."
>
> If it doesn't engage an artist, it engages people even less. The latter requires the former.

These two heartfelt declarations could be taken up by Walter Heynowski and Peter Scheumann and applied to themselves without hesitation, especially that of Vertov, with whom they have similar ideological and political preoccupations in common. In fact, the German directors never lose a chance to pay tribute to the Soviet one, and don't hide the fact that their studio is a little bit the laboratory of documentary creation that Vertov spoke of.

If officially the "H & S Studio" has existed since May 1, 1969, the team that composes it has been working together since 1965. Before that, Heynowski and Scheumann had done various work connected to written or visual journalism. The former, for example, had been editor of a satiric journal (something of this quality remains in the films) and a TV program director; the latter, a radio administrator and the director of a domestic political TV magazine. One day, these journalists decided that the cinema, oriented towards TV broadcasting, would be a privileged means for achieving their goals to ask political and philosophical questions on certain great events marking their era. That's why they chose as their method the documentary approach, based on journalistic investigation and privileging speech, and as their point of view, Marxist analysis. In doing so, they naturally fell within the Vertovian tradition of the socialist documentary.

Current affairs is a rich resource that is endlessly beckoning to us. You have to impose choices and categories on it. The first theme that attracted H & S, and that constantly returns in their films, is the permanence of fascism in the world, and especially neo-fascism in West Germany. Their career opened, then, on that of the German fascist Siegfried Müller, the head of a mercenary commando made up mainly of West Germans, and leader of the battle against those who want to liberate Africa from the colonialist yoke.

Four films are about Commando 52, run by the laughing man, "Congo" Müller.

But since German reactionaries aren't all located abroad, H & S are interested also in those who stay at home, and specifically those whom the German Democratic Republic calls the West German "avengers." If in The Hour of the Ghosts (1967), the approach was rather light and humorous (the "work" of a famous Bonn medium who is involved in politics and advises several ministers), as were the "cine-tracts" Yours Sincerely (1967) and Meier's Legacy (1975), with The President in Exile (1969) and Man without a Past (1970) the level became more serious and more consistent, and the proof of H & S's art of trapping their interview subjects is all the more masterfully established.

In the former of these two features, Dr. Walter Becher, director of the Association of Sudeten Germans, a Bundestag deputy, explains how and why Germany should once again annex the Sudeten part of Czechoslovakia and finally restore the borders of Greater Germany, Hitler's old dream. The latter feature offers a portrait of a friend of Dr. Becher, H. R. Ubelacker, a 30-year-old neo-Nazi, who channeled his college meditations into a study of the currency of the Munich Accords, which, in his opinion, were never abrogated and are thus still valid.

But aside from the German "avengers", another subject imposed itself on the filmmakers' awareness: Vietnam. Their filmic interest in this country began discreetly: by a five-minute tribute to blood donors for Vietnam. Two years later, in 1968, there followed the four-part series, Pilots in Pyjamas: H & S had been the first to be able to film a North Vietnamese camp for downed American pilots. Portraits of ten pilots become the trial of a whole wav of thinking and acting. (See photo, p. 421.) Then, aside from two shorts, including the very striking Remington 12 Calibre (1972), the filmmakers waited ten years before returning to the theme of Vietnam. But this time the situation had changed: the Americans had been defeated. In 1976-78, H & S offered four features from the series Vietnam and three shorts, including A Vietnamese Refugee, about the general who had struck down a Vietcong prisoner with a bullet to the head in cold blood, but who now, instead of being condemned as a murderer, runs a restaurant in a Washington suburb. Finally in 1979, H & S produced a new work, Our Distant Friends, the Nahs. But this time, don't forget, the situation

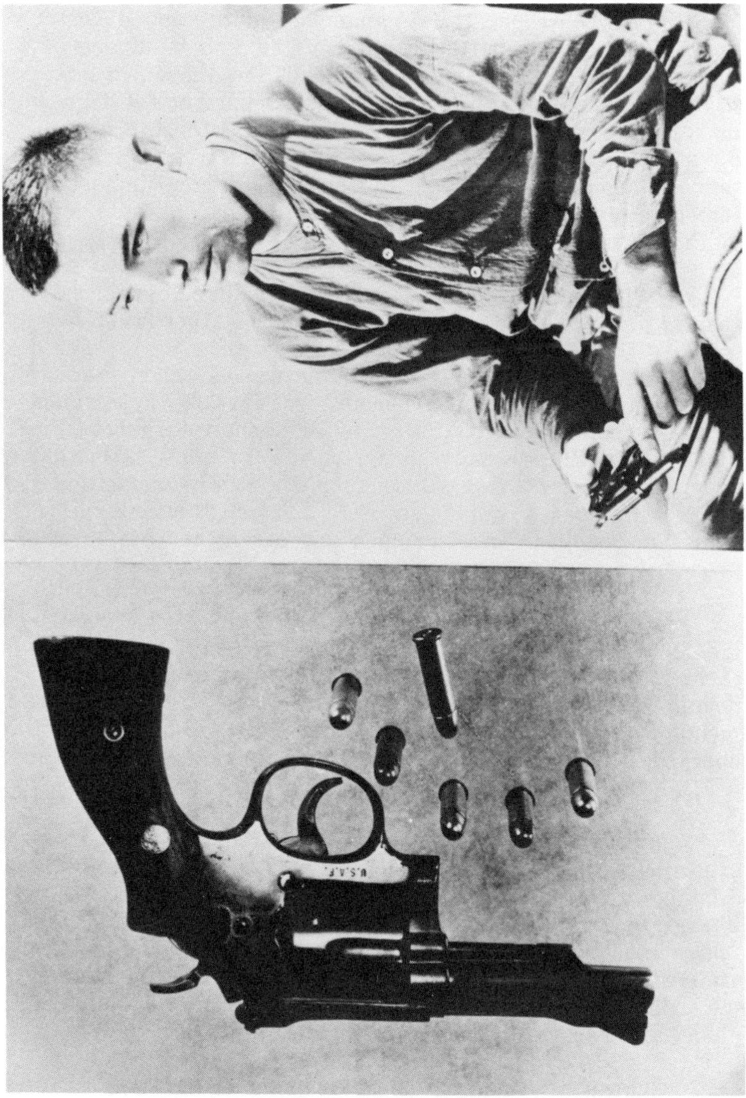

A downed American pilot in North Vietnam confronts and reflects upon his weapon in <u>Pilots and Pyjamas</u>. (Photo: Cinémathèque québécoise)

had changed once again: war among the Indochinese nations and a political re-alignment on the peninsula.

Between these two Vietnamese visits, and except for the film on the forced evacuation of the U.S.'s largest foreign base, located in the middle of the Libyan desert (Bye Bye Wheelus, 1971), the essential part of the filmmakers' work is about Chile, before and after the coup d'état. (Following this article are some extracts from their working notebooks on this subject, a very important text that helps one to understand one of the characteristics of the H & S Studio--teamwork.)

With their collaborators, the two directors investigate, prepare, and study the subject that they want to treat. If they interview someone, they know his or her life, career, and thinking. In other words, when they arrive on location, though remaining aware of the element of chance and unpredictability in the documentary enterprise, they already have an orientation in mind, a historical and political guide that allows them to choose a particular character, event, or place. And so much the better if something happens that enriches and strengthens their approach.

Such a method of proceeding, together with common ideological concerns, naturally encourages an exceptional team atmosphere, strengthened by the fact that the same people have been working together for ten years. In documentary film, when the director or directors are not the operators, the director-operator bond becomes primary and it's this that is the most fragile....

In the Heynowski-Scheumann-Hellmich triangle, operator Peter Hellmich is so familiar with the directors' thinking and method that he can guess in what direction the interview or the discussion is heading, and can frame the image with this in mind. For example, during the interview with Congo Müller, when he is questioned on Nazism, the camera zooms in on the iron cross he is wearing. This close collaboration is constantly put to the test.

These comments lead us to bring out another characteristic of H & S's films: they do not suppress the evidence of their work as filmmakers but, on the contrary, put it on display. We must remember that the representation that one gives of a thing or event is a process that lasts from before the shooting to the editing. Several documentaries hide this process to make us believe in the immanence and the transparency of reality. H & S insist rather on saying that reality is a web of contradictions within which you have to impose a selection and put things in relation to each other; the cinema maintains with this reality a dialectical relationship that alone can reveal its structures. They tell us then that it is not a question of filming several things or something other, but to film otherwise. And that becomes clear if we compare the many films shot on Vietnam or Chile with theirs. It is true that certain films are sometimes similar but only when "otherwise" takes root in the same political soil.

All this is not surprising. Vertov, whom we quoted earlier, thought similarly and acted the same. From his earliest Kinopravdas, he shows the operator filming, the editor editing, the projectionist projecting the film. In Man with the Movie Camera, this achieves the breadth of a manifesto: reality vs. its representation in the process of filmic production.

H & S also show themselves, explain themselves. For example, in I Was, I Am and I Shall Be (1974), all of the methods they followed, the subterfuges used, are explained. As yet another example, in the interviews (whose mise-en-scène, incidentally, is somewhat dry: they themselves seated behind the camera, the subject seated or standing in front), they don't cut out the question as so many directors do around the world; one therefore hears the directors questioning the subjects and the answers provided. Accordingly, they don't rely on a false sense of the natural, on the impression of life recorded unawares. This device lets us understand their method and their approach and prevents the manipulations of meanings at this very elementary level: they have more than enough chance in the editing to bring out the contradictions of the raw givens they accumulate. A last example where H & S show themselves and explain themselves: their interventions as narrators or the use (indicated as such) of objects, documents, photos, etc., that they use to introduce the film or that are supplied by chance during the interviews.

But above all their art resides in the editing, an editing that this time borrows more from Eisenstein: the montage of attractions. From the shock of two images is born a new idea, a new feeling. H & S are in marvelous possession of this associative montage (association of forms, of ideas or, most of the time, of words) that advances by complementarity and, most often, by contrast; they use it as much didactically as emotively. They therefore succeed in making essays of their films in which political, economic and social problems are represented and illuminated, without recourse to a heavy didacticism.

For editing is discourse and permits the diversion and subversion of others' discourse; and there is nothing weaker or more dangerous than words without substance, or political films that are only filmed words. It's because they've understood this well that H & S's political documentary achieves a certain kind of perfection, if not perfection itself, in the art of editing. H & S's films remind us of that great idea of Soviet filmmakers (an idea that Eisenstein saw in the rough with Griffith): editing must do more than make one understand the unfolding of events, it must teach us things that the images themselves do not show us and make in this way the qualitative leap from the narrative to the productive, or, to use a geographic metaphor to change our space without changing our place.

From such a problematic, which is not at all normative or dogmatic but on the contrary always redefined in terms of each subject, H and S could not escape because of the basic self-definition they repeat endlessly: they are filmmakers who apply historical and dialectical materialism to their work, as Vertov, Eisenstein and several others tried to do. To this effect one must remember that the G. D. R., since its creation, has shown an open attitude towards the political documentary. Already in the fifties, the G. D. R. welcomed Joris Ivens, to whom the documentary owes so much. Later, the G. D. R. produced its own documentarists of talent, from the compilationists, the Thorndikes, to H & S. What is more, to show its interest, it established a documentary film festival at Leipzig.

This then is the context in which the works of H and S were made. One can question the results, one can evaluate their impact on their audience (didactic or otherwise), one can question the political presuppositions that guide all their stages, from research to montage (with H & S, the documented point of view becomes both a political stand and a party line. Don't they often and unambiguously declare, "We are Communists," which we should probably understand to mean, "We are members of our country's party"?)--but one cannot deny the more than interesting contribition H & S have made to Marxist aesthetics and to the political documentary....

II

Heynowski and Scheumann's
The War of the Mummies, 1973-74: Working Notebook

... After each shooting day, we hold a meeting to go over the work done by the two crews. The exposed film and tapes are systematically numbered and attached to a daily report, recorded on tape, containing in addition to the technical specifications, remarks about the content, information and various notes. We have thus been able to use in the final text of the film some of the comments made on the spur of the moment. During the editing, in Berlin, these daily reports have served as reference points and have facilitated the job of the editor, Traute Wischnewski, when she had to familiarize herself with the material....

Our last daily report is dated April 13, 1973. The return was arranged for April 15. We had thus "finished shooting," with all of the unknown quantities that make up the art of documentary. In fiction films, as a general rule, you don't break the sets until you have screened all the rushes. But in documentary? Santiago, for example, presented until the elections an entirely different face than in the days following them. Thus it wouldn't have been possible to reshoot the street backdrops, not even the most simple ones.

... We had finished the shooting, and we were bringing back to Berlin at the same time numerous archival documents, photos, books, posters, etc.... During our stay in Chile, we did our best to assemble material that would give a picture at the same time rational and moving, of Chilean working class traditions. Considering that Chile had never been a center of interest before 1970, it seemed necessary to us to search for these documents of the country's history on the spot.

June 16-August 10: Finalization of the list of filmed sequences. The filmmakers and Traute Wischnewski evaluate together on the editing table the ideological and emotive value of the material, including the archival scenes. The screened rushes are numbered.

The sorting done at the same time as the list of sequences is a decisive stage of the work.

Sometimes a simple exclamation can give rise to a whole sequence. When for example Ernesto Miller, this fanatic member of the [right-wing party] Patria y Libertad, shouts "Chile!" in the mike at the same moment as the camera brutally confronts his image, it is clear that this shout translates the bitterness of the class struggle. At this point, the image and sound together give an impression that no other medium can transmit.

After many years of common experiences, we think that this way of working is rational and creative. We examine together the basic material, from which something new will be born. Examining the material with someone who has not been on location offers still another advantage. For everything that impressed the filmmakers on location does not automatically have the same effect at the screening of the rushes. Documentarists, camera operators and sound-people are always living inside of the situation they film. Given their preliminary knowledge and the commitment made on the spot, one can imagine that they "load" a certain scene with a heavier weight than would people who did not participate in the shoot and thus did not live the scene themselves, despite their knowledge of the outcome. The judgment of the latter is important for it is identical to the spectator's.

The opposite is just as true. A scene that is apparently less important for the crew can provoke an unexpected enthusiasm when the rushes are screened. Everyone knows that the camera eye is different from the human eye. It already bears a judgment when it enlarges or contracts the field of vision, something the human eye does not know how to do.

Consequently the screening of the rushes is always a rediscovery of the subject: disappointments and surprises succeed each other. But this does not mean a fetishism of the image. There are more than images in the film, there is also the sound: text, original voices, sounds, music. It's only the combination of all these elements that will produce the overall effect....

During the "Monday meetings" in the studio, at the same time as we select sequences, we get ready to draft the texts for the editing and the scenario, and we decide on the length of the subject. After several days, we have realized that the Chile theme, given the method of analysis we practiced on location, would not be exhausted in a single film. Our intention is to create a cycle on Chile, a cycle in which each film will dwell on a precise and limited topic. That will allow us in any case to stagger the release dates.

We decide to continue to work on Chile in 1974.

We have divided into four the bulk of the material brought back, which will constitute the cycle on Chile:

First part: "La Esperanza" (Hope), centered on the Unidad Popular's electoral victory of March 4, 1973.

Second Part: Vista Hermosa" (Beautiful View). The estate "Vista Hermosa" of the leader of Chilean rural landholders, Benjamin Matte, has been appropriated to be run as a cooperative. A story of the class struggle in the countryside.

Third Part: Los Caserolles (The Cooking Pots). The struggle for an increase in the bread ration, for the contents of the kettle. Copper, "Chile's wages," Unidad Popular against the monopolies.

Fourth Part: "Patria y Libertad." A study of the Chilean fascists, seen by themselves and through their program. The ideas of homeland and of freedom monopolized by the fascists, must be restored to the Chilean people by means of a panorama of the country's revolutionary traditions.

While we are working on this, news reaching us from Chile becomes more and more alarming. The forces of reaction are preparing to put the Unidad Popular to a new test.

June 29: Towards four o'clock of the afternoon, first news of an attempted military putsch.

June 30: A crew leaves for Santiago.

July 31: The crew returns.

August 1 to August 13: Detailed examination of the rushes of the second stay in Chile.

August 27: A new crew leaves for Santiago, for news out of Chile causes fears of a major move by the right. . . .

September 12: We stay listening without break to the latest news--it is now certain that President Allende has been assassinated and we are trying to see clearly what the continuation of the work will be. Results: immediate transformation of the scenario of the first part, all the while continuing to reflect on the whole cycle.

At the same time, the idea comes to us of going to interview for the second time the representatives of reaction, the "temporary winners," that we had already filmed between February and April 1973. This is a unique opportunity. We will be able to produce a document on the dealings of the counter-revolution before and after the coup d'état. . . . We will use the "relationship of trust" established during the spring with the reactionaries, not only in order to extract admissions from them after the putsch, but also to investigate the stand taken by these people with regard to the political reality of the junta.

The fascists are still sealing Chile off from the outside world. We still haven't any contact with our crew. But from today on one thing is certain: if we are to use this once-in-a-lifetime chance, we must return to Chile, but this time with a precise shooting plan, taking up in this autumn of 1973 the framework established the previous spring.

September 13: Someone says at the meeting of the cell of the United Socialist Party of Germany that "the Chilean editing table is from now on located in our studio." It is clear to everyone that the fascist junta is getting ready to come down hard on our battle comrades of the Chilean cinema. It is possible that we are the last to have possession of certain materials on Chilean history.

During a meeting of all the collaborators together, the problems of the revision of the first part of the cycle are brought up, and we talk about it.

September 27: The crew gets back from Santiago.

October 22: A new departure for Santiago We

will try to fulfil the idea we had on September 12: taking up in the new situation created by the putsch the themes that we had established in our images last spring.

We hope to succeed in this important mission with the help of an old acquaintance: Federico Willoughby, once a publicity agent for Ford, whom we have got to know better since February 1973 since he was the electoral manager for the retired colonel Alberto Labbé. After November 11, he is named the junta's press representative. It ought to be possible, with him as a go-between, to find our "old friends" again.

This new undertaking of the scouting of the terrain has been prepared in great detail. The declarations of the representatives of reaction, gathered in the spring, are once again studied, in order to be able to develop a play of questions that would permit the most accurate reflection of these characters in case we meet them again.

We are preparing questions for the representatives of the West German economic interests about the junta: Is the new Chile a good investment?

Otherwise, the crew must demonstrate the extension beyond September 11 of characteristic situations that we had filmed in the spring; there were, for example, queues in front of the stores: today, what can you buy? for what price? who can buy? in what quantities?

November 5: Presentation of the working copy of La Democracia (121 minutes) to a group of friends and comrades, who at one moment or another have been connected with our studio's productions. The discussion that follows is a decisive test for the criticism of the form and content of our material.

It comes out of the discussion of November 5, 1973 that we must make a film contrasting the historic program of the Unidad Popular to the "criminal" activity of the Chilean oligarchy and of international monopoly capital. If we succeed in mastering this essential theme from a socialist point of view, if it is then possible to deploy concrete and tangible proof, this film will be able to contribute to the formation of as broad as possible an alliance against the fascist junta.

We ask ourselves whether we can still keep the cycle

conception in the face of this new stage of the Chilean struggle. In response, we drop La Democracia and the idea of a cycle. At some point, there will surely be long extracts of La Democracia that will be used for other films. But this is not the only reason for the relevance of the work on La Democracia. Without this film and the debates it provoked, we would have trouble freeing ourselves from the emotions stored up within us. After November 5, it has been possible to quickly separate ourselves not only from La Democracia but also from all the concerns arising from the examination and the criticism of the Chilean arena.

To conclude, we must remark that without La Democracia there would not have been The War of the Mummies. The "unhappy" experience is very instructive not only for knowledge but also for art. La Democracia allowed us to measure the justice of our scope for War of the Mummies.

November 20: Our camera crew returns from Santiago. A first oral review makes one thing certain: our reflections of September 12 were right. For example, the president of the Chilean management association has expressed his frank satisfaction about the putsch. He has invited international monopoly capital to come to Chile. A deputy of the West German Bundestag finds that Chile "is regaining the path of solvency." We also have at our disposal sequences on the island concentration camp of Dawson, sequences that the junta's censors have meanwhile withdrawn from circulation.

We have also in our possession images of the Santiago stadium, images that the censors have forbidden for television broadcasting. Also photos of the assassinated president coming from the secret archives of the junta.

November 9 to February 1, 1974: elaboration of the new film.

Chapter 22

NOTES AND QUESTIONS ON POLITICAL CINEMA: FROM HOUR OF THE FURNACES TO ICI ET AILLEURS

Steve Neale

Through a reflection on the contexts of the production and reception of two very different committed documentaries, Steve Neale draws upon contemporary theoretical terms of reference to challenge the inherited conception of what is "political" as regards the cinema, and, not incidentally, the inherited dividing line between documentary and fiction.

This article seeks to raise and discuss one or two issues that center, firstly, around the term "political" when used in describing films and filmmaking, and secondly, around the term "cinema" itself. Uniting the two sets of issues will be questions to do with defining and understanding what we mean by "audience," "institution" and "address." During the course of the discussion I shall refer principally to two--very different--films, La Hora de los Hornos (The Hour of the Furnaces), a documentary on the history and politics of Argentina, made in Argentina itself in the late sixties by Fernando Solanas, and Ici et ailleurs (Here and Elsewhere), a film made about Palestine and Palestinian revolution, partly in Palestine itself and partly in France, by Jean-Luc Godard and Anne-Marie Miéville. Although neither will be treated as in any sense "typical" or "exemplary," the differences between them are such as to allow a series of important distinctions, comparisons and contrasts to be made.

All films are composed (consciously and unconsciously) of a series of discourses, each governed by a set of codes and conventions, each entering into a process of combination and mutual modification during the course of the film itself, and each marked and classified by the social spheres and social institutions from which they emanate or within which they generally circulate. A "political" film, conventionally understood, is a film which mobilizes during the course of its composition a discourse or set of discourses marked, classified and understood as "political" by society at large. This applies--or can apply--equally to mainstream Hollywood films like All the President's Men and The Parallax View, to European features like The Mattei Affair or 1900, as well as to films like Harlan County, USA, The Hour of the Furnaces, Ireland Behind the Wire, Peace and Plenty and The Wobblies. A specific set of features tends to link these discourses together, these features thus giving them their conventional social status as political discourses, enabling in turn a classification of the films themselves. They include. above all the representation either of established groups and institutions, whose own discourses articulate their primary aim as the control of government and the apparatuses of the state, and/or the representation of government and the apparatuses of the state themselves. It is this common set of features that in certain contexts--a film season, for example--allows films as diverse in origin, form and circulation as All the President's Men, Salvatore Giuliano, Ireland Behind the Wire, and even Triumph of the Will to be assembled together under a single generic heading like "Political Cinema" without the differences between them necessarily rendering such an assembly totally incoherent. This in itself raises issues about the ways in which cinematic products are categorized (something to which I shall turn in a moment), but it is worth just noting here the extent to which the general social category of politics, understood largely in the terms outlined above, has been rendered problematic in the West in recent years.

Under the impact variously of the events of 1968 in Europe, of Maoism and the Cultural Revolution in China, of the Women's Movement, of the Gay Liberation movement and of the struggles by ethnic groups and organizations in a number of countries, a series of questions has been raised as to the very definition of politics: as to the spaces political activity occupy in our lives, as to conventional distinctions between "the personal" and "the political," as to the relationships between economic and ideological struggles, as to the conventional distinctions between "reform" and "revolution," as to the traditional form of organization of "political activity" within the context of the party, and so on. Rather than uniting a specific and limited set of activities under the umbrella of conventional political organization, politics now in the West is coming more and more to be understood as involving an extremely wide and heterogeneous set of discourses, practices and struggles, so wide, heterogeneous and specific as to be impossible at present either to grasp within the terms provided by a single theoretical discourse (Marxist or otherwise) or to organize within the space provided by a single institution--even, indeed, to unify conceptually within a term like "politics" itself. This development has, in turn, shattered the previous unity of the field of discourses upon which political films have drawn hitherto, involved the representation of different spheres of social activity and different social institutions (no longer are the apparatuses of the armed forces, the judiciary and the police privileged a priori in the representation of the state and state power), and has involved also the problematization of the mechanisms of discourse and representation themselves--mechanisms hitherto largely taken for granted. It is no accident, therefore, that it is much less easy now to categorize a whole range of contemporary films (Fortini-Cani, From the Cloud to the Resistance, In the Forest, The Nightcleaners, Because I Am King, Empire of the Senses, Le Gai savoir, Ici et ailleurs and so on) as political in any conventional sense. Indeed these films take as their task the questioning of that form of categorization. It is no accident either that a number of films within this range have been made by and/or concern women and feminism: Riddles of the Sphinx, Daughter Rite, Thriller, Taking a Part, Often During the Day, Journeys from Berlin, Jeanne Dielmann, Freud's Dora, Je Tu Il Elle, News from Home, Amy!, The Song of the Shirt--I shall return to this point later too.

Although films are primarily categorized as political on the basis of the discourses they involve, there is an important sense too in which they are further categorized and differentiated, in which they are further marked as political, on the basis of the organization of their production, distribution and exhibition. It is here, for example, that distinctions are made as to whether a film constitutes political propaganda as such or whether it is simply a political film in the sense that its plot and subject matter involve the discourses of politics to a greater or lesser extent. A film like The Parallax View differs from a film like The Hour of the Furnaces not least in that the former originates and circulates within the apparatuses of mainstream cinema, within the space of the cinematic institution. It involves a production company, distribution within the cinema market, and exhibition in conventional cinemas. Hour of the Furnaces, by contrast, was produced by a group of politically militant intellectuals in collaboration with other militants, workers, and peasants. In Argentina itself, it was distributed through political, rather than cinematic, channels and was shown to small groups of militants, workers and peasants in generally clandestine circumstances. A number of very important points, distinctions, implications and consequences need at this point to be drawn out and elaborated from this initial difference.

One point worth making initially is that different modes of production and circulation have fundamental implications for the ways in which political issues can be dealt with and discussed, for the ways in which the relationships between sound and image can organize that discussion, and for the nature and composition of the audience to whom that discussion is addressed. As regards production--and the relationships between production and distribution that obtain in mainstream commercial cinema--it is worth quoting here Ben Brewster's comments on those cycles of Hollywood films dealing on the one hand with the campus revolts that occurred in America in the late sixties and early seventies, and on the other, with Watergate and post-Watergate issues and themes:

> The commercial cinema speculates on topicality, but in so doing it faces a characteristic set of difficulties. First of all, there is a very long time between the inception of a production project and the final release of the finished film. Secondly, the predominant aim of production in the USA has always been to produce films which have the widest possible market at home and abroad.... Hence a topical theme may have ceased to be topical by the time a film attempting to exploit it appears, and there is a potential audience which may have no interest in that topical theme. The original project of All the President's Men was simply to exploit the topicality of the Watergate theme, and to use completely anonymous look-alikes for the central parts, increasing the authenticity and hence the topical appeal. But it was impossible to get the

> film made on those terms. The central parts had to be allotted to major stars, since the distributors (whose guarantees were required to raise the initial capital) were not to know whether Watergate was not going to be anathema to much of the American public in six months time or whether anybody in Europe was in the slightest bit interested in it, whereas they knew very well that they would all be interested in Robert Redford and Warren Beatty [sic]. Thus they could gamble on the topicality while covering themselves by insisting on another, more general interest. Now in the campus revolt genre this process had specific political effects. An all-out concentration on the topicality of the theme was avoided by what was called "human interest." The campus revolt incident in the films was usually inserted into a plot in which an apolitical student goes up to university and gets involved in militant activity because of sexual difficulties; he then resolves his personal problems, drops out of militant activity and thereby avoids being caught in its defeat. So the campus revolt is there, but there is the more human story alongside it. It is obvious in this case that, without there necessarily being any direct political censorship or control of the subject matter, the pressures of the distribution problem, precisely the problem mentioned by Brecht of the separation of the moment of production of the film from the moment of its consumption, have imposed a plot strategy which completely diffuses any politically radical potential in the subject matter of the film made. [1]

The organization of the relations between production, distribution and exhibition, each articulated ultimately in terms of the commodity form, thus of itself tends to preclude a political address to politically topical issues. This is reinforced, as Colin MacCabe has pointed out, by the manner in which this organization determines also the articulation of such issues within the chain of images and sounds that constitutes the film itself and the constitution of the audience and its interests:

> Films are financed by the raising of money against future distribution receipts. The fact that the film is addressed to an audience which

> it cannot know except insofar as it goes to the cinema entails that it is only as <u>viewer</u> that the audience can be addressed. Immediate consequences for production follow from this fact. The spectator has no particular interest in going to see any particular film because it has not been made for him or her and it is this fact that stimulates repetition--I will go and see again what I have already seen--a repetition that takes two major forms: genres and stars. [2]

Hence Ben Brewster's point about <u>All the President's Men</u>. Hence, too, the fact that politics tends to enter mainstream cinema as genre, as, precisely, the political thriller. Overall then:

> the fact that the production of films is financed through specific forms of national and international distribution, the fact that the audience has no existence for the makers of the film except as an audience which goes to the cinema and pays money and thus has no identity except a commercial one, these features of what might be called the institution of cinema are a major determinant of the organization of sounds and images in particular films. Crucially this requires a fixed relation of dependence between soundtrack and image whether priority is given to the image, as in fiction films (we see the truth and the soundtrack must come into line with it), or to the soundtrack, as in documentary (we are told the truth and the image merely confirms). In both cases what is presupposed is the possibility of direct address to the audience, but as the audience is not addressed either as individuals or as members of particular collectivities (family, work, school) they find their place to see and hear only as members of a cinema audience. [3]

Hence, in a very real sense, the difficulty, if not the impossibility, of a <u>political</u> address through the apparatus of conventional, commercial cinema. Such an address is only possible if the audience is constituted on the basis, not of cinema, but of politics itself. It is only possible if the identity of the audience is formed on a basis other than that of having simply paid the price of admission to a cinema auditorium.

This is the importance of the alternative circuits and practices of production, distribution and exhibition constituted around films like The Hour of the Furnaces. Solanas' own comments on this illustrate some of these alternative possibilities and the thinking that lies behind them:

> Guerrilla cinema still doesn't have enough experience to set down standards in this area; what experience there is has shown, above all, the ability to make use of the concrete situation in each country. But regardless of what these situations may be, the preparation of a film cannot be undertaken without a parallel study of its future audience and, consequently, a plan to recover the financial investment. Here, once again, the need arises of closer ties between the political and artistic vanguards, since this also serves for the joint study of forms of production, exhibition and continuity.
>
> A guerrilla film can be aimed only at the distribution mechanisms provided by the revolutionary organizations, including those invented or discovered by the filmmaker himself (sic). Production, distribution, and economic possibilities for survival must form part of a single strategy.[4]

Clearly, for someone like Solanas in a country like Argentina, there is no option other than to seek to develop alternatives. But even if there were alternatives, even if it would have been possible for him to have made a feature film with potential commercial distribution and exhibition, it is clear that any degree of political effectiveness, any potential political use of the film by the audiences who saw it, would only be possible if those audiences, that seeing, were themselves constituted on a political basis, or if the presentation of the film were such as to transform both the conditions of viewing and the status of the film itself. Hence Solanas' insistence both on the importance of the nature of the audience and the viewing event ('Each showing for militants, middle-level cadres, activists, workers and university students became--without our having set ourselves this aim beforehand--a kind of enlarged cell meeting of which the films were a part but not the most important factor.'[5]), and on the importance of subsequent discussion and debate ('... we realised that the distribution of that kind of film had little meaning if it was not complemented by the participation of the comrades, if a debate was not opened on the themes suggested by the films'6). These points are particularly important when discussing the work of someone like Godard, who because of his previous work within the framework of the conventional film industry clearly in part at least had the kind of choice that Solanas did not have in that he could have gone on making films for conventional commercial distribution and exhibition. He has been accused of preaching to the converted, of making films for tiny political groupings, thus turning his back on the possibility of addressing political themes to a large (if not mass) audience. But had he made that choice then the political nature and work of such films would clearly have been different--limited and transformed by the context of their circulation and of the mode in which they were (or could have been) viewed. Politics, political effectiveness, is by no means simply a question of numbers. It is also--above all--a question of social relations and practices:

> A film about politics must enjoy a different relation with its audience from that of commercial cinema; it must be a participant in the reality that it attempts to articulate rather than presenting itself as an observer that can show us the truth of any situation. Insofar as politics is a complex set of struggles ranging from the economic to the ideological, it is impossible simply to represent it to people who, in that very relation, find themselves placed outside those struggles; rather, it must address specific audiences in specific situations. [7]

If the original context for Solanas' film clearly differed from the context provided by conventional, commercial cinema and its apparatuses, it is also the case that the different relationship between audience and film that that context provided was one which Solanas sought to inscribe within the text of the film itself, transforming it into what he has termed a "film act":

> We realised that we had at hand three very valuable factors:
>
> 1. The participant comrade, the man-actor-accomplice who responded to the summons;
> 2. The free space where that man expressed his concerns and ideas, became politicized and started to free himself; and

> 3. The film, important only as a detonator or pretext.
>
> We concluded from these data that a film could be much more effective if it were fully aware of these factors and took on the task of subordinating its own form, structure and language, and propositions to that act and to those actors.... In this way the idea began to grow of structuring what we decided to call the film act, the film action, one of the forms which we believe assumes great importance in affirming the line of a third cinema. A cinema whose first experiment is to be found, perhaps on a rather shaky level, in the second and third parts of La Hora de los Hornos ("Acto para la liberacion"; above all, starting with "La resistencia" and "Violencia y liberacion").
>
> "Comrades (we said at the start of "Acta para la liberacion"), this is not just a film showing, nor is it a show; rather, it is, above all, A MEETING--an act of anti-imperialist unity. The film is the pretext for dialogue, for the seeking and finding of wills. It is a report that we place before you for your consideration, to be debated after the show."[8]

It is significant here, however, that the example Solanas and Getino chose to give of the inscription of the characteristics of the "cinema act" into the text of the film itself consists of one of its intertitles. The question that follows is whether these titles interact with other images in the film in a way which significantly differs from the organization of image, sound and title in other documentaries. I'm not by any means sure that this is true. Although certainly the film, in the kind of exhibition context it was given, would function to provoke important political debate, it is by no means the case that that debate follows from the structure and the textual conventions that govern the film itself. And insofar as this is the case, then the adoption of the documentary form, the role allotted that form by Solanas and Getino in their article, and, just as significantly, the role allotted the spectator by the film, its intertitles and the article, again, render the claims made for the film somewhat more problematic.

As Colin MacCabe points out in one of the quotations

above, the documentary and its conventions (the relations between sound and image they involve) are central to the cinematic institution The documentary, in and of itself, is no guarantee of radical authenticity. Yet that, precisely, is what is claimed for it, not only by Getino and Solanas, but by other political filmmakers as well. The convention is that documentary deals with truth, reality and the facts. The rest is fiction. But it is this very division, and the convention that sustains it, that is central to the ways in which cinema habitually differentiates its products. And what is thereby elided, unquestioned, is any notion of the ways in which any combination of images and sounds constructs, rather than reflects, a meaning and a truth. Getino and Solanas place documentary as the radical opposite of Hollywood's fantasies and fictions, yet in so doing they are operating within (rather than against) the terms that cinema itself provides for an understanding of its products, its genres, its conventional discursive regimes:

> Imperialism and capitalism, whether in the consumer society or in the neocolonialized country, veil everything behind a screen of images and appearances. The image of reality is more important than the reality itself.[9]
>
> The cinema of the revolution is at the same time one of destruction and construction: destruction of the image that neocolonialism has created of itself and of us, construction of a throbbing, living reality which recaptures truth in any of its expressions.[10]
>
> In a world where the unreal rules, artistic expression is shoved along the channels of fantasy, fiction, language in code, sign language and messages whispered between the lines. Art is cut off from the concrete facts.[11]
>
> The cinema known as documentary, with all the vastness that the concept has today, from educational films to the reconstruction of a fact or a historical event, is perhaps the main basis of revolutionary filmmaking.[12]

As we watch the film itself, however, it will be apparent that its own "truth" is very much a question of its "language." The footage of the Peron era in itself means nothing (or rather, it is capable of meaning any number of things in any number of discursive contexts). It is only when inserted into this film, and accompanied by a verbal discourse that locates and places its meaning, that it becomes an image of a truth that the film wishes to articulate. In truly conventional fashion, the images then function merely to legitimate what the commentary has to say. Reality is never transparent--even to a camera. It is only ever available in terms of various, different and specific forms of explanation. And this is constantly, symptomatically, demonstrated in a film which seeks perpetually to order its diverse and heterogeneous visual material in terms of commentaries and intertitles which, precisely, explain, and from a specific, and specifically contentious position. That position is unchallenged, unquestioned, within the film itself. Debate and discussion can thus only be a function of the viewing situation and the nature of audience itself. With regard to the role of that audience, its place inside and outside the film, the stated claims and aims of Getino and Solanas (and of the film's own titles) can at times be confusing too.

The confusion surrounds the use of the term "spectator." The film quotes Franz Fanon: "Every spectator is a coward or a traitor." The point is then reiterated in a lengthy intertitle sequence at the beginning of Part Two:

> Comrades ... this is not just the projection of a film.... It is not just a show. It is above all an act. An act for Argentinian and Latin American Liberation ... an act of anti-imperialist unity. There is room here only for those who can identify with this struggle. This is not just a show for spectators....

There is an elision here between a use of the term "spectator" as referring to someone in the act of watching a film, and a use of the term "spectator" as referring to someone who is content merely to observe, rather than to participate in, political activity and struggle. And insofar as this is the case, there is no allowance made for the fact that simply watching the film in Argentina under the conditions of exhibition that pertained there is in itself a political act. And there is no conceptual space left for a consideration of the mode of spectatorship inscribed in the structure of the film itself.

It is precisely this kind of consideration, in alliance

with a challenging of the conventions of political documentary, that mark Godard and Miéville's Ici et ailleurs. The film involved conventional documentary footage shot in Palestine in 1970, but then uses it to consider what a film on Palestine might be for filmmakers (and audiences) located in another context, in Europe. There is a crucial distance thus built into the film from the start, one which is clearly just not possible in the same kind of way for a film like Hour of the Furnaces, made in Argentina for Argentinians. But other distances, distances from documentary, from the conventions of the "political" film, were--and are--possible. Hence, in contrast to Hour of the Furnaces, there is a questioning of the role of sound and commentary in their relations with the image, a division of the narrating instance into a set of distinct voices, each articulating different concerns, different questions, different positions. The political relationship inherent in the position of the spectator vis-à-vis the film is thus, also, a different one.

If that relationship, that position is a question of politics, then the issue as to how we identify politics in a film, as to how we recognize and classify films as political or otherwise is an open one--much more open, at any rate, than traditional and conventional criteria would allow. This is precisely the work of those films referred to earlier in this article, their appearance coinciding with a general questioning as to the constitution of politics and the political in every sphere of life and society. There can be no question of legislating theoretically the conditions necessary for considering a film either political, radical or progressive. That would be simply to replace one set of criteria for another. This is a matter for local, conjunctural debate. It is worth insisting, however, that for us, here, in the West, in societies dominated by film, television, and the modes of spectatorship they involve, the issue of politics and social change are bound up with the kinds of question a film like Ici et ailleurs attempts to articulate and to pose. (1981)

Notes

1 Ben Brewster, "The Fundamental Reproach (Brecht)," Cine-Tracts, vol. 1, no. 2, Summer 1977, pp. 49-50.

2 Colin MacCabe, Godard: Images, Sounds, Politics. Macmillan/BFI, 1980, p. 41.

3 Ibid. p. 18.

4 Octavio Getino and Fernando Solanas, "Towards a Third Cinema," Afterimage, no. 3, Summer 1971, p. 30.

5 Ibid. p. 32.

6 Ibid. p. 32.

7 MacCabe, op. cit., pp. 53-54.

8 Octavio Getino and Fernando Solanas, op. cit., pp. 33-34.

9 Ibid. p. 23.

10 Ibid. p. 25.

11 Ibid. p. 25.

12 Ibid. p. 26.

Chapter 23

THE GUERRILLA FILM, UNDERGROUND AND IN EXILE: A CRITIQUE AND A CASE STUDY OF WAVES OF REVOLUTION

Anand Patwardhan

The following account of the making of Waves of Revolution, one of the more interesting examples of Indian oppositional filmmaking in the seventies, has been excerpted with minor editorial adjustments from the filmmaker/author's much longer thesis of the same title, which provides a more thorough theoretical and historical context for the concept of "guerrilla cinema" than is possible in this space. Now, almost a decade after the film was begun, Patwardhan writes from Bombay that the film is rarely shown in India "as it is too dated and the movement it describes dead (having committed suicide by allowing opportunistic elements to take over)." Patwardhan's later films (Prisoners of Conscience, a 1977 documentary "linking the existence of political prisoners in India with the continuing poverty and injustice prevalent in the social system at large"; and his prize-winning A Time to Rise, co-directed with Jim Monro, a 1980 documentary on the struggle of East Indian farmworkers in British Columbia to organize a union) are still very much in circulation, both in alternative networks in the West and in oppositional and alternative film circles in India, where, Patwardhan notes, "the new Mrs. Gandhi regime has become more selective and sophisticated in its repression," and screenings are no longer apparently as "fraught with danger" as those described in this 1981 text. Whatever the case, Patwardhan provides a thrilling first-person chronology of the making of this apprenticeship work, a "guerrilla" film that intervened effectively in a context that has since changed. The author's current film-in-progress on "slums and squatters in Bombay is in financial trouble (as usual) but inching along."

The Emergence of Guerrilla Cinema

For militant filmmakers in the Third World, where resistance to oppression is an immediate concrete imperative, formal preoccupations necessarily become secondary. Revolutionary form becomes a by-product of revolutionary content and not the other way around.

Changes in the economic base of society precedes change in the superstructure; being determines consciousness, so in the Third World actual political struggles and victories have preceded and stirred the emergence of a radical cultural movement. In the post-Second World War period, the Chinese revolution, the decolonization of Africa and Asia (however illusory and incomplete), the Cuban revolution, the success of the Vietnamese in defending themselves against the vastly superior U.S. war machine--have been the cornerstones on which the culture of the left has built itself.

Where revolutionary movements were successful, as in China and in Cuba, the cinema to which they gave birth tried consciously to fight the myths of the bourgeois ideology that had just been overthrown. But with several exceptions from Cuba, what was generally achieved was, once again, the transvaluation of values. By and large, form was not subjected to great scrutiny or innovation and content was always perfectly synonymous with what the new State had ordained.

In those parts of the world where revolutions were not successful, and where they still continue to fight precarious underground wars against a repressive enemy, whether in the jungles of El Salvador, the parched hills of Eritrea or the bloody streets of Soweto, the cinema that has emerged clearly bears the marks of this struggle. It is the urgent cinema of the battlefield; a guerrilla cinema.

Along with the emergence of this cinema in many parts of the Third World, there have also emerged theoretical position papers which both justify and demarcate this emergence. Julio Garcia Espinosa's For an Imperfect Cinema and Fernando Solanas and Octavio Getino's Towards a Third Cinema are perhaps the clearest written pronouncements of this genre. [1]

Of the two, Espinosa, who writes and films from the relative safety of an already successful revolution, is concerned with delineating the role of the filmmaker away from the elitist conception of the "artist" and towards the revolutionary one of "film-worker." He projects into the revolutionary future a time when not only will filmmakers be workers but workers will be filmmakers. It is towards this goal that his practice is directed.

For the militant filmmaker working under pre-revolutionary, repressive and even fascist conditions, it is the writing and film practice of Solanas and Getino that provides the best example of cinema that has declared itself as a weapon of the revolution. Here cinema which began as a toy, which was soon proclaimed and protected as Art, which Vertov developed into an eye and Grierson used as a pulpit, becomes in the hands of the revolutionary, a gun. Its task is to keep old wounds from healing and being forgotten and to open new ones; to isolate the enemy and to unite the forces of change; to expose the injustice of the system, but also to point out its vulnerability in the face of the united strength of the masses--this is the recurrent theme of the guerrilla cinema.

The guerrilla cinema uses hand-held cameras; captures grainy, imperfect, jerky, on-the-run, scratched images; interviews persons in silhouette who do not wish to be identified, and so on, ad infinitum, using a whatever-is-necessary approach to what was hitherto a carefully upholstered, meticulously protected medium. And although only a handful of the guerrilla films break through into the outside world their influence can be dramatic.

The recognition that the world is divided into classes whose interests are opposed to each other results in a new approach to filmmaking. The filmmaker is forced to take sides. On one side are comrades and fellow workers, and on the other, the enemy. Especially in documentary cinema, this polarization of subjects is extremely acute and the strategies developed are very different from those developed by so called "objective" or "sociological" filmmakers.

With dominant ideology disseminated at all levels of society, it becomes the urgent task of the guerrilla filmmaker to expose it. Where the poor have been dehumanized the task is to hold up a mirror that reflects them once more as human beings possessing strengths and rights as other human beings. Where the ruling class has usurped superior attributes and privileges, the task is to strip off their mask of superiority and expose their privileges as ill-gotten.

With this purpose in mind the strategies developed by the filmmaker begin to resemble those of a soldier in a guerrilla war. The purpose behind the film is revealed to one side and hidden from the other. False identities, disguises, hidden cameras and tape recorders, surprise invasions of the film crew onto enemy property followed by strategic retreats, hiding the film once it has been shot, transporting it to safe processing labs--all these are part of the process of this form of filmmaking. After the film is completed, reintroducing it into enemy territory wherever possible is an integral component of the guerrilla film praxis. The smuggling of the film outside this territory in order to win sympathy for the revolutionary cause from without becomes a further component. In many countries where conditions are extremely repressive this is the only option left, giving rise to the genre of the guerrilla cinema in exile.

The initiating moment of the guerrilla cinema is the need to raise consciousness towards revolutionary change. A theme is chosen that will be the vehicle. It may be an incident that occurred in the past which throws light on the present, like the miners' revolt in Jorge Sanjines' The Courage of the People (Bolivia, 1971). It may be a situation still existing which needs exposing, like the anonymous documentary depicting the recent massacre of demonstrators in South Korea (Massacre at Kwangju, 1980). Or it may be a symbolic representation of reality as it is or as it ought to be, like the Uruguayan animation film In the Jungle There Is Lots to Do (1972).

Once the theme has been chosen, it is discussed. A chain reaction of discussions takes place and the original idea is repeatedly modified. Every person who comes into contact with the idea, acts upon it and is acted upon by it to one extent or the other.

The consciousness process has already begun. A rough script begins to be formed. A crew comes together. The making of guerrilla cinema is a political act and every production meeting is a political meeting. The meetings are secret or open depending on the circumstances prevailing at the time.

The number of people involved increases at each succeeding stage. From the person who types the script to the one who helps carry the equipment, all share a degree of involvement in the real-life drama they have chosen to participate in. In extremely repressive conditions, every person involved, even at the very periphery of the film-making process, takes a risk, and this conscious act of risk-taking transforms such a person into an activist.

The risk-taking does not end with the production of the film but continues, sometimes in much more acute form into the distribution process, where at times every screening of the film is a militant political act fraught with dangerous consequences if the screening is discovered by the authorities.

Guerrilla Cinema and Context

Revolutionary films turn into reformist ones and reformist films into revolutionary ones depending on the circumstances in which they are made and shown on the one hand, and on the degree to which the system under attack is capable of absorbing its own critique, on the other. A system confident of its own survival tends to allow criticism to flourish, attempting at least in part to co-opt this criticism for its own purposes. Hence we see in the U.S. potentially revolutionary films such as Emile de Antonio's Underground (1975) or The Murder of Fred Hampton (1970) being robbed of their sting and served up as reminders of the liberalism of the American system.

In another context, in the fascistic period of Emergency rule in India, an essentially reformist film such as my Waves of Revolution, dealing with a non-violent, democratic rights movements, is banned and acquires revolutionary meaning, however modest.

In post-independence India, a thriving escapist commercial feature film industry controls theatrical distribution but the documentary film has remained the exclusive domain of the State, which controls both the Films Division (similar to but with far less autonomy than the National Film Board of Canada) and TV. Another source of production and distribution of documentaries dealing with India has been the foreign market. Made with foreign or with Indian crews, these films have been meant exclusively for audiences outside India and their subject matter is generally geared to the dissemination of exotica. Occasionally a film which came too close for comfort in depicting the oppressive Indian reality, such as Louis Malle's Phantom India (1968), has enraged Indian officials. In this particular case they went to the extent of temporarily banning BBC crews from operating in India as punishment for the showing of Malle's film on British TV.

With 16mm lacking the widespread infrastructure of readily available raw stock, laboratories, sound facilities, editing tables and, worst of all, projectors, the independent production and distribution of low-budget 16mm documentary films has been virtually non-existent. The existence of the Film Censor Board has presented a further obstacle to those who wish to make films opposed to the ruling elite.

It is in this context that guerrilla films that have been made and shown in India must be viewed and analyzed; in particular, as a case study for the purpose of this anthology, my own Waves of Revolution (1975) will be examined.

The Film Concept: October 1974

Waves of Revolution was not conceived as a film until after the filmmaking process had already begun. Initially footage was shot more as a record of police violence against non-violent demonstrators. The idea to make a more complete record of the movement came as a consequence.

In October 1974 I had gone to Patna, capital of Bihar State, as a volunteer in the Bihar movement, the student- and peasant-led mass movement that was eventually to become the pretext for the Gandhi government's imposition of Emergency rule.[2] When the November 4 rally was planned, police violence was widely apprehended. There was good reason for this fear. Already thirty people had lost their lives since the Movement began in March.

Patna had been turned into a fortress in preparation

for November 4. All trains and buses into the city were cancelled except for those carrying government personnel and supplies. The landing banks of the river Ganges were barricaded to stop people from reaching by boat. All streets suspected of being on the route of the proposed march were cordoned off. Midnight raids on various Movement headquarters had resulted in the arrest of several organizers. Random checks and interrogations took place in the streets and in homes, with students and youths attracting greater scrutiny.

The Movement, for its part, was also getting prepared. Support rallies attended by thousands were held in villages all over Bihar, but more concentratedly in a wide radius surrounding Patna. People made plans to reach the outskirts of the city by train and walk the rest of the way.

In these circumstances it was decided to recruit as many cameras and photographers as possible. One purpose was to keep a record, and it was also felt that the presence of cameras might inhibit the repression that would otherwise certainly be unleashed by the police. The camera was thus both a weapon of self-defense against the atrocities of the State and an eyewitness of the courage of the people who faced these atrocities.

Several still-cameras and photographers volunteered but a movie camera could not be found. A week before the rally, I went to New Delhi to obtain one. Knowing that it might never return in one piece, no one was willing to lend a 16mm camera but I was able to borrow a Super 8 and a regular 8 camera, as well as recruit a colleague, Rajeev, as a fellow cameraman. We shaved our beards, put on "respectable" clothes, got letters of authorization from a sympathetic news journal and made up false Press cards.

Super 8 film was being sold in the black market at exorbitant prices. We had enough money for only ten rolls--a total of 30 minutes. Nine rolls of regular 8 stock were also obtained. We acquired a cassette recorder and some cassettes. That was the extent of our "equipment." Armed with this we boarded the train for Patna. Twice there were inspections along the way and a few people were taken off the train, but we reached Patna safely.

In Patna we were put up as fellow squatters in a half-completed high-rise construction site. This was one of the headquarters of the Movement. Hundreds of volunteers had made this raw brick and girder structure a living dormitory. Meals were cooked and strategies discussed, as people from different parts of the country who had come to join and work in the Bihar Movement shared their past and present experiences as well as their future aspirations. It was from this group that an ever-changing production team emerged--an assistant cameraman, an interpreter, a sound recordist and so on--none of whom had ever worked on a film before.

We began by doing cassette interviews with people in the street--a rickshaw puller, a shopkeeper, an unemployed youth. Some were happy to speak up, others were shy or afraid, a few were opposed to us and refused. The poor quality of our sound equipment was most acutely felt when we attempted to do candid interviews by hiding the microphone in our clothing. The lack of sound clarity was particularly aggravating when we felt we had done a potentially important interview at great risk--for instance, when we secretly taped a conversation with a member of the Bihar Military Police who stated that he would not shoot a demonstrator even if he were ordered to, because his own family lived in the countryside and suffered while others in the government and in business lived off the fat of the land. He told us that many of his colleagues felt the same way, but warned us against members of the Central Reserve Police who, he said, were deliberately brought in from other parts of the country in order that they might obey their commanding officers without remorse or sympathy for the local people.

Partly due to our equipment and partly because of our lack of experience we continued for a long time to make bad recordings, which we ultimately could use very little. But the very process of interviewing people gave us a much better perspective than we would have got by talking to Movement activists alone.

We met students, teachers and middle-class youths who were enthusiastic supporters of the movement. We met bureaucrats vehemently opposed to the creation of chaos and anarchy. We met landlords and the urban rich who were too clever to speak their mind. We met poor workers, rickshaw pullers, hamals (weight loaders) and chaprasis (personal attendants) who had a supportive but wary attitude to the Movement. They had been promised many things before. Now, once again, they were being tantalized by the possibility of change. They would go along with it but they wouldn't hold their breath. "Our stomachs are empty, so we are ready to fight."

The process of doing interviews helped to clarify certain issues both for ourselves and for the leadership of the Movement itself, which was forced to go beyond the rhetoric reserved for mass consumption and analyze itself. We found that while most people respected the leader, Jayaprakash Narayan, almost blindly, they did not generally think beyond toppling the existing government, as not many in the Movement spoke in class terms.

Apart from interviews, we recorded songs popularized by the Movement and sung by activists. These songs, some composed on the spot, varied from marching songs to a haunting melody sung by a single voice that called out as we crossed a river, "O boatman, turn your boat towards the storm."

Once again our equipment failed to match our material and much of the power and clarity of the songs were lost in the malevolent hiss of our cassette recorder.

Filming the November 4 Rally

In retrospect the 4th of November marked the climactic moment of the Bihar Movement, although at the time it appeared to us as only the beginning of a wave that would progressively engulf the nation.

The original plan was to march through the main arteries of Patna city and assemble at the historic Gandhi Maidan grounds, the scene of many a protest against British Rule. As the day began, despite the halting of the transport system and despite police harassment and preventive arrests well over 100,000 people had reached Patna, on foot, by bus or in boats, and were making their way to the assembly point.

With two cameras, the 8mm and the Super 8, Rajeev and I divided up our territories. He took the 8mm and went ahead with one group of marchers. I took the Super 8 and managed to get standing room on an overcrowded jeep which carried J.P. at the head of a large contingent of marchers. The view from the jeep was excellent. In front, at the top of the street you could see a police barricade. Behind was the crowd chanting slogans. The police appeared overawed by the sheer numbers of people they faced. Their instructions at this time appeared to have been to delay the marchers and thin them out rather than to stop them altogether.

As barricade after barricade fell to only minor scuffles with the police, the crowd began to exult in its own power. Finally our jeep and the crowd with it broke through to the Gandhi Maidan. Here we waited for others to join us. From two other barricaded streets which also opened up onto the Maidan we could see big groups of marchers approaching.

I got off the jeep and began to film from right behind the police cordon, waiting for it to give way. The police with their riot gear began a light attack but it was to no avail; the crowd broke through and charged right past the camera. The police attack grew heavier and skulls cracked under their clubs. They fired tear gas shells and the air became acrid and cloudy. The camera rolled as a student picked up a smoking tear gas shell and hurled it back in the direction of the police.

People ran wildly in all directions, chased by police. I clambered back onto the jeep. We circled the Maidan once, moving toward where the largest group of demonstrators, a few thousand strong, were still assembled, and decided to go with them to our next destination--the residences of the State ministers. The plan was to surround their houses and force them to resign. We never reached the houses. The approach road was blocked by a large contingent of a C. R. P. unit fully armed with pads, shields, helmets, clubs and bayonetted rifles which were pointed at us. They had obviously been instructed not to let us through whatever the cost. The District Inspector General warned us on his loudspeaker not to approach.

At this point J. P. got out of the jeep and began to walk towards the C. R. P., feeling perhaps that his age and stature as a veteran freedom fighter would protect him. He was joined by a dozen marchers. Some yards behind, the rest of us followed. The police cordon opened up to let through J. P., and the marchers abreast of him, and then closed ranks again, before we could follow. Then the attack began. We saw clubs raining down and J. P. falling. The marchers, enraged, charged the police. I attempted to stay with them and film at the same time. We were beaten back. Shots rang out, and at the sound of them the crowd appeared to panic and run. Frantic gesturing at my Press card proved fruitless as a police club hit me in the legs. I ran, partly to save myself and partly to save the camera and film. It was hard to decide whether to turn around and try once more or to keep running. Two rolls of film were already lost, dropping out of my shoulder bag. One of them had been exposed. To leave now might mean to miss the most dramatic moments of the day. To stay would jeopardize the material already filmed.

Spotting a co-worker from our dormitory, I handed over all the exposed film for safekeeping and turned back.

By this time the action was over. Police had prevented the Gherao (surrounding) of the ministers' residences, but the moral cost was high. Many marchers had been seriously injured. The injury to J. P. was not serious as he had been protected by his comrades, one of whom broke his forearm warding off the clubs. News of this attack sent shock waves throughout the country and the ruling regime's credibility reached a new low point. Because it was clear that the State government was being propped up by the Centre, and the most vicious attacks had come from the C. R. P., the Centre increasingly became the target of the Bihar Movement, which now began to develop an all-India character.

That evening I met up with Rajeev and compared notes on what we had shot. His group had been effectively blocked by the police and never reached the main point of action. His footage consisted mainly of police arresting and carrying away protesters who were offering passive resistance, as well as a sequence of demonstrators being dispersed by tear gas.

We had recorded some of the demonstration on our cassettes. In the evening we recorded an All India Radio (AIR) news bulletin which reported that the demonstration had been a failure. Later, this broadcast, played over actual footage of the march, would underline the lies told by the government-controlled media.

Upon viewing our technically disappointing 8mm rushes, much of it unusable, we decided to switch to 16mm and managed to borrow from a friend a Second World War key-wound Bell and Howell camera, along with ten rolls of black and white 16mm reversal film donated to the cause.

We went for a week's tour of the Bihar countryside, filming rallies in three villages, doing interviews with villagers and with students as they sought to transform the society in which they had grown up. Not having synchronous sound equipment, we filmed and taped (on our cassette) simultaneously, and later achieved a very rough synchronous sound effect on an editing table by adding and subtracting portions of silence from the soundtrack. Most of our shooting was done in the daytime as we had no lights. One night sequence was shot beside a campfire using a slow shutter speed.

By this time the Movement was being increasingly infiltrated by bourgeois opposition leaders of various parties--from the mildly left Socialists to the right-wing Jan Sangh, whose main interest was to replace Mrs. Gandhi's government at the Centre. As filmmakers we saw our task as being to reaffirm the grassroots nature of the Movement and to warn against putting one's faith in the corrupt, self-seeking politicians of old. Only great public vigilance and a mass awakening of consciousness could lead to a new India. So we emphasized the role of the peasantry, showing them beginning to question their age-old oppressive traditions of caste and dowry. We showed them conscious of the way landlords illegally held large plots of land, and we showed the people willing to face State repression without abandoning their struggle. Although in reality it was the students and not the poor peasants who gave the Movement its direction, because we considered this to be a weakness of the Movement and because we wished the film to serve as an organizing tool which would help to strengthen the Movement, we gave priority to the words of peasants rather than to those of students.

We already had access to many of J. P. 's speeches addressed to villagers and recorded during the Movement. These would serve as a narrative thread tying segments of the film together. We now filmed J. P. from behind as he addressed rallies, so that we could later juxtapose whichever portion of his speech we found appropriate over this footage.[3] The rallies we attended were mammoth. At the end of every speech J. P. asked for a show of hands of those who wished the Bihar ministry to resign. A sea of hands would go up. At the last rally I waited for the right moment to film this mass vote of no-confidence. Just as the hands went up, the camera wound down to a stop. Frustrated, I sent J. P. a note asking him if he could ask the people to repeat their gesture. He explained to them that the Movement had a slow-witted cameraman, and they good humoredly raised their hands once more. This time I made no mistake.

At the end of the week we had run out of film and money and were forced to stop shooting.

Post-Production

The biggest problem we now faced was to blow up the Super 8mm material to 16mm. There was no frame-by-frame optical printer that could do this in the country. With the help of a retired TV cameraman who took a liking to us, we did several experiments, setting up a Super 8 projector, a rear-screen and a 16mm camera and filming a projected Super 8 image directly onto 16mm. Afraid that the film would be discovered by the authorities, we processed it in a converted still-camera bath. The result was a hazy, flickering, off-center, scratched image of people being attacked by police. Normally such an image would have been considered totally unacceptable, but we felt that with appropriate sound, and providing we did not use too much of it, these sequences could be extremely powerful. In a sense they symbolized at once all the trials and difficulties our film and the Movement as a whole were up against.

Around this time (January, 1975), when J. P. visited New Delhi, our TV cameraman helped us to shoot the only properly lit, synchronous sound interview in the entire film, an interview in which J. P. stated that the Movement was well aware of attempts by bourgeois opposition leaders to co-opt it and would safeguard against such an eventuality.

I had found a place to edit the film at night providing I left no trace of it in the morning. The reversal original served as our workprint as we could not afford a real one. Scratches thus developed on the film before a duplicate negative was made. Because our total footage was extremely low, but we did have plenty of sound (relatively speaking), the film was first conceived as a soundtrack and then the visuals were matched to the sound.

By the time the film was edited and the negative cut, the political situation had worsened. As the Bihar Movement spread, so did State repression. Sycophancy towards the ruling government was in evidence, and in Bombay a laboratory refused to process our film after learning what the material was. The film was processed in several different laboratories. Finally, in June, the first print was ready. The film was half an hour long. It had taken a year and a half to complete and had been made with the incredibly low shooting ratio of $2\frac{1}{2}$:1 and had cost Rs. 18,000 (approximately $2,500.) No one had been paid a salary and many of the people who worked on the film contributed not only their time but materially as well. Their names did not appear in the credit titles because this could have got them into trouble at the time. We knew the film could never get a Censor's Certificate, so did not show it openly but held limited screenings in private homes. The response was enthusiastic. The picture was scratched and not always sharp, the soundtrack had several unintelligible moments in it, but the film was timely and considered valuable for the Movement. It had been made in Hindi and in Bhojpuri (a dialect of Bihar), as it was intended for use in the countryside by Movement activists, but this plan never materialized.

Underground and in Exile

On the 26th of June, 1975, Emergency rule was declared and the film went underground. Screenings became even more clandestine than they had been. Each person attending had to be personally vouched for by reliable colleagues known to us, as each screening took on the significance of a subversive act. Discovery by officials would have meant at best that the film would have been confiscated, and at worst, jail for all those present.

Because of the difficulties involved in using the film extensively in India, it was decided to send a print abroad, where it might arouse international opinion against the Emergency. One print was to remain in India to be used whenever possible. A second print was secretly made and smuggled out of the laboratory, at considerable risk to the person who volunteered for this task. This print was cut into pieces and smuggled out of the country in the personal baggage of friends.

By this time several groups, both centrist, such as Indians for Democracy (I. F. D.), and leftists such as Indian People's Association in North America (I. P. A. N. A.),[4] had sprung up outside of India in response to the repressive Emergency declared by Indira Gandhi. North American groups such as the War Resisters' League (W. R. L.) were also taking active part in condemning the loss of democratic rights in India. Some of these groups helped in raising money to make the English version, both directly and through their individual members.

Attempts to find television exposure for the new English version in North America and the U. K. were frustrating, with some stations claiming political reasons for their refusal, others technical. Even sympathetic alternative distributors would not take on the film, for reasons of technical quality or because of low interest in the Indian situation.

Consequently a self-distribution mechanism was created, relying on myself to tour with the film, and otherwise on promotion by groups opposed to the Emergency in India. Six prints circulated including the one I took across North America, often hitchhiking.

The format of the presentation varied from place to place. Where a local group of Indians existed who were fighting against the Emergency, the screenings were the best organized and attended and interest was at the highest. The program would begin with the local group introducing the general political background in India and what the anti-Emergency struggle was trying to achieve. I would then preface the film by describing the conditions in which it was made, warning the audience about its poor technical quality and attempting to fill in some of the information gaps which existed because the film had not originally been made for a foreign audience but for people much more familiar with its content.

After the film, discussions would follow, which were often long and heated. Many of the Indians living abroad were Indira supporters or felt that "we should not wash our dirty linen in public." Still others felt that non-violent protest in India was tantamount to reformism or, worse, counter-revolution. One such group, led by Chairman Hardial Bains of the Communist Party of Canada (Marxist-Leninist) took out a special pamphlet denouncing the film. The large majority of people who saw the film, however, were impressed by the genuinely mass-based character of the Bihar Movement and moved by the plight of a peaceful, democratic, people's struggle being crushed by a ruthless State machine.

While some universities were able to pay an honorarium to cover travel and other expenses, many were not, and after each screening, usually while discussions were still going on, a donation box would be passed around the room. Depending on the situation, the funds thus collected would either be used for the local group which had organized the screening, or towards the expenses incurred in the making and distributing of the film.

In this way, over a period of two years the film recuperated its original investment. Further prints were made, some to be given away at less than laboratory cost to politically active groups. The remainder of the money collected was sent back to assist the underground resistance movement in India.

In August 1976, the film was chosen for the Robert Flaherty Film Seminar in Boston, where it was screened alongside Louis Malle's Calcutta and followed by a panel discussion with Louis Malle. The general audience response to the two films was that while Calcutta was a beautifully made film, it left one with a feeling of impotent despair, while Waves of Revolution although technically far inferior, presented the Indian masses as vibrant and fighting to overcome their circumstances.

In March 1977, Indira Gandhi was defeated at the polls, bringing the Emergency to an end. Between December 1975 and March 1977, 15 prints of the film had been made, including one in French. The film had been screened in the U.K., U.S.A., Germany, Holland, France and Canada. I had personally attended over a hundred public screenings. Directly or indirectly it had raised over $4,000 and had been seen by more than 10,000 people. It had generated three TV and 12 radio interviews and 25 articles in the press.

Overground in India

With the defeat of the Emergency and the election of the Janata Party, for some months a new era of democratic consciousness appeared to have dawned in India.

I returned with the film in June 1977 and quickly obtained a Censor's Certificate for the film. The press, which had only recently emerged from its Emergency shackles, now hailed the film in glowing terms.

Five local TV stations broadcast the film. They paid only Rs. 500 ($75.) per telecast, but thousands got to see the film for the first time. Distribution remained extremely difficult even though there was no fear of censorship, for the simple reason that there is as yet no viable 16mm circuit in India for independently produced films, let alone documentaries.

In a few months the euphoria began to evaporate. The government that had replaced the Congress, while more democratic, was still a government of the ruling class, unwilling to solve and incapable of solving the problems of the vast majority.

Because there was a danger that the message of the film might be misinterpreted under the changed circumstances, to imply that the Janata government was the culmination of the revolutionary struggle, we added an epilogue to the film which stated " ... Today new parties of the ruling class replace old ones. But the long term struggle of the Indian people towards true socialism and grassroots democracy will continue to grow--from one victory to the next."

The Director of the government's Field Publicity department offered to buy 200 prints of the film if the epilogue was removed. This was naturally unacceptable and the film was distributed through a low-level, poorly financed cooperative instead.

In any case events were rapidly moving in India. The original spirit of the Bihar Movement had been replaced by the opportunism for the Janata leadership. The film was therefore a frozen moment of history and no longer an instrument of an ongoing process of change. With the end of the Emergency, it had outlived its usefulness. A new film had begun to take shape.

Conclusion

As the infrastructure of film technology spreads across the world at a faster pace than world revolution, many progressive people in countries where the revolution has yet to occur find access to filmmaking as a method to speed along the revolutionary process. It is this that has accounted for the rise, in the last two decades, of the guerrilla film.

But the spreading consciousness throughout the world of the need for change has been accompanied by a virulent increase in the repressive tactics of the threatened ruling classes. This increase in repression has severely limited the use of the guerrilla film in the country of its origin and has led to the higher incidence of the guerrilla film in exile.

Films like Patricio Guzman's The Battle of Chile (1973), Nana Mahamos' Last Grave at Dimbaza (Azania, 1975) or Diego de la Texera's El Salvador: The People's Victory (1980) could never be shown openly in their own countries until the regimes in power there have been overthrown. Further, the extent of the repression in these countries makes clandestine screenings almost impossible. Hence they are used mainly to win support from the outside.

But whether the guerrilla film has been made for internal or external consciousness-raising its primary aim remains political and not aesthetic. At times the very effectiveness of the political statement being made creates its own aesthetic, at other times conventional aesthetic beauty is deliberately suppressed or transformed in order not to upstage the political objective of the guerrilla film.

Especially for audiences in the Third World where literacy is low, films are as much a source of information as of entertainment. The dominant classes have already created the cinema of entertainment and escape. It remains for the guerrilla filmmaker to create the cinema of reality and change.

And there is evidence to show that when such films do reach audiences whose class interests are directly addressed, they are seen with rapt attention, followed by animated debate, which occasionally leads to direct political action.

On the rare occasions that Waves of Revolution was screened in India during the Emergency, it was invariably followed by fund-raising for the anti-Emergency cause and discussion on strategies for political action. Outside of India, where the opportunities for direct action were more limited, fund-raising and information exchange were the main results of showing the film.

By its very definition, the guerrilla film is

inextricably tied to its context since it is not its intrinsic nature but the nature of its function that determines whether a film is guerrilla or not. It is a film born of the consciousness for revolutionary change, in societies where revolutionary struggles have already begun or are on the verge of beginning. Its guerrilla function ceases in countries where the revolution is successful and the film becomes officially sanctioned, although it may continue to have this function in other countries where similar struggles have yet to succeed. Thus Nicaragua: Free Homeland or Death (1979) is no longer a guerrilla film in post-revolutionary Nicaragua but continues to be one in neighboring El Salvador.

The fact that a film ceases to have a guerrilla function does not mean that it automatically ceases to be of value, but merely that it now serves a different function--for instance, that of reminding people of their oppressive past and of the sacrifices made in overcoming this past. In the hands of people who continue to live by their revolutionary ideals this can be a useful and progressive tool. But in the hands of a revisionist State that rules in the name of a revolution long abandoned, it becomes yet another weapon of dominance.

For there are no fool-proof formal safeguards against content misuse. There is no democratic film form that cannot be transformed into an authoritarian instrument. The self-reflexive film is an attempt to make audiences aware of the manipulations involved in the filmmaking process, but a self-reflexive appearance may in fact be yet another manipulation, as final control remains in the hands of producers and distributors and there is no built-in mechanism for actual dialogue with the audience.

And yet, the search for a democratic film form must continue, for it is a necessary but not sufficient condition, which in combination with revolutionary content, can point the way to a truly emanicipatory process of communication.

Notes

1 Fernando Solanas and Octavio Getino, "Towards a Third Cinema," reprinted in Bill Nichols, ed., Movies and Methods (Berkeley, 1976), pp. 44-64; Julio Garcia

Espinosa, "For an Imperfect Cinema," reprinted in Jump Cut, No. 20 (May 1979), pp. 24-26.

2 Early 1974 had seen the largest railway strike in world history, ferociously suppressed by the Gandhi government, and three months of massive street protests in the western state of Gujerat aimed at political corruption and unemployment, both seeming to escalate into the Bihar Movement, originally an agitation for educational reform. The Movement broadened after 17 student demonstrators were killed by police and the charismatic founder of the Socialist Party, Jayaprakash Narayan ("J. P."), became its figurehead, a leadership stressing non-violent methods and the goal of "total revolution." An October state-wide general strike culminated in more deaths and the November 4 rally was in protest against this. The movement continued to grow. The following June, Gandhi, provoked by a crucial electoral loss and a court ruling against her, declared the suspension of India's parliamentary system, banning opposition parties and imposing censorship. Over 100,000 people were jailed in the two years of Emergency rule, including the septagenarian J. P., who would die in 1979 of an illness contracted in jail.

3 In most documentary films which use synchronous sound the cutaway shot has an important editorial function. It allows the filmmaker to select and compress the soundtrack while the camera is momentarily freed from the lip movement of the speaker, and we are shown something else. This is an example of the filmmaker's ultimate authoritarianism or control. The cutaway need not necessarily be a physical cut on film. The camera may zoom or pan away from the subject's face into a detail in the background or foreground (for instance it may focus on the hands of the speaker alone). This is the most subtle and therefore the most manipulative form of cutting. For even as the camera appears to have been in continuous motion on a "reality take," a cut has taken place on the soundtrack, and we may be listening to two sentences which were never together in the first place. Most of the cutting in Waves of Revolution draws attention to itself, and moreover, because we had no access to synchronous sound equipment, there is a built-in distancing effect in that the lip movements do not match the soundtrack. The audience understands

that the words heard were not necessarily spoken at that precise moment in that precise form. Whether it believes the film or not therefore depends on a deeper analysis of what the film is saying and not on a superficial truth claim.

4 The I. F. D. dissolved itself shortly after the end of Emergency rule, but I. P. A. N. A. is still active, with headquarters at P. O. Box 69646, Stn. K, Vancouver, B. C. V4K 4W7.

Chapter 24

THE SANDINISTA DOCUMENTARY: A HISTORICAL CONTEXTUALIZATION

John Ramirez

Like others of the contributors to this volume, John Ramirez considers the question of the audience to be central to the problematic of committed cinema; he here defines this centrality with respect to the world's youngest revolutionary state cinema, both its present aspirations and its historical determinations. Because of the abstraction inevitable in any appreciation of a cinema that has scarcely gained entrance to world markets, marginal or mainstream, we append here program-note synopses of several representative products of the new Nicaraguan documentary.

> Emphasis was placed on contextualizing the film experience. [Fernando] Birri insisted that every film begin with the concrete reality of the situation depicted and end by inserting itself into the concrete reality of those who view it. [1]

> The unrepeatable experience of filming testimony on the most devastating moments in the struggle against Somoza stands as the foundation to an emergent cinema that will serve as a cultural instrument for the recovery and development of national identity. [2]

All New Latin American film movements, past and

present, share one common historical objective, namely, to affirm the aspirations, achievements, and potentials for cultural reclamation. This representational imperative signifies, first and foremost, strategies of national advancement: from foreign domination and shattered self-image to independent cultures of restored and cohesive national identities. The New Latin American Cinema stands in integral relation to a continental complex of need for regional renovations on all fronts. The objective is "development," which is to say, independence from foreign impositions of economic, cultural, and psychological "underdevelopment." It is in light of these considerations that I shall discuss Nicaraguan national documentary cinema, by clarifying its distinct historical roots, tracing the threads of its social and aesthetic cohesion, and locating its practice in relation to this New Latin American cinematic legacy.

I

Hollywood established and maintained an unchallenged hegemony in Latin America, at least until the early 1920s when on several occasions Mexico and Panama mobilized a number of Latin American nations toward closing their film-exhibition circuits to North American productions. These efforts were in protest against Hollywood representations considered ethnically and nationally insulting to Latin American audiences.[3] The resulting boycotts and a handful of legislative actions banning Hollywood fare accomplished little more than impressing upon the North American studios that profits stood to be gained by a few calculated gestures of hemispheric goodwill. More often, this response to the protests was to avoid Hispanic representations altogether, indicating no gain for the side of cultural resistance since this response only further helped to silence a culture already displaced to the voiceless margins of colonial domination. These protest initiatives, however, did motivate existing national cinema infrastructures in Argentina, Brazil, and Mexico to pursue alternative commercial fare of their own with which to compete against Hollywood imports--a difficult task given the cultural saturation already attained by U.S. entertainment media.

An important aspect of these resistance efforts is the fact that Nicaragua, which had been under direct U.S. military occupation from 1912-1925 and again from 1927-1933, took part in the 1932 and 1935 defensive actions against Hollywood. Given this, it is historically inaccurate to assume that no film culture predates the Sandinista national film industry, since Nicaraguans definitely hold claim to a history of participation in early resistance efforts against cinema imperialism.

Furthermore, those efforts testify to a significant Pan-Latin American sensibility that prefigured the cinematic framework introduced in the 1940s by the Argentinian Fernando Birri, regenerated in the 1960s, for example, by the Cuban National Film Institute, Octavio Getino and Fernando Solanas in Argentina, and the Brazilian Cinema Novo, and continued most currently by the Sandinista documentary.

The early resistance struggles demonstrate at least two interrelated principles which can be seen as key factors of film-cultural resistance. First, a continental agenda of "anticipated spectatorship," referring the motive of opposition to the suppressed reaches of economically displaced cultural self-image. Struggles for reclamations of cultural identity target the full range of imperialist ideological mechanisms and their effects. These struggles speak to a severing determination which challenges the imbalances of power intrinsic to imperialist domination. Secondly, these resistance efforts demonstrate some of the first historical instances in which codes of visual representation and cinematic address have been interrogated at an international level. Clearly, the ramification of such interrogation is the potential for discerning film entertainment's ideological underpinnings.

Nicaragua's participation in the Latin American front against Hollywood coincided with one of the most overt U.S. occupations in recent Latin American history--an occupation that by 1935 was well on its way to guaranteeing the security of U.S. economic and political investments in Nicaragua through manipulation of internal political strife and growing civil discontent.

In opposition to the U.S. military occupation, and to accommodations to the U.S. by the Nicaraguan government, a popular revolt emerged in 1926. Organized by General Augusto Sandino, the increasingly popular peasant army caused the U.S. in 1927 to finance and direct the implementation of a National Guard with the initial objective of defeating Sandino's forces. In 1934 Sandino and two of his key generals were assassinated by the Guard which was then under the command of its first Nicaraguan chief, Anastasio Somoza Garcia. With the credit of having defeated Sandino, Somoza Garcia assumed enough leverage to make the Guard his personal army, enabling him in 1935 to secure by intimidation both the presidency and permanent command of the Guard. Somoza Garcia's appropriation of absolute power would span forty-five years, extending to two of his sons: Luis Somoza Debayle from 1956-1963, and to Anastasio Somoza Debayle from 1967-1979.[4]

Soon after taking office in 1935, Somoza Garcia assigned to the Guard administrative responsibilities for the country's major institutions, which were all eventually appropriated for the profit and aggrandizement of the Somoza family. Among those institutions were the communication industries: press, radio, film-exhibition (largely limited thereafter to low-rate Hollywood and Mexican fare), Nicaragua's own film studio established in the '50s, and television, which was introduced in the '60s. During the several years prior to his assassination in 1956, Somoza Garcia took steps to install within his political machine a film production facility, PRODUCINE. The facility never ventured beyond cheap advertisements promoting products within the family's monopoly holdings, self-serving newsreels glorifying the family's privileged lifestyle, and visual training manuals for the Guard. In spite of the facility's creative poverty, it did provide a structure for the centralization of national film-exhibition revenues. In addition, PRODUCINE's aesthetic shortcomings deepened the cultural disenfranchisement of Nicaragua's modes of public address.

Here we arrive at a factor crucial to the course of material and aesthetic integration of the Nicaraguan revolutionary experience. I refer to the alienating gap between the popular daily experience under the Somoza dynasty and that dynasty's prevailing communications apparatus. However incompetently structured and aesthetically devalued the Somoza media network was, it nonetheless was firmly bound to the exigencies of domination--both Somoza's and that of the foreign interests which the Somoza dynasty accommodated. Somoza's self-enforcing productions, together with carefully selected U. S. and Mexican films, comprised a film discourse completely closed off from the participation and input of those it addressed.

This state of affairs should be seen against the backdrop of a landscape of interrelated social disparities. For instance, by the time of the revolutionary victory in 1979, civil liberties affecting the press, public speech, artistic expression, education, labor rights, and health care were virtually nonexistent, save for a handful of nominal concessions made in the interest of sustaining U.S. financial and military aid. Illiteracy stood at 50 percent, unemployment at 28 percent; 80 percent of the employed earned a per-capita income of less than $805 a year and, for two-thirds of these, annual income was barely $300. At the same time the country's inflation rate was 60 percent.[5] Like the tip of an iceberg, these figures do not begin to reflect the full proportion of public deprivation and abuse suffered during the forty-five years of the Somoza dynasty. But this paradigm of immiserization and the acknowledgement of the contribution to it by Somoza's media apparatus have informed the course of Sandinista cinema. This leads to the question: How are the effects of that apparatus to be altered and rectified?

The Sandinista response to this question suggests a dialectical imperative: to seize the modes of cultural address and apply them against generations of de-culturation, national deformation, and psychological manipulation. The genesis of this cultural objective, to reclaim national identity by way of a historical rectification of social inequities, can be traced to the documentation practices of the Frente Sandinista de Liberacion Nacional (FSLN).

In 1962, opposition parties were united in a coalition under the leadership of the FSLN. Through the consolidation of their combined efforts, the FSLN waged a concerted program of guerrilla struggle and popular education which in 1979 successfully dismantled the Somoza dynasty. Inspired by the support of an international community of documentary filmmakers and photo-journalists covering the Liberation War, the FSLN chose to implement its own information network in April of 1979. Combatants were invited to volunteer for technical training in Mexico, to be followed by photographic and 16mm film documentation assignments in Nicaragua's strategic war zones, thus constituting the War Correspondents Corps. These documentarists were joined by a number of cineastes and photo-journalists from around the world who responded to an FSLN appeal for professional international media assistance. That appeal aimed to complement, via international solidarity, Nicaragua's own filmmaking resources and expertise which were understandably scarce.

An immediate function of the Corps was to gather evidence on the development of the war--evidence that would effectively discount Somoza's distorted official version.

Through the Corps' formation the first steps were taken to seize the modes of cultural address and turn them against the abusive practices that had prevailed. The Corps' most significant long-term effect derives from the infrastructural base it laid for Nicaragua's first national cinema. Three days after the July 1979 victory, the Government of Reconstruction offered to Corps members the task of coordinating, as a branch of the Ministry of Culture, the Instituto Nicaraguense de Cine (INCINE.)

Three men who had fought in and documented the war, Ramiro Lacayo, Carlos Ibarra, and Franklin Caldera, were invited to direct the new institute's coordination from the abandoned PRODUCINE facilities. Housing only a small studio, an editing room, a darkroom, and a recording studio, the facility was never equipped with film processing capabilities. What is more, Somoza had managed to take virtually all the filmmaking equipment with him out of the country.

In spite of severe shortages of equipment and technical expertise, INCINE coordinated an effective production and distribution policy designed to meet the needs of national reconstruction. INCINE set forth a production goal of making maximum use of some 60,000 feet of 16mm footage taken by the War Correspondents Corps during the final months of the war. Together with an estimated 300,000 feet of PRODUCINE footage left behind by Somoza, INCINE developed a tripartite agenda of projects consisting of: Noticieros or newsreels, Feature Documentaries, and Special Projects.

INCINE Noticieros, which number at least thirty-five to date, are ambitious 10-20 minutes B/W projects distributed through Nicaragua's 150 movie houses to supplement feature programming. The Noticieros treat significant events of the Sandinista resistance more broadly than either television newscast or press reportage formats allow. Noticieros also offer a training-ground for Nicaraguan filmmakers to experiment with and refine those skills acquired through war coverage experience and during their production training in Mexico and, since the victory, at the Cuban Film Institute (ICAIC.)

These tightly edited, fast-paced productions are exemplary evidence of capable and creative film practice in a context where scarcity inhibits the way to social renovation. Having to rely generally on archival footage from both the

Correspondents Corps and the Somoza collections, the Noticieros make innovative use of found objects which stand as prime evidence on the Liberation War: newspaper and magazine spreads, television newscasts, still photographs. These, together with contemporary footage depicting public participation in the reconstruction (i. e. Nicaraguans engaged in national defense, education, health care, labor, and leisure), provide an arsenal of visual elements. These elements are calculatedly matched and mismatched in dialectical juxtaposition to inject new meanings and signifying possibilities not only into the popular visual language but also into the codes of historical discourse.

Their dynamic interweaving of such visual elements accompany soundtracks that are also produced under technically unsophisticated conditions. For example, since sync sound is not always available or economically feasible, there is a recurring use of voice-over strategies such as first-person narration, anonymous public interviews and citizen opinions, crowds in revolutionary chant, traditional folk music, and radio broadcasts. In cases where sync sound is utilized, as in dialogue accompanying television newscasts or interviewees, the visuals often shift in and out of correspondence with the sound so as to make full and economical use of the signifying possibilities a continuous length of sound may have alongside different visual images. The resulting fluctuation between sync and nonsync creates a visual-aural system that reinforces such dramatic effects as irony, humor, sorrow, and horror.

A textual demonstration of these principles is especially evident in the 1983 newsreel, Historia de un Cine Comprometido (Emilio Rodriguez). This film chronicles the development of INCINE, relating its training, production, and distribution practices firmly to the concrete circumstances of reconstruction. In the course of this chronicling, the film expresses the nation's new cinematic agenda through a striking recycling of conventional commercial representation. A highly condensed montage sequence, using clips from foreign feature fictions, includes shots of bloody physical violence, then shots of female nudity, then shots of masculine heroics. These clips, shown without commentary, tend with their "entertainment" incentive to elicit responses based on one's experience. The same clips, however, are immediately shown again, this time accompanied by voice-over commentary showing how the terms of their "entertainment" value are caught up in an imperialist ideological design: the underdog, the socially marginalized figure, is typically the target for violence; the woman's narrative function typically reduces her to a sexual object; the hero is typically "Anglo" and "male" and saves the day by performing death-defying deeds against people of color, Third World nations, and communist threats.

Grounded in conditions of cultural renovation, the Noticieros provide the structural basis for a genuine Nicaraguan film discourse by informing the Feature Documentary and Special Projects categories of INCINE's production program. Feature Documentaries, which number at least ten to date, are 30-60 minute B/W and/or color productions that offer more expanded treatment on points of history and social renovation. Special Projects consist of a number of thematically specific projects designed to fulfill needs of particular ministries in the Reconstruction Government, such as an educational series that was produced for use in the Literacy Campaign. Special Projects also include international co-productions, of which perhaps the most notable to date is the 1982 Alsino y el Condor. Directed by exiled Chilean filmmaker Miguel Littin, and combining the talents and resources of Nicaragua with those of Costa Rica, Cuba, and Mexico, Alsino y el Condor stands as the first and so far only fictional narrative feature to emerge from INCINE.

INCINE's distribution policy incorporates an internal and international agenda. Nationally, INCINE utilizes Nicaragua's existing exhibition channels such as the country's movie houses, located largely in the urban centers, the nationalized television network, and the school and college circuits. This internal agenda also includes the coordination of a Mobile Film Units Department which is responsible for supplying film screenings to remote, largely rural regions of the country--regions where, in many cases, not even Somoza's aesthetically bankrupt fare had been generally available. INCINE's national distribution plans also seek to provide the population with films from Latin American, European, U.S., and other Third World alternative and independent film markets. In this endeavor, INCINE has had to rely on the generous donation of films from the international film community. Finally, INCINE includes an international distribution arm for its own productions--an enterprise which recognizes both the opportunity to share with the world the course of Nicaragua's reconstruction, and a means to raise much needed funding for future productions.

II.

> Film, here, has played an important role in ... alienation and in the colonizing process. Therefore, we conceive the new Nicaraguan cinema precisely as a front in the battle against imperialism, as a decolonizing and liberating agent, as a political instrument to fight the cultural and ideological penetration of imperalism. Our cinema will help to consolidate the Sandinista ideology among the Nicaraguan people.[6]
>
> --Ramiro Lacayo,
> co-director, INCINE

It is clear that the documentary plays a fundamental role in defining the parameters of Nicaragua's national cinema. Furthermore, the central importance of documentary, in terms of both the space it affords for an expanded popular language of representation, and the expanded space of its accessibility, indicates an aesthetic literacy that must be seen in light of the country's overall literacy increase. Within five months of the Literacy Campaign, implemented immediately following the 1979 victory, illiteracy was effectively reduced from 50 to 10 percent. As of 1982, some 1,258 new schools have been constructed, and the number of public libraries quadrupled from 8 to 34.

Developments in Nicaraguan film are concomitant with advances in the arts and media in general and all are intimately connected with the national imperative to recuperate and reclaim cultural identity. Of course, this rectification of cultural self-image encompasses the total field of factors affecting national well-being. This process encourages a renovative integration of the forces and relations of social production. Such an integration assumes the qualitative expansion of the "public sphere"--an expansion of the public social space lying between the private and state sectors--thus increasing the opportunities for dialogue that affect political and cultural dimensions of the general welfare. In terms of Nicaraguan documentary, this integration presupposes not only its broadest possible popular access, but necessarily an increasing public capacity for participation--that is to say, for film readership and production practice. It is in conjunction with an integrative social agenda that the documentary plays its crucial role in Nicaragua.

In an essay entitled, "Communication and Dramaturgy

in the Documentary Film,"[7] Mayra Vilasis, the Cuban film theorist and historian of Nicaraguan cinema, posits an ideological axis on which the classical model of fiction narrative operates. She argues that this is basically an axis of viewer anticipations invoked from an inventory of socially directed desires and anxieties. The classical model of resolution functions to further frustrate those desires through the containment of anticipation via momentary visual gratification that preempts the possibility for active spectatorship. The viewer, captive of an insatiable cycle of visual enticements and temporary indulgences, is rarely if ever equipped to comprehend her/his manipulation, much less be inclined to assume any real role in determining the course of cinematic encounters. These parameters of classical fictional address saturate the spectator's experience of visual representation such that their ideological effects carry over into the discursive operations of documentary. In the final analysis, the fiction-documentary dichotomy is one of a number of ideologically informed divisions structured to obscure the distributions of power accompanying "capitalist" modes of cultural address.

After years of imperialist impositions, the task is to displace the social and psychological effects of a univocal system of addresses which confuses the parameters of "entertainment" and information and offers false assumptions of national development. Vilasis reasserts new Latin American documentary practice as the most appropriate mode of culturally renovative film language. Rooted in tenets of Neo-Realism and of Eisensteinian dialectical montage, this mode has the capacity, she argues, to capture the drama of Latin American reality--a reality, I might add, which in its excesses of horror hovers at the cutting edge of surrealism, and which, at its most hopeful, affirms an earthly place this side of fantasy. The most significant quality of this filmmaking practice is that it invites the creative participation of the spectator. It is a representational system whose legitimation rests fundamentally on capable input and active feedback by those whose lives are concretely at stake in its address.

What is intended here is not so much an eradication of structural differences between fiction and documentary, but rather, the social attainment of a popular capacity to recognize historical ramifications and ideological underpinnings of the conventional fiction-documentary dichotomy. Only when their effects are acknowledged can the task to counter them be undertaken. Furthermore, the broader the social space of that knowledge is, the more effectively democratic the process of their deconstruction will be--which is precisely the direction in which Nicaraguan film culture has developed.

The democratization of film culture in Nicaragua indicates a popular-based demystification of film practice. This is evident for example, in the fact that virtually all INCINE's administrative and technical staff and trainees have no formal background in filmmaking. Rather than cloak the visual media in an air of exclusivity and professional elitism, the Sandinista cultural policies have opened the way for mass opportunities of aesthetic expression. For instance, "public access" on the national television network, Sistema Sandinista de Television, requires little more than a reasonably budgeted concept, a manageable production schedule, and the energy and commitment on the part of a community collective to pursue and execute production. Provided these conditions, technical resources, scarce and unsophisticated as they may be, are amply accessible; and furthermore, broadcast time is virtually guaranteed.

Not of value then in Nicaragua's visual media are representations which fit standardized, pre-determined molds of commercial appeal. Media address no longer descends from the privileged heights of personalized power and official opinion. Rather, media address radiates through a network of realigned and intersupportive sites of popular authority in accordance with the expanded field of social space and democratic process.

In support of Mayra Vilasis' propositions, the Nicaraguan example demonstrates a cinematic agenda which strives for genuine communication, for poly-vocal interchange, and participatory spectatorship. In relation to these factors emerges an important cultural self-reference in Nicaragua's film language. That dimension of self-reference signifies the degree to which Nicaragua's visual media are deeply invested in the imperative to reclaim cultural identity, thereby asserting a more authentic national point of view. (August 1983)

Notes

1 Julianne Burton, "The Camera as 'Gun': Two Decades of Culture and Resistance in Latin American," Latin American Perspectives, Vol. 5, No. 1 (Winter 1978),

p. 58. For more on Argentine filmmaker Fernando Birri's pioneering contribution to the Latin American social documentary, see Burton's "Democratizing Documentary: Modes of Address in the New Latin American Cinema, 1958-1972," ibid, pp. 344-383.

2 Mayra Vilasis, "Un Primer Noticiero: Notas Sobre el Cine Nicaragüense," Cine Cubano, No. 100, p. 91. Translation by John Ramirez.

3 Allan L. Woll, The Latin Image in American Film, (Los Angeles: UCLA Latin American Center Publications, 1977).

4 David Craven and John Ryder, Art of the New Nicaragua, Monograph, State University of New York, 1982.

5 George Black, Triumph of the People: The Sandinista Revolution in Nicaragua, (London: Zed Press, 1981).

6 "In Search of Sandino's Image," Interview with Ramiro Lacayo, Cine Cubano, No. 96 (1979), p. 18. Translation by Zuzana Pick.

7 Mayra Vilasis, "Comunicacion y Dramaturgia en el Cine Documental," Transcript from the First International Festival of New Latin American Cinema (Havana, 1979).

APPENDIX

Representative INCINE productions, 1979-1982*

A. Feature-length productions

La educación no se interrumpió (Education Was Not Interrupted). This documentary is INCINE's first production. It explores the ways in which education continued during the armed struggle, and the students' and teachers' view of their role during this difficult period. As it covers the preparatory course of study prior to the official school opening, in

*Many of these films are available in the U. S. from "Comu-Nica", P. O. Box 612, Cathedral Station, New York, NY 10025, and in Canada from DEC Films, 427 Bloor Street West., Toronto M5S 1X7.

September 1979, it outlines the goals of the new educational system. 3/4" video, color, 45 mins., 1979. Spanish/English.

Victoria de un pueblo en armas (Victory of an Armed People). This first feature-length documentary produced by INCINE utilizes powerful footage on the final offensive against Somoza, shot by the FSLN War Press Corps, as well as by international journalists. It also briefly chronicles the building of the Sandinist Front for National Liberation over a twenty-year period, with emphasis on the last stages of the war. 16 & 35mm, color, 60 mins., 1980.

La insurrección cultural (The Cultural Insurrection). Covers the 1980 crusade to eradicate illiteracy from beginning to end, its impact on society and on people's attitudes towards their cultural heritage. This documentary was produced by INCINE with the Ministry of Culture, the Ministry of Education, and the National Literacy Bureau. 16mm, color, 60 mins., 1981.

B. "Noticieros"

1: Links the present goals of Sandinismo to its origins in the 1920s and early '30s through the testimony of a combatant in General Augusto Sandino's armed resistance to the U.S. military interventions, closing with the August 1979 nationalization of Nicaragua's mines. 16 & 35mm, color, 9 mins., 1979.

2: Chronicles the main events of 1979, opening with the last months of Somoza's rule, through the uprising and the entrance of the victorious popular army into Managua, to the initial steps of the Government of National Reconstruction. 16 & 35mm, b/w, 18 mins., 1980.

4: Covers the first nationwide commemoration of the anniversary of the assassination of Nicaragua's "General of Free Men," Augusto Cesar Sandino, on February 21, 1934, including remembrances by people who knew him personally. 16 & 35 mm, b/w, 10 mins., 1980.

5: On the preparatory stages of the national mobilization for the Literacy Crusade, and how different sectors of society were contributing to it. On-the-spot interviews capture the attitudes and expectations of the students and teachers-to-be, and the importance the new government grants to raising the people's level of education. 16 & 35mm, b/w, 10 mins., 1980.

7: On the implementation of the Agrarian Reform and its place within the general plan for economic reactivation and social development. Includes footage on the views of the private sector, as well as of the Minister of Agrarian Reform, Commander Jaime Wheelock, addressing peasants on these issues. 16 & 35mm, b/w, 16 mins., 1980.

8: Captures images of the celebration of the first anniversary of the Revolution, on July 19, 1980, from the preparatory stages to the parade and key addresses. 16 & 35mm, b/w, 16 mins., 1980.

9: On the successful completion of the Literacy Crusade. It highlights the relationships developed between rural students and urban teachers, and culminates with the massive concentration of literacy teachers in Managua, and their reunion with their families, after the long journey from the most remote regions of the country. 16 & 35mm, b/w, 1980, English subtitles.

10: Portrays the working and living conditions of the banana plantation workers, and looks into the concept of democracy from different perspectives in reference to discussions on how to solve the needs posed by the workers. 16 & 35mm, b/w, 10 mins., 1980.

14: "The Military Defense" examines how the people of Nicaragua are readying to resist any possible military intervention either as civilians or in the army. Images of training, interwoven with glimpses of public opinion on this issue. 16 & 35mm, b/w, 9 mins., 1981.

15: "The Economic Defense" deals with the mechanisms the Nicaraguan people and their government are developing to face the economic aggression which is affecting the supply of food and other basic necessities. 16 & 35mm, b/w, 10 mins., 1981.

34: "Dawn Belongs to Me," through an innovative and impressionistic style, presents the life and poetry of Ruben Dario, the poet considered the father of Nicaraguan modernism. 35mm, b/w, 15 mins., 1982.

C. Other Shorts

La Otra Cara del Oro (Gold's Glitter). Rafael Vargas and Emilio Rodriguez, directors. One of the first dramatizations outside the newsreel genre to explore aesthetic avenues towards the development of a Nicaraguan cinematic style. The subject is gold mining and the ensuing exploitation and devastation of the people employed in it. 35mm, b/w, 18 mins., 1981.

Bananera (Banana Companies). Ramiro Lacayo, director. This film, one of the latest Nicaraguan documentaries, constructs with great skill and assuredness a portrait of exploitation under capitalism in Nicaragua: the raising and export of bananas by American companies before the Revolution, and its tremendous human cost. 35mm, color, 16 mins., 1982.

Historia de un Cine Comprometido (History of an Engaged Cinema). Emilio Rodriguez, director. This most recent Nicaraguan documentary concerns the history of new Nicaraguan cinema, the course of its development in relation to the Sandinista reconstruction. 35mm, color, 15 mins., 1983.

CONTRIBUTORS

John D. Barlow is Professor of German at Indiana University, Indianapolis, where he also teaches film courses. He is the author of German Expressionist Film.

Joan Braderman, speaker, video- and film-maker, writer and activist, teaches at the School of Visual Arts in New York City. She was one of the founders of Heresies, an organizer of the People's Convention in the South Bronx, and has recently been involved in cable production, as well as performing a "hysterical post-semiological reading of the National Enquirer" for Paper Tiger TV.

Julianne Burton, Associate Professor of Latin American literature and film at the University of California, Santa Cruz, has published widely on Latin American film. She has recently completed her tenure as Fellow of the Latin American Program at the Woodrow Wilson International Center for Scholars, the Smithsonian Institution, Washington, D.C., during which she wrote "Democratizing Documentary."

Russell Campbell, New Zealand scholar and activist, is the author of Cinema Strikes Back: Radical Filmmaking in the United States, 1930-1942 (Ann Arbor: UMI Research Press, 1982).

Margaret Cooper is a media programming consultant and freelance writer currently based in New York. She was formerly film editor for Branching Out, a Canadian feminist magazine, and film programmer for the Art Gallery of Ontario in Toronto.

Seth Feldman, author of Evolution of Style in the Early Work of Dziga Vertov and Dziga Vertov: A Guide to References and Resources, has been professor of film studies at the University of Western Ontario and York University, Toronto, as well as programmer for the Grierson Film Seminar.

Dan Georgakas, of the Cinéaste Editorial Board, has most recently been author of The Methuselah Factor (Simon and Schuster) and co-editor of The Cinéaste Interviews: On the Art and Politics of the Cinema (Chicago, Lake View Press, 1983).

Guy Hennebelle, Paris editor and critic, is author of Quinze ans de cinema mondial and editor of the "International Review of Art and Politics," Cinémaction.

John Hess, a founder and co-editor of Jump Cut, lectures in film at San Francisco State University.

Bert Hogenkamp, Dutch film historian, is author of a recent book on the 1933 Belgian film by Joris Ivens and Henri Storck, Borinage, and of a forthcoming book on film and the workers' movement in Britain in the thirties.

Claire Johnston, a pioneer of feminist film scholarship, has been a frequent contributor to Screen and other journals, and a member of the Screen editorial board.

E. Ann Kaplan teaches film and literature at Rutgers University. She has published numerous articles on women and film, Fritz Lang and other topics in journals such as Wide Angle, Quarterly Review of Film Studies, Millenium Film Journal, Jump Cut, Social Policy and Socialist Review. Her most recent books are Women in Film Noir and Fritz Lang: A Research and Reference Guide. Two new books, Women in Film: Both Sides of the Camera and an anthology Regarding Television will appear shortly.

Chuck Kleinhans, founder and co-editor of Jump Cut, is a Super 8 filmmaker and photographer who teaches in the Radio-Television-Film Department at Northwestern University.

Réal La Rochelle is a Montreal critic who has published widely on Quebec cinema, and teaches at Cégep Montmorency in Laval, Quebec.

Julia Lesage, Jump Cut co-editor, teacher and activist, has written on women and film and on Godard.

Barbara Halpern Martineau, now Sara Halprin, Canadian filmmaker, teacher and activist, is presently traveling around North America with her partner, Martha Keaner, showing films and documenting their search for an alternative community.

Steve Neale is the British author of Genre (BFI, 1980), programmer at the New Cinema in Nottingham, and editorial board member and frequent contributor to Screen.

Bill Nichols, author of Ideology and the Image: Social Representation in the Cinema and Other Media and editor of Movies and Methods, is head of the Film Studies Department at Queens University, Kingston, Ontario.

Anand Patwardhan, Bombay filmmaker and activist, directed Waves of Revolution (1975), Prisoners of Conscience (1978) and co-directed with Jim Monro A Time to Rise (1981), which has won several international prizes. His current film is about Bombay pavement dwellers.

Vlada Petric studied theater, literature and film in Yugoslavia and the Soviet Union as well as at NYU, and now is professor of film at Harvard. He is currently completing two books: Dziga Vertov and "The Man with the Movie Camera" and Film and Dreams: An Approach to Bergman.

John Ramirez has directed several Third World Film festivals and conferences. Currently a doctoral student at UCLA, his dissertation is an investigation of spectator positioning in the history of the Nicaraguan film and television industries.

Daniel Serceau is the Paris author of many articles on film and of the recent book Renoir l'insurgé.

Pierre Véronneau, director of publications and historical research at the Cinémathèque québécoise, Montreal, has written and edited many publications, and teaches film studies at Concordia University.

Thomas Waugh, a contributor to Jump Cut and The Body Politic, wrote his doctoral dissertation on Joris Ivens and is professor of film studies at Concordia University, Montreal.

Victor Wallis is Associate Professor of Political Science at Indiana University, Indianapolis. He is a contributing editor of Workplace Democracy and is the author of several articles on the Allende period in Chile.

Paul Willemen, a former member of the *Screen* editorial board, has published widely on film theory in *Screen*, *Framework* and other journals.

NAME INDEX

FILM TITLE INDEX

SUBJECT INDEX